BUSINESS, ENVIRONMENT, AND SOCIETY
Themes and Cases

Vesela R. Veleva
University of Massachusetts Boston

Work, Health, and Environment Series
Series Editors: **Charles Levenstein, Robert Forrant, and John Wooding**

Baywood Publishing Company, Inc.
AMITYVILLE, NEW YORK

Baywood Publishing Company, Inc.
26 Austin Avenue
PO Box 337
Amityville, NY 11701
(800) 638-7819
E-mail: baywood@baywood.com
Web site: baywood.com

Library of Congress Catalog Number: 2014025373

ISBN: 978-0-89503-882-1 (cloth)
ISBN: 978-0-89503-883-8 (paper)
ISBN: 978-0-89503-884-5 (e-pub)
ISBN: 978-0-89503-885-2 (e-pdf)
http://dx.doi.org/10.2190/BEA

Library of Congress Cataloging-in-Publication Data

Veleva, Vesela R., 1968-

 Business, environment, and society : themes and cases / Vesela R. Veleva, University of Massachusetts, Boston.
       pages cm. - - (Work, health, and environment series)
  Includes bibliographical references and index.
ISBN 978-0-89503-882-1 (cloth : alk. paper) -- ISBN 978-0-89503-883-8 (pbk. : alk. paper) -- ISBN 978-0-89503-884-5 (e-pub) -- ISBN 978-0-89503-885-2 (e-pdf)
  1. Social responsibility of business. 2. Social responsibility of business -- United States. 3. Social responsibility of business--United States--Case studies.
4. Environmental responsibility. 5. Environmental responsibility--United States.
6. Environmental responsibility--United States--Case studies. I. Title.
  HD60.V45 2014
  658.4'08--dc23

                                                      2014025373

Table of Contents

III. Case Studies in CSR and Environmental Management

Foreword

Over the past 40+ years there has been an evolution of thought regarding sustainability and the environment in corporations around the world. In the early days the focus was on risk avoidance. The establishment and expansion of the Clean Air Act and Clean Water Acts in 1970 and 1972 respectively put compliance and criminal liability squarely on the C-Suite and Boards of Directors. However basic compliance in many cases represented the lowest denominator of environmental performance. In the 1990's there emerged a new concept, CSR (Corporate Social Responsibility), where organizations began to look at environmental and social performance along with financial results. This was something that was increasingly demanded by diverse stakeholders such as NGOs, shareholders, customers and employees. Companies began to publicly report on this performance in annual sustainability reports and some transparency and standardization, such as GRI (Global Reporting Initiative) and the CDP (Carbon Disclosure Project) began to emerge. Today sustainability represents a new mega trend and progressive companies are elevating environmental performance and sustainability as key components of their core growth strategies. Companies, such as Staples and others understand that striking a balance between financial, social and natural capital is critical in order to survive and most importantly thrive in a rapidly changing global economy. By incorporating a sustainability lens on how they operate and identifying these new opportunities businesses can in fact "do well while doing good."

As sustainability and the environment are emerging as mega trends many companies are focused on the impacts within the "4 walls" of their business. They focus on energy and water efficiency, waste reduction and recycling and well they should, attention to these areas have very tangible bottom line and environmental benefits. Unfortunately this is not nearly enough. Large interdependent global supply chains, natural resource degradation and unprecedented demands on resources and ecosystem services caused by population growth and 1 billion new consumers in emerging economies demand that all businesses think very differently about their role they play in the value chain. Many are now trying to account for their direct and indirect impacts of their enterprises. The old models and assumptions of production, consumption and where corporate responsibility begins and ends are changing rapidly. All corporations need to understand and account for not only the upstream impact areas associated with raw materials, energy, carbon, water, waste and toxins but, also the consumer use and ultimately how they are recovered and/or disposed of responsibly. How can a sustainable production and consumption approach help us look at design or financing differently to unlock untapped value in the supply chain? Creating transparency related to life cycle impacts of products and services and accounting for the "externalities" in financial, social and environmental terms will identify areas of supply chain and brand risk, but more importantly uncover those opportunities for innovation and transformation.

Why isn't this transformation happening faster? The simple answer is language. It is critical that there be a common language or vernacular and accepted standards to effectively measure sustainability. These indicators help establish base line performance and set goals and targets for improvement, first within individual companies and then most importantly across large interdependent global supply chains. There are many examples of efforts within industries such as the Sustainable Apparel Coalition and the Sustainability Consortium that are convening companies, partners and competitors alike to build these standards of measure and to create "radical transparency" both up and down the supply/ value chains.

Staples and other companies have been engaging in these kinds of "uncommon collaboratives" for years and seen how the power of sharing real-life case studies can accelerate and transform our business. Finally, here is a practitioner-oriented book which focuses on these companies' actual case studies in a way that illustrates how businesses are effectively building sustainability as a major component of core business strategy and performance in this ever changing global economy. The book is building skills, capabilities and language that all students will require regardless of their field of study or future career choice. Sustainability can no longer be the job of the Sustainability, EHS and CSR department, instead it needs to be everyone's job. Our economies, our communities and our planet need talented future leaders equipped with the tools and knowledge to make a real difference and this book is a wonderful first step to help guide them on their learning journey.

Mark F. Buckley
VP Environmental Affairs
Staples Inc.

Foreword

In this important contribution to the series in *Work, Health and Environment* we look closely at the role played by the corporate and business sectors in helping to achieve a more sustainable society. Clearly, in the past several decades, and as a result of sustained pressure from unions, environmentalist and consumers, many corporations have recognized both the advantages and the value of improving their business activities to embrace greener practices and ideas. The conversations about corporate responsibility, green energy, sustainability practices and the protection of workers have begun to be more engaging and vital. In many cases, corporate values have changed. Environmental responsibility is seen not only as the right thing to do but, frequently, as the profitable thing to do. These attitudes have resulted in some very interesting developments in corporate policy, ideas and beliefs.

The *Work, Health and Environment* series has ranged widely over the challenges and issues that modern production creates—from occupational health and safety, the exploitation of children in the developing world, the dangers to humans and environment posed by petrochemicals, oil and nuclear power, and what happen to workers and communities when whole industries move away. In this series we have explored the role of science and politics, international political economy in the global system and the consequences to humans and the environment of making everything from toys to shoes. Now, in this excellent collection of research and commentary, Vesela R. Veleva has brought together important cases and examples that examine the role of industry and corporations from another perspective—the achievements as well as challenges that face socially and environmentally responsible manufacture and distribution. As she points out there are problems in the current business approach yet, within these pages, the reader will find innovative techniques and sound policies that will help achieve a more sustainable society, as well as mistakes and misssteps that raise serious questions about corporate and business willingness to protect human and environmental health.

There are many lessons here. One of the purposes of this collection is to provide a series of sophisticated cases that enable scholars and students alike to have available an up to the minute sense of what is going on in the corporate and business world around issues of sustainability. By providing examples and discussions of how corporations approach the whole issue of the green economy and the many contradictions that this brings , to looking at how we measure and evaluate corporate programs, this book we think will be invaluable. The inclusion and presentation of several lively cases that examine corporate social responsibility adds depth and insight that provide any student of these issues with important and timely knowledge. In short, we believe this work will be welcomed by all those who seed more information about the real world experience of businesses and corporations as they adapt to the demands for a more sustainable system of production and consumption.

Robert Forrant
Charles Levenstein
John Wooding
Series Editors: *Work, Health and Environment*

Preface

In the Baywood series *Work, Health, and Environment*, the conjunction of topics is deliberate and critical. We begin at the point of production—even in the volumes that address environmental issues—because that is where things get made, workers labor, and raw materials are fashioned into products. It is also where things get stored or moved, analyzed or processed, computerized or tracked. In addition, it is where the folks who do the work are exposed to a growing litany of harmful things or are placed in harm's way. The focus on the point of production provides a framework for understanding the contradictions of the modern political economy.

Despite claims to a post-industrial society, work remains essential to all our lives. While work brings income and meaning, it also brings danger and threats to health. The point of production, where goods and services are produced, is also the source of environmental contamination and pollution. Thus, work, health, and environment are intimately linked.

Work organizations, systems of management, indeed the idea of the "market" itself, have a profound impact on the handling of hazardous materials and processes. The existence or absence of decent and safe work is a key determinant of the health of the individual and the community: what we make goes into the world, sometimes improving it, but too often threatening the environment and the lives of people across the globe.

We began this series to bring together some of the best thinking and research from academics, activists, and professionals, all of whom understand the intersection between work and health and environmental degradation, and all of whom think something should be done to improve the situation.

The works in this series stress the political and social struggles surrounding the fight for safer work and protection of the environment, and the local and global struggle for a sustainable world. The books document the horrors of cotton dust, the appalling and dangerous conditions in the oil industry, the unsafe ways in which toys and sneakers are produced, the struggles to link unions and communities to fight corporate pollution, and the dangers posed by the petrochemical industry, both here and abroad. The books speak directly about the contradictory effects of the point of production for the health of workers, community, and the environment. In all these works, the authors keep the politics front and foremost. What has emerged, as this series has grown, is a body of scholarship uniquely focused and highly integrated around themes and problems absolutely critical to our own and our children's future.

Introduction

Vesela R. Veleva

PERSONAL JOURNEY

My journey in the environmental field began in 1991 when I started my first job after graduation at the Ministry of Environment, Regional Inspectorate, Varna, Bulgaria. I worked as an engineer assigned to the automatic air monitoring system. My duties included tracking, analyzing, and reporting air pollution data in the region of Varna, Bulgaria. I had always been health conscious and concerned about pollution, however, I developed a passion to study and work in the environmental field from what I saw at this first job. My realization that I wanted to work in the environmental field as a career was born on the day I came across air quality data from 1986. This data was collected a few years before socialism collapsed in Bulgaria. What the data revealed was that every measurement from the gas analyzers in the Devnya industrial region near Varna (where my father worked) was significantly above the permissible limits. In fact, the readings were at the maximum scale of the instruments. For example, concentrations of sulfur dioxide (SO_2) were recorded at 2.85 mg/m^3 compared to the ambient air standard of 0.05 mg/m.^{3} Similarly, high concentrations were recorded for the city of Varna, where I lived, for all air pollutants tracked at the time—sulfur dioxide, ammonia, nitrogen dioxide, and ozone.

It did not take long before I began to wonder if there was a correlation between my being constantly sick as a child and the extremely high levels of air pollution where I lived. I was alarmed also at the high levels of pollution my father likely was exposed to for 40 years. Since 1961, he had worked at the Devnya industrial complex, first at the soda ash factory and then at the thermal power plant that supplied energy for over a dozen large chemical facilities, including a PVC plant, fertilizer plant, and soda ash plant. (My father died of stomach cancer in 2001 at the age of 63). My realization that my family and I had lived in a period of significant pollution fostered my desire to return to school to study environmental science and management.

Yet this was not an area of study easily found at colleges and universities in Bulgaria at that time. As a result, I sought programs overseas and in 1993 was selected to attend a 2-month summer program in Environmental Science and Policy at the Central European University, Budapest, Hungary. After completing the program, I continued my study toward a Master of Science degree in Pollution and Environmental Control at the University of Manchester, UK. My studies brought a completely new understanding of the complexity of environmental problems. I also realized that pollution prevention was what I wanted to focus on rather than waste management. At Manchester, I specialized in *environmental impact assessment* (EIA), and my thesis focused on developing environmental sustainability indicators for EIA. In 1994, I first heard the terms *sustainable development* and *sustainability indicators*. During this time, there were just three organizations globally developing sustainability indicators, Sustainable Seattle being one of them. Seeing the significant potential of indicators when used as a tool, I continued my research in this area during my doctorate study in Cleaner Production and Pollution Prevention at the University of Massachusetts Lowell in the late 1990s. Based at the Department of Work Environment, this multidisciplinary program was one of three in the world at the time that trained students on how to design products and processes in order to eliminate pollution and toxic chemicals exposures to workers, communities, and the environment. Since then I have focused on working primarily with companies around sustainability measurement, management, and corporate social responsibility.

Observations From Two Decades in the Field

Looking back since I began in this field, I am amazed how much has been achieved in terms of raising awareness among companies, policymakers, and people about sustainability and environmental issues. An increasing number of companies are leveraging their sustainability strategies to reduce costs, increase market share, and innovate. Recognition of the significant impacts of climate change and energy security issues, for instance, has led to considerable growth in policies and practices around energy efficiency and clean energy development. In 2013, my home state of Massachusetts had been ranked 3 years in a row the #1 state for energy efficiency. In addition, the clean energy industry in the state had grown about 12% per year in terms of jobs over the past few years. Technological and business innovations have led to numerous green products to include green cleaning materials, electric cars, and bio-based plastics. Although there have been significant accomplishments in sustainability, there are two areas I feel we have not addressed adequately over the past two decades: *worker health and safety*, and *sustainable consumption*. Sustainability courses and business sustainability strategies rarely include these two areas, and awareness is still limited.

Protecting *workers* from toxic chemicals and work-related injuries and illness is not just an issue of developing countries such as China and Bangladesh. Millions of workers in the United States are exposed to debilitating levels of pollution, according to the U.S. Occupational Safety and Health Administration (OSHA).

Those concerned with the environment tend to focus narrowly on environmental issues such as climate change, water pollution, and biodiversity loss, but have often failed to implement a systems approach to teaching, analyzing, and addressing major problems today. The result is often shifting risks between different stakeholders. Too frequently it is workers who bear the brunt of these problems. Many clean energy sectors are promoted as "green," even though workers are exposed to highly toxic chemicals. Furthermore, definitions of "green jobs" rarely include worker health and safety (see Chapter 1). Excitement with new technology continues to outpace efforts to understand and adequately address the potential environmental, health, and safety impacts, as demonstrates the case of nanotechnology (see Chapter 5).

I have come to the realization that even the most responsible companies (I have worked with many) have business models that, understandably, focus on selling more and more products. This ultimately leads to increased materials throughput and the negative environmental impacts associated with the extraction, consumption, and disposal of goods with short life cycles. I see a need for a major paradigm shift to promote product durability, reuse, and the selling of services rather than products (dematerialization). Such a shift will require new policies, business models, and significant culture change (e.g., Zipcar model). While businesses are not entirely "in control" of the system of consumption and production, they can still play an important role, as outlined in Chapter 6. Companies must work with governments, NGOs, and other stakeholders to change the current policies, corporate structures, and consumer habits in order to enable the shift to *sustainable consumption*. As Porter and Kramer (2011) state, "Capitalism is an unparalleled vehicle for meeting human needs, improving efficiency, creating jobs, and building wealth. But a narrow conception of capitalism has prevented business from harnessing its full potential to meet society's broader challenges." The time has come to create a new, more "conscious capitalism," based on systems thinking, environmental protection, regenerative ownership, and steady-state economy that focuses on human well-being and long-term sustainability. I see that continuing our present course as a consumption-driven society will lead to a bleak future of shortages of food, fuel, and key raw materials, something I personally experienced in Eastern Europe after the collapse of socialism and the loss of critical resources and markets.

The Idea for and Organization of This Book

Having taught in higher education for a number of years, I have always found it challenging to identify texts containing up-to-date readings and teaching cases. Further, these texts typically do not fully reflect current business practices and policies related to environmental management, corporate social responsibility, or sustainability, and provoking systems thinking and critical analysis. This book aims to help fill the gap and help create a more practitioner-style training and teaching curriculum. Teaching materials in the book provide students with a broad understanding of some of the most pressing environmental and sustainability challenges today. It helps better prepare students for a career in the environmental/sustainability field.

Based on extensive work with companies, the book offers engaging readings and teaching cases that address key challenges for business today—measurement, supply-chain management, public policy, and stakeholder pressures. Part I focuses on the macrolevel and provides an overview of concepts such as the green economy, eco-industrial parks, corporate social responsibility (CSR; also known also as corporate citizenship), nanotechnology, and sustainable consumption. Part II provides specific frameworks and tools for sustainability management and measurement at the company level. Despite the wide proliferation of sustainability indicators and the important role of the Global Reporting Initiative to advance their use, most companies continue to use quantitative measures that reflect traditional and easy ways to measure inputs and outputs, such as energy use, materials, waste, and the number of volunteer hours. Chapters 9 through 11 and the Underwriters Laboratories case study in Chapter 15 aim to address this and provide guidance on how to develop and implement more effective indicators for sustainability management. Chapters 7 and 8 focus on a specific industry (the electronics and cosmetics industries, respectively) to demonstrate how, in a global economy, government policies in one market can affect companies in the rest of the world. Part III of this book includes detailed teaching cases of several well-known firms, such as Stonyfield Farm, New Balance, UL, and PerkinElmer. Detailed teaching notes can be obtained from the author or in some cases from the original publisher of three of the cases, Ivey Publishing. Each book chapter includes Discussion Questions.

The main theme of the book is that business is a key player in achieving a more sustainable development, yet its practices are often narrow in focus or shortsighted. The book provokes discussions around issues such as, Is business sustainability possible in a market economy focused on increasing consumption? Should a product or service be called "green" when it puts at risk the health and safety of workers? What can U.S. policymakers learn from their European counterparts when it comes to protecting human health and the environment? How can we ensure that the benefits of nanotechnology exceed its risks? How can sustainability indicators be used as a tool to advance sustainability by companies and policymakers? How can policymakers, companies, and NGOs work together to advance a truly sustainable development?

ACKNOWLEDGMENTS

First of all I would like to thank my former advisor and Baywood Publishing Editor Professor Emeritus Charles Levenstein, who encouraged me to write this book. He was also the one who inspired me to pursue my doctorate in Cleaner Production and Pollution Prevention. This book would not have been possible without the support and hard work of my editor, Professor John Wooding, who helped me frame the topics and provided valuable feedback on the chapters and overall book content. I would also like to thank Professor Bob Forrant for the insights and support. Special thanks go to all my co-authors, who were critical for conducting the research and writing the chapters. Finally, my greatest thanks go to my family for supporting me in writing this book. My husband, Andrew

Cronk, provided analytic constructive criticism to many of the chapters. My two loving daughters, Adela and Renee, 9 years old, have brought special meaning and passion to my work, as I hope their generation will be better prepared to address many of the complex problems we are facing today and still enjoy a high quality of life. Last but not least, I would like to thank my parents, Adela Veleva and Rayko Naydenov Velev, who raised me to be responsible, hard working, with a curious mind, passion for learning, and an appreciation for quality experiences rather than material goods.

REFERENCE

Porter, M., & Kramer, M. (2011, January/February). Creating shared value. *Harvard Business Review,* 62–77.

Section I.
Growing the Green Economy –
Challenges and Opportunities

Chapter 1

THE STATE OF THE GREEN ECONOMY AND GREEN JOBS IN THE UNITED STATES

SUMMARY

While still a small part of the U.S. economy, representing just 2.6% of all jobs in the United States, the green economy is poised to grow at a rapid rate, with some sectors such as clean energy registering double-digit growth annually. Most policies and resources to date have promoted the production side of the green economy and have focused on energy, utilities, and green building, followed by green/clean tech manufacturing and transportation. Much less attention has been paid to stimulating green consumption and focusing on the sectors related to changes in lifestyle (e.g., retail, eco-tourism, organic gardening) (Chapple, 2008). With the U.S. Congress in political gridlock, most policies to promote the green economy have come from state and local governments.

Growing the green economy is often seen as an opportunity to create new green jobs. Green jobs, however, are not necessarily safe jobs, and many of the current green technologies pose significant health and safety risks for workers. A life-cycle approach and greater emphasis on worker health and safety is necessary when promoting future policies and practices. Some of the most urgent steps for advancing the green economy require introducing energy tax changes, increasing government support for disruptive innovation, eliminating policy uncertainty, and supporting long-term financing of clean technologies. Greater emphasis on driving the demand side through government procurement, green labeling/certification policies, and education is also vital. Many researchers believe the majority of green jobs are not fundamentally different from traditional jobs but simply require "an extra layer of skills/training" (Center on Education and the Workforce, 2010). Workforce training emphasizing practical skills and knowledge is essential to meet the needs of employers.

DEFINING THE GREEN ECONOMY AND GREEN JOBS

The term "green economy" was first introduced in 1989 in the report "Blueprint for a Green Economy," prepared by a group of leading British environmental economists (Pearce, Markandya, & Barbier, 1989). The report's goal was to advise the UK government on advancing sustainable development policies and resulting implications for growth and economic progress. Green economy policy measures were discussed in the following decade by economists and academics and at international negotiations such as the 1992 Rio Summit. Principle 16 of the Rio Declaration called for "promoting internalization of environmental costs and the use of economic instruments," and Principle 8 called for "eliminating unsustainable consumption and production" (UN, 2012). In 2002, the Johannesburg Plan of Implementation also emphasized the need to change the way societies produce and consume and called for developing a 10-year framework of programs for sustainable consumption and production (UN, 2012). A decade later, the global financial crisis led to questioning the unsustainable economic development path that many countries had pursued and revival of the term "green economy." In 2008, the United Nations Environmental Program (UNEP) called for governments to implement "green stimulus packages" as a way to promote economic recovery that supports the principles of sustainable development (UN, 2012).

While there is no internationally agreed-upon definition of the green economy, UNEP offers one of the most widely used: A "green economy is economy that leads to improved human well-being and social equity, while significantly reducing environmental risks and ecological scarcities." This definition reflects the three key elements of the green economy: (a) It is low carbon, (b) it uses resources efficiently, and (c) it helps promote poverty alleviation and social justice by improving well-being for all (UNEP, 2012).

Another term used when defining the green economy is *clean tech* or *clean technology*. While many people are using it interchangeably with green technology, there is a difference. Green technology includes both new technology and "end-of-pipe" technology, while clean tech focuses on new technologies with positive environmental impact, which "are driven by market economics therefore offering greater financial upside and sustainability" (Dikeman, 2008). Examples of clean tech include solar, wind, and ethanol technologies as well as fuel cells and electric vehicles, among others.

In 2008, UNEP launched the Green Economy Initiative as a way to provide analysis and policy support for growing the green, environmentally friendly sectors. Its 2011 Green Economy Report provides an overview of the current state of the green economy globally. The UN Commission for Sustainable Development published in 2012 a guidebook for countries on how to advance the green economy (UN, 2012). In the United States, one of the most significant policies to support the green economy was the American Recovery and Reinvestment Act (ARRA) of 2009. Signed into law by President Obama in February 2009 as a response to the Great Recession, the Act committed $788 billion to support the economy through infrastructure development, tax cuts, and transfers to states. Of this amount, $93 billion was allocated to support different industry sectors representing the green economy (e.g., low carbon transportation, green building and energy efficiency, transmission and infrastructure, broadband and telecommunications, environmental management, and remediation).

With support from a broad coalition of business, labor, environmental, and civil rights organizations, the U.S. Congress passed the Green Jobs Act in June 2007. The law (H.R. 2847) authorized up to $125 million in funding for setting up various job programs to address the shortages in green workforce that might be impairing the growth of green industries, such as energy efficient buildings and construction, renewable electric power, and bio-fuels development, among others. In addition, the law aimed to help identify and track the new jobs and skills needed to further advance energy efficiency and renewable energy (Dickson, Garvey, & Larson, 2007).

While there is no universally accepted definition of a green job, several organizations have proposed working definitions. The United Nations Environmental Program defines a green job as "work in agriculture, manufacturing, research and development, administrative and service activities that contribute substantially to preserving and restoring environmental quality" (Schulte, Heidel, Okun, & Branche, 2010). The U.S. Bureau of Labor Statistics defines green jobs as jobs involved in producing green products and services and increasing the use of clean energy, energy efficiency, and mitigating negative impacts on the environment (Schulte et al., 2010).

Clearly there is no universally agreed-upon definition of the green economy or what constitutes a green job. Regardless, a number of initiatives have attempted to measure the growth of the green economy and green jobs in the United States as a way to evaluate the impact of enacted policies and support future actions. The rest of this chapter focuses on the state of the green economy and green jobs in the United States. The main goal is to examine the current size, barriers, and opportunities for growing the green economy and related employment. A separate section is devoted to the issue of the occupational health and safety of green jobs. Finally, the chapter concludes with some recommendations on how to advance the green economy and green jobs in the United States.

MEASURING THE GREEN ECONOMY AND GREEN JOBS

Measuring the green economy and green jobs is challenging since there is no separate job classification, and almost all sectors are striving to conserve energy and resources while reducing their carbon footprint. In addition, many jobs may include making "green" as well as "nongreen" products or using both green and nongreen processes. Presently there is no universally accepted definition or methodology for measuring the green economy and green jobs, but several important recent initiatives have paved the way to moving in this direction.

A U.S. Department of Commerce study, "Measuring the Green Economy," estimated the private sector green employment in the United States based on Economic Census data (but did not include agriculture, rail transportation, educational institutions, political organizations, and private households). The study found that green jobs composed between 1.5% and 2% of private employment in 2007, accounting for about 1.8 million to 2.4 million jobs (Department of Commerce, 2010).

In a 2011 study, the Brookings Institution estimated that the U.S. clean economy in 2010 employed 2.7 million workers. Based on comprehensive review of existing green jobs/industry classifications, the report offered a detailed typology of the industry sectors representing the green economy, including agriculture and natural resource conservation, education and compliance, energy and resource efficiency, renewable energy, greenhouse gas reduction (GHG), environmental management, and recycling (Brookings Institution, 2011).

Similarly, the "Greening of the World of Work" study by the Occupational Information Network (O*Net) examined the occupational requirements and demand across 12 sectors. O*NET defined the green economy as "the economic activity related to reducing the use of fossil fuels, decreasing pollution and GHG emissions, increasing the efficiency of energy usage, recycling materials, and developing and adopting renewable sources of energy." The 12 green sectors in the study were (O*Net, 2009)

- Renewable energy generation
- Energy efficiency
- Energy trading
- Research, design, and consulting
- Agriculture and forestry
- Recycling and waste reduction
- Transportation
- Green construction
- Energy and carbon capture
- Environmental protection
- Manufacturing
- Governmental and regulatory

Of all initiatives to date, the Bureau of Labor Statistics (BLS) Green Jobs Initiative offers the best approach for classifying and measuring the green economy and green jobs. Launched in March 2010, the BLS Green Jobs Initiative aims to identify the number of and trend over time in green jobs, their distribution, and the wages of workers. It is based on an annual survey launched in 2011. The first BLS Green

Jobs report was published in 2012.[1] The BLS defines green jobs as either jobs in businesses that produce goods or provide services that benefit the environment or conserve natural resources or jobs in which workers' duties involve making their establishment's production processes more environmentally friendly or use fewer natural resources" (BLS, 2013).

Category A jobs and services fall into one of the following five categories:

1. Energy from renewable resources
2. Energy efficiency
3. Pollution reduction and removal, greenhouse gas reduction, and recycling and reuse
4. Natural resource conservation
5. Environmental compliance, education and training, and public awareness

Category B jobs fall within one of the following four categories:

1. Energy from renewable resources
2. Energy efficiency
3. Pollution reduction and removal, greenhouse gas reduction, and recycling and reuse
4. Natural resource conservation

According to the BLS results, there were a total of 3.4 million green jobs in the United States in 2011, an increase of 0.1% compared to 2010 and representing 2.6% of all jobs in the United States (BLS, 2013). Of these, about 2.5 million jobs were in the private sector and about 880,000 in the public sector. Construction demonstrated the highest increase in green employment between 2010 and 2011, while manufacturing had most green jobs (see Figure 1). Looking at the state level, California had the largest number of green jobs (360,245 jobs, representing 2.5% of all jobs in the state), while the District of Columbia had the highest percentage of green employment (5.1%), followed by Oregon (4.3%).

The study also found that 75% of the businesses were using at least one green technology or practice in 2011. *Energy efficiency* and *waste reduction* were the two most frequently used practices, reported by 57% and 55% of companies, respectively. The least common green technology or practice was the generation of electricity, heat, or fuel from renewable sources, reported by about 2% of establishments. Information and educational services were the two industries reporting the greatest adoption of green technologies and practices at 84% and 81%, respectively. At the low end were mining, quarrying, oil and gas extraction (49%), and transportation and warehousing (61%) (Watson, 2013; see Figure 2).

Some states have also attempted to measure the green sector and green jobs as a way to inform and guide state policies.

---

[1] The BLS Green Jobs Initiative was cancelled in March 2013 as result of the sequestration, or the $85 billion in across-the-board cuts by the U.S. Federal Government in fiscal year 2013 (BLS, 2013).

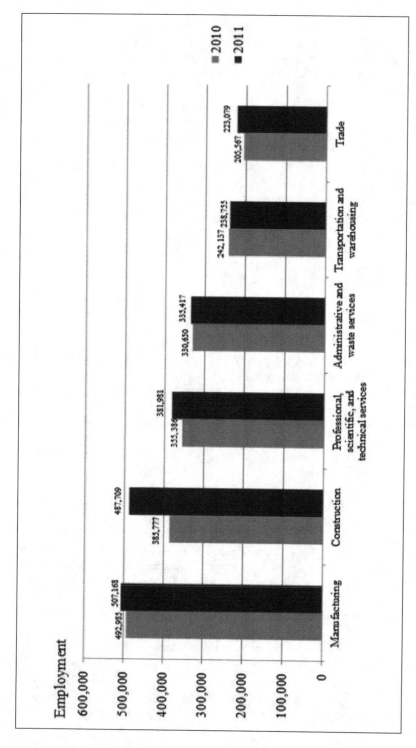

Figure 1. Green goods and services private sector employment, 2010–2011. **Source:** Bureau of Labor Statistics, http://www.bls.gov.news.release/pdf/ggqcew.pdf

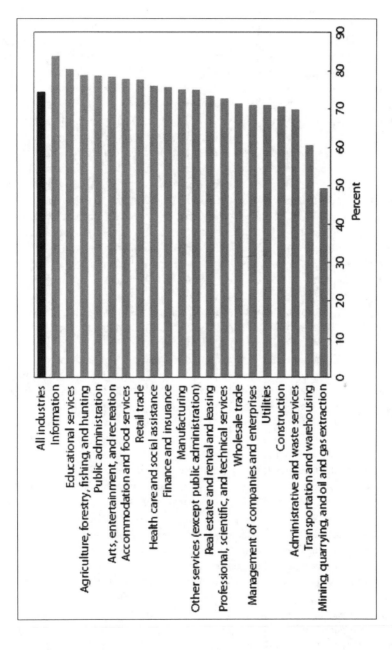

Figure 2. Percentage of establishments using at least one green technology or practice, by industry, August 2011 (Watson, 2013).

Washington State, one of the first states to attempt to measure the green economy and jobs, defined the green economy as "rooted in the development and use of products and services that promote environmental protection and energy security." The following types of business establishments were included in the study: (a) energy efficiency, (b) preventing and reducing pollution, (c) renewable energy, and (d) mitigating or cleaning up pollution. The study identified over 99,000 green jobs in 2010. The two major sectors involving green jobs were construction (mostly energy efficiency) with 38.6% of all green jobs, followed by agriculture at 15.8% (Washington State Employment Security Department, 2010).

In 2013, for the third year in a row, Massachusetts ranked first on the American Council for Energy Efficient Economy (ACEEE) State Energy Efficiency Scorecard (ACEEE, 2012). Massachusetts also ranked second after California for private clean energy investments. Local companies have received 17% (or $62.8 million) of the federal dollars awarded through the Department of Energy's ARPA-E program. As a result, the state has significantly increased its production of renewable energy with an 85-fold increase in installed solar capacity and 158% growth in electric energy savings from energy efficiency in just under 7 years (MACEC, 2013). A 2013 study found that Massachusetts had a large clean energy cluster, with 5,557 clean energy firms that employed 79,994 workers representing 1.9% of total employment in the state (MACEC, 2013). Since 2011, clean energy employment in Massachusetts has grown by 24.4%, or more than eight times faster than the overall 3% growth rate of all industries in the state. It is projected that by 2014, the sector will grow another 11.1% (MACEC, 2013). These numbers represent only part of all green jobs in the state, as no comprehensive data for other green sectors is available. The Commonwealth's success in advancing the green economy is result of bold policies passed by Governor Patrick, such as the Green Communities Act, the Green Jobs Act, and the Global Warming Solutions Act in 2008.

The year 2012 was challenging for U.S. Clean Tech due to presidential election politics, a gridlocked Congress, the "fiscal cliff," and bankruptcies of some clean tech investments such as Solyndra and A123 Systems. As a result, the U.S. venture capital investment in clean energy dropped 26% to its lowest level ($5 billion) since 2009. Regardless, there were some notable achievements: Wind power grew by 28%. Renewable energy overall (wind, solar, geothermal, biomass, and others) accounted for 49% of the added electricity capacity in the United States. Solar PV in the United States, spurred by continued price drops and innovative financing options, continued to grow. Installed PV capacity increased by 76%, with California becoming the first state to install more than 1,000 MW in a single year. The 2013 Clean Tech Leadership Index ranked California as the number one, followed by Massachusetts, Oregon, New York, and Colorado (Clean Edge 2013; see Figure 3).

In addition to states, cities are also ahead of the federal government on climate action, CO_2 reduction, and promoting green technology and jobs. More than 1,000 mayors have signed the 2005 U.S. Conference of Mayors' Climate Protection Agreement, pledging to meet or exceed Kyoto Protocol emission-reduction targets. Recently, 11 large U.S. cities became members of the global C40 Cities Climate

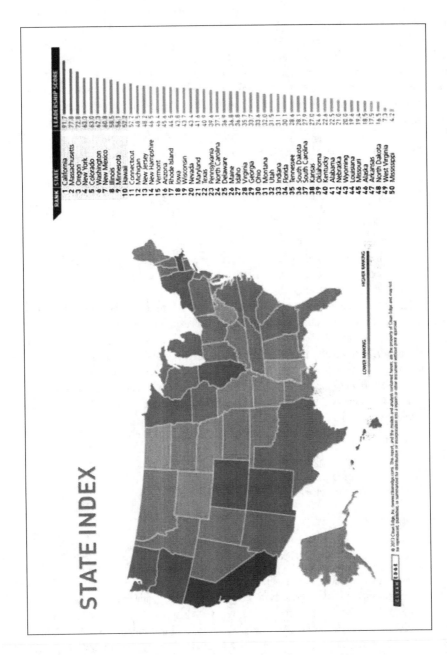

Figure 3. 2013 Clean Tech Leadership Index. Reprinted from Clean Edge (2013), with permission.

Leadership Group, in which cities around the world collaborate and share best practices on how to advance policies to promote clean tech and more sustainable energy use (Clean Edge, 2013).

Overall, the green economy is still small, representing less than 3% of all jobs in the United States. Yet it is growing at a rate faster than the overall economy, with some sectors, such as clean energy, experiencing double-digit growth annually. The advancement of the green economy is uneven, with some states such as California, Massachusetts, Oregon, and New York experiencing faster growth as a result of implementing a suite of supporting state and local policies. Manufacturing and construction presently include the largest number of green jobs, but 75% of all establishments in the United States report using at least one green technology or practice.

GOVERNMENT POLICIES TO SUPPORT THE GREEN ECONOMY

Most policies to support the green/clean economy in the United States have focused on promoting energy efficiency and clean energy development; significantly less has been done by the government to promote development of and increase demand for green products and less toxic production and manufacturing processes. With the lack of political consensus in the U.S. Congress, much of the policies driving the green economy in the United States presently are coming from state and local levels. This section provides an overview of some commonly used policies and their impacts. It does not offer a comprehensive review of all existing policies but rather aims to identify what is working and what is not, what are the barriers to business and job growth, and what are the lessons learned from existing policies.

Government policies to support the green economy generally can be classified into four main categories:

A. Laws and regulations
B. Financing sources and mechanisms
C. Green procurement requirements
D. Policies supporting cluster development

A. Laws and Regulations

Renewable portfolio standards (RPS)

RPS is one of the most commonly used policy mechanisms to increase renewable energy production. The standards typically require that a specified percentage of electricity supply comes from renewable energy. While the United States does not have a national RPS, 29 states plus the District of Columbia and Guam had such requirements or goals as of December 2010. The standards set renewable capacity goals between 4% and 30% by specified dates and often include incremental targets. They have been particularly successful in increasing the U.S. nonhydro renewable energy capacity by 60% between 1998 and 2010 (REEEP, 2010). Texas was among the first states to pass the RPS in 1999 and since has experienced a larger increase in renewable energy capacity expansion and use than any other state. A main lesson learned was that renewable energy expansion is often constrained by transmission, and government has a key role to play in supporting infrastructure development for clean energy through financing and more efficient permitting.

Energy efficiency resource standards (EERS)

The energy efficiency resource standard is a regulatory mechanism that encourages more efficient generation, transmission, and use of electricity and natural gas. Similar to the RPS, it is a performance-based mechanism wherein electricity and natural gas distributors are required to achieve a percentage of energy savings relative to baseline (typically between 1% and 20% within a specific timeframe). The United States does not presently have a national EERS, but 22 states had enacted such a standard as of December 2009. One example comes from Connecticut, which in 1998 adopted the first law related to energy efficiency. In 2007, the state adopted the Electricity and Energy Efficiency Act (H.B. 7432) to strengthen the requirements. The law mandates creation of the Connecticut Energy Efficiency fund, which is funded through a small charge in utility customers' bills (REEEP, 2010). No reliable data is available to evaluate the impact of the law in terms of energy costs, energy security, or job growth.

Public benefit funds (PBF)

PBF is a policy tool to secure stable, long-term funding for state or municipal energy programs, commonly supported by a small, fixed fee added to the customer's electricity bill each month. New Jersey was among the first states to implement such policy in 1999 as a way to support investments in energy efficiency and renewable energy. In 2001, the state adopted the Electric Discount and Energy Competition Act (EDECA), which supported the state's Energy Master Plan and its three main goals around reducing energy consumption, peak demand, and promoting renewable energy sources. Between 2001 and 2008, the state collected over $1.2 billion to support New Jersey's Clean Energy Program (NJCEP), and more than $1.2 billion was expected to be collected between 2009 and 2012. About 80% of this fund was devoted to energy efficiency programs and 20% to renewable energy programs. As result of the program, there were 4,719 renewable energy projects across the state through November 2009, providing 153.9 MW of sustainable energy (solar, wind, biomass, and fuel cells). The program helped reduce electricity and energy consumption and saved residents $4 for every dollar invested (REEEP, 2010).

Energy code implementation

This policy focuses on improving the energy profile of buildings—both commercial and residential—and requires the involvement of government agencies, nonprofit groups, design and construction industries, and other stakeholders to ensure training, information, and compliance with the mandates. Seattle was among the first places in the United States to implement such policies. The Seattle Energy Code (SEC) was originally adopted in 1980. The Seattle Department of Planning and Development is responsible for setting and enforcing the code. The code is updated every 3 years and aims for energy savings of nonresidential buildings at 20% above the current ASHRAE Standard of 90.1 (it also covers residential buildings). Seattle's experience provides valuable lessons for other communities on how to overcome challenges such as informing all stakeholders of code changes and ensuring compliance. The city has been very successful in "instilling in its building industry a culture of acceptance of the energy code requirements and enforcement" (REEEP, 2010). Another example: In 2007, Boston became the first city in the United States to require all large-scale projects to meet the U.S. Green Building Council's LEED certification standards (City of Boston, 2013). Such a mandate ensures greater adoption of building energy efficiency measures compared to a voluntary standard.

Building energy benchmarking and disclosure mandates

A growing number of U.S. cities are introducing energy benchmarking and disclosure mandates. These cities include San Francisco, New York City, Chicago, Philadelphia, and Boston. On May 8, 2013, Boston passed a mandate for such reporting and disclosure as part of its comprehensive strategy to achieve its Climate Action Plan and reduce Greenhouse Gas Emissions 20% by 2020 and 80% by 2050 (for reference, 70% of Boston's GHG emissions come from buildings, with the majority being commercial) (City of Boston, 2013). Studies have found strong correlation between building energy disclosure and improvements in energy efficiency (Keicher, 2013).

Appliances standards

Appliance and equipment standards help state and federal government achieve energy efficiency objectives while saving consumers money and reducing GHG emissions. As of 2010, the federal government had established appliances standards for over 30 product categories. Of the states, California has been a leader in this area, starting with the Warren-Alquist Act of 1974 and establishing appliances standards for over 50 products as of 2010. The state provides valuable lessons for successful implementation of an appliance standard, such as using rebates and other rewards to promote demand for new and unknown energy efficient products, providing incentives for utilities to support energy efficient products, and communicating standards to manufacturers across the United States and overseas. It is estimated that over 31% of the state's total energy savings have been achieved as result of California's appliance efficiency standards, leading to $2.5 billion annual savings in electrical bills (REEEP, 2010).

Compliance standards—The recent EPA clean air regulations

While some argue that tougher compliance standards will lead to job losses, data compiled by the Bureau of Labor Statistics shows that regulations are having "virtually no impact on job losses." In 2010, just 0.3% of the job losses were linked to stricter regulations. Conversely, several recent studies have looked into the impacts on job creation and economic development from the EPA's Cross-State Air Pollution Rule (CSAPR) and the Utility Toxics Rule. A two-phase study in 2011 commissioned by the Coalition for Environmentally Responsible Economies (CERES) and conducted by the Political Economic Research Institute (PERI) at UMASS Amherst found that meeting the two EPA rules for limiting sulfur dioxide, nitrogen oxides, mercury, and other air pollutants emitted by utilities will create nearly 1.5 million skilled construction and professional jobs between 2010 and 2015, or nearly 300,000 jobs per year (CERES, 2011). The investments in pollution controls and new generation capacity to meet the EPA's mercury and air toxics rule will also include net annual benefits between $52.5 and $139.5 billion and healthcare savings of $4.513 billion (the cost of compliance with the Utilities Toxics Rule is estimated at $11.3 billion).

In summary, most laws and regulations to support the green economy have been adopted at state and local levels, with no federal mandates in place as of 2013. Among the described policies in this section, the renewable portfolio standards and the energy codes have been among the most successful in advancing the green economy. However, limited data is available on the impact of most policies. Furthermore, no single policy instrument can effectively promote the green economy. Policymakers need to adopt "an optimal mix of instruments which are supported by national strategies and integrated policy frameworks." Such a mix should include market-based, regulatory, voluntary, and information-based instruments (UNIDO, 2011).

B. Financing Sources and Mechanisms

One of the most significant barriers to the green economy growth is the access to low-cost financing. The "Valley of Death," as defined by Bloomberg, prevents many new clean technologies from scaling up and commercialization (Bloomberg New Energy Finance, 2010). While venture capital was pouring into clean technologies at record amounts between 2004 and 2008 (a record increase from $46 billion to $173 billion), the recession reduced the available funding. In addition, federal subsidies and incentives are often short-term, and many of them expired at the end of 2012 due to the lack of action by Congress and the budget deficit (in January 2013, Congress extended the Production Tax Credit for Wind energy by another year) (see Figure 4). Such a lack of long-term subsidies and a comprehensive energy policy creates uncertainty and constrains renewable energy investments. Today's clean technologies cannot compete with incumbent dirty technologies due to perverse subsidies, the cost of switching, or customer reluctance to adopt an untested technology or products. In such an environment, providing long-term incentives and subsidies and stable, predictable environment for deployment is critical and will require a reform of the myriad tax provisions and incentives. Studies have demonstrated the correlation between the existence of federal subsidies for clean technologies and the growth of the sector, as well as its decline when such subsidies expire.

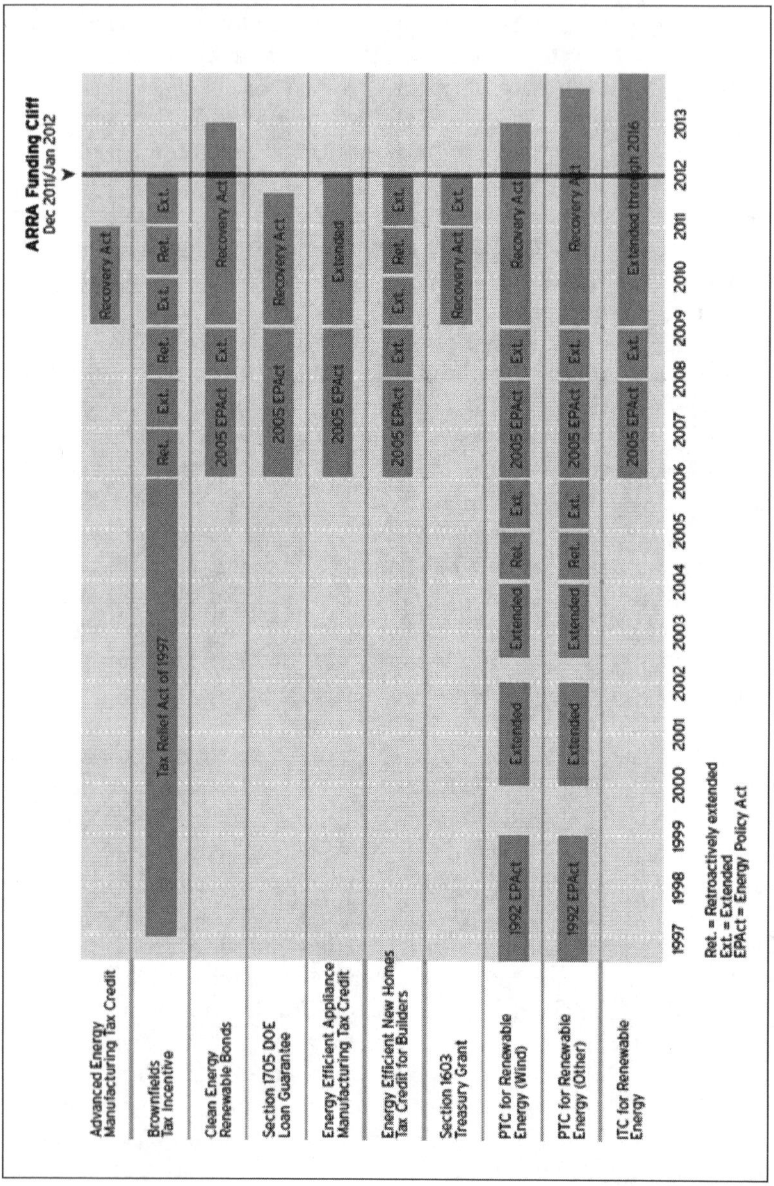

Figure 4. Expiration of many federal clean economy tax and other incentives. Reprinted from the Brookings Institution (2011), with permission from the Metropolitan Policy Program at Brookings.

China provides an example of successful government policies to promote clean technologies by leveraging long-term, low-cost financing. In just a few years, the country has emerged as the world leader in deployment of clean technologies. In 2010, China put in place $54.4 billion in clean technology investments (for comparison, the U.S. private investment in clean energy totaled $34 billion). In the first quarter of 2011, China added an additional $10.9 billion for asset finance investments compared to just $2 billion in the United States (Bloomberg New Energy Finance, 2010). While the approach taken by China cannot be replicated in a market economy like the United States, there are some steps that the U.S. government can take to support business and national competitiveness in this area, such as adopting a comprehensive long-term clean technology strategy, increase the demand side by implementing proper management regulations, provide lower cost financing for clean technologies, and consider adopting a carbon tax.

The rest of this section provides examples of present U.S. policies related to financing, their impact, and the lessons learned.

American Recovery and Reinvestment Act (ARRA) of 2009

As discussed earlier, the ARRA is one of the most significant recent laws that support (in part) the green economy in the United States. The best study of its impact was commissioned by the BlueGreen Alliance and the Economic Policy Institute in 2011. It found that the $93 billion to support the green economy helped create or save 997,000 jobs and increased the U.S. GDP by $146 billion (Walsh, Bivens, & Pollack, 2011). Under the ARRA appropriation for Electric Vehicle and Component manufacturing, the Department of Energy (DOE) has provided grants (a total of $2 billion) to support development of electric vehicles and more efficient batteries. As a result of the program, the United States increased its share of the world's hybrid batteries—manufacturing from 2% in 2009 to 20% in 2012—and is expected to reach 40% by 2020, while helping cut the price of hybrid batteries in half (Canis, 2013). As of December 2010, almost all $2 billion were obliged, over $469 million were invoiced, and 1,109 jobs were created each quarter.

The ARRA has also been instrumental in supporting state and local initiatives to grow green sectors and promote green jobs. For example, the City of Boston conducted a comprehensive study of the economic and sustainability benefits of the ARRA investments and found that the $327.6 million in investment (of this amount, $241.2 million was direct ARRA stimulus) translated into 1,276 direct full-time equivalent (FTEs) jobs in Boston and an additional 1,585 jobs statewide (direct and induced). Additional social and environmental benefits included reduction in electricity consumed, gas used, water preserved, and GHG emissions prevented (Boston Redevelopment Authority, 2010).

Yet there were problems with the implementation of ARRA. For example, the funding that states received under the Weatherization Assistance Program (a total of $5 billion) "strained capacity of states and providers to ramp up quickly while maintaining program quality." The law's new requirements also took time to understand and implement (e.g., the Davis Bacon prevailing wage requirements), all of which led to "serious and unexpected delays in implementation."

Better building initiative

Announced by President Obama in February 2011, this initiative includes a suite of legislative proposals and executive action aimed at reducing energy consumption in commercial buildings by 20% by 2020. The initiative commits $4 billion in public and private investments in building upgrades, which are projected to save American businesses approximately $40 billion per year as well as improve U.S. air quality, reduce GHG emissions, and create jobs. Key elements of the initiative include new tax incentives for building efficiency, more financing opportunities for commercial retrofits, and competitive grants to state and local governments, among others. The initiative complements the ARRA's $20 billion in funding for building energy efficiency. A study by the Political Economy Research Institute (PERI) at UMASS Amherst estimated that the initiative would create more than 114,000 jobs (direct, indirect, and induced) and save businesses over $1.4 billion in annual energy bills (Burt, Waltner, Desiderio, & Zeidenberg, 2011).

U.S. Department of Energy loan guarantee program

This program was established by the Energy Policy Act of 2005, and its main goal was to foster development of early stage technologies by leveraging federal government unconditional guarantee of up to 80% of the loans. The ARRA allocated additional $6 billion to Section 1703 of the program. However, numerous problems have been identified with this program—from the lack of proper personnel and enormous documentary burden on companies (in some cases over thousands of pages) to the lack of transparency and uncovered corruption such as the case of now bankrupt solar company Solyndra, which received $535 million from the program (GAO, 2013).

C. Green Procurement

Due to their significant purchasing power, federal and state governments can help drive the green economy by increasing the demand for green products and services. While there is no federal strategy for ramping up green procurement, several initiatives have been enacted at federal and state levels.

Executive Order 13514 for federal buildings

To lead by example and demonstrate federal government commitment to sustainability, in October 2009 President Obama signed Executive Order 13514, which set specific targets for federal agencies, such as 30% reduction in vehicle fleet petroleum use by 2020, a 26% improvement in water efficiency by 2020, a 50% recycling and waste diversion by 2015, implementation of the 2030 net-zero-energy building requirements, and 95% of all applicable contracts to meet sustainability requirements. In January 2010, President Obama announced a federal government-wide GHG emissions reduction targets for 2020 of 28% below 2008 levels. While no data is currently available on the impact of these policies, the potential for driving demand and, respectively, business and job creation, is significant (CEQ, 2009).

State and local green procurement initiatives

Many states and towns have implemented mandates and voluntary guidelines on green procurement, energy efficiency, and clean energy, which have helped grow the green economy, although good measures of the actual impacts are still lacking. California has been among the leaders with the Governor's Green Building Executive Order and AB32 (DGS, 2011). Early adopters of environmentally preferable purchasing also include Minnesota, Maine, Washington State, and Wisconsin.

Green labeling and certification

Programs such as Energy Star and Green Seal can drive demand for green products and processes by raising awareness and advancing green procurement. While no data presently exists on the impact of such programs on jobs and business growth, a recent study found a significant increase in adopting green purchasing by government agencies between 2001 and 2009 but no registered improvement in performance. Green procurement policies have been found to influence less than 20% of procurement budgets. The main obstacles identified include the incomplete and imperfect information on benefits, the lack of common standards, the real and perceived costs, and some market and technical uncertainties (Fisher, 2010).

D. Policies Supporting Cluster Development of the Clean Economy

According to a 2011 study by the Brookings Institution, U.S. efforts to advance the green economy to date have placed too little emphasis on regional and industry cluster strategies, defined as "the geographic concentration of interconnected firms and supporting or coordinating organizations" (Brookings Institution, 2011). While such efforts are beginning to emerge, they are still inadequate. Modest support for cluster initiatives is presently offered by the Economic Development Administration, the Small Business Administration, the National Science Foundation, and the DOE's Energy Regional Innovation Cluster hub, among others. The federal government and states "need to understand and embrace the fact that the clean economy is significantly region-and-metro-led." They need to empower regional clean economy initiatives. In fact, some states such as Colorado, New York, Massachusetts, and Oregon have already applied a strong regional and cluster focus on their clean economy development. The Puget Sound area in Washington State, for example, has positioned itself as a leader in energy efficiency and building solutions (McKinsey Global Energy and Materials, 2009).

GREEN JOBS AND WORKER HEALTH AND SAFETY

With the excitement and rush to advance the green economy and green jobs, many policymakers, academics, and businesses have failed to recognize the risks that such jobs and processes can create for workers, communities, and the environment. In fact, as Schulte et al. (2010) demonstrate, most of the current definitions of a "green job" do not include health and safety, including the ones provided by UNEP and U.S. Bureau of Labor Statistics and presented earlier in this chapter. Labor groups and researchers have raised concerns about the safety and health hazards related to green jobs. For instance, during the construction of the Las Vegas City Center, which earned six Leadership in Energy and Environmental Design (LEED) gold certifications, six construction workers were killed (Schulte et al., 2010). A green job is not necessarily a safe job, and much work remains to be done to identify, evaluate, minimize, and control the hazards posed by new green technologies and processes. Below are outlined some examples of the worker risks associated with common green jobs.

Much of weatherization and energy efficiency jobs include traditional hazards, such as falls, musculoskeletal stresses, and airborne chemicals. For example, fibercement is a popular concrete-like material used in roof shingles, photovoltaic (PV) panel units, floor underlayment, and siding for its strength, durability as well as mold, fire, and weather resistance. However, it contains up to 50% crystalline silica, a known occupational hazard causing silicosis and lung cancer (RICOSH, 2009).

The most common solar energy systems include PV panels, which use semiconductors and sunlight to generate electricity. The manufacturing, installation, and end-of-life disposal of such PV panels, however, include some serious occupational hazards. More than 15 hazardous materials are used in the manufacture of PV panels (ILO, 2012), such as

- *Cadmium telluride (CdTe)*: A known and highly toxic carcinogens; EPA and OSHA consider cadmium "extremely toxic" as it has the potential to cause kidney, liver, bone, and blood damage from ingestion and lung cancer from inhalation;
- *Gallium arsenide (GaAs)*: The limited toxicological data on this chemical suggest potential "profound effects on lung, liver, immune, and blood systems" if workers are exposed for extensive periods during manufacturing or if the chemical is accidentally released;
- *Silicon tetrachloride (SiCl4)*: An extremely toxic substance that reacts violently with water, causes skin burns, and is a respiratory, skin, and eye irritant;
- *Sulfur hexafluoride (SF6)*: This is used to clean the reactors used in silicon production and is classified by the Intergovernmental Panel on Climate Change (IPCC) as the most potent greenhouse gas (25,000 times more potent than CO_2);
- *Sodium hydroxide (NaOH) and potassium hydroxide (KOH)*: These are used to remove the sawing damage on the silicon wafer surfaces and are caustic chemicals that are dangerous to the eyes, lungs, and skin;

- *Lead (Pb)*: Lead is often used in solar PV electronic circuits for wiring, solder-coated copper strips, and some lead-based printing pastes. It is known for its neurotoxicity, developmental toxicity, and carcinogenicity;
- *Trichloroethylene (TCE)*: TCE used as a solvent for cleaning and is a known carcinogen;
- *Hydrochloric acid, methane, triethyl gallium, and trimethyl gallium*: These are also used in the manufacturing of solar panels and pose both environmental and worker hazards.

The occupational hazards and risks in the manufacturing of wind turbines are similar to the ones present in the automobile industry and aerospace installations; the installation and maintenance of such turbines creates hazards similar to those in construction. The main chemicals of concern in these cases include styrene, epoxy resins, solvents, harmful gases, vapors, and dusts (e.g., from fiberglass, hardeners, aerosols, and carbon fibers) (ILO, 2012). Such exposure could cause liver and kidney damage, dermatitis, dizziness, chemical burns, and reproductive effects. The most significant physical hazards during wind turbine maintenance include falling from heights, musculoskeletal disorders resulting from manual handling and awkward postures, injuries from falling objects or rotating machinery (ILO, 2012). Wind turbine manufacturing also requires the use of rare earth metals, which are associated with significant environmental and occupational hazards during mining.

With shrinking waste disposal capacity, recycling, and waste management are poised for continued growth. The ILO's green jobs program identified waste management as one of the fastest sectors for green employment (ILO, 2012). Yet these industrial sectors include a range of occupational and environmental hazards. Recycling work can be dirty, polluting, and dangerous, even in developed countries. The ILO reported a case of mercury poisoning in a UK-based electrical waste recycling facility resulting from the recycling of compact fluorescent light bulbs (CFLs)—a widely promoted green alternative to incandescent bulbs—due to their mercury content. Waste-to-energy processes "can lead to air pollution, explosions, and dangerous substances and gases in confined spaces" (ILO, 2012).

Many green technologies and green jobs present a variety of occupational risks from nanoengineered materials—substances whose physical properties are changed at the molecular level to improve performance, a process often leading to different and more hazardous toxicological impacts. The latter are still inadequately studied, and a few controls and other protective measures are in place to protect workers (SVTC, 2009).

Another concern related to the adoption of green technologies is the potential to create an electronic waste burden if the proper infrastructure is not put in place. According to the Silicon Valley Toxics Coalition report,

> Solar PV panels have the potential to create a significant new wave of electronic waste at the end of their useful lives (which is estimated to be 20 to 25 years), and they also contain a growing number of new and emerging materials

(such as cadmium telluride and gallium arsenide) that present complex recycling challenges in terms of technology, safety and health and environmental protection. (SVTC, 2009)

Numerous organizations such as the Occupational Health and Safety Administration (OSHA), the National Institute for Occupational Safety and Health (NIOSH), the Toxics Use Reduction Institute (TURI), and others are working to promote greater awareness and improved recognition and prevention of occupational hazards from green technologies. OSHA, for example, provides information on the hazards associated with different green jobs (OSHA, 2012). The main challenge, however is that majority of establishments creating green jobs are small. A 2012 report by the Massachusetts Clean Energy Center found that two-thirds of the clean energy employers had 10 or fewer employees (MACEC, 2012). Such organizations often lack the resources and the culture of creating a safety program. They are also more difficult to reach by OSHA and other occupational health and safety organizations to inspect or provide with free consultation and training.

In December 2009, about 170 representatives from labor, industry, academia, government agencies, and nongovernmental organizations attended a workshop on Making Green Jobs Safe. The experts emphasized Prevention thorough Design (PtD) as the most effective approach to risk reduction in the various green jobs (NIOSH, 2011). They identified 48 strategies for ensuring green jobs are safe, which can be grouped into four main categories: research, education, practice, and policy. Research efforts, for example, must focus on identifying the work hazards of green technologies, eliminating such hazards at the design phase using green chemistry, and developing safer alternatives. Education efforts must aim to change the culture of designers, architects, engineers, and businesses by incorporating occupational health and safety in professional training and certifications. Finally, developing new standards that incorporate occupational health and safety requirements are necessary to ensure wider adoption of safer work practices (Schulte et al., 2010). The workshop participants proposed "a product, building, or process should not be allowed to be called green unless it can also be called safe" (NIOSH, 2011).

As the Assistant Secretary of Labor for Occupational Safety and Health, David Michaels, summed up,

> It is vital, now, that we integrate worker safety and health concerns into green manufacturing, green construction and green energy. Most importantly: We must push worker health and safety as a critical, necessary, and recognized element of green design, green lifecycle analysis and green contracts. (Michaels, 2009)

ANALYSIS OF CURRENT BARRIERS AND OPPORTUNITIES TO ADVANCING THE GREEN ECONOMY

This section outlines some studies that analyze the current barriers to advance the green economy and identify potential solutions.

The Center for Community Innovation at UC Berkeley has done extensive research on the green economy and policies for development both in California and nationwide. Its research has found that most U.S. policies and resources to date have promoted production and have focused on energy, utilities, and green building, followed by green/clean tech manufacturing and transportation. Much less attention has been paid to stimulating consumption and focusing on the sectors related to changes in lifestyle (e.g., retail, eco-tourism, organic gardening) (Chapple, 2008).

A study by the Georgia Tech School of Public Policy provides comprehensive analysis of the current barriers to advancement of clean energy technologies in the United States. The study identified three main types of barriers—fiscal, regulatory, and statutory—and the specific policies under each of these that impede the development of such technologies presently. Table 1 summarizes the key barriers outlined in the study.

The Hamilton Project offered a detailed analysis and proposed a U.S. strategy of incorporating the full social costs of different energy sources (Greenstone & Looney, 2011). The latter should include the costs of the health effects of current energy sources, the social costs of carbon, other environmental and economic effects, and the impact on macroeconomic stability and international security. The study estimated a social cost of carbon at \$21 per ton of CO_2 emissions for 2010 and found that at least seven major regulations have included the social costs of carbon. The authors recommended four main approaches for addressing the present shortcomings of U.S. energy strategy: (a) appropriately price the social cost of energy production and use; (b) fund basic research, development, and demonstrations; (c) make regulations more efficient; and (d) address climate change on a global scale as most of the negative impacts of today's energy use are experienced outside the United States.

According to most national- and state-level studies on the green economy and green jobs, the construction industry and particularly, improving energy efficiency, has the greatest potential to create new jobs or preserve existing construction-related jobs. A 2009 study by the U.S. Green Building Council found that green construction could support over 7.9 million jobs by 2013 (Hamilton, 2009). The U.S. economy has steadily improved its ability to produce more with less energy. However, these improvements have emerged unevenly and are far short from achieving their potential for reducing U.S. economy carbon intensity and creating more jobs. McKinsey research outlines three main types of barriers to improving U.S. energy efficiency: structural, behavioral, and availability. For example, substantial upfront investment is needed in which the payback is over the lifetime of the measure taken; measuring the nonuse of energy is challenging, and reaching out to all players in the fragmented energy efficiency market is challenging. The study suggested some solutions to overcome these barriers and "unlock" the energy efficiency in the United States, which is projected to save more than \$1.2 trillion through 2020. These solutions include education and information, incentives and financing, codes and standards, and third-party involvement (McKinsey Global Energy and Materials, 2009).

A report by the Tellus Institute and Sound Resource Management addressed the potential impact of implementing a bold national recycling and composting strategy in the United States over the next two decades. The study authors found that mandating a 75% national waste diversion rate by 2030 could generate 2,347,000 total direct jobs—over 1.1 million more jobs than the status quo and nearly

Table 1. Fiscal, Regulatory, and Statutory Impediments to Clean Energy
Technologies. Adapted from Brown and Chandler (2008, Table 2).
Reprinted with permission of the Board of Trustees of the
Leland Stanford Junior University

Type of barrier	Specific policies	Examples
Unfavorable fiscal policies	Tax subsidies	Deductions for purchase of large light trucks under IRS rules; oil and gas companies claim depletion deduction for loss of their reserves.
	Unequal taxation of capital and operating expenses	Federal tax code discourages capital investments in general and forces depreciation of energy efficiency investments over a longer period of time.
	Unfavorable tariffs	Import tariff for ethanol raises the cost for ethanol.
	Utility pricing policies	Regulated rate structure, lack of real-time pricing; profits linked to sales
Ineffective fiscal policies		Tax credits for hybrid electric vehicles and residential PV systems have limited value due to AMT tax; state incentives to develop forested land instead of leaving it as carbon sink.
Fiscal uncertainty	Fiscal incentives	Variable production tax credits.
	Fiscal penalties	Investor uncertainty regarding GHG emissions costs.
Unfavorable regulatory policies	Performance standards	Exemptions for existing facilities from stricter emission standards.
	Connection standards	Ban on private electric wires crossing public stress.
Ineffective regulations	Regulatory loopholes	Exemption of heavy vehicles over 8,500 pounds of CAFÉ standards
	Poor land-use planning	Zoning for low-density urban development.
	Burdensome permitting processes	Slow and burdensome process for land-based wind projects, carbon capture, and hydrogen.

Table 1. (Cont'd.)

Type of barrier	Specific policies	Examples
Regulatory uncertainty		Uncertainty regarding GHG regulation.
Unfavorable statutes	Lack of modern and enforceable building codes	Building codes based on outdated technology.
	State procurement policies	Inability of state agencies to contract over more than one fiscal year.
Statutory uncertainty	Variable clean energy portfolio standards	Variable standards across states making it difficult for utility investors to improve efficiency.
	Uncertain property rights	Unclear property rights for subsurface and above-surface areas (e.g., coalbed methane, wind energy, carbon storage).

1.5 million more jobs than in 2008 (this is an additional benefit to reducing human health and ecosystem impact as well as reliance on imports for materials such as metals). Waste disposal is not labor intensive and generates just 0.1 jobs per 1,000 tons of waste. Recycling and manufacturing using recycled materials creates a relatively high number of jobs—2 jobs per 1,000 tons for processing of recyclables; 4 jobs per 1,000 tons for manufacturing using recycled paper, iron, and steel; and about 10 jobs per 1,000 tons for plastics manufacturing (Tellus Institute and Sound Resource Management, 2011). Reuse is even more labor intensive, with computer reuse leading in terms of job creation (30 jobs per 1,000 TPY) (Institute for Local Self-Reliance, 2011). Unfortunately, no federal recycling mandate exists currently in the United States; most such requirements are initiated at state and local levels.

NEW POLICIES, NEW IDEAS

Despite some success in advancing the green economy and green jobs in the United States, much remains to be done to develop and implement effective federal, state, and local policies. Here are some suggestions for strategies that provide the greatest impact:

1. Introduce Energy Tax Changes

One of the most important and urgent strategies to advance the green economy involves making changes to the current energy taxes and eliminating existing barriers and perverse tax subsidies. In his 2010 testimony to the Ways and Means Committee of the House of Representatives, Joseph Romm made the following recommendations for addressing existing tax barriers and driving the green job economy (Romm, 2010):

- Eliminate perverse tax subsidies (e.g., oil companies in 2009 were subsidized $1.3 billion at the taxpayers' expense to deplete U.S. national resources)
- Stop investing in polluting technologies like coal to liquids (CO_2 emissions of coal-to-diesel are twice as high than from conventional diesel)
- Increase transparency of tax expenditures (in 2007, approximately $6 billion in direct spending on energy and $10 billion in additional under-the-radar tax spending were not disclosed)
- Streamline and maximize beneficial subsidies that level the playing field, such as production tax credit (e.g., for wind generation), cash grant in lieu of investment tax credit, manufacturing tax credit, and 100% capital expense deduction for clean energy development (similar to the way fossil companies can currently deduct their spending on imported fuels as a business expense).

2. Increase Government Support of R&D in Clean Technologies to Promote Disruptive Innovation

According to recent analysis by the Brookings Institution, current U.S. efforts to promote innovation for the clean economy are "inadequate in terms of both their scale and their format." Studies have suggested that we need national expenditures "of at least $15 billion to $25 billion annually to bring the research intensity of the U.S. energy sector in line with that of other innovation-oriented sectors such as IT, biotech or the semiconductor industry" (Brookings Institution, 2011). Private investments have limited the ability to drive disruptive innovation as they often avoid early-stage, risky technologies. While such massive investments by the federal government are unlikely, there are still numerous approaches that can be taken—embrace incremental growth of the energy and environmental R&D budgets even in the context of deficit reduction; make incremental investments in the Energy Frontier Research Centers, ARPA-E, and the Energy Innovation Hubs; create a water sciences innovation center and establish regional clean economy consortium initiatives; focus and prioritize innovation investments at the state level.

3. Introduce a Carbon Tax to Promote Energy Efficiency and Expansion of Mature Clean Technologies

While a carbon tax has often been cited as one of the most important policies needed to support the growth of the green economy, a 2011 study demonstrated that to make clean technologies competitive with coal, a carbon tax would have to "rise to politically untenable levels of $100 or more per ton" (Hourihan & Atkinson, 2011). A modest carbon tax, however, is a valuable policy mechanism that "could help alter individual consumption as well as investment decisions in the power sector to boost the diffusion of mature, available alternatives to take advantage of the so-called low-hanging fruit, including wind at peak hours and energy efficiency measures" (Hourihan & Atkinson, 2011). A carbon tax can also serve as a revenue generator to invest in clean technology innovation.

4. Support Financing of Clean Technologies

According to the Brookings Institution's study of the clean economy,

> The single most catalytic action that could be taken to advance the scale-up of new clean economy manufacturing and infrastructure is an action by Congress to create an emerging technology deployment finance entity to address the commercialization of the Valley of Death. (2011)

Studies have proposed creation of Clean Energy Deployment Administration (CEDA) and/or Energy Independence Trust (EIT). Two other proposed approaches include emerging technology to reverse auction mechanisms and efficacy insurance (Bloomberg New Energy Finance, 2010).

5. Increase Demand for Clean Technologies

At a minimum, federal and state governments can step up their procurement of green goods and services. Each year, the federal government purchases $500 billion in goods and services, and state and local governments spend an additional $400 billion. In addition, the federal government occupies 500,000 buildings and operates more than 600,000 vehicles, which all provide "an enormous opportunity for government supply chains to create and drive the market for clean economy growth" (Brookings Institution, 2011). There is a need for better information about the environmental and social impact and benefit of such products and services.

6. Focus on Regions and Build the Clean Economy Cluster by Cluster

Efforts to advance the green economy by the United States to date have placed too little emphasis on regional and industry cluster strategies. While such efforts are beginning to emerge, they are still inadequate. In order to promote cluster development, regions need first to understand the local clean economy in detail, to identify existing barriers and constraints, and then move to formulate strong, "bottom up" action to address them. Local policymakers can play a critical role by leveraging procurement, improving zoning and permitting processes, and improving regional clean economy workforce development. Building strong public-private partnerships is critical for advancing local and regional cluster development of the clean economy.

7. Ensure That Green Jobs are Also Safe

It is an imperative to include worker safety and health concerns into green manufacturing, green construction, and clean energy and adopt life-cycle analysis for identifying all potential hazards to workers, communities, and the environment. Policymakers should promote research, education, best practices, and policy changes that ensure green jobs are also safe and emphasize Prevention through Design (PtD) strategies. New standards must incorporate occupational health and safety requirements. Policies should also aim at reaching out to smaller firms through industry associations and other local organizations.

8. Develop and Train Skilled Workforce

Ultimate success for the United States in maintaining a competitive position and advancing the green economy depends on the availability of a skilled workforce. Such policies require identifying the business needs in terms of skills and knowledge, developing better communication systems, and ultimately aligning the current curriculum with the business needs of the green economy by establishing partnerships between academia, business, and government. With funding from Massachusetts Clean Energy Center, the UMASS Boston Center for Sustainable Enterprise and Regional Competitiveness launched five interdisciplinary programs in Clean Energy and Sustainability in 2011, which help equip "green and white collar" professionals, policymakers, and business managers for the transition to a clean energy economy. Designed for both students and professionals, these new offerings blend up-to-date expertise, theory, and practice to meet the demands of a transition to a sustainable economy (for more information, see www.umb.edu/serc/sustain).

CONCLUSION

As the green economy continues to gain momentum and further grow in different forms in different regions, policymakers, businesses, and other stakeholders have an opportunity to shape its future. This is accomplished through establishing partnerships, understanding the current barriers and opportunities, and working collaboratively to build on local strengths in designing an effective long-term strategy. While the federal government has an important role to play, local policies can drive regional green economies by taking advantage of the existing capacity in job training programs, business incubators, small business assistance centers, and other organizations. It is critical in developing new policies and strategies to include a wide group of stakeholders and implement life-cycle approaches in identifying and minimizing all potential health and safety hazards of new and existing green technologies. This will help create a more sustainable and equitable green economy.

DISCUSSION QUESTIONS

Chapter 1: The State of the Green Economy and Green Jobs in the United States

1. What are the main sectors in the U.S. green economy? What green technologies and practices are most frequently used by businesses? Which states are leading in terms of advancing the green economy and green jobs?

2. What are the main government policies to support the green economy in the United States? Which policies are most effective in supporting the green economy and which are least effective?

3. Why is it said that some green jobs are not necessarily safe jobs? Provide examples of green technologies which may expose workers to health and safety risks.

4. What are the main barriers to growing the green economy in the United States? What are some strategies to overcome these barriers?

REFERENCES

American Council for an Energy Efficient Economy (ACEEE). (2012, October 3). *Massa-chusetts still #1 state for energy efficiency, while Oklahoma, Montana, and South Carolina are among most improved.* Retrieved August 21, 2013, from http://aceee.org/press/2012/10/aceee-massachusetts-still-1-state-en

Bloomberg New Energy Finance. (2010, June 21). *Crossing the Valley of Death: Solutions to the next generation clean energy project financing gap.* Retrieved August 30, 2013, from http://cleanegroup.bluehousegroup.com/assets/Uploads/CEGBNEF-2010-06-21 valleyofdeath.pdf

Boston Redevelopment Authority. (2010). *Economic and sustainability benefits of Boston's ARRA investments.* Retrieved August 20, 2013, from http://www.cityofboston.gov/Images_Documents/SROI%20Analysis%20Report_tcm3-18467.pdf

Brookings Institution. (2011). *Sizing the clean economy: A national and regional jobs assess-ment.* Retrieved August 30, 2013, from http://www.brookings.edu/~/media/Series/resources/0713_clean_economy.pdf

Brown M., & Chandler, S. (2008). Governing confusion: How statutes, fiscal policy and regulations impede clean energy technologies. *Stanford Law & Policy Review, 19*(472), 507.

Bureau of Labor Statistics (BLS). (2013). *Measuring green jobs.* Retrieved August 16, 2013, from www.bls.gov/green/

Burt, L., Waltner, M., Desiderio, D., & Zeidenberg, D. (2011, June 13). *A new retrofit industry: An analysis of the job creation potential of tax incentives for energy efficiency in commercial buildings and other components of the Better Buildings initiative.* Retrieved August 9, 2013, from http://www.usgbc.org/ShowFile..aspx? DocumentID=9531

Canis, B. (2013, April 4). Battery manufacturing for hybrid and electric vehicles: Policy issues. *Congressional Research Service.* Retrieved August 10, 2013, from http://www.fas.org/sgp/crs/misc/R41709.pdf

Center on Education and the Workforce. (2010, August). State of green: The definition and measurement of green jobs. *Georgetown University.* Retrieved August 28, 2013, from http://cew.georgetown.edu/117408.html

CERES. (2011, November). *New jobs—Cleaner air part II: An investment in American businesses and American jobs.* Retrieved August 16, 2013, from http://www.ceres.org/resources/reports/new-jobs-cleaner-air-part-two

Chapple, K. (2008, November). Defining the green economy: A primer on green economic development. *Center for Community Innovation at UC Berkeley.* Retrieved August 30, 2013, from http://communityinnovation.berkeley.edu/reports/Chapple%20-%20 Defining%20the%20Green%20Economy.pdf

City of Boston. (2013). *Green buildings.* Retrieved August 12, 2013, from http://www. cityofboston.gov/environmentalandenergy/buildings/

Clean Edge. (2013, June). *2013 U.S. clean tech leadership index.* Retrieved August 12, 2013, from http://www.cleanedge.com/sites/default/files/CTLI-2013-Report.pdf? attachment=true

Council on Environmental Quality (CEQ). (2009). *Federal leadership in environmental, energy and economic performance—Executive Order 13514.* Retrieved August 13, 2013, from http://www.whitehouse.gov/administration/eop/ceq/sustainability

Department of Commerce. (2010, April). *Measuring the green economy.* Retrieved August 14, 2013, from http://www.greenbiz.com/business/research/report/2010/05/04/measuring-green-economy?utm_source=twitterfeed&utm_medium=twitter

DGS. (2011, March). *California green goals and accomplishments.* Retrieved from http://www.documents.dgs.ca.gov/dgs/pio/green/highlights.pdf

Dickson, A., Garvey, B., & Larson, M. (2007). *Green energy options for sustainable local economic development: Policy, financing and strategies for green energy.* Atlanta: Georgia Institute of Technology.

Dikeman, N. (2008, August). What is clean tech? *CNet.* Retrieved August 15, 2013, from http://news.cnet.com/8301-11128_3-10012950-54.html

Fisher, E. (2010, April 20). Green procurement: Overview and issues for congress. *Congressional Research Service.* Retrieved August 15, 2013, from http://nepinstitute.org/get/CRS_Reports/CRS_Climate_and_Environment/Other_Environmental_Issues/Green_Procurement.pdf

General Accounting Office (GAO). (2013, May). *Status of DOE loan programs.* Retrieved August 10, 2013, from http://gao.gov/assets/660/653064.pdf

Greenstone, M., & Looney, A. (2011, May). A strategy for America's energy future: Illuminating energy's full costs. *The Hamilton Project, Strategy Paper.* Retrieved August 10, 2013, from http://www.brookings.edu/~/media/Files/rc/papers/2011/05_energy_greenstone_looney/05_energy_greenstone_looney.pdf

Hamilton, B. A. (2009, July). Green jobs study summary. *U.S. Green Building Council.* Retrieved August 20, 2013, from http://www.usgbc.org/ShowFile.aspx?DocumentID=6435

Hourihan, M., & Atkinson, R. (2011, March). Inducing innovation: What a carbon price can and can't do. *The Information Technology & Innovation Foundation.* Retrieved August 15, 2013, from http://www.itif.org/files/2011-inducing-innovation.pdf

Institute for Local Self-Reliance. (2011). *Recycling means business.* Retrieved August 8, 2013, from http://www.ilsr.org/recycling/recyclingmeansbusiness.html

International Labor Organization (ILO). (2012, April 28). *Promoting safety and health in a green economy.* Retrieved August 12, 2013, from http://www.ilo.org/wcmsp5/groups/public/---ed_protect/---protrav/---safework/documents/publication/wcms_175600.pdf#page=3

Keicher, C. (2013, April 8). How benchmarking makes cities smarter. *BuildingRating.org.* Retrieved July 29, 2013, from http://www.buildingrating.org/content/how-benchmarking-makes-cities-smarter

Massachusetts Clean Energy Center (MACEC). (2012). *2012 Massachusetts clean energy industry report.* Retrieved August 30, 2013, from http://www.masscec.com/content/2012-clean-energy-industry-report

Massachusetts Clean Energy Center (MACEC). (2013). *2013 Massachusetts clean energy industry report.* Retrieved December 2, 2013, from http://www.masscec.com/content/2013-clean-energy-industry-report

McKinsey Global Energy and Materials. (2009, July). *Unlocking energy efficiency in the U.S. economy.* Retrieved August 30, 2013, from http://www.greenbuildinglawblog.com/uploads/file/mckinseyUS_energy_efficiency_full_report.pdf

Michaels, D. (2009, December 16). Making green jobs safe: Integrating occupational health and safety into green and sustainability. *NIOSH Going Green Workshop.* Retrieved August 14, 2013, from https://www.osha.gov/pls/oshaweb/owadisp.show_document?p_table=SPEECHES&p_id=2119

National Institute of Occupational Health and Safety (NIOSH). (2011, August). *Summary of the Making Green Jobs Safe 2009 workshop.* Retrieved August 14, 2013, from http://www.cdc.gov/niosh/docs/2011-201/pdfs/2011-201.pdf

Occupational Health and Safety Administration (OSHA). (n.d.). Green job hazards. Retrieved August 7, 2013, from https://www.osha.gov/dep/greenjobs/index.html

Occupational Information Network (O*Net). (2009, February). *Greening of the world of work.* Retrieved August 10, 2013, from http://www.onetcenter.org/dl_files/Green.pdf

Pearce, D., Markandya, A., & Barbier, E. (1989). *Blueprint for a green economy.* Earthscan: London, UK.

Renewable Energy and Energy Efficiency Partnership (REEEP); Alliance to Save Energy; American Council on Renewable Energy (ACORE). (2010, April). *Compendium of best practices: Sharing local and state successes in energy efficiency and renewable energy from the United States.* Retrieved August 1, 2013, from http://www.acore.org/wp-content/uploads/2011/02/Compendium_of_Best_Practices_-_Final.pdf

Rhode Island Committee on Occupational Safety and Health (RICOSH). (2009, February). Going green, safely. Retrieved August 5, 2013, from http://www.coshnetwork.org/node/259

Romm, J. (2010, April 14). *Written testimony before the Ways and Means Committee of the House of Representatives hearing on energy tax incentives driving the green job economy.* Retrieved August 8, 2013, from http://www.americanprogressaction.org/issues/2010/04/pdf/Romm_testimony.pdf

Schulte, P., Heidel, D., Okun, A., & Branche, C. (2010). Making green jobs safe [editorial]. *Industrial Health, 48,* 377–379.

Silicon Valley Toxics Coalition (SVTC). (2009, January). *Towards a just and sustainable solar energy industry.* Retrieved August 9, 2013, from http://svtc.org/wp-content/uploads/Silicon_Valley_Toxics_Coalition_-_Toward_a_Just_and_Sust.pdf

Tellus Institute and Sound Resource Management. (2011). *More jobs, less pollution: Growing the recycling economy in the U.S.* Retrieved August 4, 2013, from http://www.teamster.org/sites/teamster.org/files/11911RecyclingJobsFullReport.pdf

United Nations (UN). (2012, August). *A guidebook to the green economy.* Retrieved August 29, 2013, from http://www.uncsd2012.org/content/documents/528Green%20Economy%20Guidebook_100912_FINAL.pdf

United Nations Environmental Program (UNEP). (2012). *Green Economy Initiative.* Retrieved August 7, 2013, from http://www.unep.org/greeneconomy/AboutGEI/WhatisGEI/tabid/29784/Default.aspx

United Nations Industrial Development Organization (UNIDO). (2011, May). *UNIDO green industry: Policies for supporting green industry.* Retrieved August 29, 2013, from http://www.unido.org/fileadmin/user_media/Services/Green_Industry/web_policies_green_industry.pdf

Walsh J., Bivens, J., & Pollack, E. (2011, February). Rebuilding green: The American Recovery and Reinvestment Act and the green economy. *BlueGreen Alliance and the Economic Policy Institute.* Retrieved August 29, 2013, from http://www.bluegreenalliance.org/admin/publications/files/BGA-EPI-Report-vFINAL-MEDIA.pdf

Washington State Employment Security Department. (2010, March). *2009 Washington State green economy jobs.* Retrieved August 30, 2013, from http://www.energy.wsu.edu/ Documents/2009_Green_Economy_Jobs_FINAL_Report.pdf

Watson, A. (2013, January). Green technologies and practices: A visual essay. *Monthly Labor Review.* Retrieved January 4, 2014, from http://www.bls.gov/opub/mlr/2013/01/ art4full.pdf

Chapter 2

THE STATE OF CORPORATE CITIZENSHIP 2009: THE RECESSION TEST[1]

Is corporate citizenship[2] simply a fashionable trend for a few leading companies, or is it becoming a business imperative for the 21st century? The recession of 2007–2009 provided almost perfect conditions for testing the value of corporate citizenship. Tough times call for tough decisions, and initiatives that are not seen as critical tend to be scaled back or eliminated.

This chapter presents key findings from the 2009 State of Corporate Citizenship Study, a biennial survey of top executives from small, medium, and large companies in the United States. Funded by the Hitachi Foundation, the survey was launched in 2003 to track how executives' attitudes and actions change over time and provide comparisons and insights about key trends and differences among U.S. businesses by size, type of ownership, and industry, among others.

The 2009 survey found that some initiatives have been scaled back, but corporate citizenship overall expanded at a significant rate.[3] Some 54% of respondents, the majority of whom were CEOs and vice presidents, stated that corporate citizenship is even more important during a recession. As the *Economist* summed up, "During an economic expansion, corporate citizenship is an opportunity. . . . In an economic downturn it can be a vital competitive advantage" (Economist Intelligence Unit, 2008).

[1] Reprinted from Veleva V., "The State of Corporate Citizenship 2009: The Recession Test," Corporate Finance Review, Vol. 14, No. 4, pp. 17-25, January/February 2010, by permission of the publisher ©2010 Thomson Reuters.

[2] Corporate citizenship is defined as the way a company takes responsibility and is accountable for managing its social and environmental impacts on society. It covers the design of its products and services, the management of its operations, and the way it works beyond the fenceline to address social and environmental challenges. Other terms used interchangeably with corporate citizenship include corporate social responsibility, sustainability, and corporate responsibility.

[3] The survey defined small companies as establishments with 1–99 employees, medium-size companies as those with 100–999 employees, and large companies as those with 1,000+ employees.

Research Methodology

The 2009 State of Corporate Citizenship Survey was conducted by GlobeScan, a professional polling firm based in Toronto, Canada, using a nationally representative sample of 756 companies of all sizes. The online survey was completed between June 4 and June 23, 2009. To ensure a representative sample of U.S. companies, sample control quotas were set in advance of the fieldwork for company-headquarter location, size (measured by number of full-time equivalent employees), and industry. Large companies were oversampled in order to produce a significant number of responses for separate analysis. The data has been weighted by the geographic distribution of establishments,[4] number of employees (company size), and industry sector to reflect national U.S. census data.

The survey included 26 multipart questions in addition to questions about company size, industry, ownership, headquarter location, and financial performance, among others. Some of the questions were tracking questions used in the previous three surveys (2003, 2005, and 2007). Only direct comparisons to the 2007 survey results can be made, as the earlier two surveys used different sampling methodologies.

Context for Corporate Citizenship in the United States

The 2009 survey is a snapshot taken during a period of economic and financial turbulence unequaled since the Great Depression of the 1930s. Companies of all sizes were attempting to navigate through a swift and seemingly unrelenting tide of negative economic developments. While about half (48%) of companies in the survey reported a decrease in revenues/sales, about one in four saw an increase in revenues/sales (26%), with the remaining 26% reporting no changes.

To survive the recession, many businesses had to implement drastic cost-cutting measures: 27% reported increased layoffs (for large companies, 54%); 24% reported reduced wages, benefits, or work hours (for large companies, 31%); and 38% reported reduced charitable giving. Almost one in five (19%) reduced research-and-development investments in new sustainable products and services, whereas 22% of large companies (compared to 15% for all American companies) increased such investments, which indicates the value they see in integrating corporate citizenship into their business strategy.

Despite the severe economic environment, the past 2 years mark a period of significant developments in the field of corporate citizenship:

- Increasing regulatory pressures: With the Obama administration, policies have begun to emerge for climate change, health care, education, products safety, consumer protection, the taxation of corporate profits overseas, and the gap between the rich and poor.

---

[4] Establishments (i.e., a "branch" of a firm) were used in weighting rather than entire firms (main company enterprise).

- Increasing consumer demand for sustainable products and services: Though the economy and health care emerged as the top concerns for Americans, studies have shown that demand for green and sustainable products and services has continued to grow (Boston Consulting Group, 2009; GMA/Deloitte, 2009).
- Increasing public distrust in business: Not surprisingly, trust in business dropped to a record low as 77% of Americans said they trusted business less than they did a year ago (Edelman, 2009).
- Increasing investor pressures: Investors have long been accused of pressing for quarterly profits and ignoring the long-term value creation of social and environmental initiatives, but there is evidence that this is beginning to change. Mainstream investing is slowly moving toward incorporating social, environmental, and Governance criteria (Eurosif, 2008), and venture capital for clean-technology projects doubled between 2007 and 2008 and reached a record $7.6 billion (Makower, 2009).
- Increasing pressures from employees: Employees, and in particular generation Y, have emerged as a strong driver for corporate citizenship. Employees today increasingly value work-life balance and the idea of corporate culture aligning with their own values. Despite the high unemployment rate, attracting and retaining top talent continues to be a key challenge for companies and one of the most critical factors for business success.
- Senior executives getting onboard with corporate citizenship: There is growing evidence that top leadership is beginning to see the business value of social and environmental initiatives for improving reputation, differentiating products, and attracting and retaining top talent. A recent McKinsey survey found that two-thirds of CFOs agreed that environmental, social, and governance activities create measurable value for their shareholders (Bonini, Brun, & Rosenthal, 2009).

Key Findings

What emerged from the 756 executives in the survey was that despite the deep recession, American companies of all sizes have generally maintained their support for corporate citizenship initiatives. Although charity and donations and community investment registered statistically significant but relatively small declines, U.S. businesses put more efforts into integrating corporate citizenship with their business strategy and expanding environmental sustainability initiatives. Over half of the surveyed senior executives believed that corporate citizenship was even more important in a recession. Following is a summary of the key findings from the study.

Drivers for corporate citizenship

The 2009 State of Corporate Citizenship confirmed the trend that corporate citizenship was moving from "doing what's right" to doing what's good for business and society. In the previous three surveys, the top driver for social and environmental responsibility was companies' traditions and values. In the 2007 survey, reputation emerged as a strong second driver, and in 2009 it shared first place (at 70%) with company traditions and values in motivating business actions. For large companies, it is now the top driver of corporate citizenship practices (82%). Other reasons for pursuing corporate citizenship, according to executives, include customer/consumer demands (58%), the integration with business strategy (56%), and the importance for recruiting and retaining employees (42%).

Ethical business practices and valuing employees

In the light of the recent scandals, a greater number of American companies believe the most important way to be a good corporate citizen is to operate with ethical business practices (91%, up from 87% in 2007). Valuing employees and treating them well remains strong at 81%, followed by managing and reporting finances accurately (76%) (see Exhibit 1).

Community support has declined, but not for all companies. The survey found that the recession has had a negative impact on philanthropy and community support but smaller than expected by the research team. As corporate donations and sponsorships are closely linked to corporate profits, 38% of companies reduced their philanthropy and giving in 2008, compared to the 2007 survey. Despite the drop in total dollar amount, the number of companies providing cash donations and sponsorships to communities has remained stable,[5] (68% versus 69% in 2007), perhaps in part recognizing the increased need in many communities. There was a statistically

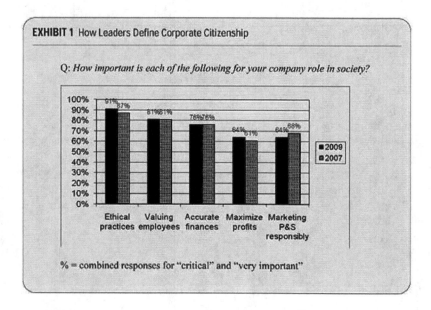

EXHIBIT 1 How Leaders Define Corporate Citizenship

Q: *How important is each of the following for your company role in society?*

% = combined responses for "critical" and "very important"

---

[5] It should be noted, however, that the 2007 survey asked for cash donations only, while the 2009 survey asked for cash donations and sponsorships.

significant but relatively small drop in the number of companies providing in-kind donations (from 65% to 60%), employee volunteering opportunities (from 64% to 57%), and community investments (from 30% down to 21%).

Large companies maintained and in some cases increased their support:

- 44% of large companies provided volunteering opportunities for employees in 2007 and 2009.
- 33% reported increased hiring from poor communities compared to 23% in 2007.
- 31% reported increased involvement in improving community conditions compared to 29% in 2007.

The top three areas supported by U.S. companies in 2009 were education (46%); health care, including nutrition and physical fitness (33%); and environmental issues (29%). Comparing the present survey results to the 2007 results, the most significant change is the increased support for environmental issues (from 19% to 29%) as companies of all sizes continue to expand their environmental initiatives and align with their business strategy.

Despite layoffs, employee support remained strong. Numerous public studies have found that treating employees well is one of the most important criteria for demonstrating good corporate citizenship (Fleischman-Hillard/National Consumer League, 2007). Such practices improve company reputation and productivity, help to attract and retain top talent, and reduce turnover costs. In today's world of blogs and social networking, unethical practices or poor treatment of employees can very quickly put a company at reputational risk. American executives seem to recognize the importance of employee support. Following are results of the 2009 survey compared to the results of the 2007 survey.

- 81% of the survey respondents (the same percentage as that in the 2007 survey) stated that valuing employees and treating them well is critical or very important.
- 71% of all companies (84% of large corporations) hired women and/or minorities in management positions, compared to 63% in the 2007 survey.
- 60% of all companies (79% of large corporations) supported work-life balance practices for all employees, compared to 46% in the 2007 survey.
- 45% of all companies (57% of large corporations) compensated employees for ideas that benefited the bottom line and the environment/community, compared to 37% in the 2007 survey.
- Large and midsize companies significantly increased their offering of health insurance to all employees, including hourly workers, from 76% to 91% for large companies, and from 77% to 87% for midsize companies.

Senior executives increasingly see the business value of corporate citizenship. When resources are limited, finding ways to cut costs, differentiate products and services, and improve reputation and employee morale are critical. The survey found that the top three corporate citizenship business opportunities implemented by U.S. companies in 2008 included reducing costs through improved materials efficiency (72%), manufacturing or sourcing domestically/locally (58%), and increasing brand awareness as green or socially responsible (53%).

Among large companies, 65% aim to design and offer sustainable products/ services, 59% offer energy-efficient products, and 59% provide customers with more information about social and environmental impacts of their products and services.

Increasing integration of CC in the business strategy

Integration of environmental, social, and governance factors into the business strategy has increasingly been linked to better financial performance (Kearney, 2009; Mercer, 2009). Despite the challenging economic times, the survey found that U.S. companies of all sizes committed more resources and increasingly aimed to integrate corporate citizenship with their business strategy:

- In three out of four companies, the CEO is leading the corporate citizenship initiative.
- 40% (compared to 25% in the 2007 survey) have an individual or a team responsible for corporate citizenship issues
- 43% (compared to 39% in the 2007 survey) report that corporate citizenship is an integral part of their business-planning process (for large companies, the increase is from 46% to 61%)
- An increasing number of companies (33% compared to 28% in the 2007 survey) have policies or written statements about corporate citizenship (for large companies, the increase was from 55% to 65%)

Large companies reported having explicit corporate citizenship goals around employee education, training, and career advancement (80%); diversity (76%); community support (71%); environmental responsibility (63%); sustainable products/ services (63%); and human rights within the supply chain (58%). Almost half (47%) of large U.S. corporations reported that their board reviews and approves corporate citizenship programs.

The green transformation of American companies has begun. Environmental sustainability efforts expanded significantly as a growing number of business leaders saw these as a win-win strategy: good for the bottom line and an integral part of being a "good corporate citizen." Companies of all sizes significantly increased their initiatives to develop and launch green or sustainable products and services (see Exhibit 2).

These findings correlate to other studies that have found that the recession slowed but did not stop business investment in green initiatives. Various powerful factors are driving the green agenda: the regulatory landscape, market incentives for clean energy, nongovernmental organization (NGO) pressures, and investor/ consumer interest.

Emerging citizenship gap between large and small companies

The survey found an increasing gap between how large and small companies see their role in addressing social and environmental issues. While large companies maintained or even increased their support for communities, small companies focused on protecting jobs (comparisons are between the 2007 and 2009 survey):

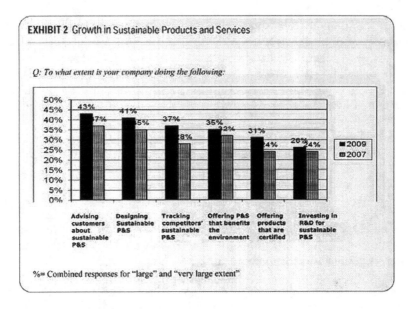

EXHIBIT 2 Growth in Sustainable Products and Services

Q: To what extent is your company doing the following:

%= Combined responses for "large" and "very large extent"

- Large companies reported an increased importance in improving conditions in their communities (from 59% to 63%); small companies reported a decrease from 53% to 44%.
- Large companies maintained their support for employee volunteering (44% in both the 2007 and 2009 survey); small companies significantly reduced volunteering opportunities for their employees (from 42% down to 33%).
- More large companies offered health insurance to all employees (from 76% to 91%); small companies reduced health insurance coverage (drop from 38% to 34%).
- Large companies increased hiring from poor communities (from 23% to 30%); small companies reduced such hiring (from 23% to 18%).
- 54% of large companies reported increased layoffs; only 14% of small companies used layoffs as a cost cutting measure.

New role for business in public policy

The majority of U.S. senior executives believe business should be more involved than it is presently in solving major public policy issues:

- 67% said business should be more or much more involved in solving product safety issues.
- 65% said business should be more or much more involved in health care.
- 56% said business should be more or much more involved in public education.
- 53% believed business should be more or much more involved in addressing climate change.

Executives from large privately held companies support at a much higher rate of business involvement in health care (74% versus 60% for publicly held large companies) and public education (65% versus 51% for public companies).

At the same time, greater federal or global regulation was not seen as the solution. About 66% of respondents believed that more ethical and value-based leadership in the C-suite was the solution to the current economic crisis, and 61% cited the need for more effective corporate governance practices (see Exhibit 3). Just about one in three executives believed greater regulatory oversight by federal government was important or very important for solving the current crisis and ensuring a more stable American economy going forward.

Discussion and Recommendations

The recession provided an almost ideal opportunity to test corporate citizenship. Corporate citizenship will increase in importance in the future as pressures from consumers/customers, government, NGOs, investors, and employees intensify and companies recover from the recession.

The green economy continues to expand, and U.S. businesses are slowly catching up with their European and Asian peers. The gap between public and executive views on the most important corporate citizenship issues is also closing, as both see education, health care, and environment as the most important issues to address.

However, many of the social and environmental initiatives are still marginal and considered "greenwash" by consumers.

True sustainability requires reducing material output and selling more services instead of products. In a way, the recession of 2007–2009 was a wakeup call for

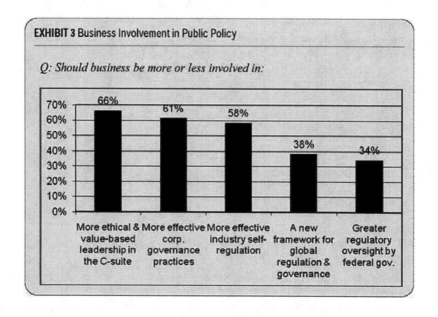

EXHIBIT 3 Business Involvement in Public Policy

Q: Should business be more or less involved in:

American consumerism—a McKinsey survey conducted in March 2009 found that 90% of U.S. respondents said their households had reduced spending as a result of the recession, the majority of them (55%) by choice and not necessity. People today drive their cars longer, keep their computers longer, and look for smaller houses. Businesses of all sizes need to adjust to such consumption shifts and change the way they design and market their products and services.[6]

In order to capture the full benefit of corporate citizenship practices, companies need to address the following challenges:

- *Define the business case*: According to a recent MIT Sloan/BCG study, 92% of respondents said their company was addressing sustainability, but more than 70% admitted they have not developed a clear business case for sustainability (MIT Sloan Management Review/Boston Consulting Group, 2009). The latter requires a comprehensive assessment of risks and opportunities, and measuring the return on investment or other intangible benefits from social and environmental initiatives. Without such measures, corporate citizenship becomes "vulnerable and subject to changing corporate leadership, public priorities and financial cycles" (Epstein, 2008).
- *Lead from the top*: Successful corporate citizenship strategy starts from the top, with a clear vision and strategy that is supported by the CEO. Obtaining CEO support can be challenging. Without CEO leadership, however, a successful citizenship strategy will not happen.
- *Align and integrate corporate citizenship with the business strategy*: Integration with the business strategy requires committing resources (people and funding), building cross-functional teams, developing internal competencies, and setting clear policies and principles to support implementation. Effective integration requires setting performance measurement goals for managers as they may face conflicting objectives (e.g., for sales/revenue growth in addition to ensuring supplier compliance).
- *Increase transparency to build "trust" and good reputation*: To generate value, financial and other reporting needs to be an integral part of performance management and include both the good news and the bad news. The Reputation Institute has found that a 10% improvement in perceived citizenship translates to 11% improvement in reputation and 14% improvement in a company's market value (Veleva, 2008).
- *Seek partnerships*: Partnering with NGOs, government, and peers not only helps address material issues for business but also helps build good reputation and market share. According to our survey, executives are increasingly recognizing the business benefits of such partnerships: 79% seek these partnerships to improve reputation, and a striking 69% see financial benefits of such partnerships

---

[6]Examples of successful business strategies come from leading companies such as IBM, HP, and Xerox, which have increased their offerings of services versus products and thus secured stable revenue even during the recession.

as providing opportunities for innovation. Only 3% seek such partnerships because it is the right thing to do.

- *Build a sustainable supply chain*: Nothing will be more important for business success in the future than building a sustainable supply chain. Companies have learned the hard way that they must track the social and environmental performance of suppliers, know all ingredients in their products, and partner with suppliers to promote innovation and avoid liabilities and market exclusion.

- *Empower employees*: Smart companies see their employees as their greatest asset. Employees are best positioned to come up with ideas that benefit both the bottom line and society. Creating a system to promote and reward employees' corporate citizenship ideas can bring numerous business benefits.

- *Empower consumers*: Studies have shown that consumers want to have more information about products in order to make better decisions. When given a choice between products of equal quality and price, they are more likely to buy green or sustainable products from a company they trust. Walmart has made some bold steps in this area by partnering with NGOs and peers to launch the first sustainability labeling system for rating consumer products (GreenBiz.com, 2009).

CONCLUSION

Business and government leaders such as Bill Gates, Larry Summers, Ben Bernanke, and President Obama have called for a new type of capitalism ("kinder capitalism" or capitalism 2.0) to address various issues—the widening gap between rich and poor, health care, and climate change, among others. A new social contract,[7] is needed, and government has taken some bold steps in this direction. No one knows for sure what capitalism 2.0 will look like, but the 2009 survey revealed that despite the extremely difficult economic environment, American companies—small, medium, and large—see business benefits in corporate citizenship strategies. In these times of major change, business needs to find the most effective ways to create a new framework for building a more sustainable and prosperous American economy and avoiding future economic crises.

ACKNOWLEDGMENT

The author would like to thank the Hitachi Foundation for supporting this study and the research team working on the 2009 State of Corporate Citizenship Survey: Bradley Googins, Phillip Mirvis, Christopher Pinney, Margaret Connolly, Mark Popovich, Ryan Raffaelli, and Rene Carapinha.

---

[7]Social contract is defined as the roles and responsibilities of the three major actors in society: government, business, and NGOs/civil society.

DISCUSSION QUESTIONS

Chapter 2: The State of Corporate Citizenship 2009: The Recession Test

1. What is corporate citizenship? How do companies define corporate citizenship? Is their definition different from yours, if so, describe the differences?
2. Why, despite the recession of 2007-2009, did American companies of all sizes maintain their support for corporate citizenship initiatives?
3. How do small and large companies differ in their approach to corporate citizenship?
4. What are the main methods applied to integrate corporate citizenship with a core business strategy?

REFERENCES

Bonini, S., Brun, N., & Rosenthal, M. (2009, February). Valuing corporate social responsibility. *The McKinsey Quarterly*.

Boston Consulting Group. (2009, January). *Capturing the green advantage for consumer companies.* Retrieved from http://www.bcg.com/documents/file15407.pdf

Economist Intelligence Unit. (2008, November). *Corporate citizenship: Profiting from a sustainable business.* Retrieved from http://graphics.eiu.com/upload/Corporate_Citizens.pdf

Edelman. (2009). *2009 Edelman trust barometer Executive Summary.* Retrieved from http://www.edelman.com/assets/uploads/2014/01/2009-Trust-Barometer-Executive-Summary.pdf

Epstein, M. (2008, January). Implementing corporate sustainability: Measuring and managing social and environmental impacts. *Strategic Finance*, 25–31.

Eurosif. (2008). *High net worth individuals and sustainable investment.* Retrieved from http://www.eurosif.org/publications/hnwi_sustainable_investment

Fleischman-Hillard/National Consumer League. (May 2007). *Rethinking corporate social responsibility.* Retrieved from http://www.franchise-kwt.com/mazeedi/mazeedi/media/pdf/mosoh5.pdf

GlobeScan. (2008). *CSR Monitor.* Retrieved from www.globescan.com

GMA/Deloitte. (2009). *Finding the green in today's shoppers: Sustainability trends and new shopper insights.* Retrieved from http://www.ahcgroup.com/mc_images/category/93/deloitte_on_competing_on_green_with_shoppers.pdf

GreenBiz.com. (2009, December 2). *Inside the sustainability consortium: What you need to know* [webinar]. Retrieved from www.greenbiz.com

Kearney, A. T. (2009). *Green winners: The performance of sustainability-focused companies in the financial crisis.* Retrieved from http://www.pwnetwork.com.au/kb/jeremy-barker---green-winners-paper-1.pdf

Makower, J. (February, 2009). *The state of green business 2009.* Retrieved from http://www.greenbiz.com/business/research/report/2010/02/02/state-green-business-2009

Mercer. (2009, November). *Shedding light on responsible investment: Approaches, returns and impacts.* Retrieved from http://www.mercer.com/ri

MIT Sloan Management Review/Boston Consulting Group. (2009, September). *The business of sustainability.* Retrieved from http://www.mitsmr-ezine.com/busofsustainability/2009#pg1

Veleva, V. (2008). Financial performance and corporate citizenship: The chicken or the egg. *Boston College Center for Corporate Citizenship.* Retrieved from http://www.bcccc.net/

UPDATE TO CHAPTER 2: THE STATE OF THE CORPORATE CITIZENSHIP 2009: THE RECESSION TEST

The State of Corporate Citizenship 2012 confirmed the trend that leaders see significant business benefits of corporate citizenship, including increasing company market share and improved risk management (BCCCC, 2012). Eighty percent of all executives in the 2012 survey confirmed that social, environmental and governance initiatives create financial value for their company. The study found that environmental sustainability programs continued to receive most funding and are expected to continue to grow. Pressure to deliver short-term results was identified as the main barrier to greater corporate citizenship.

Consumer demand for green product has continued to grow and a 2012 study by Accenture found that many executives struggled to meet demand (Accenture, 2012). While not willing to pay a premium, consumers continue to seek products that are energy-efficient, free of toxic chemicals, made of recycled content, or biodegradable.

On the clean-tech investment side, developments were not so positive with global clean-tech investments dropping 12% in 2012 to $244 billion. Developing countries, and in particular China, are presently leading in clean-tech investments, while the United States and Europe have scaled back. Some reasons for the decline in clean-tech investments in developed countries include the expiration of the stimulus funding in the United States and the relatively poor economy in Europe. On the other hand, sectors such as solar and wind have matured sufficiently and new clean-tech investments are increasingly focused on energy efficiency, water management, waste-to-energy and "clean-web' software (software applications and data analytics) (Forbury Investment Network, 2014).

REFERENCES

Accenture. (2012). *Long-Term Growth, Short-Term Differentiation and Profits from Sustainable Products and Services; A global survey of business executives*. Retrieved from http://www.accenture.com/SiteCollectionDocuments/PDF/Accenture-Long-Term-Growth-Short-Term-Differentiation-and-Profit.pdf

Boston College Center for Corporate Citizenship. (2012). "Commitment to Value: The State of Corporate Citizenship 2012 Highlights." Retrieved from http://www.bcccc.net/pdf/SOCC2012HighlightPresentation.pdf

Forbury Investment Network. (2014). Trends in clean-tech investing: the search for leader and less capital-intensive investment. Retrieved from http://www.forburyinvest.com/Content.aspx?id=105

Chapter 3

THE BUSINESS BENEFITS OF ECO-INDUSTRIAL PARKS: INSIGHTS FROM DEVENS, MASSACHUSETTS

With Svetlana Todorova, Peter Lowitt,
Neil Angus, and Dona Neely

INTRODUCTION

There is no waste in nature. The waste from one organism becomes food for another. Nature is highly efficient at using resources and maintaining a balance within a system of interlinked groups of organisms. Can human systems be redesigned in a similar way? One main goals of *industrial ecology* is to change the current linear nature of our industrial systems and move to a circular system "where the wastes are reused as energy or raw materials for another product or process." Within the broader field of industrial ecology, which examines the flow of physical resources through systems at different scales, the subfield of industrial symbiosis (IS) focuses on these flows at the level of industrial clusters and industrial parks. *Eco-industrial parks* (EIPs) are defined as

> A community of businesses that cooperate with each other and with the local community to efficiently share resources (information, materials, water, energy, infrastructure and natural habitat), leading to economic gains, gains in environmental quality, and equitable enhancement of human resources for the business and local community. (PCSD 1997)

In a world of constrained resources and growing population, EIPs are increasingly seen as a means for green growth and reduced resource consumption. In 2010, the Organization for Economic Cooperation and Development (OECD) recognized industrial symbiosis "as a systemic innovation vital for green growth" (Lombardi,

Lyons, Shi, & Agarwal, 2012). China became the first country to globally launch an eco-industrial park standard in 2006 and presently has at least 1,568 national- and provincial-level industrial parks, which are seen as critical for achieving a circular economy and national competitiveness (Geng, Zhang, Cote, & Fujita, 2008; Shi, Tian, & Chen, 2012). The standard, developed by the State Environmental Protection Administration (SEPA), includes a comprehensive guidance, criteria, and indicators for EIPs (Geng et al., 2008).

Early literature on eco-industrial parks argued qualitatively that these sorts of arrangements were likely to be advantageous for participating firms (Côté & Cohen-Rosenthal, 1998; Esty & Porter, 1998). With the Sarbanes-Oxley Act's requirement for disclosing the cost of retiring old polluted manufacturing facilities, a growing number of U.S. companies will be trying to remove these off their balance sheets. Presently, there are approximately 490,000 sites and almost 15 million acres of potentially contaminated properties across the United States that could benefit from sustainable redevelopment (EPA, 2012). Yet there are very few developers interested in redeveloping such sites despite the fact that the latter often have an ideal infrastructure for clean energy/clean tech industry development (McKittrick, 2012). To promote redevelopment of this and other sites as eco-industrial parks, it is critical to understand and communicate the benefits for companies and developers as well as examine the key factors for success. These benefits include not just savings from reduced energy and materials efficiencies but also intangibles such as improved reputation, innovation, resiliency, and ability to attract and retain employees.

This chapter presents insights from a study of the business needs and sustainability practices of companies located in the Devens eco-industrial park. A former military site listed under the Comprehensive Environmental Response, Compensation, and Liability Act (CERCLA), Devens has had a sustainability vision from the very beginning and the goal to improve regional economic base by employing the principles of industrial ecology. Today, Devens is a regional enterprise zone, which has attracted 95 organizations and contributed over $1.45 billion and 3,200 high quality jobs to the Massachusetts economy while cleaning up the local environment and advancing more sustainable infrastructure such as a rail and green buildings (Veleva, 2012).

Yet little is known about the business benefits of locating to an eco-industrial park and what helps attract and retain companies. The authors seek to address this gap by examining the following questions: What are the main reasons for companies to move to an eco-industrial park like that in Devens? What are the business benefits from being a part of an eco-industrial park? Are large or small facilities more likely to be engaged in collaborations with others? What is the role of the organizational and human factors, including the Devens Enterprise Commission (DEC) and Devens Eco-Efficiency Center (DEEC), in supporting business and sustainability goals? The chapter begins with a section discussing eco-industrial parks, business sustainability, and firm competitiveness. The case of Devens is presented next, including its sustainability vision and process for redevelopment. The main part of the chapter includes data and analysis of the interviews with 29 local organizations. The authors conclude with discussion of the limitations of the study and recommendations for future research.

Eco-Industrial Parks, Business Sustainability, and Firm Competitiveness

The business benefits of industrial ecology and EIPs have received somewhat limited attention by both researchers and practitioners. An early study by Esty and Porter (1998) concluded that industrial ecology

> can help companies find ways to add value or reduce costs both within their own production processes and up and down the supply chain, but it cannot always be counted upon to yield competitive advantage at the firm level since the costs of closing loops will exceed the benefits.

The authors outline three key places where industrial ecology can help uncover business opportunities: (a) within the firm; (b) within the chain of production, including suppliers or customers; and (c) beyond the chain of production. The greatest opportunities to find "hidden sources of opportunity can be discovered by looking to reduce costs up or down the chain of production, which offers real opportunities for improved competitiveness" (Esty & Porter, 1998). The authors, however, caution about the limited time and capacity of corporate managers to identify such opportunities.

A more recent study of a smelter in China found that industrial ecology "can improve the competitive advantage of supply chains by reducing production cost and improving environmental performance" (Yuan & Shi, 2009). Rao and Holt (2005) examined greening of firms' supply chains and found that the process "leads to integrated green supply chains which ultimately leads to competitiveness and economic performance." The study builds on an earlier work by Bacallan (2000), which suggested that improved competitiveness is a result of improved performance and ability to meet a growing number of environmental regulations, the ability to address environmental concerns of customers, and to mitigate the environmental impact of production and service activities.

More broadly, the literature on sustainability clusters has identified the importance of supporting infrastructure and other local factors in promoting productivity, innovation, and competitiveness (Martin & Mayer, 2008; Maskell & Malmberg, 1995; Porter & Kramer, 2011). Diverse industrial clusters include not only the local businesses but also institutions such as schools, universities, trade associations, and nonprofit organizations. Local governments can play a particularly important role in promoting cluster development and firm competitiveness by setting clear and measurable social goals that can promote social development and business sustainability (e.g., around energy use, health and safety, or infrastructure improvement).

Research has brought attention to the importance of diversity of sectors represented at an EIP in promoting greater collaborations, resilience, and competitiveness (Geng et al., 2008). Increasing diversity "broadens the knowledge and resource base available to the industrial symbiosis network, and fosters innovation and variety in solutions" (Lombardi & Laybourn, 2012; see also Boons & Berends, 2001; Duranton & Puga, 2000). Cross-sectoral knowledge transfer has been shown to promote innovation and thus firm competitiveness (Hargadon, 2003). Including educational, research, and governmental entities to the network creates unique opportunities to create and share knowledge, advance workforce skills, and promote development of supportive policies.

In their work on creating shared value, Porter and Kramer (2011) emphasize the "profound effect" of a business location on a firm productivity and innovation, which still remains understudied by researchers. They argue that companies can create economic value by creating societal value. There are three distinct ways to do that: (a) by reconceiving products and markets, (b) by redefining productivity in the supply chain, and (c) by building supportive industry clusters at the firm's location. A company's supply chain clearly affects and is affected by various societal issues, claim Porter and Kramer, including natural resource and water use, infrastructure development, health and safety, and working conditions. The increasing costs of energy and transportation, growing political and other supply-chain risks "may lead companies to remake their value chains by moving some activities closer to home and having fewer major production locations." Such trends will make the location increasingly important. Porter and Kramer argue that "shared value helps uncover new needs to meet, new products to offer, new customers to serve and new ways to configure the value chain, where the resulting competitive advantage will often be more sustainable than conventional cost and quality improvements." The ability to increase self-reliance within the network of collaborating firms is another indicator of improved business competitiveness.

Historically, industrial ecology has focused on material and energy flows, including water and by-products. Developing EIPs around a narrow definition of physical exchanges among closely located firms has been problematic. Studies have identified the main barriers to such eco-industrial development, including technical, economic, informational, organizational, and legal (Gibbs & Deutz, 2007). In the 21st century knowledge-based economy, business success is increasingly determined by factors such as skills and knowledge (human capital), innovation, and infrastructure. Recently, Lombardi and Laybourn (2012) proposed expanding the definition of EIPs to include "the exchange of knowledge, information, and expertise," which they find also "positively influences the physical flows of materials and energy" and are seen as sources of innovation.

Concerns about global warming, weather-related business disruptions, energy and materials security are also becoming important sources of innovation and competitiveness (Drucker, 1985). Nidumolu, Prahalad, and Rangaswami (2009) demonstrate how sustainability today is becoming a key driver of innovation for small and large companies. By focusing on creating more sustainable supply chains, operating their facilities more efficiently, designing more sustainable products and services, enhancing reputation, and attracting employees by improving the workplace, companies can reduce their operating costs and increase market share. In a 2010 McKinsey study, 76% of the executives said that "engaging in sustainability contributes positively to shareholder value in the long term" (McKinsey, 2010). A study on competitiveness and sustainability outlined four ways in which sustainability can enhance firm competitiveness (Bent, 2008):

- Growing profits and reducing risk through pollution prevention,
- Enhancing reputation and legitimacy through product stewardship,
- Accelerating innovation through clean technology, and
- Creating a growth path by meeting unmet needs

Hoffman (2003) was among the first to call for examining the role of the social systems—social interaction, culture, and institutions—in implementing industrial ecology in practice. He argued that the physical and social systems are closely interconnected, and the full potential of industrial ecology cannot be achieved without understanding and leveraging the power of the social systems. Implementing industrial ecology in practice requires developing network embeddedness by connecting firms and individuals, developing trust and shared actions toward eco-industrial development and sustainability (Paquin & Howard-Grenville, 2012). Such embeddedness occurs over time and has been found to accelerate the formation of relationships and, in the case of EIPs, leads to reduced transaction costs, including the search and negotiation costs involved in identifying exchange partners (Chertow & Ehrenfeld, 2012).

Having the right institutional setting in a region is among the most important elements for successful development of eco-industrial parks (Mirata, 2004). But trust and cooperation must be developed between firms "before they are prepared to link processes together in ways that have an impact upon the economic viability of the firm" (Gibbs & Deutz, 2007). Thus, supportive local policies and champions can play a critical role in advancing eco-industrial development that leads to environmental and business benefits. They can serve as "network brokers and institutional anchor tenants' initiating the actor networks and providing political and managerial support as well as informational and educational services and infrastructure support for the other participants of the industrial ecosystem" (Korhonen, von Malmborg, Strachan, & Ehrenfeld, 2004). Given the limited time and resources of company managers, there is a need for a coordinating organization that can facilitate such collaboration and "create interaction spaces where firm members could meet and share ideas" (Lombardi et al., 2012).

Embracing sustainability as a driver for innovation, however, is not easy for most companies. It requires continuous education, supportive government policies, and understanding of the business benefits that such a strategy brings. The case of Devens, Massachusetts, provides valuable lessons on the role of DEC and MassDevelopment in examining business needs and providing a variety of programs to advance sustainability awareness, create a network of collaborating local businesses, and communicate the business benefits of eco-industrial park activities.

DEVENS ECO-INDUSTRIAL PARK—HISTORY AND PROCESS FOR SUSTAINABLE REDEVELOPMENT

Devens is a regional enterprise zone created by the Massachusetts legislature in 1993 to aid the redevelopment of the former Fort Devens (see Figure 1). First created in 1917 by the U.S. Congress and the Department of the Army as a military base, Fort Devens consisted of predominantly rural lands from the adjacent towns of Ayer, Shirley, Harvard, and Lancaster. When the closure of Fort Devens was announced in 1991, a local and regional movement toward base reuse planning was initiated. The Massachusetts legislature adopted Chapter 498 of the Acts of 1993, which created the Devens Enterprise Commission (DEC) to take regulatory and permit-granting responsibilities for Devens. MassDevelopment, a quasi-state agency, retains the infrastructure, police, fire, public works, and is responsible for the sale and leasing of real estate within the Devens Regional Enterprise Zone (DREZ) (Devens Sustainability Indicator Report, 2000).

The 1993 Fort Devens Charrette and the Devens Reuse Plan began the process of establishing the vision and goals for Devens redevelopment. Sustainability for Devens was defined as "the thoughtful and careful redevelopment of the base for the purpose of promoting economic development, social welfare, environmental protection, and natural resources" (Devens Sustainability Indicator Report, 2000).

Redevelopment of Devens was focused on attracting a diverse set of companies to provide a range of employment opportunities in order to provide "resilience from impacts associated with the loss of a single primary employer." Business development efforts were particularly focused on attracting employers from the clusters that were seen as good fit for the community, for example, military defense, life sciences, medical devices, plastics, and renewable energy technology (Hammer, Babcock, & Moosbrugger, 2012).

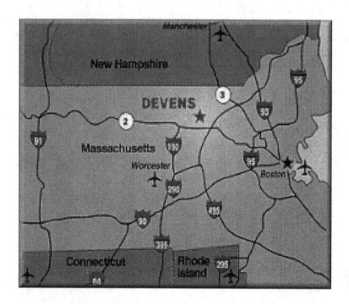

Figure 1. Map of Devens, Massachusetts (Lowitt, 2012).
Reprinted with permission from the Devens Enterprise Commission, Copyright 1999.

In 2000, Devens developed a framework of sustainability issues and indicators as a tool to measure and communicate progress toward its sustainability vision (see Figure 2). These indicators were updated in 2012 when a comprehensive assessment of Devens sustainability achievements was undertaken. The assessment revealed that overall, Devens has made significant progress in most areas over the past decade (Veleva, 2012). Most progress has been made in the following areas:

- The number of organizations based in Devens increased from 60 to 95;
- Since its launch in 2007, the Devens Eco-Efficiency Center had interacted with more than 80% of the establishments in Devens;
- The number of people participating in community events increased from 120,000 to 300,000 annually;
- All 324 CERCLA sites have been cleaned up and all known undergraduate storage tanks (USTs) removed;
- The total linear feet of sidewalks has doubled from 40,673 to 65,482, representing 57% of the Devens roads in 2012;
- The total linear miles of trails increased from 5.44 miles to 12.46 miles;
- Percentage of commuters using alternatives to driving increased from 4% to 10%;
- Freight rail available to local businesses increased from 8,000 linear feet to 14,300 linear feet;
- Percentage of sustainable/high performance (green) buildings reached 14% of the total square footage of all occupied space in 2012 (no green buildings existed in 2000).

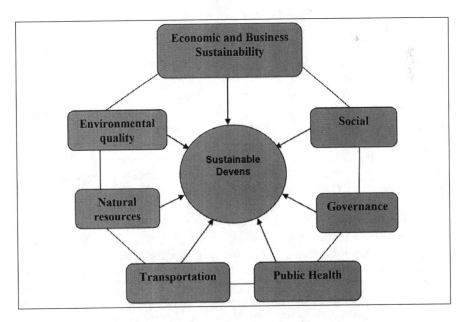

Figure 2. Sustainable Devens: Framework and seven key issues (Veleva, 2012).

Devens Enterprise Commission (DEC)

In this process, the DEC and its Director, Peter Lowitt, have played a critical role in working toward achieving the Devens sustainability vision. As a Chair of the Eco-Industrial Development Council of North America and the key person behind the development of the Londonderry Ecological Industrial Park, Mr. Lowitt focused on three main aspects in redeveloping Devens as an internationally recognized EIP: (a) promoting supportive local policies, (b) establishing a separate entity to focus on providing education and building a network of collaborating firms, and (c) implementing an open and inclusive process for measuring achievements and identifying gaps.

For instance, the initial Sustainable Indicator Report in 2000 identified two major issues that DEC worked to address over the past 12 years: (a) lack of public transportation and alternatives to single-occupancy passenger vehicles to commute to and from Devens, and (b) lack of green buildings. To address the first issue, the Fitchburg Line Working Group was established with chair DEC Director Mr. Lowitt. The group managed to secure $200 million investment to double track the rail between South Acton and Ayer and thus enable a viable reverse commute. To address the second issue, DEC adopted the Green Building Incentive Program and various regulatory changes to encourage the deployment of green buildings in Devens. The DEC has also adopted policies for low-impact development and water resource protection (Lowitt, 2012).

Devens Eco-Efficiency Center (DEEC)

To engage local organizations and promote building linkages and advance Devens' development as an eco-industrial park, DEC Director Mr. Lowitt brought in a sustainability consultant in 2001 to develop the membership program EcoStar, which was launched in 2005 as a voluntary branded program "to enable businesses and organizations in the Devens (MA) area to gain eco-efficiencies by pursuing strategies that improve environmental and economic performances" (EcoStar, 2012). In 2007, EcoStar transitioned to become the Devens Eco-Efficiency Center, a nonprofit organization with the goal of assisting local businesses and organizations in reducing operating costs and environmental impacts through efficiency, reuse, and recycling. The Center offers workshops around more sustainable operational practices, environmental, health, and safety (EHS) roundtable (a monthly open forum for EHS professionals to discuss experiences, trends, and best practices as well as potential collaborations); energy efficiency assistance; recycling assistance; the Great Exchange (a forum for exchanging and repurposing waste); and educational tours, among others. For example, Eglomise Designs saved more than $1,800 per year by implementing an employee engagement program to promote energy conservation. The Great Exchange helped repurpose 61 tons of materials in 2012, saving $24,000 for the 50 entities participating in it (see Text Box 1).

Text Box 1. The Great Exchange, Devens

The Great Exchange was launched in 2007 as a forum to divert unwanted items and materials from the landfill to reusable opportunities. Managed by Dona Neely, Executive Director of the DEEC, the program repurposed 61 tons of materials in 2012 saving $24,000 for the 50 entities participating in it. Some of the main materials exchanged included foam packing sheets, bubble wrap, elastics, cloth bags, furniture, equipment, and small boxes. Waste such as 10 gallon pails, plastic jars, styrofoam block, and fabric scrap are "turned into art" by local schools and museums. Since the first Exchange took place in 2008, the program has partnered with over 100 global firms, small businesses, service providers, daycare facilities, nonprofits, and municipalities and repurposed 500 tons of materials, helping participants avoid over $200,000 in purchase and disposal costs (DEEC, 2012).

Research Methods

In order to examine the main reasons for locating in Devens and the sustainability practices of local organizations, the research team designed a 20-question survey. A simple random sample from the finite population of 95 Devens organizations was used. The main reason to conduct a sample study and not a census was that the research team had limited resources. To determine a sample size for the estimation of the proportion from the finite population, the researchers took into consideration the 95% confidence interval and maximum error of 0.15. Thus, the conservative estimate of the sample size was determined to be 29. To obtain additional feedback from companies, DEC scheduled interviews with all 29 survey participants.

The interviews were held in the period January–March 2013 and were open-ended, semi-structured, and conversational in style. The interview team included representatives from DEC, DEEC, MassDevelopment, and UMass Boston. Company representatives included senior executives such as CEOs, CFOs, or a vice president, as well as other personnel involved in implementing sustainability practices such as environmental health and safety managers and sustainability/recycling coordinators. Questions addressed issues such as the main reasons for locating in Devens, top sustainability challenges, current collaborations with other Devens organizations, product take-back, waste management practices, and contingency planning for weather and other business disruptions, among others. Study participants were provided with the survey in advance of the interview. In addition to responding to the survey questions, participants were encouraged to provide additional input into the sustainable redevelopment of Devens, as well as identify areas in which Devens Enterprise Commission and Devens Eco-Efficiency Center services can help support their sustainability mission and business goals.

In addition, the study sought to analyze the association between facility size and collaborations with others. Collected data were analyzed using SPSS software package. Only questions for which sufficient number of responses was available are reported in the results. To examine the impact of facility size, the researchers created a new binary variable—organizations with fewer than 50 FTEs at Devens (small facility) and 50 or more FTEs at Devens (larger facility).

For deeper and precise analysis, the research team used not only the proportions of selected indicators, but also the 95% confidence intervals (CI), presented in Table 1.

Study Results and Analysis

As Devens moved into its second decade of promoting sustainable local development, the DEC wanted to better understand, measure, and communicate Devens' achievements as well as existing barriers to greater collaborations among local companies. The study aimed to examine local organizations' current practices, challenges, and opportunities in advancing mutually beneficial collaborations with other Devens organizations to improve efficiency and business competitiveness. Table 2 lists all 29 organizations participating in the study (30% of Devens' organizations). Of these, 79% were businesses, 14% were nonprofit, and 7% were government entities. The majority of participating companies (90%) were manufacturing entities. More than half of the organizations (59%) had a small number of employees in Devens (fewer than 50 FTEs). About 41% of participants reported having 50 or more FTEs in Devens. In terms of total number of U.S. employees, more than half (53%) reported having over 500 FTEs, and 47% reported fewer than 500 FTEs in the United States. About 76% of participants (CI, 55%–91%) were familiar with the DEEC EcoStar program and other offerings, and 45% (CI, 26%–64%) knew that Devens is internationally recognized as EIP (see Table 1).

Main reasons for locating to Devens

The majority of study participants (67%) identified the access to good infrastructure—rail, green building and roads—as the main reason for locating to Devens (see Figure 3). A large number of firms mentioned traditional business factors such as the lower cost of real estate (59%) and tax benefits (52%) as key reasons for locating to Devens. One in three organizations (33%) identified the ability to collaborate with other businesses as one of the top three reasons for locating to Devens; 22% said that Devens' sustainability vision and policies were a factor in their decision. After an international search, Bristol Meyers Squibb (BMS) chose to locate a large biopharmaceutical manufacturing plant in Devens "because the site had the necessary infrastructure capacity, a unified and expedited permitting process and competitively priced utilities. Devens' commitment to sustainability aligned with the company's mission was an additional selling point" (Hammer et al., 2012).

Key sustainability challenges of Devens organizations

The top two sustainability challenges identified by study participants included reducing the cost of energy (improving energy efficiency) and reducing the cost of materials (improving materials efficiency), each mentioned by 61% of interviewed organizations (see Figure 4). In this area, DEEC offers a range of services designed to help businesses decrease their energy consumption and save money. These services

Table 1. Sample Proportions and 95% CI for Devens Organizations, April 2013[a]

No.	Indicators	Number of respondents	Sample proportion (success = "yes")	95% Confidence Interval	
1	Does your firm have walking clubs or other programs to encourage employee fitness?	28	0,39286	0,21504	0,59423
2	Does your firm encourage the use of flex time for employees? (e.g., working from home a day or more, compressed work week, reduced work hours, job sharing)	29	0,37931	0,20687	0,57740
3	Do you encourage alternatives to the single-occupancy vehicle to get to work? (e.g., carpool, commuter rail, biking)	27	0,29630	0,13753	0,50181
4	Did you know that Devens is internationally recognized as an Eco-Industrial Park?	29	0,44828	0,26446	0,64306
5	Product take-back for reuse or remanufacturing	24	0,70833	0,48905	0,87385
6	Offering services versus selling products (e.g., leasing vs. selling products)	19	0,31579	0,12576	0,56550
7	Using other companies' waste as a raw material in your facility	24	0,54167	0,32821	0,74470
8	Contingency planning for improved resilience in cases of weather disruptions (e.g., hurricanes), including telecommuting, sharing infrastructure with others, etc.	25	0,56000	0,34928	0,75598
9	Increasing the use of local/U.S. suppliers to reduce supply-chain risks	25	0,76000	0,54871	0,90644
10	Does your organization currently partner with any other organizations in Devens or the surrounding region?	28	0,85714	0,67335	0,95966
11	Are there areas/opportunities within your organization that you feel could benefit from partnerships with other organizations in Devens?	28	0,78571	0,59047	0,91704
12	Are you familiar with the Devens Eco-Efficiency Center's EcoStar program and other service offerings?	29	0,75862	0,56460	0,89702

[a]95% CI indicates that we are 95% confident that the interval constructed from the sample will contain the true population proportion. There are several ways to compute a confidence interval for a proportion. If the sample size is small, as in the present study, symmetrical confidence limits that are approximated using the normal distribution may not be accurate enough for this application. The method that provides a more reliable confidence interval with small sample is the Clopper-Pearson interval. The Clopper-Pearson interval is an "exact" interval since it is based directly on the cumulative probabilities of the binomial distribution rather than any approximation of the binomial distribution (Sauro & Lewis, 2005).

Table 2. Devens Organizations Participating in the Study,
April 2013

AMSC	Mount Wachusetts College
Biognostics	Nashoba Valley Chamber of Commerce
Bristol Myers Squibb	NBKenney
Comrex	New England Sheets
Devens Recycling	Parker Charter School
Eglomesie Designs	Parker Hannifin
Guild of St Agnes	Patterson Veterinary
Integra	Red Tail Golf Course
Johnson Matthew	Rofin Baasel
Laddawn	Ryerson
Learning Express	Sabic Polymer
Liberty Tire recycling	True North Hotel Group
Loaves and Fishes	UNACC
Magnetmotion	Waiteco
Media News	

include employee outreach and engagement guidelines, energy consumption bench-marking with Energy Star's Portfolio Manager, and professional audit service by the Industrial Assessment Center at UMass Amherst to help identify efficiency opportunities with a payback period of 2 years or less (DEEC, 2013).

About one in five Devens organizations (21%) identified reducing waste generation among its top three sustainability challenges. The study found that most organizations did not track waste generation, reuse, and recycling, and therefore no reliable information was available to measure progress and cost savings. With the growing waste-reduction mandates, including the 2014 Massachusetts Organics Ban, it is expected that waste management will grow in importance (Massachusetts EEA, 2013). In all, 45% of study participants reported using other companies' waste as a raw material, a traditional EIP indicator. With the Great Exchange Forum, DEEC has helped facilitate such connections and save companies' money.

Many companies identified employee-related issues as key challenges: 39% reported difficulties with access to highly skilled employees, 21% mentioned employee health and well-being, and another 21% the challenges in engaging employees around sustainability initiatives. These findings confirm the growing importance of knowledge, skills, and employee health and well-being for improving business performance and competitiveness and is an area in which DEC and DEEC have played an important role. For instance, with its monthly workshops and round-tables around Green Building, Environmental Health and Safety, and Regulatory

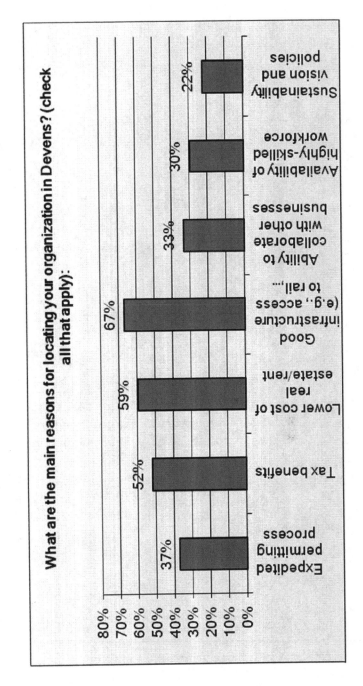

Figure 3. Main reasons for locating to Devens, April 2013.

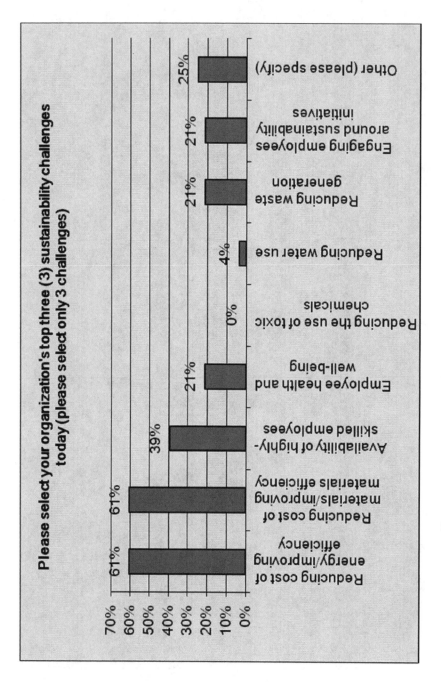

Figure 4. Top sustainability challenges for Devens organizations, April 2013.

Compliance, each attracting around 20 people, DEEC has provided a forum for area businesses to share best practices, discuss challenges, exchange resources, and build partnerships, thus helping them run more efficiently and sustainably. Expanded trails and sidewalks are supporting local firms' wellness programs. In all, 39% of study participants reported having walking clubs or other programs to encourage employee fitness (see Table 1).

Other sustainability practices of Devens organizations

With the increasing costs of raw materials globally, a growing number of companies are adopting strategies for product take-back and reuse or dematerialization (selling services instead of products), which can bring significant bottom-line benefits (Veleva, Montanari, Clabby, & Lese, 2013). The study found that 71% (CI, 49%–87%) of Devens organizations were taking back old products for reuse or remanufacturing (this question was applicable only to manufacturing facilities), and 32% (CI, 13%–57%) of study participants reported offering services instead of selling products.

Over a half or 56% (CI, 35%–76%) of study participants reported being engaged in contingency planning for improved resilience in cases of weather or other business disruptions, including telecommuting and sharing infrastructure with other businesses. Such planning has become increasingly important after the widespread business disruptions caused by hurricane Sandy in October 2012. During the interviews, several companies expressed interest in collaborating with others in Devens to find space for employees in cases of fire or other emergency. A few firms were planning to expand and looking for new space, while others had space they were looking to lease. In such cases, MassDevelopment and the Devens Enterprise Commission played a critical "broker" role in helping companies make the connection and thus reduce transaction costs, leading to improved business competitiveness.

Some 76% (CI, 55%–91%) of participants reported increasing the use of local/U.S. suppliers to reduce supply-chain risks. While many companies were involved in sourcing materials and selling products globally, they recognized increasing supply-chain risks and costs and were looking for local opportunities.

Collaborations between Devens companies

The level of collaboration by companies in an EIP is an important indicator of building local networks, which enable cost savings (e.g., resulting from materials exchanges or joint sourcing) and knowledge sharing. The study found that 86% (CI, 67%–96%) of Devens organizations partnered with others locally. On average, each organization partnered with 2.5 others; three companies—Laddawn, Integra, and Devens Recycling—reported partnerships with eight other organizations. The presence of nonprofit organizations such as the Parker Charter School (secondary school), Mount Wachusetts Community College (higher education), and Loaves and Fishes (food pantry) has helped increase the diversity of local organizations and thus create additional opportunities for collaborations—from student internships to waste repurposing, donations, and volunteering.

When asked about future opportunities for collaboration, 79% (CI, 59%–92%) of study participants said their organization could benefit from partnerships with others, such as joint purchasing, co-op bidding for snow plowing, landscaping and waste disposal, joint safety and other training, contingency space use during fire and other business disruptions, cardboard exchange, and employee offerings such as walking clubs, gym facilities, and field trips. Such collaborations are important for successful development of eco-industrial networks because they create "short mental distance," "trust," "openness," and "communication" (Ashton & Bain, 2012).

Small versus large facilities

Data analysis did not reveal a statistically significant difference in sustainability practices of small versus large facilities in Devens (defined as having fewer or more than 50 FTEs, respectively). Over 80% of both small and large facilities reported partnering with others and seeking additional opportunities from local collaborations (88% and 82%, respectively). About three quarters of both small and large facilities reported increasing the use of local/U.S. suppliers to reduce supply-chain risks (75% and 78%, respectively). Significant numbers of both small and large facilities were likely to take back their old products for reuse or remanufacturing despite the challenges of managing a global supply-chain logistics of product take-back (71% and 70%, respectively).

On the other hand, smaller facilities were more likely to encourage the use of flex time by employees (41% vs. 33%) and promote employee health and fitness by having walking clubs or other health programs (44% vs. 33%). About the same percentage of large and small facilities were likely to encourage alternatives to single-occupancy vehicles to get to work (31% vs. 30%). By supporting development of sidewalks and trails as well as commuter rail, DEC can further assist local organizations advance such practices.

Intangible benefits from locating in an eco-industrial park like Devens

Devens' offerings have helped local organizations advance their sustainability practices, often seen as key to their business success and firm competitiveness. Maura Peeler, Area General Manager of the True North Hotels Group (personal communication, August 15, 2013) shared,

> Being part of Devens EIP has helped us become more competitive with prospective national and local accounts that use our hotels for corporate travel. Many large companies inquire as to sustainability practices and methods during the "RFP" (request for pricing) process. If they themselves have a sustainability initiative, they often won't do business with vendors that don't hold similar values.

For other organizations, being a part of an EIP and participating in Devens programs has helped improve employee morale and satisfaction, as Melissa Fetterhoff, President and CEO, Nashoba Valley Chamber of Commerce shared (personal communication, August 15, 2013).

CONCLUSION

This study demonstrates that a large number of Devens organizations see sustainability practices as a key business issue and source of competitive advantage. By identifying and addressing local firms' key sustainability challenges and priorities—energy efficiency, materials efficiency, good infrastructure, and employee skills and well-being—the DEC has supported and advanced these practices. Most importantly, local government policies and initiatives to increase access to rail and promote green building development as well as companies' collaborations are in line with business needs and can serve as a valuable lesson for other policymakers and developers interested in attracting and retaining companies.

By simultaneously pursuing environmental and community goals, Devens EIP provides empirical evidence in support of Porter and Kramer's (2011) theory on creating shared value. The case demonstrates in practice how the right kind of government approach (including tax breaks and regulations) can encourage companies to pursue shared value. This approach includes setting clear and measurable social goals, establishing performance standards to meet these goals without being too prescriptive (e.g., the Green Building incentives and regulations encouraging the use of low-impact development stormwater management techniques), investing in the development of a measurement and reporting system to benchmark progress (Devens Sustainability Indicators), and efficiently and timely reporting of results to all stakeholders.

Continuous communication about available programs for local organizations is key for advancing local sustainability goals and increasing collaborations. With its workshops and roundtables as well as the Great Exchange, the DEEC has played a critical role in promoting shared knowledge and learning, building trust, and encouraging environmentally favorable behavior among firms located in Devens and neighboring communities. This confirms previous studies that have examined the role of social factors, including champions, in advancing collaborations and cooperative approaches to resource management (Ashton & Bain, 2012; Boons & Spekkink 2012). By creating a separate entity focused on promoting industrial ecology principles and greater collaborations among local firms, Devens has put in place the necessary institutional infrastructure to ensure activities will continue, even in case of personnel changes and loss of key industrial ecology champions.

The fact that despite its two-decade-long redevelopment, Devens still does not have any major exchanges of materials or by-products confirms earlier studies that have identified a range of technical, legal, economic, and organizational barriers (Gibbs & Deutz, 2007). In addition, since most heavy manufacturing has moved abroad, there is less heavy material usage available for major by-product exchanges. In this sense, Devens represents an eco-industrial model for light industrial parks, which is more relevant to the U.S. industry presently. In the 21st century knowledge-based economy, the Devens case provides empirical evidence in support of Lombardi and Laybourn's (2012) proposal to expand the definition of EIPs to include exchanges of knowledge, information, and expertise, which are all sources of innovation.

The case of Devens confirms that "developing EIPs is likely to be a long process where immediate results are unlikely to be forthcoming" (Gibbs & Deutz, 2007). While EIP policies and initiatives cannot force companies to change their behavior, providing educational and networking opportunities, knowledge, and guidance (especially when associated with costs savings or reduced business risks) can promote greater participation, collaboration, and ultimately advance the sustainability and competitiveness of local firms.

Limitations of the Study and Recommendations for Future Research

Due to the limited resources, the study used a small sample, which did not allow for conducting more sophisticated statistical analysis and moving beyond descriptive statistics. Future research could include stratified sampling from several eco-industrial parks to examine the business benefits of locating to an eco-industrial park, the differences between small and large facilities, and the impact of offered programs on sustainability practices and firm competitiveness. Potential analysis to use includes inferences about differences between two or several population proportions, such as confidence intervals and hypothesis testing.

Another limitation of the study is the lack of financial data to quantitatively evaluate firm performance. Part of the challenge is the fact that many of the Devens firms have other facilities in the United States and abroad. Future research could focus on a few companies and collect time-series data to compare the performance of their facilities in Devens to others in the United States, controlling for variety of other factors.

More research is needed to examine the role of environmental technologies (e.g., recycling, composting, co-generation, and clean energy generation) on building greater number of mutually beneficial collaborations that can promote costs and risk reduction as well as knowledge creation. Such work can build on the research by Geng et al. (2008) on the role of scavengers and decomposer businesses in increasing firm collaborations and competitiveness.

Limited research has been done on the link between business-cluster development and EIPs. Porter (1998) has pioneered this concept and his most recent work on shared social value outlines the need to focus on cluster development for advancing business competitiveness and local and regional sustainability (Porter & Kramer, 2011). In examining how industrial symbiosis happens, Chertow (2007) also makes the parallel to the development of business clusters. Research into the business benefits of EIPs can build on the literature around diverse cluster development and how the latter promotes greater firm competitiveness and sustainability. Clusters of similar industries create similar by-products. A diverse industrial base has been shown to produce a greater number of by-product exchanges and collaborations (Bain, Shenoy, Ashton, & Chertow, 2010).

Key to Devens' EIP success is its vision that serves community and business interests, a plan to achieve that vision, a collaborative structure to implement the plan, and a viable process to measure progress, revisit goals, and refine plans and strategies as conditions change. The present study demonstrates the importance of examining and addressing business sustainability challenges as well as establishing an organization focused on identifying and facilitating networking activities and collaborations. It provides valuable insights for policymakers and developers about the business benefits of eco-industrial parks. Finally, the case of Devens EIP demonstrates that eco-industrial parks today can be less about physical exchanges of materials, energy, water, and by-products and more about infrastructure and knowledge sharing, joint sourcing, building local supply chains, and reducing the risks from weather and other business disruptions, all critical components of business competitiveness in the 21st century knowledge-based economy.

DISCUSSION QUESTIONS

Chapter 3: The Business Benefits of Eco-Industrial Parks: Insights from Devens, Massachusetts

1. What is an eco-industrial park? What are the main business and societal benefits of developing eco-industrial parks?
2. What are the key driving forces for establishing eco-industrial parks? What are the main barriers?
3. What is the best strategy for the Devens Enterprise Commission to measure and communicate the business benefits of locating to Devens eco-industrial park as a way to attract additional companies?

REFERENCES

Ashton, W., & Bain, A. (2012). Assessing the "short mental distance" in eco-industrial networks. *Journal of Industrial Ecology, 16*(1), 70–82.

Bacallan, J. J. (2000). Greening the supply chain. *Business and Environment, 6*(5), 11–12.

Bain, A., Shenoy, M., Ashton, W., & Chertow, M. (2010). Industrial symbiosis and waste recovery in an Indian industrial area. *Resources, Conservation and Recycling, 54*, 1278–1287.

Bent, D. (2008). Competitiveness and sustainability: Building the best future for your business. *Forum for the Future. Sustainable Business Initiative.* Retrieved August 25, 2013, from https://www.icaew.com/~/media/Files/Technical/Sustainability/competitiveness-and-sustainability-building-the-best-future-for-your-business.pdf

Boons, F., & Berends, M. (2001). Stretching the boundaries: The possibilities of flexibility as an organizational capability in industrial ecology. *Business Strategy and the Environment, 10*(2), 115–124.

Boons, F., & Spekkink, W. (2012). Levels of institutional capacity and actor expectations about industrial symbiosis. *Journal of Industrial Ecology, 16*(1), 61–69.

Chertow, M. (2007). Uncovering industrial symbiosis. *Journal of Industrial Ecology, 11*(1), 11–30.

Chertow, M., & Ehrenfeld, J. (2012). Organizing self-organizing systems. *Journal of Industrial Ecology, 16*(1), 13–27.

Côté, R., & Cohen-Rosenthal, E. (1998). Designing eco-industrial parks: A synthesis of some experiences. *Journal of Cleaner Production, 6,* 181–188. Retrieved May 25, 2013, from http://www.umich.edu/~indecol/EIP-cote.pdf

Devens Eco-Efficiency Center (DEEC). (2012). *Annual report.* Retrieved May 28, 2013, from http://www.ecostardevens.com/index_files/annualreport.htm

Devens Eco-Efficiency Center (DEEC). (2013). *Energy efficiency and conservation.* Retrieved May 29, 2013, from http://www.ecostardevens.com/index_files/ee.htm

Devens Sustainability Indicator Report. (2000). Retrieved May 28, 2013, from http://www.devensec.com/sustain/indicators/sustainreport.html

Drucker, P. F. (1985). *Innovation and entrepreneurship: Practice and principles.* Oxford, UK: Butterworth-Heinemann.

Duranton, G., & Puga, D. (2000). Diversity and specialization in cities: Why, where and when does it matter? *Urban Studies, 37*(3), 533–555.

EcoStar. (2012). *Program overview.* Retrieved May 28, 2013, from http://www.ecostardevens.com/index_files/ecostar.htm

Environmental Protection Agency (EPA). (2012). *Re-powering America's land: Renewable energy on potentially contaminated land and mine sites.* Retrieved August 26, 2013, from http://www.epa.gov/renewableenergyland/docs/repower_contaminated_land_fact sheet.pdf

Esty, D., & Porter, M. (1998). Industrial ecology and competitiveness: Strategic implications for the firm. *Journal of Industrial Ecology, 2*(1), 35–43.

Geng, Y., Zhang, P., Cote, R., & Fujita, T. (2008). Assessment of the national eco-industrial park standard for promoting industrial symbiosis in China. *Journal of Industrial Ecology, 13*(1), 15–26.

Gibbs, D., & Deutz, P. (2007). Reflections on implementing industrial ecology through eco-industrial park development. *Journal of Cleaner Production, 15,* 1683–1695.

Hammer, J., Babcock, J., & Moosbrugger, K. (2012). *Putting concepts into practice: Triple bottom line economic development.* Retrieved August 26, 2013, from http://www.tbltool.org/files/CUPA_Casebook.pdf

Hargadon, A. (2003). *How breakthroughs happen.* Boston, MA: Harvard Business School.

Hoffman, A. (2003). Linking social systems analysis to the industrial ecology framework. *Organizations & Environment, 16,* 66–86. Retrieved May 28, 2013, from http://webuser.bus.umich.edu/ajhoff/pub_academic/2003%20O&E.pdf

Korhonen, J., von Malmborg, F., Strachan, P., & Ehrenfeld, A., Jr. (2004). Management and policy aspects of industrial ecology: An emerging research agenda. *Business Strategy and the Environment, 13,* 289–305.

Lombardi, R., & Laybourn, P. (2012). Redefining industrial symbiosis: Crossing academic-practitioner boundaries. *Journal of Industrial Ecology, 16*(1), 28–37.

Lombardi, R., Lyons, D., Shi, H., & Agarwal, A. (2012). Industrial symbiosis: Testing the boundaries and advancing knowledge. *Journal of Industrial Ecology, 16*(1), 2–6.

Lowitt, P. (2012, November 13). *Devens—A sustainable community.* Presentation at UMass Boston.

Martin, S., & Mayer, H. (2008). Sustainability, clusters and competitiveness. *Economic Development Quarterly, 22*(4), 272–276.

Maskell, P., & Malmberg, A. (1995, October). Localized learning and industrial competitiveness. *eScholarship University of California.* Retrieved August 20, 2013, from http://escholarship.org/uc/item/66n1527h#page-36

Massachusetts Energy and Environmental Affairs. (2013, July 10). *Patrick administration announces plan to ban disposal of commercial food waste.* Retrieved August 26, 2013, from http://www.mass.gov/eea/pr-2013/commercial-food-waste-ban.html

McKinsey. (2010, March). *How companies manage sustainability: McKinsey global survey results.* Retrieved August 20, 2013, from http://www.mckinsey.com/insights/sustainability/how_companies_manage_sustainability_mckinsey_global_survey_results

McKittrick, T. (2012, September). *ReVenture Park: Charlotte's first eco-industrial park.* Presentation at US Industrial Eco-Park Development Networking Event, Devens, MA. Retrieved July 25, 2013, from http://www.devensec.com/sustain/ReV_Clean_Energy.pdf

Mirata, M. (2004). Experiences from early stages of a national industrial symbiosis programme in the UK: Determinants and coordination challenges. *Journal of Cleaner Production, 12,* 967–983.

Nidumolu, R., Prahalad, C. K., & Rangaswami, M. R. (2009, September). Why sustainability is now the key driver of innovation. *Harvard Business Review.* Retrieved from http://hbr.org/2009/09/why-sustainability-is-now-the-key-driver-of-innovation/

Paquin, R., & Howard-Grenville, J. (2012). The evolution of facilitated industrial symbiosis. *Journal of Industrial Ecology, 16*(1), 83–93.

Porter, M. (1998). Clusters and the new economics of competition. *Harvard Business Review, 67*(6), 77-91.

Porter, M., & Kramer, M. (2011, January/February). Creating shared value. *Harvard Business Review,* 62–77.

President's Council on Sustainable Development (PCSD). (1997). *Eco-industrial park workshop proceedings.* Cape Charles, VA. Retrieved July 28, 2013, from http://clinton2.nara.gov/PCSD/Publications/Eco_Workshop.html

Rao, P., & Holt, D. (2005). Do green supply chains lead to competitiveness and economic performance? *International Journal of Operations & Production Management, 25*(9), 898–916.

Sauro, J., & Lewis, J. R. (2005). Estimating completion rates from small sample using binomial confidence interval. Comparison and recommendation. *Proceedings of the Human Factors and Ergonomics Society 49th annual meeting* (pp. 2100–2104).

Shi, H., Tian, J., & Chen, L. (2012). China's quest for eco-industrial parks, Part I: History and distinctiveness. *Journal of Industrial Ecology, 16*(1), 8–10.

Veleva, V. (2012). *Devens sustainability indicator report 2000–2012: Progress report.* Retrieved August 21, 2013, from http://www.devensec.com/sustain.html

Veleva, V., Montanari, A., Clabby, P., & Lese, J. (2013, January). PerkinElmer: Old instrument reuse and recycling. *Richard Ivey School of Business.* University of Western Ontario, Canada, Case#9B12M115w.

Yuan, Z., & Shi, L. (2009). Improving enterprise competitive advantage with industrial symbiosis: Case study of a smeltery in China. *Journal of Cleaner Production, 17,* 1295–1302.

Chapter 4

PRODUCT STEWARDSHIP IN THE UNITED STATES: THE CHANGING POLICY LANDSCAPE AND THE ROLE OF BUSINESS[1]

AUTHOR'S PERSONAL STATEMENT

Since I came to the United States almost 12 years ago, I have been astonished by the rate of consumption and the enormous amount of waste generated by people and organizations. Could Americans wake up one day without electricity, gasoline, or bread, as happened to many Eastern European countries in the early 1990s? It was a tough lesson that many people of my generation will never forget. It is clear to me that the current rate of consumption and environmental pollution is unsustainable. Every few years, people change cars, computers, televisions, other appliances, and even their homes! It is often said that if every person on this planet consumed like Americans, we would need several planets Earth. But why should people in other countries not have the right to own a car, travel to exotic destinations, and purchase prepackaged food, modern appliances, and toys for their children?

As an engineer and scientist trained in cleaner production, I have always believed in the unlimited potential of humankind to find solutions to seemingly unsolvable problems. But we need to have the right incentives. This does not mean people and organizations should not change their consumption patterns, but rather that we can build the economy from a systems perspective, considering the entire lifecycle of products and services and the social, economic, and environmental impact of our actions today and in the decades to come. The current global recession makes it even clearer that a systems approach is critical in going forward to ensure stable and sustainable development in an increasingly interconnected world. Business, government, and civil society organizations all need to work together to design the

[1] Reprinted from Veleva, V. (2008, Fall/Winter). Product stewardship in the U.S.: The changing policy landscape and the role of business. *Sustainability: Science, Practice and Policy*, 4(2). Retrieved from http://ejournal.nbii.org/archives/vol4iss2/communityessay.veleva.html

rules of the new economic system in which products last longer, have no toxic chemicals, and are reused and recycled; society as a whole consumes less, and people spend more time with family and friends and less time working to maintain their "standard of living."

* * *

Back in 2001, the Product Stewardship Institute (PSI) convened its first dialogue around electronic waste issues and began to explore the challenges of handling leftover paint. Seven years later, the Fourth PSI Forum was an exciting and over-whelming experience. Despite a lack of federal regulation, business in the United States is beginning to work with federal and state governments to address product stewardship, and companies are taking increasingly active positions. In the current economic downturn, and with the Obama administration, product stewardship issues will be an even more important source of competitive advantage (Economist Intelligence Unit, 2008). This chapter provides an overview of the changing policy landscape in the United States, reviews some emerging practices, and explores the role of business in product stewardship.

What is Product Stewardship?

The PSI defines product stewardship as "a principle that directs all participants involved in the life cycle of a product to take shared responsibility for the impacts on human health and the natural environment that result from the production, use, and end-of-life management of the product" (PSI, 2008). The main objective of product stewardship is to promote waste reduction by encouraging manufacturers to redesign products so they contain fewer toxics, last longer, can be reused and recycled, and/or contain recycled materials.

The PSI was created to alleviate the financial and logistical burden of managing waste on state and local governments. As of November 2008, PSI membership included 45 states and 60 local governments (representing over 85% of the United States population) and had more recently expanded to create an adjunct council comprising 30 businesses, environmental and academic organizations, and other stakeholders. Through conference calls, meetings, and information exchange, PSI has helped consensus building, policy development, and regulation adoption in many states.[2]

In most cases, the process begins with regulation overseas, typically in the European Union (EU), which the *Economist* (Brussels Rules OK, 2007) calls "the world's chief regulator." Rules such as the EU Waste Electrical and Electronic Equipment (WEEE) Directive, the Restrictions of Hazardous Substances (RoHS) Directive, the End-of-Life Vehicle (ELV) Directive, and the Packaging Directive

[2]For information on past dialogues, potential new product initiatives, or details on membership in PSI's Adjunct Council, see the Product Stewardship Institute website, http://www.product stewardship.us

have been quickly adopted by other countries, including Canada, China, Japan, Korea, and Australia. Typically, some American states such as California, Minnesota, and New York then began introducing similar bills. For example, in the electronics waste area—the first issue tackled by PSI—as of November 2008, some 16 states and New York City had already passed laws on electronic waste, and more than 15 other states were considering such bills (Electronics TakeBack Coalition, 2008).

The Role of Business in Product Stewardship

Whether realizing it or not, companies play an important role in shaping the product stewardship policy landscape. PSI has shown that successful initiatives require the involvement of all key stakeholders, such as manufacturers, retailers, recyclers, governments, nongovernmental organizations (NGOs), and others. On the one hand, successful policies require building a consensus around responsibilities, performance goals, incentives, and implementation. If a state or local government drafts a bill, lack of agreement with key industry players may lead to aggressive lobbying and defeat. On the other hand, without business input, regulators might support a bill that is either unfeasible or can hurt local businesses.

While European companies have traditionally been more supportive of environmental regulations, American businesses have preferred voluntary initiatives (see the carpet take-back program described in Box 1). Historically, the United States federal government has also avoided environmental protection or health and safety issues, because "most government leaders believed that this responsibility should be chiefly shouldered by private industry, the states, and professional organizations" (Geiser, 2001). Moreover, many economists, policymakers, and businesses in the country believe that environmental regulation retards productivity despite numerous

---

Box 1. Addressing Carpet Disposal

- Product stewardship efforts: Driven largely by manufacturers such as Interface and C&A.
- Memorandum of Understanding (MOU) signed in January 2001: Agreed to develop "negotiated outcomes" for collecting and processing discarded carpet, establish reuse and recycling goals, and develop model procurement goals.
- Carpet dialogue: Determined recycling and reuse rates with participants including EPA, the states of Minnesota, Iowa, Massachusetts, North Carolina, California, Oregon, and Maryland; industry and NGOs.
- New MOU, signed in January 2002: Agreed by 2012 to achieve 40% landfill-diversion goal, roles and responsibilities, evaluation criteria, and schedule.
- 2007: Midcourse review conducted by Zero Waste Alliance found efforts significantly lag behind established targets. Identified new strategies including increased marketing of recycled products, developing forms of sustainable financing, and expanding collection and processing infrastructure.

studies demonstrating the opposite (e.g., Jorgenson & Wilcoxen, 1990). This view is, to some extent, related to the burdensome and highly prescriptive and complex regulations like Best Available Control Technology (BACT), which have been previously implemented in the United States. By comparison, regulations in Europe have generally been simpler and more flexible, based on setting goals and targets and letting businesses decide how to get there (Vig & Faure, 2004). One example is the standard for occupational exposure to cadmium; the provision is about 15 pages long in Sweden versus several hundred in the United States.

At the same time, individual American states continue to lead the way with environmental regulations, an approach that poses a logistical difficulty for many American companies (Rabe, 2004). Having to meet numerous different standards in various jurisdictions can be an enormously complex task. At the Take It Back! annual conference in 2005, electronic industry manufacturers asked the Environmental Protection Agency (EPA) to pass a federal take-back regulation to provide a "common playing field" (Veleva, 2005). Without such uniform standards, companies risk fines, litigation, and damaged reputation, as Microsoft experienced in 1999 when the Mateel Environmental Justice Foundation sued the company for noncompliance with California's Proposition 65, which mandates labeling wire and cable products containing a high lead concentration (Veleva & Sethi, 2004).

More recently, American toy manufacturers have faced similar challenges. After numerous large recalls in 2007 and 2008, a Mattel spokeswoman stated, "Fifty different state standards will create a confusing patchwork of regulations, limit certain toys sold in some states, drive up costs for consumers and will not substantively increase toy safety" (Trottman & Williamson, 2008). Therefore, Mattel and many other manufacturers support tougher federal standards that give the industry "clear and uniform rules." Working with state and federal regulators, NGOs, industry peers, and other stakeholders is one way for businesses to advance uniform rules and policies.

Major companies in the United States have long realized the importance of being active players in dialogues around product stewardship. For instance, Dell came under significant pressure from environmental groups across the EU to assume responsibility for its old products, an experience that sensitized company officials to the risks and opportunities of state and federal e-waste regulations and the need to take proactive steps (Cole & Vozick, 2002). The computer manufacturer drafted and successfully campaigned for the passage of the so-called Dell Model Bill in several American states, including Kansas, Texas, and Oklahoma. While states with poor capacity to enact such policies believe it is better to have the "Dell Bill" than no regulation at all, some federal regulators and the Electronics TakeBack Coalition consider it weak regulation and a cause for concern as it may prevent passage of a stricter bill nationwide.

Companies want to be involved in the discussion and the framing of product-stewardship policies, as government and NGOs expect them to pay for product end-of-life disposal. While in most cases firms are able to pass these costs on to the end consumer, global competition from companies overseas with no such regulations sometimes leads to manufacturers absorbing the cost of take-back and disposal. For example, while some computer manufacturers charge a fee for taking back old computers, others, such as Dell, Lenovo, and Toshiba, have free take-back programs. In addition, with limited state and local government resources for waste treatment and disposal, there has been a movement globally toward shifting the responsibility to manufacturers. In California, for example, local governments responsible for hazardous waste collection met in 2001 and recognized that their costs had tripled due to the large stream of electronic waste. Since they did not want to increase tipping fees or taxes to pay for it, "industry needs to take responsibility and fund a program" (Fraser, 2009). As a result, the state passed Senate Bill 20, which imposes a recycling fee on all electronics that contain lead.

Known as Extended Producer Responsibility (EPR) in Europe and Product Stewardship (PS) in the United States, this approach to environmental management typically requires collecting and recycling or safely disposing of old or unused products at the end of their useful life (e.g., EU's WEEE and ELV directives). EPR, though, differs from PS in two important ways: (a) it shifts responsibility (physically and/or financially) upstream to the producer and away from municipalities, and (b) it provides incentives to producers to take environmental considerations into the design of the product. PS, by comparison, considers all parties involved in producing, selling, or using a product (e.g., suppliers, designers, manufacturers, distributors, retailers, customers, recyclers, remanufacturers, and disposers) to be responsible for the full environmental and economic impact of that product. Such "shared" accountability provides less clarity and weaker incentives for manufacturers to redesign their products to reduce end-of-life impact.

In both cases, however, taking back old or unused products is expensive. Manufacturers typically do not do so, and taxpayer money is required to fund take-back programs at state and local government facilities to properly recycle such products so they do not end up in the landfill or get incinerated and thus contaminate air or groundwater. Many regulators and NGOs in the United States are calling on manufacturers to fund take-back programs and for retailers to collect waste products in their stores (the most convenient option for consumers). Group Health, for example, participated with its 25 pharmacies in a voluntary take-back pilot program for secure medicine returns in Washington State (see Box 2). In 2001, Benjamin Moore was involved in a voluntary take-back pilot program in Massachusetts, coordinated by PSI and the Massachusetts Department of Environmental Protection. This initiative later helped inform the PSI dialogue on this issue (see Box 3).

Walmart Driving Product Stewardship?

Whether inspired after Hurricane Katrina (Creno, 2008; Scott, 2007) or as a result of stakeholder pressures and an attempt to improve its image and reputation, Walmart's transformation to embrace sustainability is a phenomenon that has begun to attract considerable attention. The historic speech by Walmart Chief Executive Lee Scott in the fall of 2005 put the giant retailer on a fast track called "Sustainability 360."

Box 2. Pharmaceutical Waste

- **Problem**: Improperly disposed-of drugs can be a source of childhood poisoning and teenage and adult abuse. They are also increasingly showing up in the environment and, according to the U.S. Geological Survey, are found in 80% of the country's streams and in the drinking water supply of many cities.

- **Global status**: Some jurisdictions such as British Columbia have enacted regulations and created agencies such as the Post-Consumer Pharmaceutical Stewardship Association (PCPSA) with active participation by pharmacies to safely collect and dispose of medications.

- **United States status**: No federal regulation and only guidelines on safe disposal by consumers exist. PSI convened a dialogue in three phases:

  - Phase I: Literature search that identified and interviewed stakeholders, summarized efforts, invited participation in a national dialogue, developed the Product Stewardship Action Plan for Unwanted/Waste Pharmaceuticals.

  - Phase II: Launched in June 2008 to convene four national dialogue meetings, to organize workgroup meetings, to develop priority agreements, and to disseminate project results.

  - Phase III: Will jointly implement priority projects and initiatives identified in dialogue process.

- **Funders**: Waste Management; EXP Pharmaceuticals; King Pharmaceuticals; Water Environment Federation; National Association of Clean Waters; States of Minnesota, California, and Idaho; King County (Washington State) and Los Angeles County (California); and cities of Santa Monica and San Francisco in California.

Box 3. Leftover Paint Disposal

- **Goal**: Develop nationally coordinated leftover paint management system
- 2003–2004: Four dialogue meetings held
- 2005: First MOU signed
- 2007: Second MOU signed by 45 parties thus far:
  - "Invisible" eco-fee paid by consumers at retail locations
  - Industry-run system of collection
  - Industry pays for the collection and reuse/recycling of leftover paint and passes costs onto the consumer
  - Industry will enhance existing collection infrastructure
  - No mandatory retail take back
  - Consumer education on proper paint disposal
- 2008: Minnesota legislation passed by both Houses; supported by industry, manufacturers, retail, and government; vetoed by the governor, but will be reintroduced in the 2009 session.
- 2008–2010: Based on demonstration in Minnesota, system will roll out to Oregon, Vermont, Washington, California, Iowa, Florida, North Carolina, and Connecticut.

According to Scott, sustainability is the single biggest business opportunity today. In a subsequent lecture to the Prince of Wales's Business and the Environment Programme in February 2007, Scott declared that, "Hurricane Katrina changed Walmart forever. And it changed us for the better. We saw our full potential—with absolute clarity—to serve not just our customers, but our communities, our countries, and even the world. We saw our opportunity and our responsibility" (Scott, 2007).

To begin this process, the company held a meeting at its headquarters in Bentonville, Arkansas, in March 2006, inviting many sustainability specialists to devote a day to analysis, discussion, and action planning (Googins, Mirvis, & Rochlin, 2007). Representatives from the Boston College Center for Corporate Citizenship (BCCCC) were among the invited participants.[3] The company's journey started with defining three main inspirational goals, two of which—Goal 2 and Goal 3 below—are related to PS:

- Goal 1: Use 100% renewable energy
- Goal 2: Generate zero waste
- Goal 3: Sell sustainable products

---

[3] The Boston College Center for Corporate Citizenship is a membership-based research organization associated with the Carroll School of Management. It is committed to helping business leverage its social, economic, and human assets to ensure both its success and a more just and sustainable world. As a leading resource on corporate citizenship, the Center works with global corporations to help them define, plan, and operationalize their corporate citizenship. Through the power of research, education, and the insights of its 350 corporate members, the Center creates knowledge, value, and demand for corporate citizenship. The Center offers publications, including a newsletter, research reports, and white papers; management and leadership programs, including three certificate programs; events that include an annual conference, roundtables, and regional meetings; peer-to-peer learning forums; and a corporate membership program.

To progress, Walmart established three networks to focus on key opportunities under each goal. The networks start with a "captain," or senior business leader, whose performance review includes sustainability criteria (Waddoups, 2008). To measure achievements toward the three goals, Walmart developed specific targets and initiatives, such as

- Increasing fleet efficiency by 25% in 3 years (achieved).
- Selling 100 million compact fluorescent light (CFL) bulbs in 2007 (exceeded the target by selling 137 million).
- Partnering with suppliers like General Mills to reduce product packaging (prevented the generation of 890,000 pounds per year of waste; launched packaging scorecard for suppliers in 2006).
- Reducing supply-chain greenhouse gas emissions by sourcing locally (by partnering with Mississippi farmers, Walmart reduced by two thirds the miles traveled to source corn).
- Selling 100% sustainably harvested seafood (currently working with the Marine Stewardship Council [MSC] to develop guidelines and certification; selling 22 MSC-certified seafood products as of December 2008).
- Introducing chemical-safety standards for suppliers that are more stringent than current federal regulations in the United States (e.g., for lead, phthalates, mercury, antimony, arsenic, barium, cadmium, chromium, and selenium; three priority chemicals have been identified in 2008 for phase-out by suppliers: propoxur, permethrin, and nonyl phenol ethoxylates).

There is growing evidence that Walmart is walking the walk, and its actions have begun to affect the market (Ethical Performance, 2009; Plambeck & Denend, 2008). Using its large purchasing power, Walmart is changing the way companies design and deliver products. Many of the member companies of the BCCCC, such as Teradata, Tennant, and General Mills, admit they are making product changes or committing to corporate citizenship reporting because "Walmart asked us to do so" or because "our customers are demanding it." With over 60,000 suppliers around the globe, Walmart is able to bring changes that no government can enact as fast (Birchall, 2008; CSR Wire, 2008). By introducing tougher requirements for suppliers, making longer-term commitments, and partnering with NGOs for product testing and certification (Plambeck & Denend, 2008), Walmart is becoming one of the driving forces for product innovation and stewardship, as are many other large companies such as Nike, Target, Dell, and Intel.[4]

[4]Nike, for example, is taking back and recycling old sneakers. Pressured by socially responsible investors and NGOs, Target agreed in 2008 to phase out from its stores all products containing polyvinyl chloride (PVC). Dell became the first computer maker in the United States to take back its old or unused computers. Intel was among the founding members of the Electronics Industry Code of Conduct—a voluntary initiative promoting better supply-chain management, which includes guidelines for designing and manufacturing greener products.

At the same time, most business support for PS in the United States is around product design, manufacturing, and use rather than end-of-life management. An example of this approach is Walmart's commitment to influencing consumers to switch to more energy efficient CFLs. By actively promoting these bulbs, Walmart has probably helped reduce energy use, but at the same time, the company's actions have indirectly contributed to another problem: mercury emissions from discarded products. While CFLs are an environmentally preferable option from the standpoint of energy conservation, not all consumers know that the bulbs contain mercury and need to be properly disposed of at the end of their life.

Collecting old CFLs has proved difficult and costly, and currently Walmart does not want to get involved. The EPA considers discarded CFLs to be "hazardous waste" and the subject of special requirements for collection, personnel training, and transportation due to the health risks that they pose (Appell, 2007). While studies show that the mercury used in CFLs is less than the mercury emitted from a coal-fired power plant that would otherwise power incandescent lightbulbs, the former is still a concern due to its "dispersed" nature. If a consumer throws an old CFL in the trash, there is no way to separate it from the other household waste that is typically incinerated or disposed of in a landfill. Moreover, recycling CFLs containing mercury can expose workers to this toxic chemical. In contrast, mercury from coal-fired power plants is "concentrated" at the source, and new technologies exist to capture much of it before emission (Feeley, Murphy, Hoffmann, Granite, & Renninger, 2003).

Some environmental groups, such as the Natural Resource Defense Council (NRDC), are considering whether other innovations, such as light-emitting diodes (LEDs), which do not contain mercury or any other toxic chemicals, could be an alternative to CFLs (Roman, 2008). This approach, however, could be costly and require systems thinking, life-cycle assessment, and collaboration by various stakeholders, including government.

To address both the presence of mercury in fluorescent lightbulbs and the lack of collection options, PSI is convening a national dialogue that seeks to develop a comprehensive solution for CFL product responsibility. The goal is to negotiate acceptable and accountable roles for key stakeholders involved in the product life cycle, including retailers, manufacturers, and government officials. The key objectives of the dialogue are to reduce the environmental impact of the manufacture of fluorescent lightbulbs, to increase the manufacture and procurement of environmentally preferable lighting, and to maximize the safe collection and recycling of spent lamps from households and businesses by developing a nationally coordinated system that is financially sustainable.

WHAT SHOULD COMPANIES DO TO PREPARE FOR THE PRODUCT STEWARDSHIP "WAVE"?

Momentum is growing both globally and in the United States for greater environmental responsibility and PS. With the Obama administration, it is widely expected that government involvement and oversight of business will increase. To prepare for this coming "wave" in PS policies and regulations, companies can do the following:

- *Educate yourself:* If you manufacture products, parts, or materials, educate yourself about what happens to your goods once they reach the end of their life and whether there are social, environmental, or health risks. The BCCCC has numerous offerings and works with companies to map and address key social and environmental impacts and to help their bottom line.
- *Know your supply chain:* Knowing and tracking all ingredients and suppliers of your products, parts, and materials is one of the most critical business challenges today for companies across industries. Visionary companies like HP and Intel have developed a sustainable supply chain and see their suppliers as key partners (Veleva, 2007).
- *Track the regulatory landscape:* Learn about any regulatory action, NGO campaigns, or other initiatives that target your industry's products, parts, or materials, not just in the United States, but also overseas. In a global marketplace, it is just a question of time before such actions affect domestic companies. Think of NGO campaigns, customer requirements, and regulatory restrictions on mercury, cadmium, lead, polybrominated diphenyl ethers (PBDEs), phthalates, PVC, bisphenol A (BPA), transfats, and more recently, nanomaterials.
- *Participate in a dialogue:* Find out if someone is already working on PS issues and join a group, such as the PSI dialogues, to participate in the development of new policies.
- *Be proactive:* New regulations will emerge whether you take action or not. To be better prepared, start with some pilot initiatives to explore the costs and benefits of various product redesigns and take-back schemes. Companies including Benjamin Moore, Staples, Dell, Nike, and Best Buy were among the first in their industries to explore take-back options.
- *Be transparent:* Customers, consumers, regulators, and NGOs want to know what your company is doing to address issues of concern. Communicating your initiatives builds trust and improves your reputation, both crucial resources for your business and bottom line.
- *Look at product stewardship as a process, not a destination:* Today, we cannot possibly foresee all the changes in scientific knowledge, environmental issues, and consumer preferences. As nicely summarized by Tod Arbogast (2008), director of sustainable business at Dell, "You get a lens into the future if you engage with stakeholders." The best way to prepare for the coming PS "wave" in your industry is to join a network, engage with stakeholders, learn, talk, and act.

In times of product oversupply and increasing global competition, deepening economic crisis, and changing consumer preferences, PS provides unique opportunities for innovations that can increase market share, profits, and shareholder value. Proactive companies can play a key role in shaping emerging PS policies and regulations in the United States.

DISCUSSION QUESTIONS

Chapter 4: Product Stewardship in the United States: The Changing Policy Landscape and the Role of Business

1. What is "product stewardship"? How does it differ from "extended producer responsibility" concept used in Europe?
2. What are the main drivers for product stewardship initiatives in the United States?
3. How is Walmart driving product stewardship in the United States?
4. Research a specific product from the Product Stewardship Institute website (http://www.productstewardship.us/?page=Product__Work) and report on recent product stewardship developments in the U.S. for this product. Are these developments adequate to address the problem?

REFERENCES

Appell, D. (2007, October). Toxic bulbs: Recycling rules vary for mercury-containing fluorescents. *Scientific American.*

Arbogast, T. (2008, April 29–30). Building Leadership, Creating Solutions, CERES annual conference, Boston, MA. Retrieved from http://www.ceres.org

Birchall, J. (2008, September 30). Walmart boycotts Uzbek cotton. *Financial Times*, p. 27.

Brussels Rules OK. (2007, September 22). *The Economist.*

Cole, S., & Vozick, E. (2002). Digging Dell to take it back. *EcoCycle Times, 26*(2). Retrieved from http://www.ecocycle.org/zerowaste/aroundtheworld#dell

CSR Wire. (2008). *Walmart sets goal to reduce its global plastic shopping bag waste by one-third.* Retrieved January 1, 2009, from http://www.csrwire.com/press_releases/24221-Wal-Mart-Sets-Goal-to-Reduce-Its-Global-Plastic-Shopping-B

Creno, C. (2008, May 26) Walmart sustainability efforts draw praise. *The Arizona Republic.* Retrieved from http://www.azcentral.com/business/articles/2008/05/26/20080526biz-greenretailers0526-ON.html

Economist Intelligence Unit. (2008). *Corporate citizenship: Profiting from a sustainable business.* New York, NY: Economist Intelligence Unit Limited. Retrieved from http://graphics.eiu.com/upload/Corporate_Citizens.pdf

Electronics TakeBack Coalition. (2008). *Computer takeback campaign.* Retrieved January 1, 2009, from http://www.electronicstakeback.com/home/

Ethical Performance. (2009). Walmart is most improved. *Ethical Performance, 10*(8), 12.

Feeley, T., Murphy, J., Hoffmann, J., Granite, E., & Renninger, S. (2003, October16–23). DOE/NETL's mercury control technology research program for coal-fired power plants. *EM.*

Fraser, R. (2009, January, 18–24). Managing electronic waste in a climate of constant change. *EM.* Retrieved from http://c.ymcdn.com/sites/www.productstewardship.us/resource/resmgr/imported/EM_eWaste_article_an2009.pdf

Geiser, K. (2001). *Materials matter.* Cambridge, MA: MIT Press.

Googins, B., Mirvis, P., & Rochlin, S. (2007). *Beyond good company: Next generation corporate citizenship.* New York, NY: Palgrave Macmillan.

Jorgenson, D., & Wilcoxen, P. (1990). Environmental regulation and U.S. economic growth. *RAND Journal of Economics, 21*(2), 314–340.

Plambeck, E., & Denend, L. (2008, Spring). The greening of Walmart. *Stanford Social Innovation Review*, 53–59.

Product Stewardship Institute (PSI). (2008). [Home page]. *The Product Stewardship Institute*. Retrieved January 5, 2009, from http://www.productstewardship.us

Rabe, B. (2004). *Statehouse and greenhouse: The emerging politics of American climate change policy*. Washington, DC: Brookings Institution.

Roman, B. (2008). *LED lighting—Cool technology heats up*. Retrieved January 5, 2009, from http://www.onearth.org/node/724

Scott, L. (2007). *Sustainability Progress to Date 2007-2008*. Retrieved January 4, 2009, from http://www.walmartstores.com/sites/sustainabilityreport/2007/companyMessage.html

Trottman, M., & Williamson, E. (2008, June 18). Children's product industry put in regulatory bind. *The Wall Street Journal*, p. A3.

Veleva, V. (2005, March 8). *Navigating investment risk in a new regulatory environment: An investor perspective*. 2005 Take It Back! Conference, Alexandria, VA.

Veleva, V. (2007). Take the gamble out of your supply chain: Lessons from the electronics industry journey. *The Corporate Citizen, 2*, 31–34.

Veleva, V., & Sethi, S. (2004). The electronics industry in a new regulatory climate: Protecting the environment and shareholder value. *Corporate Environmental Strategy, 11*(9), 207–224.

Vig, N., & Faure, M. (Eds.). (2004). *Green giants: Environmental policies of the United States and the European Union*. Cambridge, MA: MIT Press.

Waddoups, R. (2008, June 3–5). Presentation at fourth National Product Stewardship forum, Boston, MA. *Product Stewardship Institute*. Retrieved from http://www.product stewardship.us/?284

UPDATE TO CHAPTER 4: PRODUCT STEWARDSHIP IN THE UNITED STATES: THE CHANGING POLICY LANDSCAPE AND THE ROLE OF BUSINESS

As of 2014, there was still no federal legislation on product stewardship in the United States. The states continued to lead the efforts in this area with support from the Product Stewardship Institute (PSI). The PSI's members and collaborators increased further to include 47 state environmental agencies, hundreds of local government members, 95 corporate, business, academic, non-U.S. government, and organizational partners (PSI, 2014).

Product stewardship efforts expanded to include a greater number of products in the United States. As of May 2014, PSI work covered 17 different product categories, including electronics, batteries, fluorescent lighting, mattresses, medical sharps, packaging, tires, pharmaceuticals, paint and carpet, among others.

- *Electronics* recycling continued to grow in importance as people were replacing their old TVs and CRT monitors with flat screens, leading to further growth in e-waste. According to PSI, more than 3.4 million tons of electronic waste was generated in 2011, of which just 29% was recycled. As of May 2014, 23 states had passed extended producer responsibility (EPR) laws mandating manufacturers' responsibility for taking-back and recycling their electronic products (PSI, 2014).
- After more than 10 years working to address *leftover paint* issues, in 2007 PSI reported the establishment of a Memorandum of Understanding for the establishment and rollout of an industry-funded paint stewardship plan. Oregon became the first state to implement paint stewardship program in 2010 and as of

2014 there were a total of 7 states which had passed paint stewardship legislation based on the agreed model.

- While some retailers such as Home Depot have voluntarily begun to offer take-back and recycling for *fluorescent lights*, such efforts are insufficient to ensure wider adoption of product stewardship (Rosenbloom, 2008). As of May 2013, three states – Maine, Washington, and Vermont – had passed EPR laws for mercury-containing lighting.

Detailed information about product stewardship initiatives for specific product categories is available on the Product Stewardship Institute website (PSI, 2014).

REFERENCES

Product Stewardship Institute, Product Specific Work, 2014, http://www.productstewardship. us/?page=Product__Work

Rosenbloom, "Home Depot Offers Recycling for Compact fluorescent bulbs," *New York Times,* June 24, 2008, http://www.nytimes.com/2008/06/24/business/24recycling.html?_r=0

Chapter 5

GODS OF SMALL THINGS: UNDERSTANDING AND ADDRESSING EMERGING ENVIRONMENTAL, HEALTH, AND SAFETY RISKS OF NANOTECHNOLOGY

INTRODUCTION

Nanotechnology, or the science of manipulating materials at the level of atoms and molecules to achieve new properties and design better products, has been growing quickly and is considered by many the technology to drive the next industrial revolution. Governments, companies, and research centers around the world are spending billions of dollars on new applications that incorporate nano-technology—from more efficient solar cells and desalination devices to lighter and smaller computers and electronic devices to more effective medical therapies and personal care products. Yet the technology brings new risks for workers, consumers, and the environment, which are still insufficiently studied and poorly understood. With its seemingly limitless amount of applications, it is hard to imagine an industry or a company that will not be affected by nanotechnology in the future. As new uses of nanotechnology proliferate, we need to establish what companies should do to ensure responsible use of nanomaterials and minimize potential risks of liability, damaged reputation, consumer rejection, and nongovernmental organi-zations (NGO) campaigns. This chapter offers some background information and recommendations for companies on how to better prepare and minimize the risks while maximizing the benefits of this important new technology.

WHAT IS NANOTECHNOLOGY?

Nanotechnology is the science of manipulating matter on the nanoscale. One nanometer (nm) is one billionth of a meter. While some nanomaterials exist in nature, nanotechnology is about engineered nanomaterials (ENMs). The Environmental Protection Agency defines nanomaterials as "an ingredient that contains particles that have been intentionally produced to have at least one dimension that measures between approximately 1 and 100 nanometers" (Project on Emerging Nanotechnologies, 2013) (see Figure 1). To put it in perspective, an engineered carbon nanotube is 2 nm, human DNA has a width of 2.5 nm, a virus is 100 nm, and the width of human hair is 75,000 nm.

The term *nanotechnology* was first introduced in 1974, but the technology really took off with the discovery of carbon nanotubes in 1991. Since the beginning of the 21st century, the technology has grown rapidly. According to the Project on Emerging Nanotechnologies, which maintains inventory of nano-enabled consumer products, there were 54 reported nano products in the United States in 2005; this number exceeded 1,600 in 2013 and has continued to grow (Project on Emerging Nanotechnologies, 2013). Over half of the reported products fall under the category "health and fitness," which includes cosmetics, clothing, personal care, sporting goods, sunscreens, and filtration. The main nanoengineered materials include silver, carbon, zinc, silicon/silica, titanium, and gold. Nanoengineered membranes are now being developed for desalination of water and for bioremediation of contaminated sites. Nano-enabled technologies allow for more targeted treatment of cancer and avoiding the side effects of chemotherapy. Nanotechnology also promises to bring to market cheaper and more efficient solar and wind energy applications. According to Lux research, the global market for goods incorporating nanotechnology in 2007 was $147 billion and is projected to reach $2.5 trillion by 2015 (Lux Research, 2010).

Figure 1. Graphene (carbon atoms in a single layer). Source: James Hedberg, http://www.jameshedberg.com/scienceGraphics.php?sort=all&id=graphene-atomic-structure-sheet. This work by James Hedberg is licensed under a Creative Commons Attribution-NonCommercial-ShareAlike 3.0 Unported License.

Government Support for Nanotechnology

Governments around the world have provided significant support for research and development of nanotechnology as a way to promote their national competitiveness in the global market. It is estimated that in 2005, the European Union (EU) invested approximately $1.5 billion and Japan $1.8 billion (NNI, 2013). Countries such as China, South Korea, Russia, India, and Mexico are also moving quickly toward developing nano-enabled applications and investing in their development.

The U.S. government has provided strong support for the technology development. In 2000, President Clinton launched the National Nanotechnology Initiative, a collaboration of 25 government agencies, to better coordinate federal efforts to position the United States as the leader in the world for development and commercialization of the technology (NNI, 2013). In 2003, the U.S. Congress enacted the 21st Century Nanotechnology Research and Development Act, which provided a legislative foundation for the research (Sargent, 2010). Since fiscal year 2001, the U.S. government has spent close to $20 billion on nanotechnology development (NNI, 2013). This includes $1.7 billion for fiscal year 2014. While no good statistics are available, it is estimated that the private sector has invested at least as much as the federal government.

As a result of these significant investments by governments and private industry, nanotechnology patents have increased more than 5,000%, from 224 in 1991 to 12,776 in 2008 (Dang, Zhang, Fan, Chen, & Roco, 2010). The United States continues to lead in nanotechnology patents with more than 5,000 for the period 1990 to 2009 (Roco, Hersam, & Mirkin, 2011). At the same time, U.S. government support for environmental, health, and safety research of engineered nanomaterials (ENMs) has lagged, with only an estimated $750 million in grants since 2006, or between 5% and 6.5% of the NNI annual budget (NNI, 2013). Companies are seen by regulators and consumers as having the primary responsibility for conducting studies on the potential environmental and health effects of the technology. This, however, can be a problem, since many companies do not have the resources to invest in such expensive studies. They are also not required by law yet to conduct such studies before bringing their products to the market.

Nanotechnology applications are expanding fast in many sectors; it is therefore worth reviewing a sample of present and future applications.

Sustainable energy

Nanotechnology catalysts for energy production can lead to cleaner burning fuel and help avoid the reliance on precious metals, the majority of which are controlled by China. Nanotechnology is seen as critical for increasing the efficiency and reducing the cost of solar energy. It can also be used for generating energy from biofuels (e.g., as catalysts for corn or sugarcane). Advances in the technology are expected to lead to more efficient and faster charging batteries for storing energy and thus further promoting development of renewable energy sources such as wind and solar. The technology is helping increase fuel cell efficiency through improved hydrogen storage and using water instead of natural gas to obtain hydrogen (Bell, 2009).

Water treatment

Nanotechnology holds the promise of addressing some pressing challenges related to the water availability, costs, and decentralization. For instance, new nano-enabled sensors will be able to detect biological and chemical contaminants at very low concentrations. Advanced filtration materials using nanoparticles enable water reuse, recycling, and desalination as well as implementing chlorine-free biocides such as nano-silver. Nanotechnology also allows for improved filtration of wastewater at the source of pollution (Qu, Alvarez, & Li, 2013).

Electronics and information technology

Nanotechnology has brought forth powerful tools for the electronics and information technology sectors, "enabling the development and cost efficient production of state-of-the-art components that operate faster, have higher sensitivity, consume less power, and can be packed at much higher densities" (Nanoconnect Scandinavia, 2013). With the discovery of *graphene* in 2004 (a single layer of carbon atoms; see Figure 1), the opportunities to develop faster, smaller, and flexible electronic devices have increased further.

Transportation

Nanotechnology has enabled building lighter and more efficient automobiles, airplanes, and ships. In the future, the technology is expected to improve the transportation infrastructure by creating more durable and less expensive nano-engineered steel, concrete, and asphalt for highways as well as sensors for continuous monitoring of bridges, tunnels, railroads, and other structures (NNI, 2013).

Medical and health applications

Some of the most exciting medical applications of nanoparticles involve targeted cancer treatment (using nanoparticles to target the tumors only instead of chemotherapy that typically damages healthy cells as well), improved medical diagnostics for a variety of diseases (often years before the disease has developed any symptoms), stem cell applications, and tissue engineering, among others (Mirkin, 2010).

Cosmetics and personal care

Nanotechnology has enabled improved formulation of skin care and cosmetics products to deliver greater benefits to users. For instance, due to their small size nano-engineered titanium dioxide (TiO_2) and zinc oxide (ZnO) in sunscreens are able to penetrate deeper and ensure better sun protection. Anti-aging creams such as L'Oreal's Revitalift can penetrate deeper below the skin's surface to deliver nutrients and repair, thus improving skin results. Figure 2 provides a list of cosmetics and

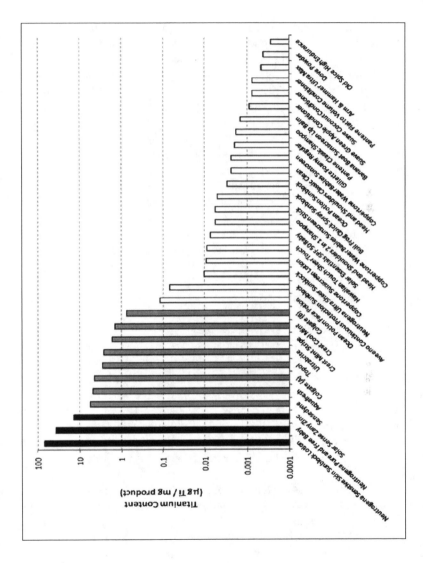

Figure 2. Cosmetics and personal care products with nano-engineered TiO$_2$.
Reprinted with permission from Weir et al. (2012). Copyright American Chemical Society.

personal care products that were found to contain nano-engineered TiO_2 according to a recent study (Weir, Westerhoff, Fabricius, Hristovski, & von Goetz, 2012).

Food and nutrition

Nanotechnology has spurred innovations around food production, packaging, and storage. Nanofood is defined as food in which "nanoparticles, nanotechnology techniques or tools are used during cultivation, production, processing, or packaging of the food" (Nanowerk, 2013). Figure 3 provides examples of various applications of nanotechnology in food and nutrition. For instance, in agriculture, nanotechnology is used to more efficiently deliver pesticides, fertilizers, or other agrichemicals. In food processing, the technology provides opportunities for enhancing food flavor and removing chemicals or pathogens. Antimicrobial and antifungal surface coatings with nanoparticles ensure longer shelf life for food. Nano-supplements allow for better absorption and stability of delivered nutrients. A recent study identified at least 89 applications in which the technology was utilized for food, including ice cream, salad dressing, sauces, diet beverages, and chewing gum (Weir et. al. 2012; see Figure 4).

The promise of the technology for both business and society is clearly significant. Yet our knowledge about potential risks to human health and the environmental is still very limited, leading to great regulatory uncertainty and potential risks for companies. The next section outlines some recent findings about nanotechnology's impacts on human health and the environment.

Emerging Knowledge of Environmental, Health, and Safety Risks of Nanotechnology

Environmental release of ENMs typically happens during manufacturing, product use, or product end-of-life disposal (e.g., in landfills or from wastewater treatment plants). Typical pathways for human exposure include inhalation in the workplace, ingestion of water and food with ENMs, and dermal contact from use of cosmetics and personal care products. It was not until the early 2000s when research begun to emerge on the toxicity and potential risks of ENMs for biota, vertebrates, and humans.

Carbon-based and metal-based nanomaterials have been found to have the most adverse effects on human health. *Carbon nanotubes*, which resemble asbestos, were shown to behave like asbestos and cause severe lung inflammation and cancer (Poland et al., 2008; Wang, Gerlach, Savage, & Cobb, 2013). A recent study found that carbon nanotubes cause DNA damage in rats (Kisin et al., 2011).

Titanium dioxide and *zinc oxide* nanoparticles in sunscreens have been associated with increased free radical production and damage to the DNA (Barnard, 2010; Friends of the Earth, 2006; Guix et al., 2008). In addition, dermal exposure has been found to lead to "abnormally rapid or uncontrolled cell turnover relating to apoptosis and cell growth" (Cui, Tian, Ozkan, Wang, & Gao, 2005). Animal studies have demonstrated increased incidence of lung cancer after 2 years exposure

Agriculture	Food Processing	Food Packaging	Supplements
• Single molecule detection to determine enzyme/substrate interactions • Nanocapsules for delivery of pesticides, fertilizers and other agrichemicals more efficiently • Delivery of growth hormones in a controlled fashion • Nanosensors for monitoring soil conditions and crop growth • Nanochips for identity preservation and tracking • Nanosensors for detection of animal and plant pathogens • Nanocapsules to deliver vaccines • Nanoparticles to deliver DNA to plants (targeted genetic engineering)	• Nanocapsules to improve bioavailability of neutraceuticals in standard ingredients such as cooking oils • Nanoencapsulated flavor enhancers • Nanotubes and nanoparticles as gelation and viscosifying agents • Nanocapsule infusion of plant based steroids to replace a meat's cholesterol • Nanoparticles to selectively bind and remove chemicals or pathogens from food • Nanoemulsions and -particles for better availability and dispersion of nutrients	• Antibodies attached to fluorescent nanoparticles to detect chemicals or foodborne pathogens • Biodegradable nanosensors for temperature, moisture and time monitoring • Nanoclays and nanofilms as barrier materials to prevent spoilage and prevent oxygen absorption • Electrochemical nanosensors to detect ethylene • Antimicrobial and antifungal surface coatings with nanoparticles (silver, magnesium, zinc) • Lighter, stronger and more heat-resistant films with silicate nanoparticles • Modified permeation behavior of foils	• Nanosize powders to increase absorption of nutrients • Cellulose nanocrystal composites as drug carrier • Nanoencapsulation of neutraceuticals for better absorption, better stability or targeted delivery • Nanocochleates (coiled nanoparticles) to deliver nutrients more efficiently to cells without affecting color or taste of food • Vitamin sprays dispersing active molecules into nanodroplets for better absorption

Figure 3. Examples of nanotechnology applications in food and agriculture.
Source: Nanowerk (2013). Reprinted with permission from Nanowerk LLC (www.nanowerk.com).

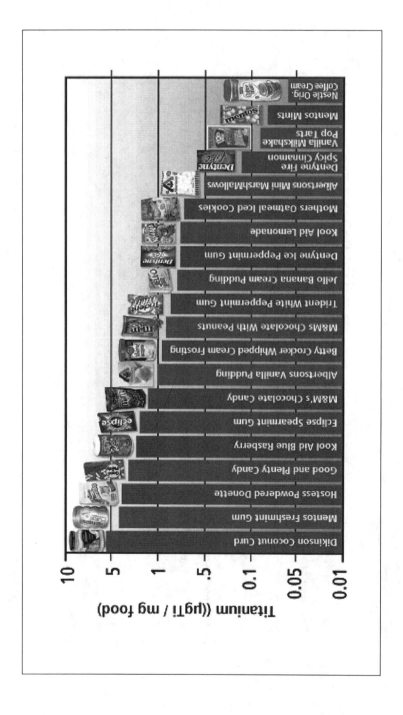

Figure 4. Nano-engineered TiO$_2$ in food products. Reprinted with permission from Weir et al. (2012). Copyright American Chemical Society.

to ultrafine TiO_2 (Heinrich et al., 1995). Recent studies have linked exposure to TiO_2 through food with increased incidence of developing Crohn's disease and possibly cancer (CCOHS, 2006). In 2006, the International Agency for Research on Cancer (IARC) classified TiO_2 as a *possible human carcinogen (Category 2B)* based on sufficient evidence in experimental animals and inadequate evidence from epidemiological studies (IARC, 2006). Of particular concern is a recent finding that children have the highest exposure to TiO_2 from food due to its presence in candy and other sweets (see Figure 4; Weir et al., 2013).

Occupational exposures to *heavy metal nanoparticles,* such as nano-engineered cadmium-telluride used in solar panels, have been shown to accumulate in the nodes, bone marrow, and liver, causing chronic inflammation and possibly cancer (Iannitti et al., 2010). When released in the environment, such nanoparticles can be absorbed by plants and aquatic organisms, leading to bioaccumulation and greater exposure of humans through the food chain (Smita et al., 2012).

Silver nanoparticles used in clothing such as socks and shirts have been found to be toxic to aquatic life (Navarro et al., 2008). Due to their antibacterial properties, silver nanoparticles are increasingly used in Tupperware, packaging, or as a pesticide and applied directly on fruit, vegetables, and meats, where they can penetrate the outside layer after washing and enter the human body (Zhang, Kong, Vardhanabhuti, Mustapha, & Lin, 2012). A growing number of in vitro studies indicate, "silver nanoparticles are toxic to mammalian cells derived from skin, liver, lung, brain, vascular system and reproductive organs" (Ahamed, Alsalhi, & Siddiqui, 2010). According to the study authors, the brain appeared to be most sensitive to silver nanoparticles. Furthermore, some studies have demonstrated that such particles have the potential to cause DNA damage and affect the mechanism of cell division and apoptosis, increasing the risk of cancer (Ahamed et al., 2010).

At the same time, a small but growing number of studies have demonstrated that, through chemical and physical redesign of the nanoparticles, it is possible to reduce and even completely mitigate their negative environmental health and safety impacts. In 2013, an international research team created a carbon nanotube that was 10 times shorter than typical nanotube fibers, and it caused much less irritation in the mouse lungs (Ali-Boucetta et al., 2013). An earlier study had demonstrated that "short or curly carbon nanotubes did not behave like asbestos," which means that products could be made to be safer (Poland et al., 2008).

Stakeholders Target Nanotechnology Risks

While public awareness of nanotechnology has remained low (Hart Research, 2009), various stakeholders have begun to raise awareness and demand greater transparency in relation to the health and safety impacts of ENMs.

NGOs such as Friends of the Earth have conducted research and launched campaigns to raise public awareness of the potential health risks of sunscreens and other cosmetic products that contain nano particles (Friends of the Earth, 2006). As You Sow, a shareholder advocacy group, examined the use of nanomaterials in food and food-related products and in a recent report highlighted the potential risks of the technology for public health, as well as for companies that are knowingly or unknowingly using it in their products (As You Sow, 2013).

Investors have been filing resolutions at companies using ENMs, demanding policies for safer use, greater transparency, and reporting of ENMs. Since 2008, socially responsible investors representing the Investors Environmental Health Network have filed resolutions for nanomaterial product safety at companies like Avon, Colgate-Palmolive, McDonalds, Kraft, Kellogg, and Walmart (IEHN, 2013).

Some insurers such as Swiss Re, Munich Re, and AIG have begun to examine and address nanotechnology risks by marketing products designed to cover nano-tech losses related to general liability, product liability, workers' compensation, environmental liability, and product recalls (Monica, 2010).

News media has continued to bring attention to the potential risks of nano-technology to consumers. An AOL investigation in 2010 was among the first to reveal that nanotechnology was widely used not only in cosmetics and personal care products but also in food to extend shelf life, improve flavor and texture. ENMs have been added to ice cream, salad dressing, sauces, diet beverages, muffins, and pancakes mixes (Schneider, 2009).

Emerging Policies and Frameworks

Due to the fast pace of nanotechnology development and its complex nature, adopting policies to ensure safe use is challenging. Regardless, some governments and policymakers have begun to introduce regulations and guidelines to ensure safer development and use.

A. Regulations

The European Union (EU) has moved to regulate ENMs under the REACH Directive (Regulation, Evaluation and Authorization of Chemicals) (EU, 2013). The EU also introduced mandatory disclosure of ENMs in cosmetics and personal care products under the cosmetics directive 2003/15/EEC. Some European Union countries have taken further steps: Germany's Federal Institute for Risk assessment announced that "nanosilver has no place in food, textiles and cosmetics" (BfR, 2010); Denmark banned sales of "nanofilm" floor sealant sprays in 2010 after a study showed lung damage in mice. In 2011, the Belgian minister called for "caution" and applying the precautionary principle when introducing new ENMs (EurActiv, 2010).

In 2010, Canada became the first nation in the world to require businesses to disclose the use of engineered nanomaterials (Montague-Jones, 2009). It also banned the use of nanotechnology in organic products (Organic & Non-GMO Report, 2010). Furthermore, Health Canada, the federal department responsible for public health issues in Canada, requires the assessment of potential risks and benefits of products to the health and safety of Canadians before they can be approved for sale (Health Canada, 2011).

Regulatory oversight of nanotechnology in the United States is still lacking and inadequate. A 2010 report by the U.S. Government Accountability Office (GAO) concluded that the U.S. Environmental Protection Agency (EPA) faces challenges regulating ENMs and recommended the agency take specific steps within its authority (GAO, 2010). An earlier EPA voluntary program for reporting of nano-materials use led to responses from just 29 companies (EPA, 2009). As a result, the agency moved to regulate nanotechnology under the Significant New Use Rule (SNUR) of the Toxics Substances Control Act (TSCA) (EPA, 2011). In addition, it regulates nanoscale materials used as pesticides under Federal Insecticide, Fungicide, and Rodenticide Act (FIFRA) (Wang et al., 2013). The law requires chemicals used as pesticides to undergo EPA review before marketing and use. The Food and Drug Administration (FDA) has not adopted any regulations yet but published two draft guidance documents in 2012 that address the use of nanotechnology in food and cosmetics products (FDA, 2012). Both guidance documents encourage assessment of nanomaterials safety and recommend consulting the agency before taking the products to market (but do not require providing information to the agency or consumers).

At a state level, California has taken the boldest step to regulate ENMs under its Green Chemistry Regulation for Safer Consumer Products, released in June 2010[1] (DiLoreto, 2011). The law, passed in 2008, requires companies that manufacture or import goods or services to California to provide toxico-logical information on chemicals in their products or manufacturing processes that is available to consumers and other stakeholders (California Green Chemistry Initiative, 2008).

B. Voluntary policies and frameworks

In 2012, the National Institute for Occupational Safety and Health (NIOSH), the research arm of the Occupational Safety and Health Administration (OSHA) and part of the Centers for Disease Control, released guidelines for safe handling of ENMs in research laboratories (CDC, 2012).

The Organization for Economic Cooperation and Development (OECD) has estab-lished a Working Party on Manufactured Nanomaterials (WPMN) to coordinate the research, testing, and risk assessment of the ENMs among member and nonmember states (OECD, 2013).

The International Organization for Standardization (ISO) has been working on several international guidance standards on nanotechnology risk management and product stewardship. Its nanotechnology working group—ISO TC 229—is tasked with focusing on "developing standards for terminology and nomenclature; metrology and instrumentation, including specifications for reference materials; test methodologies; modeling and simulations; and science-based health, safety, and environmental practices" (ISO, 2013). The American National Standards Institute (ANSI) is working closely with the ISO on the development of such new standards.

[1] See http://www.dtsc.ca.gov/PollutionPrevention/GreenChemistryInitiative/gc_draft_regs.cfm

Environmental Defense Fund (EDF)-DuPont Nano Framework

In 2007, the EDF and DuPont partnered to develop a comprehensive, practical, and at the same time, flexible framework for companies to help them evaluate and address the potential risks of nanoscale materials (see Figure 5). The framework includes six stages and presents a systematic and disciplined process for identifying, managing, and reducing potential environmental, health, and safety risks of ENMs across a product's "life cycle"—from initial sourcing, through manufacture, use, and final disposal. The framework also requires transparency and accountability as it emphasizes documenting and communicating the key impacts (EDF, 2007). As of 2013, no information was available on the number of companies that have used the framework as part of their nanotechnology risk management.

Challenges to Managing Nanotechnology Risks

While the past decade has seen tremendous growth in nanotechnology applications and growing research on potential risks, some key challenges remain:

- Our knowledge about potential health, safety, and environmental impacts is still poor, therefore companies will have to operate under great uncertainty.
- Insufficient research has been conducted to support decision-making of the complex issues around ENMs management, such as evaluating the benefits and costs in specific applications.

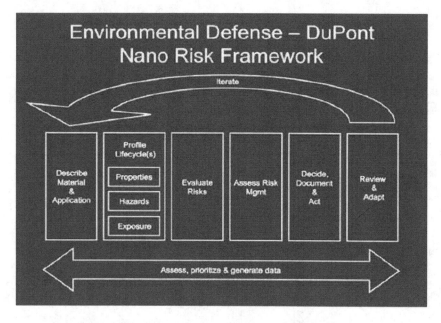

Figure 5. Environmental Defense-DuPont Nano Risk Framework.
Source: EDF (2007).

- The multidisciplinary nature of nanotechnology requires communication and collaboration between various groups, such as physical scientists, social scientists, biologists, oncologists, and bioengineers, among others, which is challenging.
- There is still a lack of best practices and information about how leading companies are managing ENMs. A growing number of large corporations are publicly stating their commitment to safer development and use (see Text Box 1), but no information is available on how they implement such practices internally.
- Senior executives and environmental/EHS managers are either unaware of or underestimate the potential risks of the technology and the impacts on their company. A 2013 study on how the industry views nanotechnology risks found that companies involved in commercializing the technology acknowledged the uncertainty and the responsibility of their companies to ensure safe products, but "did not see nanotechnology as novel or risky" (Becker, 2013). When asked about risks, study participants talked about financial, business, and social risks before mentioning environmental, health, and safety risks.
- There are no generally acceptable frameworks for managing the societal and life-cycle impacts of ENMs, although some organizations are working in this area (e.g., the EDF-DuPont Nano Risk Framework and the EU code of conduct for responsible nanosciences and nanotechnology research) (European Commission, 2009).
- Most companies involved in developing the technology are small and difficult to identify, engage, reach, or educate. An international survey of nanotechnology organizations found that 84% of respondents worked for companies that had

---

Text Box 1. Sample Statements on Safe Nanotechnology Use

Avon Statement on Nanotechnology Use,
http://www.avoncompany.com/corporatecitizenship/corporateresponsibility/resourcecenter/policies_and_procedures/nanotechnology.html

DuPont Position Statement on Nanotechnology, http://www.dupont.com/corporate-functions/news-and-events/insights/articles/position-statements/articles/nanotechnology.html

EMD, Nanotechnology, http://reports.emdgroup.com/2012/cr-report/products/nanotechnology.html

Evonik Nanomaterials Statement,
http://corporate.evonik.com/en/responsibility/eshq/product-stewardship/new-technologies/nanotechnology/pages/default.aspx

Johnson & Johnson Guidelines: Responsible Use of Nanotechnology,
http://www.jnj.com/sites/default/files/pdf/Nanotechnology_march2013.pdf

Kellogg Statement on Nanotechnology, 2011 CSR Report, page 32,
http://www.kelloggcompany.com/content/dam/kelloggcompanyus/corporate_responsibility/pdf/2011CR/2011_Kelloggs_CRR.pdf

McDonalds Statement on Nanotechnology,
http://www.aboutmcdonalds.com/mcd/sustainability/library/policies_programs/sustainable_supply_chain/product_safety/Nanotechnology.html

fewer than 50 employees (Conti et al., 2008). Another study found that about 75% of nanotechnology companies had fewer than 20 employees and 50% had fewer than 10 employees (NCMS, 2009).

• Testing for health and safety is expensive and unable to keep pace with the speed that nanomaterials are introduced in a variety of products. A 2009 study by the University of Minnesota found that the testing of all existing nano-materials would cost between $249 million and $1.18 billion and would take 53 years if continued at the present level of 1% of companies' R&D budgets. Yet, if manufacturers spend 10% of their R&D budget on testing, they could do it in 3–5 years (Chaterjee, 2009).

What Should Companies Do To Be Better Prepared to Manage EHS Risks?

As presented in this chapter, nanotechnology has enabled a full range of new applications that may improve our lives and may help address many sustainability challenges today. Yet it can present a variety of financial, business, social, and environmental health and safety risks for companies. While a growing number of companies are adopting policies on safer nanotechnology use, there is still very limited information on how these are implemented in practice. What can companies, particularly small ones, do to manage and minimize the business risks of nano-technology and maximize the benefits?

Responsible management of ENMs requires understanding and managing the risks of this emerging technology across a company's supply chain as well as its impact on the society and communities where it operates. This section provides some recommendations for EHS staff, CSR practitioners, and other company staff on how to identify and manage such risks in four main domains: governance, community, products and services, and operations (see Figure 6).

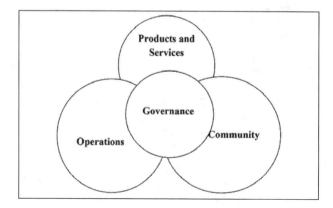

Figure 6. Framework for understanding and managing nanotechnology risks in four main domains.

Governance

This dimension addresses how a company's core values, mission, vision, and governance structures support or prevent the company from understanding and managing EHS and sustainability as an integrated part of business strategy.

- Track emerging science: Stay informed about emerging research and the potential hazards of nanoparticles used or manufactured by your company.
- Monitor regulatory and other policy developments: Keep track of emerging regulatory and voluntary initiatives both in the United States and abroad. Consider getting involved through your industry association or other collaboration. Be proactive and stay ahead of any regulatory requirements to avoid fines, violations, and lawsuits.
- Educate your CEO and board about emerging risks of ENMs.
- Adopt a framework for responsible management of ENMs: Get familiar with existing approaches such as the EDF-DuPont Nano Risk Framework or implement your own framework for ENMs across the entire supply chain.
- Be transparent and report on ENM use and health and safety data on your website and/or your CSR report.

Products and Services

This domain of the framework relates to addressing societal needs with marketplace solutions that return a profit to the company. This can range from ensuring product safety, redesigning of existing products and services to be more eco-efficient or socially beneficial, to a fundamental reinvention of a company's product line or services as well as its marketing and delivery.

- Work with suppliers to obtain EHS data about ENMs in your products and ingredients.
- Know all of the ENMs used in your products in order to be prepared to report to customers, to seek substitutes, or to phase out if necessary.
- If developing ENMs, follow the five principles for design for safer nanotechnology, including increasing the nanoparticle's size/surface, using less-toxic materials, functionalization, encapsulation, and reducing the quantity of materials used (Morose, 2010).
- Communicate with consumers/customers about ENMs benefits and how to use products safely. Getting the right message to consumers is key to ensuring acceptance and safe use of products with ENMs.

Operations

This domain involves assessing and minimizing potential negative impacts on the environment and employees and maximizing positive impacts.

- Implement a life-cycle approach to evaluating potential risks from ENMs (see EDF-DuPont Nano-Risk Framework for more guidance).
- Adopt the precautionary principle and err on the safe side when there is insufficient scientific information about the potential impacts; a few studies have raised "red flags."
- Implement worker training and procedures for safe handling of ENMs following the NIOSH guidelines.

Community/Society

This domain relates to understanding a company's impact on its surrounding communities and society as a whole and mobilizing its assets to address social issues and support social well-being beyond creating jobs and paying taxes.

- Keep track of and engage with key stakeholders such as consumer groups and NGOs focused on nanotechnology safety. Engage with them in meaningful dialogue to address concerns early and avoid boycotts, media campaigns, and damaged reputation.
- Participate in research and support the development of best practices, case studies, and data on environmental, health, and safety impacts by collaborating with research institutions, industry peers, and/or suppliers.
- Support the enactment of effective regulatory and voluntary frameworks for responsible management of ENMs to ensure a level playing field, avoid uncertainty, and reduce liability risks.

CONCLUSION

Nanotechnology presents a wide range of opportunities to address many of our most pressing sustainability challenges today, such as promoting clean energy, clean water, and improved food production. Any new technology, however, brings associated risks and uncertainty. It is critical for companies, large and small, to take appropriate measures to minimize business risks even in the present scientific and policy uncertainties. Such an approach will ensure that this technology does not follow the path of previous inventions and technological innovations such as DDT, asbestos, and GMOs, to name a few. Nanotechnology provides some unique opportunities. It remains to be seen whether careful assessment and analysis, coupled with voluntary guidelines and government regulation (both national and international), can mitigate or completely eliminate any environmental, health, and safety risks. By increasing awareness, transparency, and promoting cross-disciplinary collaborations and implementation of tools, such as green chemistry, companies can reduce business risks and ensure that nanotechnology becomes the engine for the 21st century sustainable economic development.

DISCUSSION QUESTIONS

Chapter 5: Gods of Small Things: Understanding and Addressing Emerging Environmental, Health, and Safety Risks of Nanotechnology

1. What is nanotechnology? What are some of its current and future applications in sectors such as energy, water, electronics, transportation, medicine, cosmetics, and food?
2. What are some environmental, health and safety risks identified to date for the technology?
3. How are different stakeholders working to promote greater awareness and address the risks of nanotechnology?
4. What are some emerging policies in the U.S. and abroad aiming to address the risks of nanotechnology?
5. What are the main challenges faced by companies and policy makers in managing nanotechnology risks? What should companies do to minimize nanotechnology risks and avoid future liabilities, reputational and regulatory risks?
6. Select a nano-enabled consumer product from the inventory provided by the Project on Emerging Nanotechnologies (http://www.nanotechproject.org/inventories/). Discuss: a) how nanotechnology has helped improve product performance; b) what are the potential risks to consumers, workers, and the environment; and c) who should be responsible for mitigating these risks, and d) what would you like to know as a consumer before buying the product?

REFERENCES

Ahamed, M., Alsalhi, M. S., & Siddiqui, M. K. (2010). Silver nanoparticle applications and human health. *Clinica Chimica Acta, 411*(23/24), 1841–1848.

Ali-Boucetta, H., Nunes, A., Sainz, R., Herrero, M. A., Tian, B., Prato, M., Kostarelos, K. (2013, February 18). Asbestos-like pathogenicity of long carbon nanotubes alleviated by chemical functionalization. *Angewandte Chemie International Edition, 52*(8), 2274–2278.

As You Sow. (2013). *Slipping through the cracks: An issue brief on nanomaterials in food.* Retrieved September 22, 2013, from http://www.asyousow.org/health_safety/nanoissue brief.shtml

Barnard, A. S. (2010, March 7). One-to-one comparison of sunscreen efficacy, aesthetics and potential nanotoxicity. *Nature Nanotechnology,* (5), 271–274. Retrieved from http://www.nature.com/nnano/journal/v5/n4/full/nnano.2010.25.html

Becker, S. (2013). Nanotechnology in the marketplace: How the nanotechnology industry views risk. *Journal of Nanoparticles Research, 15,* 1426.

Bell, T. (2009, Summer). Is downsizing to atomic scale one way forward: Nanotechnology for energy. *The Bent of Tau Beta Pi.* Retrieved September 4, 2013, from http://www.tbp.org/pubs/Features/Su09Bell.pdf

BfR (Federal Institute for Risk Assessment in Germany). (2010, August). *Nano-silver has no place in food, cosmetics and textiles.* Retrieved September 16, 2013, from http://www.bfr.bund.de/en/press_information/2010/08/nanosilver_has_no_place_in_food__textiles_or_cosmetics-50960.html

California Green Chemistry Initiative. (2008, December). Final report. *State of California; California Environmental Protection Agency; Department of Toxic Substances Control.* Retrieved September 16, 2013, from http://www.dtsc.ca.gov/PollutionPrevention/ GreenChemistryInitiative/upload/GREEN_Chem.pdf

Canadian Centre for Occupational Health & Safety (CCOHS). (2006). *Titanium dioxide classified as possibly carcinogenic to humans.* Retrieved September 9, 2013, from http://www.ccohs.ca/headlines/text186.html

Centers for Disease Control and Prevention (CDC). (2012, May). *General safe practices for working with engineered nanomaterials in research laboratories.* Retrieved September 16, 2013, from http://www.cdc.gov/niosh/docs/2012-147/

Chaterjee, R. (2009). Calculating the costs of nanohazard testing. *Environmental Science and Technology, 43*(10), 3405.

Conti, J. A., Killpack, K., Gerritzen, G., Huang, L., Mircheva, M., Delmas, M., Holden, P. A. (2008). Health and safety practices in the nanomaterials workplace: Results from an international survey. *Environmental Science & Technology, 42,* 3155–3162.

Cui, D., Tian, F., Ozkan, C. S., Wang, M., & Gao, H. (2005). Effect of single wall carbon nanotubes on human HEK293 cells. *Toxicology Letters,* (155), 73–85.

Dang, Y., Zhang, Y., Fan, I., Chen, H., & Roco, M. (2010). Trends in worldwide nano-technology patent applications: 1991 to 2008. *Journal of Nanoparticle Research,* (12), 687–706.

DiLoreto, J. (2011, March 22). *State regulation of nanotechnology: All politics are local.* SOCMA Nanotechnology Coalition, GlobalChem conference, Baltimore, MD.

Environmental Defense Fund-DuPont Nano Partnership (EDF). (2007, June). *Nano Risk Framework.* Retrieved January 6, 2014, from http://www.nanoriskframework.com/files/ 2011/11/6496_Nano-Risk-Framework.pdf

Environmental Protection Agency (EPA). (2009, January). *Nanoscale materials stewardship program: Interim report.* Retrieved September 16, 2013, from http://www.epa.gov/oppt/ nano/nmsp-interim-report-final.pdf

Environmental Protection Agency (EPA). (2011). *Control of nanoscale materials under the Toxic Substances Control Act.* Retrieved September 16, 2013, from http://www.epa.gov/ oppt/nano/

EurActiv. (2010, September 30). REACH register to regulate nanomaterials. *Institute of Nanotechnology.* Retrieved from December 13, 2010, from http://www.nano.org.uk/ news/984/

European Commission. (2009, April). *A code of conduct for responsible nanosciences and nanotechnologies research.* Retrieved November 1, 2013, from http://ec.europa.eu/ research/science-society/document_library/pdf_06/nanocode-apr09_en.pdf

European Union (EU). (2013). *Nanomaterials in REACH and CLP.* Retrieved September 9, 2013, from http://ec.europa.eu/environment/chemicals/nanotech/reach-clp/index_en.htm

Food and Drug Administration (FDA). (2012, April 20). *FDA news release.* Retrieved September 16, 2013, from http://www.fda.gov/NewsEvents/Newsroom/PressAnnouncements/ ucm301125.htm

Friends of the Earth. (2006, May). *Nanomaterials, sunscreens and cosmetics: Small ingredients, big risks.* Retrieved December 9, 2010, from http://www.foeeurope.org/activities/ nanotechnology/nanocosmetics.pdf

Government Accountability Office (GAO). (2010, May 25). *Nanotechmology: Nanomaterials are widely used in commerce, but EPA faces challenges in regulating risk.* Retrieved September 16, 2013, from http://www.gao.gov/Products/GAO-10-549

Guix, M., Carbonell, C., Comenge, J., Garcia-Fernandez, L., Alarcon, A., & Casals, E. (2008). Nanoparticles for cosmetics. How safe is safe? *Science, 4*(2), 213–217.

Hart Research Associates. (2009). Nanotechnology, synthetic biology, and public opinion. *Project on Emerging Nanotechnologies.* Retrieved December 9, 2010, from http://www. nanotehproject.org/publications/archive/8286/

Health Canada. (2011). *Nanotechnology-based health products and food.* Retrieved September 22, 2013, from http://www.hc-sc.gc.ca/dhp-mps/nano-eng.php

Heinrich, U., Fuhst, R., Rittinghausen, S., Creutzenberg, O., Bellmann, B., & Koch, W. (1995). Chronic inhalation exposure of wistar rats and two different strains of mice to diesel engine exhaust, carbon black, and titanium dioxide. *Inhalation Toxicology, (7),* 533–556.

Iannitti, T., Capone, S., Gatti, A., Capitani, F., Cetta, F., & Palmieri, B. (2010). Intra-cellular heavy metal nanoparticle storage: Progressive accumulation within lymph nodes with transformation from chronic inflammation to malignancy. *International Journal of Nanomedicine, (5),* 955–960.

International Agency for Research on Cancer (IARC). (2006). *Titanium dioxide.* Retrieved September 9, 2013, from http://monographs.iarc.fr/ENG/Publications/techrep42/ TR42-4.pdf

International Organization for Standardization (ISO). (2013). *ISO/TC 229 nanotechnologies.* Retrieved September 22, 2013, from http://www.iso.org/iso/iso_technical_committee? commid=381983

Investor Environmental Health Network (IEHN). (2013, December 9). *Shareholder resolu-tions.* Retrieved from http://www.iehn.org/resolutions.shareholder.php

Kisin, E. R., Murray, A. R., Sargent, I., Lowry, D., Chirila, M., & Siegrist, K. J. (2011). Genotoxicity of carbon nanofibers: Are they potentially more or less dan-gerous than carbon nanotubes or asbestos? *Toxicology and Applied Pharmacology, (252),* 1–10.

Lux Research. (2010, February). *The recession's impact on nanotechnology.* Retrieved from http://www.luxresearchinc.com/blog/2010/02/the-recessions-impact-on-nanotech nology/

Mirkin, N. (2010). *Nanotechnology long-term impacts and research directions 2000–2020: Chapter 7: Nanobiosystems, medicine and health.* Retrieved October 14, 2013, from http://www.wtec.org/nano2/docs/PdfPresentations/10-Ch7MIRKINPRESENTATION.pdf

Monica, J. (2010, March 31). First nano-specific insurance: Lexington Insurance Com-pany introduces LexNanoShield. *Nanotechnology Law Report.* Retrieved December 9, 2010, from http://www.nanolawreport.com/2010/03/articles/first-nanospecific-insurance-lexington-insurance-company-introdu/

Montegue-Jones, G. (2009, February 16). Canada expected to demand data on suppliers of nanomaterials. *Cosmetics Design-Europe.com.* Retrieved September 9, 2013, from http://www.cosmeticsdesign-europe.com/Hot-Topics/Nanotechnology/Canada-expected-to-demand-data-from-suppliers-of-nanomaterials

Morose, G. (2010, February). The 5 principles of design for safer nanotechnology. *Journal of Cleaner Production, 18*(3), 285–289.

Nanoconnect Scandinavia. (2013). *Nanotechnology for electronics and sensors applications.* Retrieved September 16, 2013, from http://www.nano-connect.org/content/download/ 83041/493148/

Nanowerk. (2013). *Nanotechnology food.* Retrieved September 9, 2013, from http://www. nanowerk.com/nanotechnology-in-food.php

National Nanotechnology Initiative (NNI). (2013). About the NNI. Retrieved September 1, 2013, from http://www.nano.gov/about-nni

NCMS. (2009). *Study of nanotechnology in the U.S. manufacturing industry.* National Center for Manufacturing Sciences, Ann Arbor, MI.

Navarro, E., Piccapietra, F., Wagner, B., Marconi, F., Kaegi, R., Odzak, N., . . . Behra, R. (2008). Toxicity of silver nanoparticles to *Chlamydomonas reinhardtii. Environmental Science & Technology,* (42), 8959–8964. Retrieved December 9, 2010, from http://pubs.acs.org/doi/abs/10.1021/es801785m

OECD. (2013). *Working Party on Nanotechnology: Vision statement.* Retrieved from http://www.oecd.org/sti/nano/oecdworkingpartyonnanotechnologywpnvisionstatement.htm

Organic & Non-GMO Report. (2010). *Canada bans nanotechnology in organics.* Retrieved September 22, 2013, from http://www.non-gmoreport.com/articles/may10/canada_bans_nanotechnology_organics.php

Poland, C., Duffin, R., Konloch, I., Maynard, A., Wallace, W., Seaton, A., . . . Donaldson, K. (2008). Carbon nanotubes introduced to the abdominal cavity of mice show asbestos-like pathogenicity in a pilot study. *Nature Nanotechnology, 3,* 423–428. Retrieved September 29, 2013, from http://www.nature.com/nnano/journal/v3/n7/abs/nnano.2008.111.html

Project on Emerging Nanotechnologies. Inventories. (2013). Retrieved September 16, 2013, from http://www.nanotechproject.org/inventories/

Qu, X., Alvarez, P., & Li, Q. (2013, August). Applications of nanotechnology in water and wastewater treatment. *Water Research, 47*(12), 3931–3946.

Roco, M. C., Hersam, M. C., & Mirkin, C. A. (2011). *Nanotechnology research directions for societal needs in 2020: Retrospective and outlook* (Vol. 1). Boston, MA: Springer.

Sargent, J. (2010, March 12). Nanotechnology: A policy primer. *Congressional Research Center.* Retrieved November 24, 2010, from http://www.fas.org/sgp/crs/misc/RL34511.pdf

Schneider, A. (2009, March 24). Amid nanotech's dazzling promise, health risks grow. *AOL News.* Retrieved December 9, 2010, from http://www.aolnews.com/nanotech/article/amid-nanotechs-dazzling-promise-health-risks-grow/19401235

Smita, S., Gupta, S., Bartonova, A., Dusinska, M., Gutleb, A., & Rahman, Q. (2012). Nanoparticles in the environment: Assessment using the causal diagram approach. *Environmental Health,* (11). Retrieved September 9, 2013, from http://www.ehjournal.net/content/11/S1/S13

Wang, J., Gerlach, J., Savage, N., & Cobb, G. (2013). Necessity and approach to integrated nanomaterial legislation and governance. *Science of the Total Environment,* (442), 56–62.

Weir, A., Westerhoff, P., Fabricius, L., Hristovski, K., & von Goetz, N. (2012). Titanium dioxide nanoparticles in food and personal care products. *Environmental Science & Technology, 46,* 2242–2250.

Zhang, Z., Kong, F., Vardhanabhuti, B., Mustapha, A., & Lin, M. (2012). Detection of engineered silver nanoparticle contamination in pears. *Journal of Agricultural and Food Chemistry,* (60), 10762–10767.

Chapter 6

SUSTAINABLE CONSUMPTION IN TODAY'S MARKET ECONOMY: CHALLENGES AND OPPORTUNITIES FOR BUSINESS

ABSTRACT

Some 26 years after the Brundland Commission introduced the concept of sustainable development, it has become evident that to make any real progress toward sustainability in a world of 7 billion people and growing, we need to address the issue of resource consumption. This chapter discusses the challenges and opportunities for business to advance such practices in today's market economy. The chapter first defines sustainable consumption and examines some emerging frameworks and studies that outline the business opportunities in sustainable consumption. A new 6-stage framework is proposed to guide companies in their journey to sustainable consumption. The chapter concludes with a discussion of the current barriers and emerging drivers for business in promoting sustainable consumption. Some of the questions explored include What does the journey toward sustainable consumption look like? Are companies moving toward such an approach despite a current lack of overall policy framework? What are the emerging drivers and best practices? What are the key barriers? How are some companies overcoming these barriers and adopting new business models for promoting sustainable consumption? What larger-scale policies are needed to change the current market system and promote a paradigm shift toward more conscious capitalism?

INTRODUCTION

Some 26 years after the Brundland Commission introduced the concept of sustainable development, it has become evident that to make any real progress toward sustainability in a world of 7 billion people we need to address the issue of consumption. With projections to reach 9 billion by 2050, the pressures on environmental resources and constraints will be tremendous. Companies in all sectors will be impacted by increasing material and energy costs, environmental disasters, and shortages of critical resources such as agricultural land, clean water, and rare-earth metals. This chapter primarily focuses on reducing consumption in developed countries. More than 1 billion people globally live on less than one dollar a day, and 2.7 billion live on less than two dollars per day (UN Millennium Project, 2006). Growth and consumption are much needed to lift people out of poverty in many developing countries, but they must be sustainable and within the ecological limits (Jackson, 2011).

The Great Recession of 2007–2009 has heightened anxieties that Western capitalism is unable to ensure long-term prosperity and well-being for people globally. As Porter and Kramer (2011) state, "The capitalist system is under siege. In recent years business increasingly has been viewed as a major cause of social, environmental, and economic problems. Companies are widely perceived to be prospering at the expense of the broader community." It is extremely challenging for companies to consider long-term consumption effects when their economic models are focused on growth and short-term market returns. Porter and Kramer argue that

> a big part of the problem lies with companies themselves, which remain trapped in an outdated approach to value creation that has emerged over the past few decades. They continue to view value creation narrowly, optimizing short-term financial performance in a bubble while missing the most important customer needs and ignoring the broader influences that determine their longer-term success.

Businesses can and should consider new strategies and business models for ensuring long-term success. One such strategy is building business practices around the concept of sustainable consumption. Such practices can reduce the rate of resource consumption, waste, and environmental impacts, while at the same time create jobs, reduce income inequality, and promote long-term prosperity and well-being. Such a strategy can also open new business opportunities for companies willing to take the risk and make the transition.

In what follows, this chapter aims to examine the emerging drivers and business initiatives in the area of sustainable consumption and offer a new framework for businesses committed to advancing sustainable consumption. The main questions explored include: What does the journey toward sustainable consumption look like? Are companies moving toward such an approach despite a current lack of overall policy framework? What are the emerging drivers and best practices? What are the key barriers? How are some companies overcoming these barriers and adopting new business models for promoting sustainable consumption?

BUSINESS AND SUSTAINABLE CONSUMPTION

Sustainable consumption is defined as

> the use of services and related products which respond to basic needs and bring a better quality of life while minimizing the use of natural resources and toxic

materials as well as emissions of waste and pollutants over the life cycle of the service or product so as not to jeopardize the needs of future generations. (Norwegian Ministry of Environment, 1994)

The World Summit on Sustainable Development in 2002 called for regional and national initiatives to "accelerate the shift toward sustainable consumption and production to promote social and economic development within the carrying capacity of ecosystems" (UN, 2002).

Despite a few government actions (mostly in the European Union, Africa, and Asia-Pacific), policymakers have not taken the necessary steps to create the right incentives and conditions for moving toward more sustainable consumption. It is becoming increasingly clear that technological innovation cannot help solve today's environmental problems without significantly reducing consumption. Business has a major role to play in such societal transformation, both through adopting more sustainable consumption practices and educating its consumers to use less "stuff." Such an approach, however, will require innovative thinking and new business models, as the current economic system is based on selling more stuff—companies make more money by selling more products.

Recent business initiatives demonstrate a growing movement toward developing new frameworks and practices to advance sustainable consumption. In response to the mandate of consumer industry chief executives at Davos in January 2008, the World Economic Forum (WEF) became one of the first business organizations to examine the business case for sustainable consumption. Its 2009 report, "Sustainability for Tomorrow's Consumer," focused on the opportunities for the consumer industry and identified four business imperatives for a more sustainable future. First, companies need to meaningfully engage consumers to raise awareness and change their behavior. Second, innovation is seen as the only way forward as incremental improvements will not help address today's challenges and the long-term need to dematerialize the economy. Third, companies need to rethink core business models that value externalities and focus on selling "value" instead of selling "stuff." Fourth, businesses need to collaborate along the value chain and close the loop to reduce consumption and related environmental impacts (WEF, 2009).

In its three subsequent studies, "Redesigning Business Value: A Roadmap for Sustainable Consumption" (2010), "The Consumption Dilemma Leverage Points for Accelerating Sustainable Growth" (2011), and "More with Less: Scaling Sustainable Consumption and Resource Efficiency" (2012), WEF offered a roadmap and specific recommendations for how individual companies can promote sustainable consumption. The roadmap includes four steps that focus on setting up the foundation of integrating sustainability into the business, rebuilding business using new business models, identifying new value chains, and finally, redefining value to include all stakeholder perspectives (WEF, 2010).

The study also identified some emerging drivers for sustainable consumption, such as shifting consumer preferences, the rise of sustainable investing, the impacts of the great recession, and the evolving public policy framework for sustainable consumption. While still slow and insufficient, policy frameworks have been adopted by 35 countries. In Europe, for example, the July 2008 Action Plan on Sustainable Consumption and Production is expected to boost demand for sustainable products. In the Asia-Pacific region, several countries have introduced tax system reforms, green procurement, enhanced disclosure requirements, or product stewardship policies to advance development of sustainable products and services (WEF, 2012).

Building on its 2008 study, "Sustainable Consumption Facts and Trends," in 2011, the World Business Council for Sustainable Development (WBCSD) proposed a new vision for what sustainable consumption could look like in 2050: "9 billion people living well, and within the limits of the planet" (WBCSD, 2011). The study acknowledged that such a vision cannot be achieved with technological innovation alone. There will be a need for deep transformation in lifestyles and consumption patterns. The study identified three major challenges to achieving the vision. The first is a demand-side challenge, which relates to the gap between consumer aspirations and actions. This is often attributed to a lack of awareness, confusing information, higher prices or up-front costs, poorer product performance, or lower convenience. The second challenge relates to the supply side. Most businesses have spent many years refining their supply chains to maximize efficiency and profit. Sustainability will likely require major changes to these supply chains, which could be complex and costly. Finally, the lack of regulations and financial incentives to promote more sustainable consumption practices present a "tough challenge" that will require collaboration among business, government, and other stakeholders in order to design effective new policies. Vision 2050 further recognizes the importance of designing better products and services: "The practice of building in obsolescence merely to stimulate replacement purchases will have been abandoned. Modular design will help products to be useful for longer, even as new technologies reach the market." New measures for success will also be used and "at the company level success will be defined in terms of true value: the company's contribution to human and environmental wellbeing" (WBCSD, 2011).

Another business group that had examined the issue of business and sustainable consumption is Business for Social Responsibility (BSR). In its 2010 study, "The New Frontier in Sustainability: The Business Opportunity in Tackling Sustainable Consumption," BSR analyzed the consumption challenge today and highlighted the opportunities for business in creating value while addressing this challenge. While "the current economic system and most of its measures of success promote more consumption," some new drivers are emerging that create opportunities for business. These include changing economics (e.g., financial slow down, fluctuating prices for energy and other materials, and growing consumer debt), values shift, technology as enabler of better consumer engagement and new business models, and the rise of emerging markets, which requires radical changes in the way we do business. To move to sustainable consumption, companies need to examine segments of their value chains "that have been overlooked in the first generation sustainability efforts." A new framework is proposed as a way to help companies define their strategies in sustainable consumption by looking through the lenses of innovation, education, collaboration, and measurement in the three key stages of a product's life cycle: product design, engagement and use, and end-of-use (BSR, 2010).

STAGES IN SUSTAINABLE CONSUMPTION: PROPOSED FRAMEWORK

Embracing sustainable consumption strategies is an evolutionary process and not a destination. Some companies will move faster while others will remain stuck in an efficiency-improvement stage. It is critical to be able to measure and benchmark progress. While the growing number of sustainable consumption studies and frameworks demonstrates increasing business awareness about the issues, none of them helps companies evaluate where they are in that journey. The new 6-stage framework proposed here aims to guide companies in their journey to sustainable consumption (see Figure 1). The framework includes specific questions that help businesses find out where they are in the journey to sustainable consumption, explore new opportunities, and learn from other companies that have moved to a higher stage.

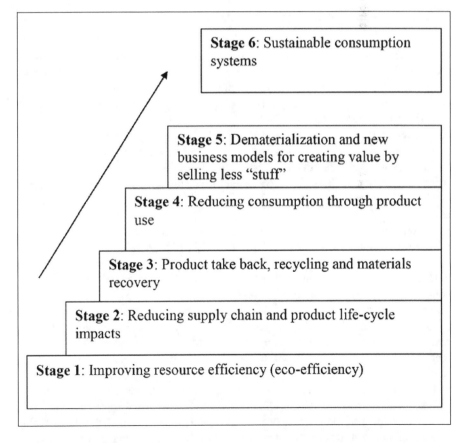

Figure 1. The 6-stage framework for moving toward sustainable consumption.

Underlying the framework are five basic assumptions:

- Developing sustainable systems of consumption is a continuous, evolutionary process of setting goals, taking action, and evaluating progress.
- Different companies and different industries are starting at different places in the evolutionary process.
- Moving to a higher stage requires the company to permanently adopt lower-stage strategies in its business operations.
- While the proposed model is most relevant for manufacturers, it can also be applied to service-providing businesses, which also need to consider the entire life cycle of their offerings.
- Developing truly sustainable systems of consumption cannot be achieved by companies or industry alone but rather requires government involvement to change the current market rules and promote greater coordination and collaboration among key stakeholders.

Stage 1: Improving Resource Efficiency (Eco-Efficiency)

Promoting more efficient use of resources in manufacturing and operations is the first stage in adopting more sustainable consumption practices. Known as eco-efficiency, this approach is currently implemented by majority of companies for its bottom-line benefits (e.g., reduced costs of energy and material use). In the middle of the Great Recession, 72% of American companies reported reducing costs through improved materials efficiency (Veleva et al., 2009). One of the first companies to recognize the value of greater resource efficiency was 3M, with its Pollution Prevention Pays (3P) Program. Between 1974 and 2005, the company reported aggregate savings of over $1 billion as a result of improved efficiency (EPA, 2011). Interface, one of the world's largest producers of commercial floor covering, saved over $200 million from 1996 to 2002 through its eco-efficiency efforts. Dupont reduced energy use by one-third at one facility, saving over $17 million per year on power while reducing greenhouse gas pollution per pound of product by half (WBCSD, 2009).

Rising energy and commodity prices and the drive to continuously improve competitiveness are propelling a greater number of companies to adopt eco-efficiency strategies. Companies interested in moving to this stage need to ask the following questions: Can we find ways to reduce energy, water, and raw materials? Are we leveraging our workforce and rewarding employees for eco-efficient ideas? What are our competitors doing? Can we change transportation practices (e.g., use rail, local suppliers, alternative fuel vehicles) to reduce costs?

While an important first stage, eco-efficiency is insufficient to address today's environmental, social, and economic challenges. Moreover, improved efficiency can in fact increase consumption and thus make environmental problems worse (Owen, 2011). Known as the "rebound effect" in economics, improved energy efficiency, for example, lowers the cost of a given activity, which causes people to engage in that activity more, canceling out not only savings but also environmental benefits (Owen, 2011).

Stage 2: Reducing Supply-Chain and Product Life-Cycle Impacts

The next stage in advancing sustainable consumption requires examining a company's impacts throughout its supply-chain and product life-cycle, since these typically contribute most to the overall environmental footprint. Understanding such impacts requires using tools such as life-cycle assessment (LCA) and supply-chain analysis. After analyzing its greenhouse gas emissions (GHG) along the supply chain, Staples found that 93% of its GHG footprint is embedded in the products they sell (just 7% was the result of company operations) (Staples, 2011). A growing number of companies are using LCA tools and launching green products, which help reduce energy, water, material use, or eliminate toxic chemicals (LCA Links, 2013). Levi's new line of "waterless jeans" is using between 28% and 96% less water in the stage of the manufacturing process compared to traditional jeans (Kuhn Associates, 2013). In the green cleaning sector, Seventh Generation, Clorox, and Tenant have been particularly successful as consumers have demanded safer products.

The main drivers for moving to Stage 2 include changing customer preferences; desire to differentiate from competitors by using green labels such as the EPA Design for Environment, EnergyStar, and Cradle-to-Cradle; and reducing risks from resource shortages, regulation, and liability (e.g., California Green Chemistry Law, the European Union RoHS Directive). In 2009, almost a third of U.S. companies (31%) reported offering products that were certified as green or "sustainable," up from 24% in 2007. About 41% of companies reported designing products and services considering their life-cycle impacts (Veleva et al., 2009).

Despite the growing number of companies adopting supply-chain and product life-cycle strategies, barriers exist. The price of green products is often higher, as environmental externalities are not included in the cost of production, thus making it difficult to compete with conventional products. Consumer awareness about the environmental and social impacts of many products is still low, and government regulation supporting more sustainable product design is lacking. Therefore, such strategy typically works for particular product categories (e.g., organic food, green cleaning supplies, energy efficient appliances) and in particular markets such as the European Union, California, and Japan. While the number of companies moving to this stage of sustainable consumption is growing, it is still relatively small. Furthermore, many green claims are seen as "greenwashing" (TerraChoice, 2010). There is a need to adopt a widely recognized "sustainable product label" that incorporates all key aspects of sustainability and is easy to use by consumers, something the Sustainability Consortium has been working on for several years (Sustainability Consortium, 2013). The greater challenge remains the lack of government policies mandating full-cost accounting or including the cost of environmental externalities in the price of products and services.

Companies interested in moving to this stage need to ask the following questions: What are the impacts of our products throughout their life cycle, from raw material extraction to final disposal? Do we know all ingredients in our products and understand supplier practices in making them (both social and environmental)? Can we use existing LCA databases to estimate our impacts or collaborate with other companies in commissioning a LCA? Do we look at our suppliers as partners in helping us launch innovative, more sustainable products? Do we track customer expectations and preferences for more sustainable products?

Stage 3: Product Take-Back, Recycling, and Materials Recovery

Driven primarily by regulations and, in some cases, customer demand or sustainability commitments, a small but growing number of companies are taking back, recycling, and properly disposing of their products at the end of their useful lives. Examples include recycling of packaging, metal, plastics, and wood, taking back old electronics products for recycling at the end of their useful life (for specific examples, see Text Box 1).

Recycling allows for the extraction of valuable materials such as metals, plastics, and glass, which are then used in the manufacture of new products. A reduction in waste generation not only lessens the environmental burden but can also have bottom-line benefits as the cost of waste disposal declines or additional revenue is

---

Text Box 1. Examples of Product Take-Back and Recycling

Since 2001, Stonyfield Farm has been partnering with Preserve to take back its yogurt containers and make toothbrushes from the recycled plastic (O'Loughlin, 2007). In 2009, the partnership expanded to include Whole Foods Market and start the Gimme 5 program, which collected more than 45,000 pounds of material in its first year (an equivalent of about 2.9 million yogurt cups) (Stonyfield Farm, 2011).

Initially required by the European Union Waste Electrical and Electronic Directive of 2002 (WEEE), Dell Computer became the first U.S. company to take back all its products worldwide to recycle, recover useful materials, and dispose of them properly. It partnered with Staples and other retailers to collect used computers and worked with the National Cristina Foundation to promote product donations (Palmer & Walls, 2002).

Nike's Reuse-A-Shoe program helps recycle old shoes into athletic surfaces like basketball courts and playgrounds. Since 1990, the company has taken back 28 million pairs of shoes, generating 36,000 tons of scrap material for use in more than 450,000 locations around the world (Nike, 2013).

obtained (when recyclers pay for the materials). Presently, the recycling of complex products is challenging, however, due to the assortment of varied materials that are not always properly labeled. Paying for collection and shipping is another challenge, since often the extracted value could be insufficient to cover this cost, compared to reuse or remanufacturing. Nike's Reuse-A-Shoe program, for example, is revenue negative, therefore not adopted by smaller footwear manufacturers (Nike, 2013; Veleva, 2010). As a growing number of mandates require elimination of toxic chemicals from products and shortages of raw materials increase, recycling is expected to become more financially viable in the future. For example, a growing number of states have been enacting container recycling laws whereby some types of beverage containers require a small deposit that customers get back when they return the empty bottle for recycling. A study of the 10 U.S. states with such mandates found that recycling rates for bottles were 2.5 higher than in the states without such mandates (EMagazine, 2011). At the present, however, few companies have moved to take back and recycle old products or packaging.

Businesses interested in moving to this stage should examine the following issues: Is there forthcoming legislation that may require taking back our products? What are competitors doing in this area? What are some tangible and intangible benefits of taking back products for recycling and disposal? What are the associated costs? Who should we partner with in order to implement such a strategy?

Stage 4: Reducing Consumption During Product Use

This stage of sustainable consumption involves two types of strategies. The first one relates to extending the useful lives of products through design for durability, product reuse, and remanufacturing. The second strategy involves educating consumers on different practices around product use that can reduce associated environmental impacts (e.g., energy, water, waste).

Often customers will replace their products for new ones with better capabilities while their old products are still working. In such cases, reselling or donating the old products allows the extension of a product's useful life and thus reducing related environmental and health impacts from the manufacture of new products and the disposal of existing ones. Such an approach can also yield financial benefits for the owner of the product. Cars, furniture, baby clothes, and toys are all examples of products with well-established and profitable business models for product reuse. Among electronics, cell phones have a thriving reuse market; data show that in the United States, 65% of all collected cell phones are reused rather than recycled (Geyer & Blass, 2010). Remanufacturing not only minimizes the environmental impacts but can also create new market opportunities and higher profits than the manufacture of new equipment. India and China, for example, provide excellent market opportunities for the selling of remanufactured medical instruments. Research has demonstrated that the average profit margin for product reconstruction activities is 20%, compared to typical profit margins of 3%–8% in the manufacturing industry (Pearce, 2009).

Xerox was among the first companies that began taking back and remanufacturing its copiers in addition to offering customers competitive leasing contracts, achieving significant savings and inhibiting competition. In the area of medical instruments, Siemens has adopted a robust companywide program for take-back, refurbishing, and remarketing of preowned medical equipment. The company has found that "recycling and remarketing can be a successful business model in some product segments." Its refurbished ecoline systems include a wide range of medical systems such as angiography, computer tomography, and radiography (Siemens, 2012).

Design for durability or remanufacture faces many market challenges today. For many global supply chains this option is not viable as the processing costs of remanufacturing are often higher than the selling price of new products (Pagell, Zhaohui, & Murthy, 2007). Other market barriers involve consumer perceptions that a remanufactured product is "secondhand" and therefore of lower quality than a new product. The fast-changing technology lifestyles and fashion also make it difficult to design products with long-lasting functionality (Hatcher, Ijomah, & Windmill, 2013). In addition, the current market system rewards selling more products, therefore the latter are often designed to have short life spans or become obsolete quickly. Consumers also face barriers to using products longer as the cost of repair often exceeds the cost of purchasing new products.

Moving to this stage requires product life-cycle thinking and incorporating design for remanufacture criteria in product design (Stage 2). In some cases, another company could collect an old product and create a completely new business, which could be a risk for the original manufacturer. While in the 1990s, Kodak considered used cameras a waste, another company, Jazz Camera, saw them as new business opportunity. It began taking back, refurbishing, and reselling such cameras at lower prices and "soon ate up 25–40% share of the Kodak USA market, selling the cameras under many names. The cameras were cheap and they worked fine" (Good Point Ideas Blog, 2003).

Educating consumers on how to reduce consumption during product use is the second key strategy for companies seeking to move to Stage 4. Large consumer-facing brands can play a significant role in educating consumers to reduce environmental impacts during product use. In 2010, Levi's began a marketing campaign to encourage people to wash their jeans less often, in cold water only, and line-dry them, after finding out that consumers were responsible for 60% of the energy use and 45% of the water use during the lifetime of a pair of 501 jeans (Berfield, 2012). Unilever moved a step further to educate its consumers to adopt more sustainable lifestyles. In 2011, the company launched its framework for inspiring sustainable living, which includes five levers for change: make it understood, easy, desirable, rewarding, and a habit (Unilever, 2011). Changing consumer habits, however, is challenging. A significant barrier to green consumers is the high cost of effort and time. "Consumers need help from government in the form of incentives and single-issue labels to show them where they should be concentrating their limited efforts. More fundamentally, however, people need more time and space, something lacking in today's increasingly busy lifestyles" (Young, Hwang, McDonald, & Oates, 2010).

Companies committed to advancing more sustainable consumption through product use need to ask some key questions: Is there a business model for designing products to last longer or take back and refurbish? What are the risks of not doing so? Who do we need to partner with to pilot such a strategy? How do we educate consumers about the value of refurbished products or about using products in a more sustainable way? What are the benefits and risks for first movers? How do we work with policymakers to create business and consumer incentives for extending products' useful lives?

Stage 5: Dematerialization and New Business Models for Creating Value by Selling Less "Stuff"

Moving to this stage is particularly challenging, as it requires developing new business models for selling less "stuff," which in general goes against the current market system wherein profits are linked to the point of sale. It requires out-of-the-box thinking and "understanding how companies can meet customers' needs differently" (Nidomolu, Prahalad, & Rangaswami, 2009).

One viable approach is the concept of Product Service System (PSS), which is a way to promote a more dematerialized economy. In PSS, companies develop a new business model wherein they offer a service instead of a product, which ideally should lead to reduced environmental impacts through reduced product sales and extended product life (Besch, 2004). Interface was among the first companies to consider such a revolutionary business model. Under the visionary leadership of its founder and former CEO Ray Anderson, the company launched its Evergreen Service Agreement (ESA) in 1995. It aimed to "move the business model from selling carpets as product to selling "long-term floor-covering services" (Oliva & Quinn, 2003). In the car business, Zipcar pioneered car-sharing services as an alternative to car ownership. Electronic product companies like Xerox, IBM, and HP have increasingly sought to recast themselves as "service providers." Xerox, an early mover in PSS with its strategy to lease instead of sell copiers in the 1990s, aggressively pursued further business opportunities from offering services as a way to ensure more stable revenue and customer base. Half of its revenues in 2010 came from services, up from 23% the year before (Blumenthal, 2010).

Technology has enabled a significant growth in new business opportunities in the area of PSS and collaborative consumption. As Botsman and Rogers (2010) conclude, collaborative consumption in particular

> describes the rapid explosion in traditional sharing, bartering, lending, trading, renting, gifting, and swapping reinvented through network technologies on a scale and in ways never possible before. It is disrupting outdated modes of business and reinventing not just what we consume but how we consume.

Businesses of all sizes and in all sectors will be forced to reevaluate their business models if they want to stay competitive and relevant in an era of fast technological transformation of the way people consume.

Another approach to reducing consumption is to educate consumers to buy less. Patagonia, a leader in the environmental and CSR movement, shocked both businesses and consumers with its recent campaign, "Don't Buy That Jacket."

Launched in November 2011 (for "Black Friday" and then "Cyber Monday"), this one-page ad in the *New York Times* asked consumers not to buy Patagonia products if they do not need them (Patagonia, 2011). A follow-up from its earlier initiative, the Common Threads Initiative, this campaign asked consumers to think about the 5 Rs—reduce, repair, reuse, recycle, and reimagine—when they consider purchasing clothes. The company is partnering with eBay to promote consumer resale of Patagonia clothing. In addition, in January 2012, it became the first "benefit corporation" in California. This B-Corp status enables Patagonia to focus not just on shareholders but on its wider group of stakeholders and "commit to creating an overarching general public benefit." It is still too early to examine the financial impacts of this campaign, but a Terapeak (2011) analysis of the 2 weeks prior to the launch of the program and the 2 weeks after the launch of the program showed that total sales increased over 41%, total listings went up over 27%, and the sell-through rate increased by almost 3%.

Yet very few companies will follow Patagonia's approach in today's market economy. Significant barriers face traditional businesses interested in moving to Stage 5. With the lack of government policies to support leasing versus selling products, there is significant financial risk for the service provider, difficult market conditions, and inertia. In addition, consumer lifestyles focused on consumption and fast-changing fashion and design as a demonstration of social status are preventing successful adoption of product durability strategies. Therefore, implementation of Stage 5 sustainable consumption strategies will remain limited under the current market conditions.

Stage 6: Sustainable Consumption Systems

This stage shows how an individual company's consumption processes fits into the larger picture of a sustainable society. Sustainable consumption is not an isolated activity. It is a part of the larger economic, social, and environmental systems of a community. Stage 6 considers the effects of consumption on the long-term quality of life and human development within the ecological carrying capacity. In most cases, Stage 6 cannot be achieved by an individual company but rather requires coordinated efforts by government, business, and other stakeholders to establish the policies and underlying structures to move to sustainable consumption system.

Tukker, Charter, Vezzoli, Sto, and Anderson (2008) discuss two types of emerging drivers that underline the transition to such a system that he calls "an experience economy." The first is external to the firms and relates to customer fulfillment becoming less material-intensive and more focused on service and experience. Numerous studies have demonstrated the link between happiness and environmental quality and that increasing GDP above a particular point is not associated with greater quality of life. The second type of driver for transition to sustainable consumption systems is internal to the firm and relates to "an interesting group of entrepreneurs who have deliberately changed the course of their firms or who have invested heavily in sustainability."

The Benefit Corporation movement, for example, is enabling a growing number of companies to use business as a tool to solve social and environmental problems. Some 12 states have already passed legislation, and 14 are currently working on such legislation (B Labs, 2012). Such policies provide legal protection to Benefit Corporations to pursue the triple bottom line. According to Massachusetts legislation, "Benefit corporations are similar to traditional for-profit corporations but they differ in one important respect . . . their directors and officers are expressly permitted to consider and prioritize the social and environmental impacts of their corporate decision-making" (Foley Hoag LLP, 2012). Changing corporate structure is one of the most crucial factors for changing corporate practices toward greater social responsibility and triple bottom line strategies (Kelly, 2012).

Companies interested in advancing sustainable consumption systems need to align their governance structure and business strategy with sustainability; work with policymakers, NGOs and other stakeholders to promote supportive legislation; and ultimately contribute to changing consumer shopping values and habits.

SUSTAINABLE CONSUMPTION: BARRIERS AND OPPORTUNITIES

Presented research demonstrates that the movement toward more sustainable consumption practices by business is growing. While most companies are still in Stage 1 (eco-efficiency), an increasing number of businesses are evaluating and minimizing supply-chain and product life-cycle impacts (Stage 2). Driven primarily by regulation, companies in some sectors are adopting product take-back, recycling, and materials recovery strategies (Stage 3). A small number of businesses are implementing business models to expand product use or educate consumers on how to minimize environmental impacts during product use (Stage 4). Such an approach often includes product service models and does not presently work for every sector and every product category. With the exception of Patagonia, the research did not identify other businesses who have taken the radical approach of advising their customers to buy less (Stage 5). In today's market system, wherein profits are based on growing consumption and sales, such an approach is seen as a sure path to bankruptcy. Regardless, a small but growing number of companies are embracing the "slow living" movement. Born out of the "slow food" and "slow money" movement of the 1980s, slow living is about "investing in local communities and food systems that help people lead slower, more fulfilling lives" while at the same time helping reduce consumption and climate change" (Johnson, 2012).

Moving toward sustainable consumption systems (Stage 6) cannot be achieved by any single company but requires concerted efforts by government, business, and citizens to design a new economic system that promotes quality of life and prosperity for all instead of endless pursuit of economic growth. Such a paradigm shift demands moving away from the current "extractive ownership" structures to adopt "regenerative ownership" structures for companies (Kelly, 2012). The Benefits Corporation movement is one step in this direction.

The short-term thinking in capital markets (known as investment myopia or excess discounting) is another key barrier preventing companies from moving toward Stage 4 and Stage 5 sustainable consumption strategies. Haldane and Davies (2011) demonstrate the trend toward increasing investment myopia and the use of high discount rates. In a survey of 401 executives, Graham, Harvey, and Rajgopal (2005) found that executives would reject a positive-NPV project if that lowered earnings below quarterly consensus expectations. In addition, over 75% of the survey respondents admitted that "they would give up economic value in order to smooth earnings." Another study of FTSE-100 and 250 executives found that the majority of them "would choose a low return option sooner (£250,000 tomorrow) rather than a high return later (£450,000 in 3 years)," suggesting annual discount rates of over 20% (PwC, 2011).

Another challenge to moving to higher-stage sustainable consumption strategies is the value-chain manufacturing model that is still taught in business schools. As Unruh (2010) explains, we teach students "a simple model that describes the value adding steps that take a low value material like iron ore and turn it into a high value product like a Ferrari Testarossa but there are a few sustainability problems with the model." First, it does not recognize that the value chain is connected to the environment and includes endless resource extraction and dumping of used products back into the environment. An even greater challenge, according to Unruh, are the incentives that the value chain creates for sales people, who are rewarded on the "margin" or the profit made on each sale of a product. Such a process, by design, goes against the principles of sustainable consumption, which seeks to minimize material throughput and extend product use.

The process of ever-increasing consumption is reinforced by the widely adopted use of Gross Domestic Product (GDP) as an indicator of economic development. GDP "has been the single most important policy goal around the world for most of last century" (Jackson, 2009). Policymakers and companies have been aggressively pursuing growth as a way to increase income, employment, and prosperity. However, recent studies demonstrate that GDP is a poor measure of prosperity and well-being (Jackson, 2009). In addition, it does not consider environmental externalities and thus further distorts the market system by promoting environmentally destructive activities and faster consumption rates. There can be no indefinite growth within the physical limits of the Earth's natural resources, and a group of economists have proposed moving toward a steady state economy, or

> economy with constant stocks of people and artifacts, maintained at some desired, sufficient levels by low rates of maintenance "throughput," that is, by the lowest feasible flows of matter and energy from the first stage of production to the last stage of consumption. (Daly, 1991)

Implementing sustainable consumption systems will also require a shift in people's values, habits, and lifestyles, which requires a concerted effort by policymakers, business, and nonprofit organizations to change the way people live, work, and enjoy free time. Business "has the power to influence both the level and the nature of consumption through shaping perception, wants and needs" (Tukker et al., 2008).

Regardless of the numerous barriers to more sustainable production, several emerging trends are acting as powerful enablers of the sustainable consumption paradigm shift. Companies are beginning to recognize and experience the business impacts of volatile commodity prices, increasing unemployment, and a related decline in consumption, resource shortages, and other environmental constraints, which is prompting changes in their business strategies. Technology is empowering a growing number of consumers to identify, demand, and pursue more sustainable products and companies. It has also opened opportunities for business in building closer relationships with its customers, thus enabling new business models such as product remanufacturing, sustainable product use, and product service systems. Finally, people are increasingly dissatisfied with the consumerism culture.

CONCLUSION

As Michaelis (2003) concludes in his analysis of the role of business in sustainable consumption, "Businesses are not 'in control' of the system of consumption and production, nor are they necessarily caught in a web." Larger companies in particular have greater leverage with their competitors, suppliers, the media, and government and can work to promote technological innovation, new economic incentives, and cultural change needed to achieve sustainable consumption. Businesses must work with governments, NGOs, and other stakeholders to change the current policies, corporate structures, and consumer habits in order to enable the shift to sustainable consumption. As Porter and Kramer (2011) state, "Capitalism is an unparalleled vehicle for meeting human needs, improving efficiency, creating jobs, and building wealth. But a narrow conception of capitalism has prevented business from harnessing its full potential to meet society's broader challenges." The time has come to create a new, more "conscious capitalism," based on systems thinking, environmental protection, regenerative ownership, and steady-state economy that focuses on human well-being and long-term sustainability.

DISCUSSION QUESTIONS

Chapter 6: Sustainable Consumption in Today's Market Economy: Challenges and Opportunities for Business

1. What is "sustainable consumption"? What are the main drivers for companies to embrace sustainable consumption?
2. What are the six stages in the sustainable consumption framework? Select a specific company and discuss at which stage of the framework is the company presently.
3. What are the main barriers to wider adoption of sustainable consumption strategies by business? (stages 4 and 5) How can we overcome these barriers and move to a more sustainable system of production and consumption where "9 billion people can live well within the limits of the planet"?

REFERENCES

Berfield. (2012, October 18). Levi's goes green with waste<less jeans. *Bloomberg BusinessWeek*. Retrieved from http://www.businessweek.com/articles/2012-10-18/levis-goes-green-with-waste-less-jeans

Besch, K. (2004, October). *Product service systems for office furniture: Barriers and opportunities on the European market*. Master's thesis. Lund. Switzerland. Retrieved January 12, 2013, from http://lup.lub.lu.se/luur/download?func=downloadFile&recordOId=1329194&fileOId=1329195

B Labs. (2012). *Legislation*. Retrieved January 11, 2013, from http://www.bcorporation.net/what-are-b-corps/legislation

Blumenthal, R. (2010, September 19). Xerox copies IBM and HP, boosts services—and profits. *Wall Street Journal*. Retrieved from http://online.wsj.com/article/SB10001424052748703470904575500521535643454.html

Botsman, R., & Rogers, R. (2010). *What's mine is yours: The rise of collaborative consumption*. New York, NY: HarperCollins.

Business for Social Responsibility (BSR). (2010, July). *The new frontier in sustainability: The business opportunity in tackling sustainable consumption*. Retrieved from http://www.bsr.org/reports/BSR_New%20Frontier%20in%20Sustainability.pdf

Daly, H. (1991). *Steady-state economics: Second edition with new essays*. Washington DC: Island.

EMagazine. (2011, October 30). *Bottle bills*. Retrieved October 14, 2013, from http://www.emagazine.com/earth-talk/bottle-bills

Environmental Protection Agency (EPA). (2011). *3M Lean Six Sigma and sustainability*. Retrieved from http://www.epa.gov/lean/environment/studies/3m.htm

Foley Hoag LLP. (2012, August 17). *Massachusetts passes legislation recognizing benefit corporations*. Retrieved January 11, 2013, from http://www.foleyhoag.com/NewsCenter/Publications/Alerts/Business/Business_Alert-081712.aspx

Geyer, R., & Blass, V. (2010). The economics of cell phone reuse and recycling. *International Journal of Advanced Manufacturing Technology, 47*, 515–525. Retrieved from http://www.escholarship.org/uc/item/8z18c5h6

Good Point Ideas Blog. (2003). *Disposable recyclable camera wars*. Retrieved January 10, 2013, from http://retroworks.blogspot.com/2010/11/disposable-recyclable-camera-wars.html

Graham, J. R., Harvey, C. R., & Rajgopal, S. (2005). The economic implications of corporate financial reporting. *Journal of Accounting and Economics, 40*, 3–73.

Haldane, A., & Davies, R. (2011, May). The short long. *Bank of England. Brussels*. Retrieved from http://www.bankofengland.co.uk/publications/Documents/speeches/2011/speech495.pdf

Hatcher, G., Ijomah, W., & Windmill, J. (2013). Integrating design for remanufacture into the design process: The operational factors. *Journal of Cleaner Production, 39*, 200–208.

Jackson, T. (2011). *Prosperity without growth: Economics for a finite planet*. London, UK: Earthscan.

Johnson, L. (2012, June 11). Will "slow living" movement pick up speed in the U.S.? *E&E Publishing*. Retrieved from http://www.eenews.net/public/climatewire/2012/06/11/1

Kelly, M. (2012). *Owning our future: The emerging ownership revolution*. San Francisco, CA: Berrett-Koehler.

Kuhn Associates. (2013). *Levi's water footprint*. Retrieved January 3, 2013, from http://www.kuhnassociatesllc.com/water/levis-water-footprint.html

LCA Links! (2013). *Companies using LCA.* Retrieved January 12, 2013, from http://www. life-cycle.org/?page_id=11

Michaelis, L. (2003). The role of business in sustainable consumption. *Journal of Cleaner Production, 11,* 915–921.

Nidomolu, R., Prahalad, C., & Rangaswami, M. (2009, September). Why sustainability is now the key driver of innovation. *Harvard Business Review.*

Nike. (2013). *Reuse a shoe.* Retrieved January 2, 2013, from http://www.nikereuseashoe.com/

Norwegian Ministry of Environment. (1994). Elements of an international work programme on sustainable production and consumption. The Oslo Ministerial Roundtable Conference on Sustainable Production and Consumption. February 1994.

Oliva, R., & Quinn, J. (2003, June 4). Interface's evergreen service agreement. *Harvard Business School.* Case 9-603-112.

O'Loughlin, S. (2007, April 23). Toothbrush touts recycling program. *Brandweek.*

Owen, D. (2011). *The conundrum*: How scientific innovation, increased efficiency, and good intentions can make our energy and climate problems worse. New York, NY: Penguin.

Pagell, M., Zhaohui, W., & Murthy, N. (2007). The supply-chain implications of recycling. *Business Horizons, 50,* 133–143.

Palmer, K., & Walls, M. (2002, February). *Economic analysis of extended producer responsibility movement: Understanding costs, effectiveness, and the role for policy.* International Forum on the Environment.

Patagonia. (2011, November). *Don't buy this jacket.* Retrieved January 11, 2013, from http://www.patagonia.com/email/11/112811.html

Pearce, J., II (2009). The profit-making allure of product reconstruction. *MITSloan Management Review, 50*(3).

Porter, M., & Kramer, M. (2011, January). Creating shared value. *Harvard Business Review.* Retrieved from http://hbr.org/2011/01/the-big-idea-creating-shared-value/ar/1?referral= 00060

PriceWaterhouseCoopers (PwC). (2010, December). *Green products: Using sustainable attributes to drive growth and value.* Retrieved January 8, 2013, from www.pwc.com/en_US/ us/corporate-sustainability-climate-change/assets/green-products-paper.pdf

Siemens. (2012). Product take-back and conservation of resources. Retrieved November 25, 2012, from www.siemens.com/sustainability/en/core-topics/product-responsibility/ facts-figures/product-return-and-conservation-of-resources.htm

Staples. (2011, December 1). Staples and sustainability. *BizNGO.* Retrieved from http://www. bizngo.org/pdf/bizngo-agm2011-markbuckley-bizngo-staples-and-sustainability.pdf

Stonyfield Farm. (2011). *Partnering for the planet.* Retrieved October 14, 2013, from http:// www.stonyfield.com/healthy-planet/partnering-planet/preserve

Sustainability Consortium. (2013). The sustainability measurement and reporting system. *SMRS.* Retrieved from http://www.sustainabilityconsortium.org/smrs/

Terapeak. (2011). *Terapeak reviews initial results and trends of the Patagonia Common Threads Initiative and eBay campaign.* Retrieved January 4, 2013, from http://blog. terapeak.com/2011/09/26/terapeak-reviews-initial-results-trends-of-the-patagonia-common-/

TerraChoice. (2010). *Ten sins of greenwashing.* Retrieved January 9, 2013, from http:// sinsofgreenwashing.org/index5349.pdf

Tukker, A., Charter, M., Vezzoli, C., Sto, E., & Anderson, M. (2008). *System innovation for sustainability: Perspectives on radical changes to sustainable consumption and production.* Sheffield, UK: Greenleaf.

Unilever. (2011). *Inspiring sustainable living.* Retrieved January 10, 2013, from http://www. unilever.com/images/slp_5-Levers-for-Change_tcm13-276807_tcm13-284877.pdf

United Nations (UN). (2002). *Report of the World Summit on Sustainable Development*. United Nations. Johannesburg, South Africa.

UN Millennium Project. (2006). *Fast facts: The faces of poverty*. Retrieved October 14, 2013, from http://www.unmillenniumproject.org/resources/fastfacts_e.htm

Unruh, G. (2010, September 8). Sustainable consumption rising on the business agenda. *Forbes*. Retrieved January 4, 2013, from http://www.forbes.com/sites/csr/2010/09/08/sustainable-consumption-rising-on-the-business-agenda/

Veleva, V. (2010). New Balance: Developing an integrated CSR strategy. Case 9B10M011W. *Richard Ivey School of Business*. University of Western Ontario, Canada.

Veleva, V., Googins, B., Caraphina, R., Mirvis, P., Connolly, P., Pinney, C., & Raffaelli, R. (2009). Weathering the storm: State of corporate citizenship in the U.S. 2009. *Boston College Center for Corporate Citizenship*. Retrieved from http://www.bcccc.net/index.cfm?pageId=2053

World Business Council for Sustainable Development (WBCSD). (2009). *Eco-efficiency learning module*. Retrieved January 9, 2013, from http://www.greenbiz.com/sites/default/files/document/CustomO16C45F67109.pdf

World Business Council for Sustainable Development (WBCSD). (2011). *A vision for sustainable consumption*. Retrieved January 9, 2013, from http://www.wbcsd.org/Pages/EDocument/EDocumentDetails.aspx?ID=13758&NoSearchContextKey=true

World Economic Forum (WEF). (2009). *Sustainability for tomorrow's consumer: The business case for sustainability*. Retrieved January 9, 2013, from https://members.weforum.org/pdf/ConsumerIndustries/Sustainabilityfullreport.pdf

World Economic Forum (WEF). (2010, January). *Redesigning business value: A road map to sustainable consumption*. Retrieved January 10, 2013, from http://www3.weforum.org/docs/WEF_RedesigningBusinessValue_SustainableConsumption_Report_2010.pdf

World Economic Forum (WEF). (2012). *More with less: Scaling sustainable consumption and resource efficiency*. Retrieved January 11, 2013, from http://www.weforum.org/reports/more-less-scaling-sustainable-consumption-and-resource-efficienc

World Economic Forum (WEF) (2011) *The consumption dilemma leverage points for accelerating sustainable growth*. Retrieved January 11, 2013 from http://www3.weforum.org/docs/WEF_ConsumptionDilemma_SustainableGrowth_Report_2011.pdf

Young, W., Hwang, K., McDonald, S., & Oates, C. (2010). Sustainable consumption: Green consumer behavior when purchasing products. *Sustainable Development, 18*, 20–31. Retrieved from http://www.astepback.com/EP/Sustainable%20Consumption.

Note: A version of this chapter was first presented in June 2013 at the SCORAI International Conference, June 12-14, Clark University, Worcester, MA, 2013.

Section II.
Sustainability Measurement
and Management

Chapter 7

THE ELECTRONICS INDUSTRY IN A NEW REGULATORY CLIMATE: PROTECTING THE ENVIRONMENT AND SHAREHOLDER VALUE[1]

With Suresh Sethi

With the adoption of the Waste Electrical and Electronic Equipment (WEEE) and Restriction of Hazardous Substances (RoHS) Directives in February 2003 and their coming into force in August 2005 and July 2006, respectively, the European Union has paved the way toward greater environmental responsibility and sustainability in the electronics industry. The directives require complete phase out by July 2006 of several of the most toxic chemicals commonly used in the electronics industry—lead, cadmium, hexachrome, mercury, and two brominated flame retardants. In addition, companies are required to assume responsibility for their products at the end of their useful lives. Other major markets such as Japan, Taiwan, China, and California have initiated similar legislative and voluntary requirements. What does this all mean for electronics companies and their shareholders?

This chapter provides an overview of recent environmental requirements as they relate to electronic component manufacturers. Results of background research and a survey conducted by Citizens Advisers are presented to evaluate industry preparedness to meet the new environmental requirements. The authors found that many suppliers are actively working to meet the requirements and build a stronger market position, however the effort is not uniform across all companies. Producers who are lagging in their compliance efforts may incur higher costs or market exclusion. The chapter concludes with recommendations on what role investors can play to promote greater environmental responsibility in the electronics sector while at the same time helping to increase shareholder value. © 2004 NetLogex, LLC. All rights reserved.

[1] Reprinted from: Veleva, V. & Sethi, S. (2004, October). "The electronics industry in a new regulatory climate: Protecting the environment and shareholder value." *Corporate Environmental Strategy: International Journal for Sustainable Business, 11*(9), 2-207–2-225. By permission of the publisher NetLogex, LLC. © 2004 NetLogex, LLC.

INTRODUCTION

With the adoption of the Waste Electrical and Electronic Equipment (WEEE) and Restriction of Hazardous Substances (RoHS) Directives in February 2003 and their coming into force in August 2005 and July 2006, respectively, the European Union (EU) has paved the way toward greater environmental responsibility and sustainability in the electronics industry. The directives require complete phase out by July 2006 of several of the most toxic chemicals commonly used in the electronics industry. These include lead, cadmium, hexachrome, mercury, and two brominated flame retardants. In addition, companies are required to assume responsibility for their products at the end of their useful lives. Other countries such as Japan, Taiwan, and China have initiated similar legislative and voluntary requirements. In the United States, California is leading the way, followed by Maine, Massachusetts, Washington, and a few other states. What does this all mean for shareholders? What are the consequences of investing in companies that are not working to meet these global environmental requirements? What can socially responsible investors do to promote greater environmental responsibility and protect shareholder value?

This chapter provides an overview of recent environmental requirements as they relate to electronics manufacturers. In order to evaluate industry preparedness to meet these requirements, Citizens Advisers[2] conducted a survey among a group of electronics manufacturers making semiconductor and other electronic parts for computers, telephones, household and other equipment. Most research to date has focused on original equipment manufacturers (OEMs), but much less is known about how informed their suppliers are and whether they are taking action to redesign their products to phase out restricted chemicals. Citizens' survey results demonstrate that many suppliers are actively working to meet the requirements and build a stronger market position, however the effort is not uniform across all companies. The longer a company waits, the higher the costs to both the company and its shareholders. The chapter concludes with recommendations on what role investors can play to promote greater environmental responsibility in the electronics sector while at the same time helping to increase shareholder value.

Electronic Products and the Environment

Many consumers and shareholders are not aware that the same products that have dramatically improved our quality of life—computers, cell phones, household appliances—are also some of the largest sources of environmental pollution. For example, the average computer is a very complex machine and requires roughly 1,000 different materials to be manufactured. Many of these are highly persistent (do not easily degrade in the environment), toxic (able to kill living organisms), and bioaccumulative (able to accumulate in living organisms and thus increase

---

[2]Citizens Advisers is the investment adviser to Citizens Funds, one of American's oldest and largest socially responsible mutual funds families.
http://investing.businessweek.com/research/stocks/private/snapshot.asp?privcapId=988918

their concentration through the food chain). Below are listed some of the toxic chemicals currently targeted under many global and domestic environmental regulations and initiatives:

- *Cadmium (Cd)* and its compounds are classified as highly toxic, persistent, and bioaccumulative. Cadmium causes kidney cancer and developmental and reproductive damage. It is a suspected endocrine disrupter, cardiovascular and blood system toxicant, immunotoxicant, and respiratory toxicant (EDF, 2002). In electrical and electronic equipment, cadmium is often used in chip resistors, infrared detectors and semiconductors, and as a pigment and plastic stabilizer. It is estimated that the 315 million computers, which became obsolete at the end of 2004, contained almost two million pounds of cadmium (SVTC, 1999).
- *Lead (Pb)* is also a persistent, bioaccumulative, and toxic chemical. In high concentrations, it can cause brain damage, kidney damage, and gastrointestinal disorders. Long-term exposure affects the blood, central nervous system, blood pressure, kidneys, and vitamin D metabolism. In children, it causes slowed cognitive development and reduced growth, among other effects (EPA, n.d. a). Lead has been known for its toxic effects for centuries. In fact one hypothesis suggests lead poisoning from drinking water from lead pipes played a major role in the decline of the Roman Empire. Lead accumulates in the environment and has both high acute and chronic toxic effects on plants, animals, and microorganisms. Consumer electronics contribute to 40% of the lead found in the landfills (SVTC, 1999).
- *Mercury (Hg)* is a confirmed developmental toxicant and suspected blood and cardiovascular toxicant, immunotoxicant, respiratory toxicant, and gastrointestinal toxicant, among others (EDF, 2002). In its organic form, methylmercury easily accumulates in living organisms and concentrates through the food chain. When ingested, usually from eating fish, methylmercury damages the brain. The fetus, infants, and young children are under greatest risk for irreversible brain damage. A 2003 study by the Centers for Disease Control and Prevention found 8% of women of childbearing age had blood mercury levels above what the EPA deemed safe (0.1 μg per kilogram body weight per day or 5.8 ppb mercury in blood) (EPA, n.d. b). Estimates of the sources of mercury demonstrate that 22% of its yearly world consumption is used in electrical and electronic equipment (e.g., in thermostats, sensors, switches, printed circuit boards, discharge lamps, telecommunications, and cell phones) (SVTC, 1999). When incinerated at the end of their useful lives, these products release mercury, which ends up in the air, and then in lakes, rivers, and the ocean through rain.
- *Hexavalent chromium (Cr6+)* is a carcinogen and a respiratory toxicant. It can cause dermatitis and asthmatic bronchitis. In addition, hexachrome may damage the DNA. It is particularly toxic to the aquatic environment (EDF, 2002). Probably one of the best examples of the dangers of hexavalent chromium was the 1970s case of childhood leukemia in a community near a PG&E plant in California. The case was featured in the movie *Erin Brokovich* and demonstrated how toxic chemicals can contaminate groundwater and thus endanger

children and surrounding communities. Hexachrome is often used for corrosion protection of untreated and galvanized steel plates and as a decorative element and a hardener for steel housing.

- *Polybrominated diphenyl ethers* (PBDEs) are a class of brominated chemicals used in electronic products to reduce flammability and the spread of fire. They are often found in computer housings, TV sets, kitchen appliances, cables, printed circuit boards, and other components. A growing number of studies in recent years show that PBDEs are steadily increasing in the environment and in humans (see Figure 1). In May 2004, the Clean Production Action and the Computer Take Back Campaign released the results from the first nationwide tests for brominated flame retardants in dust on computers. PBDEs were found on every one of the 16 computers sampled in various states (CPA, 2004). PBDE's structure is very similar to PCBs, which are known to cause thyroid hormone disruption. Similarities to PCBs also suggest that PBDEs may affect fetal brain and nervous system development resulting in learning and motor deficits in newborns (McDonald, 2002). The United States is currently using almost 98% of the penta-PBDE globally, the most toxic, persistent, and bioaccumulative PBDE, which explains why U.S. women have strikingly higher concentrations of PBDEs in their breast milk, when compared to European women (see Figure 1).

Main Sources of the Restricted Chemicals

While environmental controls have significantly improved over the past 20 years and emissions from manufacturing have declined, the problems with soil and ground-water contamination have continued to grow. The main reason for this is that about

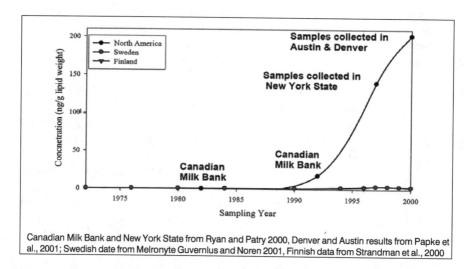

Canadian Milk Bank and New York State from Ryan and Patry 2000, Denver and Austin results from Papke et al., 2001; Swedish date from Melronyte Guvernlus and Noren 2001, Finnish data from Strandman et al., 2000

Figure 1. Comparison between concentrations of PBDEs in breast milk from North America and Europe (Blake, 2004).

95% of all toxic chemicals used today end up in the products and not in the manufacturing waste or emissions. These products make their way across the globe, and their disposal is largely unregulated. At the end of their useful lives, products are typically landfilled or incinerated. This leads to air pollution and soil and groundwater contamination, endangering drinking water supplies, fish, plants, and ultimately, human health.

In order to outline the magnitude of the problem with toxic chemicals, the Silicon Valley Toxics Coalition (SVTC) put together a background report on electronic waste (SVTC, 1999). An estimated 315 million computers will become obsolete in the United States by the end of 2004. Using data for the amounts of the toxic chemicals in an average computer monitor, the SVTC estimated that disposing of 315 million obsolete computers between 1997 and 2004 will generate about 1.2 billion pounds of lead, 2 million pounds of cadmium, 400,000 pounds of mercury, and about 1.2 million pounds of hexavalent chromium.

Americans are buying more computers than people in any other nation. Currently, more than 50% of the households in the United States own a computer. Despite the fast-growing industry, recycling is extremely low: In 1998, only 6% of older computers were recycled. The rest end up in peoples' basements, landfills, or get exported to Taiwan and China, where unprotected workers and sometimes even children collect scrap metal and burn the rest of the waste (Puckett et al., 2002). Computer models have estimated that toxic dioxin clouds,[3] created by electronic scrap incineration in China, can reach the U.S. East Coast in about a week.

To reduce the generation of toxics by the electronics manufacturers, two main environmental problems in the industry need to be addressed: the use of toxic chemicals and the large amounts of *electronic waste* generated, which were the main drivers for the recent global environmental regulations.

Use of toxic chemicals: In order to manufacture products such as computers, cell phones, and TVs, the electronics industry uses many chemicals that have good manufacturing characteristics but unfortunately are toxic, persistent, and/or bioaccumulative. Examples include lead, mercury, cadmium, hexavalent chromium, copper, PBDEs, and PVC, among others. These chemicals pose hazards to humans and the environment during extraction, processing, and manufacturing of final goods. During manufacturing, workers are exposed to toxic fumes and dust and may develop different occupational diseases, despite the presence of environmental controls such as local exhaust ventilation, training, and personal protection equipment. Some products pose hazards during use. Potential liabilities from exposure to toxic chemicals during manufacturing or product use are a serious business risk and thus a threat to shareholder value.

Electronic waste (e-waste): Electronic products are becoming an increasing part of the waste stream as consumers attempt to keep up with advancing technology. The

---

[3] Dioxins are a family of chemicals that are generated when burning PVC. They are some of the most toxic chemicals known, causing cancer, endocrine disruption, and developmental damage, among others.

rapid growth of consumer electronics sales in the past 15 years and the relatively short life span of these products are becoming major concerns for solid waste administrators. A manager at Lucent Technologies pointed out that the company used to design its products to last for 40 years; nowadays it designs them to last for only about 5-10 years (TURI, 2002). As a result, the pile of e-waste is growing fast. The EU estimates each person generates about 14 kg of e-waste per year for a total of 5 million tons per year. E-waste is growing three times faster than the average growth of all other waste (TURI, 2002). Due to their high population density, Japan and the EU were the first to face serious problems with e-waste. Electronic waste not only endangers the health of our communities, environment, and workers, but also indicates production inefficiencies. Instead of mining for new metals and raw materials, we could and should be recovering many valuable materials from electronic scrap.

Some of the regulations outlined in the next section refer to electronic waste problems, but the authors believe a considerable amount of literature and initiatives exists targeting recycling of electronics products both in the United States and abroad. Therefore, this research and the Citizens' survey aim to shed more light on the issue of toxic chemical use in electronic products and how suppliers are preparing to meet the global environmental regulations.

Global and Domestic Environmental Regulations

Global environmental regulations are driving changes in the electronics industry at a fast pace. Below are listed only a few of the recent international and domestic laws, which have been powerful drivers for change.

WEEE and RoHS: On February 19, 2003, the European Waste Electrical and Electronic Equipment (WEEE) Directive[4] and the Restrictions on Hazardous Substances (RoHS) Directive[5] were formally adopted as European law. European Union member states were obliged to implement the regulations by enacting national laws and enforcement mechanisms by August 13, 2004, and must start to enforce them in August 2005. Beginning July 1, 2006, the RoHS directive bans the use of six toxic chemicals: lead, mercury, cadmium, hexavalent chromium, penta-PBDE, and octa-PBDE in electronic and electrical equipment. The WEEE Directive requires manufacturers to assume responsibility for their products at the end of their useful lives, which will necessitate labeling, collection, and recycling of the old products. The EU has specific targets for recycling of the e-waste that have to be achieved by each of the member states. The ultimate goal of the directive is to make manufacturers improve the design of their products in order to avoid the generation of waste and

---

[4]Directive 2002/96/EC of the European Parliament and of the Council of 27 January 2003 on waste electrical and electronic equipment (WEEE):
http://europa.eu/legislation_summaries/environment/waste_management/121210_en.htm
[5]European Commission, Directive 2002/95/EC of the European Parliament and of the Council of 27 January 2003 on the restriction of the use of certain hazardous substances in electrical and electronic equipment (RoHS): http://ec.europa.eu/environment/waste/rohs_eee//legis_en.htm

promote easier disassembly and recycling of electronic scrap. As of August 13, 2004, only one EU country, Greece, had met the deadline to transpose the WEEE and RoHS directives into national legislation (European Commission, 2004). However, most other Member States are currently adopting legislation. The European Commission can open infringement procedures against Member States that do not meet transposition deadlines. More information and updates about the EU directives and their implementation can be found at http://europa.eu.int/comm/environment/waste/weee_index.htm.

Specified Home Appliances Recycling Law in Japan: With over 70% of electronic goods produced by Japanese manufacturers, it is not surprising that Japan was among the first countries to address the challenge. The Specified Home Appliances Recycling Law was enacted in 1998 and became fully enforced in 2001. The main driving forces behind the disposal ban on several main categories of household appliances were the scarcity of disposal sites, the increase of electrical and electronic equipment (EEE) in the waste stream, and the inadequacy of existing treatment plants to handle EEE. Under the program, manufacturers and importers of four large electrical home appliances (TVs, refrigerators, air conditioners, and washing machines) are required to take back the discarded products they manufactured and dismantle and recover the components and materials that can be reused or recycled (Greiner & Veleva, 2002). For computers and other large scale appliances not covered by this law, Japan enacted the Reused Law for Promotion of Effective Utilization of Resources, which requires manufacturers of computers, copy machines, and large electrical home appliances to design their products for disassembly, recycling, waste reduction, and "longevity of use" (repair, reuse, and recycling). Recent revisions of the law require producers to take back computers and appliances from commercial and institutional customers (IGES, 2009).

In 2003, China drafted a new law, Management Methods for Pollution Prevention and Control in the Production of Electronic Information Products, very similar to the European Union RoHS Directive. The law requires complete elimination of lead, cadmium, hexachrome, mercury, and penta- and octa-PBDEs from electronic products. The compliance deadline was July 1, 2003, however manufacturers were given a grace period until July 1, 2006, to fully comply. Chinese authorities announced that to enforce the law, they will use all possible means, including "nontraditional" ones, such as providing financial rewards to people who report cases of noncompliance (Industry Puzzles, 2003).

California Proposition 65 and Assembly Bill 302: In November 1986, California voters approved an initiative to address growing concerns about exposures to toxic chemicals. That initiative became the Safe Drinking Water and Toxic Enforcement Act of 1986, better known by its original name: Proposition 65. The Act requires the governor to publish a list of chemicals that are known to the state of California to cause cancer, birth defects, or other reproductive harm. Businesses are required to provide clear and reasonable warnings prior to knowingly and intentionally exposing individuals to chemicals that have been listed in Proposition 65, that is, they must label their toxic-containing products. Warnings are not required when the manufacturers can show that the toxics exposure occurs at a level that poses no significant risk of cancer.[6] Currently, many chemicals used in electronic products are on this list and are used at levels that may require labeling. For example, in 1999, the Mateel Environmental Justice Foundation (MEJF) sued Microsoft for violating Proposition 65 in its marketing of PVC-coated wire and cables. A series of lab tests revealed a sufficient amount of lead leaching from the wire and cables and other PVC-lead products during wire handling to require Prop 65 labeling. The case was settled and Microsoft agreed to pay a civil penalty of $65,000, label its products or reformulate them to contain less than 300 ppm lead (0.03%).[7] Since then, many more electronic manufacturers have been sued for not labeling toxics-containing products. To specifically address the concerns with brominated flame retardants, California passed a law in June 2003, Assembly Bill 302, which bans manufacturing, processing, or distributing products that contain penta-PBDE or octa-PBDE, effective in 2008. In addition, California has banned the landfill of CRTs and its recent SB 20 bill would require manufacturers to collect 50% of waste electronic cathode ray tubes or related devices by 2006 and increase this rate to 90% by 2010 (California Electronics, 2003).

Maine became the first state to ban all three PBDE flame retardants: penta-, octa-, and deca-. In April 2004, the governor signed a bill that bans penta- and octa-BDE by January 1, 2006, and deca-BDE by January 1, 2008. The governor also signed into law an electronic recycling bill, entitled "An Act To Protect Public Health and the Environment by Providing for a System of Shared Responsibility for the Safe Collection and Recycling of Electronic Waste." This bill will require manufacturers of electronic equipment to accept some of the responsibility for shipping and recycling their discarded products. The bill is expected to go into effect in the summer of 2004 and to require manufacturers to create consolidation centers by the beginning of 2006, where municipalities may drop off computers, television sets, and other types of electronic equipment (IFAI, 2004; Maine DEP, 2004).

A few other states have enacted similar electronics industry regulations. Massachusetts passed legislation that bans the disposal of discarded cathode ray tubes (CRTs) in landfills beginning January 1, 2004, because of their high lead content. Manufacturers have until July 1, 2005, to implement collection plans and have them approved by the Department of Environmental Protection. If they fail to do this, they will not be allowed to sell their products in the state. Washington State is moving toward a phase-out of all three PBDEs. New York and Wisconsin also are working toward legislation restricting the use of some toxic chemicals in electronic products (SVTC, n.d.). In March 2004, three U.S. Representatives introduced legislation in the U.S. Congress to ban penta- and octa-BDE nationwide (CPA, 2004).

---

[6] Proposition 65: http://www.oehha.ca.gov/prop65.html
[7] Superior Court of the State of California for the County of San Francisco, Amended Consent Judgment No. 313908, Mateel Environmental Justice Foundation vs. Microsoft Corporation, April 23, 2001.

Why is This Important for Electronic Suppliers and Shareholders?

The recently enacted environmental regulations will place new demands on the electronic equipment industry and require operational changes by producers. According to Mr. Harvey Stone, consultant with the GoodBye Chain Group,[8] this is "the biggest compliance issue the industry has ever faced." It could cost the electronics industry $1 billion to redesign products, and the effects would be most significant for smaller suppliers. Component suppliers that cannot provide heavy metal-free products will not be able to sell to their international OEMs, warns Mr. Stone (Raymond Communications, 2004). While these changes will clearly carry short term costs, they also present opportunities for market expansion and product differentiation.

The electronics industry is broadly organized into two main categories: components producers and original equipment manufacturers or OEMs. Components producers make the individual parts that go into consumer electronics products, such as integrated circuitry and processors. Familiar companies in this category include Texas Instruments and Intel. OEMs are the companies that assemble components into consumer electronic products and sell them under their own brand name, such as IBM or Dell computers.

The recent environmental regulations place the burden of action on the end-of-the-line electronics producers, that is, the OEMs. These companies rely heavily on brand name recognition and market share in the highly competitive consumer electronics industry. Exclusion from a market due to environmental regulations is a serious financial risk to OEMs. For example, in 2001, the Dutch government stopped a shipment of Sony PlayStations after discovering too much cadmium in a power cable polymer. This cost Sony about $160 million and damaged its retail channel and customer base (Smith, 2001). Studies have showed that up to 75% of a company's valuation may result from intangibles such as reputation, brand, trust, and credibility (BATE, 2004). As a result, OEMs have become particularly concerned with the toxic content of their products and the materials used by their suppliers. Motorola, Sony, Hitachi, Microsoft, and Dell, among others, have been working for several years now on redesigning their products to be lead-free and/or halogen-free.

The preparedness of electronics component manufacturers is less well known, and most of the toxics in electronics products enter the product life cycle at the components manufacturing level. Though the regulations specifically target the end-of-life consumer products manufacturers, the OEMs, compliance responsibility will be shared down the supply chain as OEMs pass these requirements to their suppliers. Such requirements would most likely include reporting and phase-out of restricted chemicals (e.g., cadmium, lead, and brominated flame retardants), labeling products, and designing parts for easy disassembly, reuse, and recycling. In some cases, OEMs may also require components suppliers to defray product end-of-life recovery costs.

---

[8]The GoodBye Chain Group is a consulting company specializing in RoHS compliance issues: http://www.goodbyechain.com

Compliance with the new environmental regulations and customer demands will require action by electronic component producers through research and development, manufacturing redesign, and recycling and recovery programs. These changes will carry some costs for the industry, at least in the short run. Toxic-free alternatives to current materials are generally more expensive. The European Commission estimates that the switch to tin-based solders, which are RoHS compliant, will cost the European electronics industry around $184 million per year in additional materials costs.[9] Component manufacturing equipment will require modification to accommodate the working properties of nontoxic alternative materials. For example, soldering machinery will need to produce higher temperatures to melt tin-based solder.

The cost of inaction, however, will certainly outweigh the cost of action. Companies will face fines and exclusion from markets if they do not take action to comply with the impending regulations. Noncompliance actions could be considerable, as was the case in the SONY example discussed earlier in this section. By far, the greatest cost associated with these environmental regulations and the greatest financial risk will be the possibility of market exclusion due to noncompliance. In 2003, Intel earned 23% of its revenues from sales in Europe and 9% from Japan, approximately $6.9 billion and $2.7 billion, respectively. In the same year, IBM earned 36% of its revenues from sales in Japan, approximately $29.1 billion.[10]

While the new demands placed on the electronics industry will result in some short-term costs, they also provide an opportunity for proactive companies to increase their market share. Companies that learn how to manufacture products that are less hazardous and easier to recycle will develop a competitive advantage, since their overall costs will be lower in the long run. As a result, some companies will see their earnings grow while others will face significant losses. The main question facing shareholders becomes, Is the company you have invested in an early adopter, mainstream, or laggard? Time is going by quickly and the deadline of July 2006 is approaching fast for the entire supply chain. The risks to companies and shareholders are very real and could be material. So are the opportunities. By deepening their understanding and initiating steps today, shareholders can protect their investments and increase shareholder value.

Are Companies Ready for the New Environmental Requirements?

To gain insight on the preparedness of electronic component manufacturers to meet the new environmental regulations, Citizens Advisers initiated a survey of 26 companies in the electronic component sector (see Appendix A). Companies with an

[9]UK Department of Trade and Industry (UK DTI), Partial Regulatory Impact Assessment on Directive 2002/95/EC of the European Parliament and of the Council on the Restriction of the Use of Certain Hazardous Substances in Electrical and Electronic Equipment, March 28, 2003: https://www.gov.uk/government/consultations/implementation-of-the-restriction-of-hazardous-substances-in-electrical-and-electronic-equipment-rohs-directive-2011-65-eu-consultation

[10]U.S. Securities and Exchange Commission (SEC): http://www.sec.gov/http://www.sec.gov/edgar/searchedgar/companysearch.html

industry classification of SIC 3674 (NAICS 334413) were selected from Citizens Funds' portfolios in January 2004. This SIC category encompasses the majority of consumer electronic components producers, whose customers include large OEMs such as HP, Microsoft, Dell, IBM, Sony, Samsung, Siemens, and Compaq. Component manufacturers often outsource in part or in full their manufacturing to contractors in Asia. This, however, does not relieve them of their responsibility under the new environmental regulations, as they need to certify that their products do not contain any of the restricted chemicals. Companies need to monitor their own suppliers to make sure they meet the requirements and provide all the necessary information on product chemical content. Many OEMs, such as Dell and Microsoft, are testing suppliers' products to verify compliance (see Text Boxes 1 and 2).

Citizens' Survey Results

Of the 26 companies contacted by Citizens Advisers, 12 responded to the survey (46%). Of the 12, three declined to provide information (25% of the respondents) and 9 completed and returned the questionnaire (75% of the respondents). A copy of the questionnaire is included in Appendix B. It was designed to be brief and take minimum time and effort to complete. In addition to the survey, Citizens Advisers conducted its own background research on the 26 selected companies by using publicly available information, such as companies' websites, environmental reports, and Securities and Exchange Commission (SEC) filings. Results from the survey and the background research are presented in Figure 2 and summarized below.

Awareness about the new environmental regulations

All of the companies that completed the survey stated that they were aware of the new environmental regulations; 62% of all companies in the sample provided information on their website or elsewhere about the requirements and their efforts to redesign products to phase out the toxic chemicals (see Figure 2). It is likely that many of the companies that did not respond are also aware of the new environmental regulations through industry associations and customer requests. Phone calls to companies revealed that in two cases, electronics suppliers thought they would not be affected by the new regulations, and therefore they might not be taking actions yet to redesign their products. The first case involves "fabless" manufacturers (who outsource production, mostly to Asia) and the second one, companies who sell mostly in the United States. In both cases, however, manufacturers will be affected by the new regulations since they operate in a global economy, where their customers, the large OEMs, want to sell the same products worldwide and not develop different products for different markets (see Text Boxes 1 and 2). Even if an outside contractor does the manufacturing, the company will still be required to certify that its products are free of the restricted chemicals.

Text Box 1
Dell's Approach

In its position on RoHS, Dell states that it understands the environmental risks associated with the targeted toxic chemicals and is committed to reduce their use and the use of other environmentally-sensitive substances in its products. It has a company-wide strategy to phase-out restricted chemicals before the July 2006 deadline. In 2002 the company launched a program for suppliers, where the latter are required to complete a *supplier declaration* for each new part provided to Dell. The declaration has two main sections: the first one includes substances banned for use in Dell's products (e.g. cadmium, hexavalent chromium, lead in paints, packaging, cables and connectors, halogenated flame retardants, except for printed circuit boards, cables, interconnected parts, non-TCO displays, printer fuser assemblies, and mercury except for lamps) and the second one – substances "under consideration" (e.g., antimony, arsenic, phthalates, and organic tin compounds). Collecting data on the substances in the second category would allow Dell to track chemicals that may be subject to future restrictions and thus be able to take proactive actions. "When our customers start demanding [RoHS-compliant or green products] and all our competitors are doing it, we don't have much choice," said Scott O'Connell, environmental program manager at Dell. The company plans to implement RoHS compliance in all its products sold worldwide, not just those for Europe.

Source: "Dell Restricted Materials Supply Chain Management Program", TURI Wire and Cable Supply Chain Workshop, March 23, 2004, http://www.turi.org/business/wire_and_cable.htm.

Text Box 2
Microsoft's Approach

The main goal of environmental compliance efforts at Microsoft is to maintain and expand market access for its products. In 2000 the company was sued for violating Proposition 65 in California for lead content in a cable product. Since then the company has been very active in ensuring compliance. This is not an easy process. Microsoft does not control its suppliers and it has a long supply chain with some six or seven levels of suppliers. Its pre-RoHS/WEEE compliance program includes testing for lead and cadmium in cables, requesting certificates of compliance for the other restricted substances, and completing materials disclosure declarations. In mid-2004 the company will launch a *compliance plan for all suppliers* with a deadline for implementation by early 2005. "Compliance violations are bad for the image, cost money, and undermine all other work," pointed out Joe Johnson, environmental regulatory manager at Microsoft. "If we do least today we'll have to do a lot tomorrow, and that is a big concern," said Mr. Johnson. On the question whether Microsoft is willing to pay more for the RoHS compliant and "green" products the answer was "probably not." "Suppliers are on their own and they need to plan for these changes, otherwise they will not be able to sell their products. The costs are high in the short-term but will go down in the long-term," explained Mr. Johnson.

Source: "Dell Restricted Materials Supply Chain Management Program", TURI Wire and Cable Supply Chain Workshop, March 23, 2004, http://www.turi.org/business/wire_and_cable.htm.

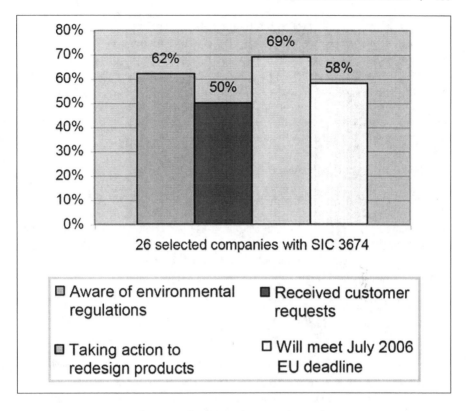

Figure 2. Survey and research results.

Customer Requests for RoHS-Compliant and Green Products

All of the companies that completed Citizens' survey mention that they had received requests from customers for green products. Combined with publicly available information, 50% of the 26 companies received requests for green products. Texas Instruments, for example, processes about 400 such requests each month. Most of the requests are for lead-free products. Many suppliers, such as Intel, are working with their customers to design and incorporate alternative materials. Japanese OEMs were among the first ones to request green products, with some U.S.-based corporations such as Dell and Microsoft beginning to make similar requests (see Text Boxes 1 and 2).

Action to redesign products

All of the companies that completed Citizens' survey are currently taking actions to redesign their products and phase out restricted chemicals. Overall, 69% of the 26 companies in the sample released information about such initiatives (e.g., lead-free, halogen-free products). It is not clear whether the remaining companies are not taking any action or are considering this information proprietary. Amkor Technology, for example, has been working for over 3 years to develop green products and considers its greening efforts to be proprietary information. Texas Instruments has had a lead-free initiative since the mid-1980s and has already manufactured over a billion lead-free products. Many companies already offer RoHS-compliant or green products in addition to their conventional products.

Timeline for toxic chemical phase out

Only 58% of the researched companies claimed that they will meet the July 1, 2006, deadline, established by the European Union Restriction of Hazardous Substances Directive (RoHS). All nine companies that completed Citizens' survey said they will meet this deadline. The majority of the survey respondents claimed that they are already fully prepared to offer RoHS-compliant and green products or will be ready in the near future, well before the EU deadline.

Major challenges in complying with the new environmental requirements

Two thirds of the survey respondents pointed out the lack of harmonized regulatory language as a key challenge. There are different regulatory requirements in the different regions, and the allowable values for the restricted chemicals are not specified yet. For example, lead is a naturally existing chemical in many materials and reaching a threshold of zero would be technically not feasible. An allowable limit of 100 ppm is a more realistic one. Regulators have also not defined clearly what a green product is and what are its standardized technical characteristics, such as peak reflow temperature, moisture sensitivity, and flammability. Customers are often unclear about what is needed and what the exemptions are. They often have different timelines for incorporating the changes, and not all of them are currently able to adjust production processes to use the new green products. Suppliers, however, cannot afford to make different products for different markets. Collecting the necessary data for qualifying the new products is another major challenge. Industry associations have been working diligently to harmonize both the regulatory requirements and reporting practices among electronics manufacturers. A couple of respondents mentioned technical difficulties as a serious challenge-for some applications there are currently no technically feasible toxic-free alternatives.

Cost estimates

In many cases, cost data are compiled on an individual-product basis, making it difficult to generalize compliance costs for all products. One company disclosed that their green products will have on average about a 5% "cost adder." Five of the nine companies that completed the survey mentioned that there will be a small "price adder" for RoHS-compliant and green products, at least in the beginning, but it will depend on the volumes ordered, time for delivery, and other market forces. Most companies admit that compliance costs are "not trivial" and "very significant," but they are working very hard to offset these costs with efficiency gains or by collaborating with their suppliers to avoid price increases. Large customers, such as Dell and Microsoft, are asking for green products at no price increase (see Text Boxes 1 and 2). Suppliers who have not begun to work toward compliance will face high costs and possible market exclusion after July 1, 2006.

What Can Shareholders Do?

Electronic products permeate almost every aspect of our modern lives, from home to school to work. Exposure to toxic chemicals in electronic equipment has become a serious environmental and health concern. As discussed in this chapter, there are numerous government initiatives designed to reduce toxics in electronic equipment; investors, however, can take action on their own.

For investors whose portfolios include electronics manufacturers, learning about the new environmental requirements and how companies are responding to them is a way to avoid risk and ensure long-term financial returns. Financial advisers may not always be familiar with changes in the regulatory climate for a particular sector. In February 2004, a *Financial Times* article warned that "the world's biggest tech manufacturers will soon feel the force of European directives on hardware disposal" (Harvey, 2004). According to the author, the cost or recycling could add $50 to the cost of a desktop PC; avoiding hazardous materials would cost an additional $10 per PC. The author concludes that "the future of PC manufacturers may lie in the taking of a more innovative approach to environmental concerns." And this is true for many other electronic products affected by the new global environmental requirements.

A good first step for any investor is to learn more about toxics-reduction initiatives both in the investor's local area and at the companies currently held or targeted for investment. There are numerous nonprofit organizations dedicated to toxics reduction in industry with well-maintained websites. Two respected organizations, which provide a starting point for learning about toxics reduction and recycling in the electronics industry, are the Silicon Valley Toxics Coalition (SVTC: www.svtc.com) and the Toxics Use Reduction Institute (TURI: www.turi.org).

As partial owners, shareholders have a direct link to the way electronic manufacturing companies are managed. Investors can use their position to engage companies in one of several ways. They can contact management by writing or calling them to find out whether the company is taking action to meet the new environmental requirements. This may include expressing a shareholder's position and reminding management that these new requirements provide an opportunity to differentiate from competitors and increase the company's market share.

Shareholders can go a step further and file a shareholder resolution to encourage compliance and greater disclosure of a company's actions in phasing out the restricted toxic chemicals. If filing a resolution is not feasible, voting in favor of other shareholders' resolutions that call for proactive toxics reduction and recycling action is another option. The socially responsible investment community has been active in the past several years in filing and supporting toxics reduction and recycling proposals. Reading through such proposals on the proxy statement and voting in support of those encouraging product redesign to phase out toxics and promote recycling is another way to use shareholder power to help protect the environment, human health, and shareholder value. This is also an excellent opportunity to make new informed investment choices that can result in good long-term financial returns.

CONCLUSION

Requirements to address toxics use in the electronics industry are growing worldwide. Beginning July 1, 2006, the European Union will ban the manufacturing and import of consumer electronic products that contain any of the following chemicals: lead, cadmium, mercury, hexavalent chromium, penta-BDE, and octa-BDE. Many other major markets such as Japan, California, and China have also initiated similar restrictions. In the remaining time, the electronic component manufacturers will have to make considerable efforts to ensure compliance. OEMs are expected to demand RoHS-compliant and green products from their suppliers at no price increase, thus further increasing the challenges faced by the electronic component producers. Some companies will benefit from these changes; others will be left behind.

Citizens' research on the issue has shown that the industry is largely aware of the novel environmental regulations and is taking action to address the issue of toxic chemicals. The effort, however, is not uniform. Some companies have already incorporated all necessary changes and can provide compliant products at low or no additional cost to their customers. Others are still working on changing their materials and manufacturing processes. Some do not provide any information on the issue and may not have begun to work toward compliance. Major challenges faced by companies include the lack of harmonized regulatory language, customer demands, and technical specifications for the RoHS-compliant and green products. The longer a company waits to make the shift, the higher the costs to both the company and its shareholders. The cost of compliance is not trivial, according to survey respondents, but the risks of noncompliance are far more significant. Fines, market exclusion, and damaged reputation could adversely affect the bottom line. On the other hand, proactive toxics management and product redesign could allow a company to diversify its products from its competitors and thus increase its market position and long-term value. By educating themselves and encouraging companies' disclosure and proactive environmental management, shareholders can play a vital role in protecting the environment, human health, and shareholder value.

ACKNOWLEDGMENTS

The authors would like to thank Citizens Advisers for supporting this research and Ms. Joanne Dowdell, Director of Corporate Responsibility, for her valuable contribution.

APPENDIX A:
LIST OF SURVEYED COMPANIES

Companies selected for the survey include semiconductor and related devices manufacturers, which Citizens held in its portfolios in January 2004. They all are classified under the Standard Industrial Classification systems (SIC) as SIC 3674 and under the North American Industrial Classification System (NAICS) as NAICS 334413.

Company Name	Ticker
1. Amkor Technology Inc.	AMKR
2. Analog Devices Inc.	ADI
3. Applied Micro Circuits Corp.	AMCC
4. Broadcom Corp.	BRCM
5. Conexant Systems Inc.	CNXT
6. Fairchild Semiconductor Corp.	FCS
7. Integrated Circuit Systems	ICST
8. Intel Corp.	INTC
9. Intersil Corp.	ISIL
10. International Rectifier Corp.	IRF
11. Linear Technology Corp.	LLTC
12. LSI Logic Corp.	LSI
13. Marvell Technology Group Ltd.	MRVL
14. Maxim Integrated Products Inc.	MXIM
15. Microchip Technology Inc.	MCHP
16. Microtune Inc.	TUNE
17. National Semiconductor Corp.	NSM
18. Nvidia Corp.	NVDA
19. Omnivision Technologies Inc.	OVTI
20. Qlogic Corp.	QLGC
21. Skyworks Solutions Inc.	SWKS
22. Standard Microsystems Corp.	SMSC
23. Texas Instruments Inc.	TXN
24. Trident Microsystems Inc.	TRID
25. Vitesse Semiconductor Corp.	VTSS
26. Xilinx Inc.	XLNX

APPENDIX B:
NEW ENVIRONMENTAL REGULATIONS FOR THE ELECTRONICS
INDUSTRY-A MANUFACTURER SURVEY

New environmental regulations on the electronics industry have been enacted in most major electronics markets, including the European Union, Japan, Taiwan, China, California, and a few other U.S. states. These regulations ban the use of hazardous substances such as lead, cadmium, mercury, and PBDEs in electronics products, and require producers to assume responsibility for end-of-life recovery and recycling of their products.

The purpose of this survey is to gather information on the preparedness of electronics producers for these new environmental regulations, the main challenges currently, and what this all means for shareholders. Your participation in this survey will provide valuable information on the effects of these regulations on the producer side of the electronics industry.

1. Are you aware of the following environmental regulations, which will affect the electronics industry?
   - The EU Restriction of Hazardous Substances Directive (RoHS)
   - The EU Waste Electrical and Electronic Equipment Directive (WEEE)
   - California toxics regulations (e.g., Prop 65 and Assembly Bill 302)
   - MA, ME, MN electronics waste regulations
   - Japan, Taiwan, China, and other Asian countries' toxic waste regulations and initiatives

2. Have you received requests from your customers for "greener" electronics products?

3. Is your company currently taking actions to redesign your products and/or prepare for end-of life recovery obligations to meet these environmental regulations?

4. If so, do you have a timeline for implementing the necessary product changes and end-of-life efforts? WEEE and RoHS, for example, will come into force in July, 2006.

5. What do you feel are the major challenges for your company in complying with these new environmental regulations for the electronics industry?

6. Has your company estimated the costs of compliance to these regulations?

Disclaimer

If you do not want your company's name to be disclosed in connection with this survey, please check the "do not disclose my company's name" box below.

☐ Do not disclose my company's name.

DISCUSSION QUESTIONS

Chapter 7: The Electronics Industry in a New Regulatory Climate: Protecting the Environment and Shareholder Value

1. How do electronics industry products affect the environment and human health (consider the impacts over their full life-cycle—from extraction, to production, transportation and final disposal)?
2. What are the main global and domestic regulations driving changes in the electronics industry? Analyze their impact on the electronics industry, human health and the environment.
3. How are shareholders driving environmental responsibility and product stewardship in the electronics industry? Research and report on a recent shareholder resolution at an electronics company using the Investor Environmental Health Network website (http://www.iehn.org/resolutions.shareholder.php). Why are investors concerned about these issues?

REFERENCES

Blake, A., Brominated Flame Retardants in Consumer Products: Health and Environmental Concerns, Northwest Hazardous Waste Conference, April 13, 2004, http://www.ecy.wa.gov/programs/swfa/mrw/pdf/Presentations/Ann%20Blake%20Brominated%20Flame%20Retardants.pdf

Business and the Environment (BATE). (2004). *Managing Mega Risks, 15*(5), 1-4.

California Electronics Take Back Bill Clears Two Policy Committees. (2003, July). *Recycling Laws International, 12*(7).

Clean Production Action (CPA) and Computer Take Back Campaign (CTBC), Brominated Flame Retardants in Dust on Computers, June 2004, http://www.electronicstakeback.com/wp-content/uploads/bfr_report_pages1-43

Environmental Defense (EDF). (2002). *Scorecard*. Retrieved from http://www.scorecard.org

Environmental Protection Agency (EPA) (n.d. a). *Integrated risk information system (IRIS)*. Retrieved from http://www.epa.gov/iris/

Environmental Protection Agency (EPA). (n.d. b). America's Children and the Environment: Third Edition, http://www.epa.gov/ace/biomonitoring/mercury.html

European Commission. (2004, August 13). *Electronic waste: Two important directives due to be implemented in EU member states* [Press release IP/04/1033]. Retrieved from http://europa.eu/rapid/press-release_IP-04-1033_en.htm

Greiner, T., & Veleva, V. (2002, April). Environmental, health and safety issues in the coated wire and cable industry. Technical Report No. 51. *Toxics Use Reduction Institute*. Retrieved from http://www.turi.org/TURI_Publications/TURI-Technical-Reports/Environmental_Health_and_Safety_Issues_in_the_Coated_Wire_and_Cable_Industry._20022

Harvey, F. (2004, February 4). PC makers set to face costs of recycling. *Financial Times*, p. 9.

Industrial Fabrics Association International (IFAI). (2004). *Maine moves to ban flame retardant*. Retrieved from http://www.ifai.com/NewsDetails.php?ID=2005

Industry Puzzles Over China WEEE Draft. (2003, July/August). *Recycling Laws International, 9*(4), 1.

Institute for Global Environmental Studies, Extended Product Responsibility Policies in East Asia, 2009, http://pub.iges.or.jp/modules/envirolib/upload/2607/attach/i-xiv.pdf

McDonald, T. (2002). A Perspective on the Potential Health Risks of PBDEs. *Chemosphere,* *46*, 745-755.

Puckett, J., Byster, L., Westervelt, S., Gutierrez, R., Davis, S., Hussain, A., & Dutta, M. (2002, February 25). *Exporting harm: The high-tech trashing of Asia.* Retrieved from http://www.ban.org/E-waste/technotrashfinalcomp.pdf

Maine Department of Environmental Protection, Electronics Recycling, 2014, http://www.maine.gov/dep/waste/ewaste/index.html Raymond Communications. (2004, June 28). *RoHS implementation called a "disaster."* Retrieved from http://www.raymond.com/

Silicon Valley Toxics Coalition (SVTC). (1999). Poison PCs and Toxic TVs: California's biggest environmental crisis that you've never heard of, 2004, Retrieved from http://svtc.org/wp-content/uploads/ppc-ttv1.pdf

Silicon Valley Toxics Coalition (SVTC). (n.d.) *Our Work.* Retrieved from http://svtc.org/our-work/

Smith, T. (2001, December 5). Dutch officials seize cadmium-packed PlayStation kit. The Register. Retrieved from http://www.theregister.co.uk/2001/12/05/dutch_officials_seize_cadmiumpacked_playstation/

Toxics Use Reduction Institute (TURI). (2001, June). Wire and Cable Supply Chain Meeting. Worcester, MA. Retrieved from http://www.turi.org/content/content/view/full/1294

Toxics Use Reduction Institute (TURI). (2002, June). Wire and Cable Supply Chain Meeting, Marlborough, MA. Retrieved from http://www.turi.org/content/content/view/full/1257

UPDATE ON CHAPTER 7: THE ELECTRONICS INDUSTRY IN A NEW REGULATORY CLIMATE: PROTECTING THE ENVIRONMENT AND SHAREHOLDER VALUE

As of 2014, U.S. electronics manufacturers selling globally had achieved compliance with the Restrictions on Hazardous Substances (RoHS) and Waste Electrical and Electronic Equipment (WEEE) Directives of the European Union without suffering negative impacts on performance or profits.

While no federal mandates similar to WEEE and RoHS have been enacted in the United States, a growing number of states have moved to pass similar laws. As of May 2014, 23 states had product take-back mandates (PSI, 2014). California became the first U.S. state to pass a RoHS legislation in 2007 banning the use of some toxic substances in electronic devices (CDTSC, 2010).

The European Union passed an update on the RoHS directive in January 2013 - The Restriction of Hazardous Substances Directive 2011/65/EU (RoHS2). RoHS2 covered two previously exempt product categories - medical/electrical equipment (Category 8) and monitoring and control instruments (Category 9) (Omega, 2014). The EU also conducted assessment of the costs and benefits of RoHS and WEEE directive implementation (RSJ Consulting, 2008). U.S. companies have continued to track and comply with the new mandates. For example, in 2013 PerkinElmer was actively working to comply with RoHS2 which will impact some of its medical instruments and monitoring devices in 2016 and 2017, respectively (Veleva et al., 2013).

Investors, in particular those working with the Investor Environmental Health Network (IEHN), have recognized the industry compliance with RoHS and WEEE and moved to engage primarily with retailers such as Amazon, Best Buy and AT&T

around safer chemicals policies and recycling (IEHN, 2014). A 2013 study in California found that as a result of the state ban on PBDEs and the industry voluntary phase out in the United States, the blood levels of these chemicals in pregnant women dropped significantly (Kurtzman, 2013).

REFERENCES

California Department of Toxic Substances Control. "Restrictions on the use of certain hazardous substances (RoHS) in electronic devices." 2010. Retrieved from https://dtsc.ca.gov/HazardousWaste/RoHS.cfm

Investor Environmental Health Network (IEHN), Shareholder resolutions, 2014, Retrieved from http://www.iehn.org/resolutions.shareholder.php

Kurtzman, L., Flame retardants in pregnant women's blood drop significantly after state ban, University of California at San Francisco, Retrieved from http://www.ucsf.edu/news/2013/09/109061/flame-retardants-blood-drop-after-state-ban

Omega, Restriction on Hazardous Substances RoHS2, 2014, Retrieved from http://www.omega.com/rohs/index.html

Premier Farnell, RoHS2 (Updated): How will it impact you, December 2008, Retrieved from http://uk.farnell.com/images/en_UK/rohs/pdf/rohs2_updated_ec.pdf

Product Stewardship Institute, Electronics, 2014, Retrieved from http://productstewardship.site-ym.com/?page=Electronics

RSJ Consulting, "EU studies RoHS costs and benefits," 2008, Retrieved from http://www.rsjtechnical.com/NewsRoHScost&benefit.htm

Veleva, V., Montanari, A., Clabby P. and J. Lese, "PerkinElmer: Old Instrument Reuse and Re-cycling," Richard Ivey School of Business Publishing, January 2013, Case # 9B12M115.

Chapter 8

NEW EU RULES FOR THE COSMETICS INDUSTRY: WHAT DO THEY MEAN FOR U.S. COMPANIES AND STAKEHOLDERS?[1]

OVERVIEW

On February 27, 2003, the European Union adopted Directive 2003/15/EEC,[2] which bans the use of substances identified as carcinogens, mutagens, or reproductive toxins (CMRs) in cosmetic products. EU Member States had until October 1, 2004, to transpose the directive into their national legislation; the directive entered into force in the spring of 2005. This new, precautionary[3] approach to cosmetics products, with the goal of protecting human health and the environment, will have far reaching

---

[1] Reprinted from: Veleva V., "New EU Rules for the Cosmetics Industry: What do They Mean for U.S. Companies and Stakeholders?" Corporate Environmental Strategy: International Journal for Sustainable Business, Vol. 12, Issues 3 & 4 (April-May 2005), by permission of the publisher Netlogex, LLC. © 2005 NetLogex, LLC.

[2] European Commission, Cosmetics Legislation Updates, Directive 2003/15/EEC of the European Parliament and of the Council of February 27, 2003, amending Council Directive 76/768/EEC on the approximation of the laws of the Member States relating to cosmetics products: http://eu.vlex.com/vid/approximation-laws-relating-cosmetic-37779602

[3] The precautionary principle is a key principle of European environmental law. Found in the Treaty Establishing the European Community Art. 174 2., the principle provides that when there are threats of serious or irreversible damage, lack of full scientific certainty should not be used as a reason for postponing cost-effective measures to prevent environmental degradation (Agenda 21, Principle 15): http://www.un.org/documents/ga/conf151/aconf15126-1annex1.htm. One American writer has gone so far as to say that "This relatively new term is the most radical idea for rethinking humanity's relationship to the natural world since the 18th century European Enlightenment" (Rifkin, 2004). In 2001, the EU Court of First Instance said that the precautionary principle allows public authorities to act "even before any adverse effects have become apparent." *Pfizer Animal Health SA v Council of the European Union*, Case T-13/99 [2002] ECR II-3305, decided September 11, 2002; see http://curia.europa.eu/juris/showPdf.jsf?docid=104172&doclang=EN

consequences for the global cosmetics industry. First, companies that sell to the 25 Member States will have to remove all restricted chemicals from their products if they want to continue to sell their products to existing markets and customers. Second, consumer groups and NGOs worldwide will demand safer cosmetics products in their own countries. Third, shareholders will be concerned with potential liabilities from identified CMRs and will push for global reformulation. This chapter introduces the new EU directive and compares it to the current U.S. regulations regarding cosmetics. It concludes with discussion on what this means for U.S. companies, their consumers, and shareholders.

The Personal Care and Cosmetics Products Industry

Personal care and cosmetics products are a big business in the United States and worldwide. The $35 billion U.S. industry has introduced tens of thousands of products in the market that promise to reduce wrinkles, soften skin, eliminate spots, or make hair, lips, or eyes shinier. Surveys show that the average U.S. adult uses nine personal care products each day, which combined contain about 126 ingredients. Over 25% of women and 1% of men use 15 or more products each day.[4] With baby boomers reaching their mid-40s and 50s, the personal care and cosmetics industry will continue to grow. Each day, new formulations are introduced in the market, but are they properly regulated to ensure consumers' health and safety? This chapter aims to shed more light on this topic and particularly on the recent European Union Cosmetics Directive, which will affect the industry worldwide.

The EU Cosmetics Directive

Adopted in February 2003 by the European Union, Directive 2003/15/EEC bans the use of chemicals classified as carcinogens, mutagens, and reproductive toxins (CMRs). Article 4b of the directive states, "The use in cosmetic products of substances classified as carcinogenic, mutagenic or toxic for reproduction, or category 1, 2 and 3, under Annex I to Directive 67/548/EEC shall be prohibited." This means that no company will be allowed to market or sell products containing any of the restricted chemicals in the 25-country European Union.

Currently, the list of restricted chemicals includes over 1,000 substances.[5] These substances are classified in three categories by the Dangerous Substances Directive 67/548/EEC. A Category 1 classification means the substance is a *proven* hazard to humans, while Category 2 means the substance is a *probable* hazard (two independent animal tests have shown the product is not safe for use). Category 3 refers to *possible* hazards and includes substances for which only very limited hazard information is available. The new cosmetics directive bans all Category 1

---

[4]Environmental Working Group, Cosmetics Research, 2004: http://www.ewg.org/skindeep/
[5]These are listed in Annex II and Annex III of Directive 76/768/EEC, amended by Commission Directive 2004/93/EC on September 21, 2004: http://eur-lex.europa.eu/legal-content/EN/ALL/?uri=CELEX:32003L0015

and 2 CMRs but allows some Category 3 CMRs to be exempt if the EU Scientific Committee on Cosmetic Products and Non-Food Products (SCCPNFP) evaluated them and found them to be safe for use. As of May 2004, five Category 3 CMRs were submitted for risk assessment and are currently under review for potential exemption from the list: acetaldehyde, 4-aminophenol, furfural, glyoxal, and octa-methyltetrasiloxane.[6] The remainder of the Category 3 CMRs are either banned or allowed with some restrictions.

As a result of the new rules, some of the commonly used ingredients in cosmetic products such as diethylhexyl phthalate (DEHP) and dibutyl phthalate (DBP) (both used in nail polish) and coal tar (used in shampoos and hair dyes) are now banned by the directive. DEHP and DBP are associated with developmental and reproductive disorders and coal tar is a proven carcinogen.

The directive also bans testing of cosmetic ingredients on animals as well as the sale of cosmetics that have been tested on animals in the 25-country European Union. The animal testing ban will go into effect in 2009. American and other global corporations that sell cosmetic and personal care products to the European Union will have to implement alternative testing methods if they want to continue to sell their products in the EU marketplace.

Cosmetics Regulations in the United States

In the United States, cosmetic products are regulated under the Federal Food, Drug and Cosmetics Act (FD&C Act) and the Fair Packaging and Labeling Act (FPLA). The FD&C Act does not require cosmetic manufacturers or marketers to test their products for safety before bringing them to the market. With the exception of color additives and a few prohibited ingredients, "a cosmetic manufacturer may, on its own responsibility, use essentially any raw material as a cosmetic ingredient and market the product without approval."[7] The Act "strongly urges" cosmetic manufacturers to conduct toxicological and other tests for safety of their products but does not require them to do so. The FDA typically begins an investigation into the safety concerns of a cosmetic product or ingredient only after it has been placed on the market.

The organization that periodically reviews scientific information regarding cosmetic ingredients and products in the United States is the Cosmetics Ingredient Review (CIR) Panel,[8] an independent group of academics, physicians, and scientists. The CIR panel was established in 1976 with funding from the Cosmetic, Toiletry and Fragrance Association (CTFA), U.S. Food & Drug Administration, and the Consumer Federation of America. The group meets 3 or 4 times each year to

---

[6]Scientific Committee on Cosmetic Products and Non-Food Products Intended for Consumers (SCCPNFP), "Opinion concerning chemical ingredients in cosmetic products classified as carcinogenic, mutagenic or toxic to reproduction according to the Chemicals Directive 67/548/EEC."

[7]Federal Drug Administration, Cosmetics, http://www.fda.gov/cosmetics/default.htm

[8]Cosmetics Ingredient Review: http://www.cir-safety.org/

review different chemicals in cosmetics. Since its establishment, the CIR panel has classified nine[9] chemicals as unsafe for use in cosmetics. This is in addition to the nine[10] chemicals banned or restricted by the FDA since it was established in 1927.

Recent Cosmetic Safety Initiatives

In 2004, the Campaign for Safe Cosmetics, a coalition of health and environmental groups, issued the "Compact for the Global Production of Safe Health and Beauty Products."[11] The compact is a pledge by manufacturers to reformulate globally following the EU standards and to introduce a rigorous system for evaluation and public reporting on cosmetics ingredients safety. In March 2005, a state legislator in California introduced a bill that would ban two phthalates (DBP and DEHP), which have been linked to birth defects and reproductive disorders, and which the EU has already banned (Beauty, 2005). In February 2005, the FDA sent a letter to the Cosmetic, Toiletry and Fragrance Association announcing that it has made cosmetic safety a top priority for 2005.[12]

Implications for U.S. Companies and Consumers

According to the "Skin Deep" report[13] published in 2004 by the Environmental Working Group (EWG), 89% of 10,500 ingredients used in personal care products have not been evaluated for safety by the CIR, the FDA, or any other publicly accountable institution. Only 28 of the 7,500 products analyzed by the group have been fully assessed for safety by the CIR; the rest of the products (99.6%) contained one or more ingredients that were never evaluated for their potential health impacts. On the U.S. market, 1 of every 120 products contains ingredients certified by government authorities as known or probable human carcinogens. For example, the International Agency for Research on Cancer (IARC) has classified coal tar as a proven carcinogen, yet 71 hair-dye products examined by the EWG contained ingredients derived from coal tar. Nearly 70% of all 7,500 evaluated products contain impurities that can be linked to cancer or other health problems. The EWG is currently updating its findings and is expected to release a new version of the Skin Deep report in the fall of 2005.

---

[9] The nine chemicals are chloroacetamide, ethoxyethanol and ethoxyethanol acetate, HC Blue No. 1, p-hydroxyanisole, 4-methoxy-m-phenylenediamine, 4-methoxy-m-phenylenediamine hydrochloride, 4-methoxy-m-phenylenediamine sulfate, and pyrocatechol: http://www.cir-safety.org/sites/default/files/U-unsafe062013.pdf

[10] The banned or restricted ingredients are bithionol, mercury compounds, vinyl chloride, halogenated salicylanilides, zirconium complexes in aerosol cosmetics, chloroform, methylene chloride, chlorofluorocarbon propellants, and hexachlorophene: http://www.fda.gov/Cosmetics/GuidanceRegulation/LawsRegulations/ucm127406.htm

[11] Campaign For Safe Cosmetics: http://www.safecosmetics.org/

[12] The FDA letter can be found at http://static.ewg.org/files/FDA2CTFA_letter.pdf; see also FDA to Investigate, 2005.

[13] Environmental Working Group, Skin Deep Cosmetics Database: http://www.ewg.org/skindeep/

With the growing awareness about the potential health effects of cosmetic and personal care products and the recent EU legislation, there will be growing pressure on U.S. companies to reexamine and reformulate their products in order to eliminate unsafe ingredients. According to the vice president of the Cosmetic, Toiletry and Fragrance Association, the EU cosmetics directive "if unaltered, could have a significant impact on the cosmetics industry."[14]

Socially responsible investors, such as Citizens Advisers, Domini Social Investments, and Trillium Asset Management, have already initiated a dialogue with about a half dozen U.S. corporations to encourage global reformulation to EU standards as a way to protect both public health and shareholder value. With growing scientific evidence of the adverse health effects of some cosmetics ingredients, companies may face lawsuits and liabilities, market exclusion, and damaged reputation.

In this climate of emerging scientific evidence about the health effects of toxic chemicals at low concentrations and growing regulatory and public pressures, several companies, such as Revlon, L'Oreal, and Unilever, already announced they have eliminated phthalates and other ingredients of concern so that all their products sold worldwide conform to the European standards. Proactive companies will be in a better position to gain market share not only in the EU but also in all markets that later enact similar regulations. They may also avoid fines, costly litigation, and damaged reputation. The longer a company waits to reformulate, the higher the cost of compliance will be—a key lesson from the electronics industry experience with EU environmental regulations on materials restrictions and product take-back (Veleva & Sethi, 2004). Instead of lobbying or waiting until new regulation is passed or additional chemicals are restricted for use, cosmetic and personal care manufacturers should have their own system in place to periodically review and phase out ingredients of concern.[15] This could be a key approach to build a competitive advantage in an industry that has been struggling to find new markets and opportunities for growth.

CONCLUSION

With the increasing publicity about and awareness of some negative health effects of cosmetics and personal care products, consumers will demand safer products. With the EU cosmetics legislation paving the way, American consumers will demand the same level of safety as Europeans. Companies that do not reformulate their products globally to the highest (in this case EU) safety standards could face reduced market demand, potential liabilities, and damaged reputation, which would ultimately hurt their bottom line. At the same time, the EU directive provides an opportunity for proactive corporations to move ahead with new products and gain a market share in a global economy where no market exists in isolation and where, with the power of the Internet, consumers are better informed than ever before.

---

[14] *Chemical Regulations Reporter,* 26(47), December 2, 2002.

[15] One valuable tool for businesses committed to identifying safer alternatives to toxic chemicals is the benchmarking framework developed by Richard Liroff (2005).

ACKNOWLEDGMENTS

The author would like to thank Citizens Advisers for supporting this research and Ms. Joanne Dowdell, Vice President of Social Responsibility and Marketing, for her valuable contribution.

DISCUSSION QUESTIONS

Chapter 8: New EU Rules for the Cosmetics Industry: What Do They Mean for U.S. Companies and Stakeholders?

1. How do European Union policies for the cosmetics industry differ from these in the United States? What is the basis for some of the differences?
2. What is the European Union Directive 2003/15/EEC and how has it affected companies in the United States?
3. How are shareholders driving development of safer cosmetics and personal care products in the U.S. even with a lack of significant regulatory action by the U.S. Food and Drug Administration (FDA)? Research and report on a recent shareholder resolution at a cosmetics company using the Investor Environmental Health Network website (http://www.iehn.org/resolutions.shareholder.php). Why are investors concerned about these issues?

REFERENCES

Beauty and the Beast. (2005, March 17). *The Hartford Advocate*.

FDA to Investigate Safety of Cosmetics. (2005, April 8). *Baltimore Sun*.

Liroff, R. (2005, January/February). Benchmarking corporate management of safer chemicals in consumer products—A tool for investors and senior executives. *Corporate Environmental Strategy: International Journal for Sustainable Business, 12*(1), 25–36.

Rifkin, J. (2004, May 12). Analysis: A precautionary tale. *The Guardian*.

Veleva V., & Sethi, S. (2004, October). The electronics industry in a new regulatory climate: Protecting the environment and shareholder value. *Corporate Environmental Strategy: International Journal for Sustainable Business, 11*(9), 207–225.

UPDATE TO CHAPTER 8: NEW EU RULES FOR THE COSMETICS INDUSTRY: WHAT DO THEY MEAN FOR U.S. COMPANIES AND STAKEHOLDERS?

As of May 2014, there was still no federal regulation in the United States similar to the EU cosmetics directive, which had banned the use of more than 1,100 substances in cosmetics and personal care products. However, momentum was building around enacting a new law - *The Safe Cosmetics and Personal Care Products Act of 2013 (H.R. 1385)*. The legislation was first introduced in 2010 as the Safe Cosmetics and Personal Care Act of 2010 (H.R.5786) but did not pass and was subsequently revised in 2011 and 2013. States continue to lead the efforts to restrict the use of toxic chemicals in cosmetics and personal care products.

California, Oregon, Connecticut and Washington had either passed or in a process of passing such laws (Safer States, 2012).

Investors continued to engage with cosmetics and personal care manufacturers and retailers around safer chemicals policies and elimination of substances restricted by the EU cosmetics directive. Some of the notable achievements over the past several years include:

- After several shareholder resolutions CVS published a safe cosmetics policy in 2008 (IEHN, 2014);
- Johnson & Johnson agreed to reformulate many of its cosmetic and toiletry products to remove toxic or cancer-causing ingredients such as formaldehyde, triclosan, diethyl phthalate and parabens, among others (EWG, 2012);
- Walmart committed to target 10 toxic chemicals for removal from products sold in its stores (Campaign for Safe Cosmetics, 2012).

The increasing use of nanotechnology in cosmetics and personal care products, in particular nano-engineered titanium dioxide and zinc oxide, have led to concerns among regulators, investors and NGOs as emerging studies have revealed potential risks to consumers. Investors have been pressing companies like Avon to disclose the use of nanomaterials in their products as well as establish a policy for safer use of nanotechnology. The European Union has moved to regulate nanotechnology under the EU Cosmetics Directive (European Commission, 2013). For more information on the use of nanomaterials in cosmetics and personal care products see Chapter 5.

REFERENCES

Campaign for Safe Cosmetics, Walmart Will No Longer Sell Cosmetics, Cleaners, Made with Targeted List of Toxic Chemicals, September 12, 2013, http://safecosmetics.org/article.php?id=1157

Environmental Working Group (EWG), Johnson & Johnson Takes a Big Step in the Right Direction, August 17, 2012, http://www.ewg.org/enviroblog/2012/08/johnson-johnson-takes-big-step-right-direction-0

European Commission, Cosmetics containing nanomaterials, 2013, http://ec.europa.eu/consumers/sectors/cosmetics/cosmetic-products/nanomaterials/index_en.htm

Govtrack.us, H.R. 1385: Safe Cosmetics and Personal Care Products Act of 2013, March 2013, http://www.govtrack.us/congress/bills/113/hr1385

Investor Environmental Health Network, Shareholder Resolutions, 2014, http://www.iehn.org/resolutions.shareholder.php

Safer States, States lead the fight against toxic chemicals lurking in cosmeters, March 2012, http://www.saferstates.com/2012/03/cosmetics.html#.U24FVm2RVo0

Chapter 9
INDICATORS OF SUSTAINABLE PRODUCTION[1]

With M. Hart, T. Greiner, C. Crumbley

ABSTRACT

Over the past 10 years, firms, government, and the public have increasingly focused on measurement tools to assess the environmental aspects of sustainability. While there are numerous lists of environmental performance indicators (see, for example, International Organizations for Standardization's ISO 14301, Global Reporting Initiative, and World Business Council for Sustainable Development), these lists provide little insight into how firms might revise the indicators they currently have to more accurately measure sustainability. The Lowell Center for Sustainable Production at the University of Massachusetts Lowell has developed a tool to enable companies to evaluate the effectiveness of sustainability indicator systems. The tool includes a framework that consists of five levels for categorizing existing indicators relative to the basic principles of sustainability. The purpose of the framework is not to rank indicators as better or worse but rather to provide a method to evaluate the ability of a set of indicators to inform decision-making and measure progress toward more sustainable systems of production. In its current state, the framework focuses on environmental, health, and safety aspects of production. Work is underway to expand it to include social and economic aspects.

Key words: indicators, sustainable production, indicator framework, indicators of sustainable production

[1] Reprinted from *Journal of Cleaner Production,* Vol. 9 (5), 2001, Veleva V., Hart M., Greiner T., and C. Crumbley, "Indicators of sustainable production," pp. 447-452., Copyright (2001), with permission from Elsevier.

INTRODUCTION

The concept of *sustainable production* emerged in 1992 at the United Nations Conference on Environment and Development (UNCED) and is closely linked to the concept of *sustainable development*.[2] The conference concluded that the major cause for the continued deterioration of the global environment is the unsustainable pattern of consumption and production, particularly in industrialized countries (UN Conference, 1992). The Agenda 21 Action Plan called on governments, business, and others to implement measures for more sustainable production and consumption patterns. However, the term *sustainability* is still very vague, particularly in the business context in which it has been used to describe everything from organic yogurt to petroleum production.

Regardless of how it is defined, market leaders in a number of industries are realizing the strategic advantages of being more sustainable and measuring their progress (Farrow, Johnson, & Larson, 1999; Greiner, 1999). Many other companies are beginning to understand the importance of sustainable development, although they are not certain how the concept applies to their business activities. This challenge was one impetus behind the establishment of the Lowell Center for Sustainable Production (LCSP)[3] at the University of Massachusetts Lowell. The Center focused its work on sustainable systems of production. In 1999, it began developing a framework for indicators of sustainable production. This chapter presents the framework and describes the key findings from using it in a series of trainings so far. It is still a work in progress. As presented here, the framework addresses only environmental aspects of sustainable production. Work is underway to expand the framework to include the social and economic aspects as well. The LCSP is interested in receiving comments and suggestions for improvement.

Sustainable Production

The LCSP defines *sustainable production* as "the creation of goods and services using processes and systems that are: non-polluting; conserving of energy and natural resources; economically viable; safe and healthful for workers, communities, and consumers; and socially and creatively rewarding for all working people" (LCSP, 2014).

The LCSP *principles* of sustainable production, derived from this definition, are presented in Appendix A. They emphasize the interconnections between the

---

[2]Although the term *sustainable development* has been used for many years, its meaning still defies simple explanation. The most commonly cited definition is "development that meets the needs of the present without compromising the ability of future generations to meet their own needs" (World Commission on Environment and Development, 1987).

[3]The Lowell Center for Sustainable Production (LCSP) was started in 1996 to promote new forms of industrial production that are safe, healthy, environmentally sound, socially responsible, and economically viable over the long term. The Center is composed of a core of faculty and staff from several academic departments and research centers, which work directly with industrial firms, nonprofit organizations, and government agencies to promote sustainable production.

environmental, social, and economic systems within which production and consumption occur. The LCSP's definition and principles of sustainable production present a vision and the long-term objectives for companies that choose to become more sustainable. However, the vision and long-term objectives alone may not be sufficient for a company to develop a more sustainable production system. There is a need for tools to assist companies in understanding the problems with existing production systems and then defining specific objectives and measuring progress toward sustainable production. One such tool being developed by the Lowell Center is a framework for indicators of sustainable production. Its purpose is to increase companies' understanding of the concept of sustainable production and promote its practical application.

Indicators, Indicators, Indicators Everywhere

Indicators are typically numerical measures that provide key information about a physical, social, or economic system. They go beyond simple data to show trends or cause-and-effect relationships. Indicators have three key objectives:

- To raise awareness and understanding
- To inform decision-making
- To measure progress toward established goals

Indicators have increasingly been used as a tool to measure progress toward sustainable development at different levels—national, regional, local, and company/facility. Examples include the Organization for Economic Cooperation and Development (1998), U.S. Interagency Working Group on Sustainable Development (1998), Sustainable Seattle (1998), International Organization for Standardization ISO 14031 (1998), Global Reporting Initiative (2000), among others. This chapter focuses on only company/facility-level indicators.

Given the difficulty some have defining sustainable development, one can imagine the greater difficulty in measuring it! While numerous environmental indicators exist, such as the ones developed under the International Organization for Standardization Environmental Performance Evaluation Guidelines ISO 14031, Global Reporting Initiative, or World Business Council for Sustainable Development (1999), none of them advances our understanding of corporate sustainability. They provide simple lists of indicators with little or no guidance as to how to select or apply them over time in order to become more sustainable (Veleva, 1999). For example, indicators of corporate compliance rates and permit exceedances, while useful, provide little "sustainability information." A firm can be in full compliance with government requirements but still making little progress in reducing its impacts on global or local sustainability. Additional indicators are needed to examine, for example, the firm's greenhouse gas emission over time and include estimates of supply-chain and product life-cycle contributions.

Other examples of indicators of sustainable production specifically related to the environment include

- Percentage of raw materials from renewable resources
- Acidification potential, measured in SO_2 equivalent
- Kilograms of emissions into the air
- Amount of energy used per unit of product made or service provided

Existing business-related sustainability indicators tend to emphasize the environmental aspects of production (Adriaanse, 1993; Veleva & Ellenbecker, 2001a). However, indicators of sustainable production (ISPs) should include not only production measures but also measures of the relationship between production and the economic, social, and environmental systems within which it exists. The types of issues that ISPs should address include energy and material use, natural environment, economic viability, social justice, community and worker development, and product life cycle. Such indicators can show the extent to which an organization is moving toward more sustainable production practices. In this respect, indicators of sustainable production are a useful tool both for companies and community groups as well as government. Companies need to "measure" in order to "manage" their achievements. NGOs, community organizations, and governments need to evaluate companies' performance in order to reward the leaders and determine how best to encourage the laggards to improve their performance.

LCSP Indicator Framework

The LCSP framework presently focuses primarily on the environmental, health, and safety aspects of sustainable production. Additional work is underway to expand the framework to include the social and economic aspects of production.

Underlying the framework are three basic assumptions:

- Developing sustainable systems of production is a continuous, evolutionary process of setting goals and measuring performance.
- Different companies and different industries are starting at different places in the evolutionary process.
- Developing truly sustainable systems of production cannot be achieved by companies or industry alone but rather requires cooperation and coordination among companies, communities, and government at many different levels—local, regional, national, and international.

These assumptions are reflected in a framework of Indicators for Sustainable Production, which consists of the following five levels (see Figure 1):

- Level 1: Facility Compliance/Conformance
- Level 2: Facility Material Use and Performance
- Level 3: Facility Effects
- Level 4: Supply Chain and Product Life Cycle
- Level 5: Sustainable Systems

Note that the levels are evolutionary. As a company begins to develop indicators at higher levels, the framework does not suggest dropping indicators at the lower

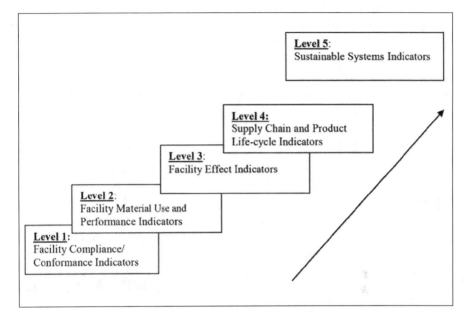

Figure 1. Lowell Center for Sustainable Production
indicator framework.

levels. It is necessary for companies to comply with regulations and industry standards (Level 1). It will always be important that companies monitor their efficiency and productivity (Level 2). In order to move toward sustainable production, however, an organization needs to look beyond its boundaries at the impacts of suppliers, distributors, and products (Levels 3 and 4) as well as its contribution in moving toward sustainable society (Level 5).

Level 1: Facility Compliance/Conformance includes measures that many companies already track. They evaluate the extent to which a facility is in compliance with regulations (e.g., Toxic Release Inventory, Occupational Safety and Health Act, Clean Air Act) or in conformance to some industry/association standards. The environmentally oriented indicators at this level tend to be measures of activities undertaken by the Environmental Health and Safety (EHS) staff or the regulatory agencies. They are primarily focused on activities within facility boundaries but are often developed in response to external regulations or requirements. Examples of Level 1 indicators include

- Number of reportable spills
- Number of notices of noncompliance

- Number of employees receiving hazardous material training
- Number or dollar value of fines paid

Level 2: Facility Material Use and Performance includes measures of facility/company inputs, outputs, and performance, such as emissions, by-products, waste, or occupational injuries. These indicators are commonly used and often critical for maintaining a competitive advantage, since they measure resource-use efficiency. Level 2 indicators can be reported as a total or adjusted for production amount (per unit of product/service or per value added). Examples include

- Tons of TRI (toxic release inventory) emissions released to air
- Total kWh energy consumed per kilogram or dollar of product output
- Tons of sludge generated
- Number of facility accident-free days

Level 3: Facility Effects indicators are a step further and measure the potential effects of a facility on environmental, worker, and public health; community development; and economic viability. They can be reported as a total or adjusted for production amount (per unit of product/service). Examples of EHS oriented indicators at this level include

- Kilograms of greenhouse gas (GHG) emissions per year measured in CO_2 equivalents (Global Warming Potential—GWP)
- Kilograms of photochemical ozone creating emissions per year measured in ethylene equivalents (Photochemical Ozone Creating Potential—POCP)
- Kilograms of acidifying substances per year measured as SO_2 equivalents (Acidification Potential).

Environmental effect categories parallel those developed in The Netherlands and include climate change, ozone depletion, acidification, eutrophication, dispersion of toxic substance, solid waste, and disturbance of local environments (Adriaanse, 1993). Note that up to this point, the indicator levels have been focused primarily on the company's internal production processes. Even at Level 3, indicators are developed to measure effects of the internal production processes on the external environment. Unlike Levels 1 and 2, these measures aim to aggregate the contribution of different sources of these effects. For example, methane and CO_2 emissions can be added to calculate global warming potential.

At *Level 4: Supply-Chain and Product Life-Cycle*, the measurement focus goes beyond the boundary of the company/facility processes to look at supply chain as well as product distribution, use, and ultimate disposal. These indicators aim to measure impacts throughout the product life cycle. At this level, a company or facility can use indicators found in Levels 1 through 3 but include the impacts from suppliers, distributors, and end users. Level 4 indicators look at using raw materials from renewable sources and/or reusing or recycling products at the end of their life. Examples of Level 4 indicators include

- Percentage of products designed to be easily reused or recycled
- Percentage of suppliers receiving safety training per year

- Embodied energy in key raw materials and packaging
- Tons of GHG emissions generated during product transportation

Level 5: Sustainable Systems contains indicators that show how an individual company's production processes fit into the larger picture of a sustainable society. Sustainable production is not an isolated activity. It is a part of the larger economic, social, and environmental systems of a community. In this context, community refers to both local community (where a company's facility is located) and global community (where a company sells its products or receives raw materials and parts). Level 5 indicators measure the effects of production on the long-term quality of life and human development within the ecological carrying capacity. They look at the extent to which materials and ecosystem services used by the company (throughout the supply chain and life cycle of the products) have been consumed within the renewable rates or assimilation capacity of nature. In most cases, Level 5 indicators cannot be developed by an individual company but rather need input from community and government in determining limits and thresholds. Examples of level five indicators include

- Percentage of water from local sources used within the average local recharge rate
- Percentage of total energy used from renewable sources harvested sustainably

Using the Framework

In 2000-2001 the LCSP used the framework in two types of training: awareness raising and skill building.

The *awareness raising* training introduces the concepts of sustainable development, production, and consumption. It defines indicators and outlines their key dimensions. Specific exercises are included to improve participants' understanding of indicators. This type of training also includes illustrative cases of companies developing sustainable production indicators as well as a bibliography on alternative indicator frameworks and resources.

The *skill building* training focuses on metrics and measures and how existing indicators fit within the LCSP framework. Participants are provided with some existing sets of indicators (e.g., 3M, Amoco, Global Reporting Initiative, Center for Waste Reduction Technology), and asked to classify them according to the LCSP 5-level framework. This type of training involves developing sustainable production indicators within the LCSP framework, in which participants list indicators that they presently use and indicators that they would like to use. The training also includes examples of companies developing sustainable production indicators and a bibliography of additional sources of information and quantitative data for indicator calculation.

Training workshops and presentations have been given for the Northeast Business Environmental Network (NBEN), the National Pollution Prevention Roundtable (NPPR), Massachusetts Toxics Use Reduction Planners Conference (TURP), the Coalition for Environmentally Responsible Economies (CERES), the Greening of

Industry Conference, and the Northern Sustainable Community Network. Participants have included companies' Environmental Health and Safety staff; representatives from local, state, and federal environmental agencies; and community activists. According to participants, the framework is extremely useful in raising their understanding of sustainable production and indicators and how to apply these in practice.

Other key findings from the sessions given to date include

- Most firms in United States are using Level 1 and 2 indicators only. This is due to the fact that U.S. firms are not required by law to prepare higher level indicators. In the few cases in which there is such an interest, firms typically lack the expertise to develop the indicators.
- Workshop participants find that classifying indicators into the five levels reveals much about their company/facility indicator systems. Placing an indicator within the 5-level framework is not always easy. However, the process of discussing different viewpoints about where an indicator fits within the framework has proven very successful in increasing participants' overall understanding of sustainable production.
- Level 5 indicators (sustainable systems indicators) are difficult for companies to understand, develop, and implement, since these require community and government support, expanded databases, and information on limits and thresholds. Without such support, business will be able to make only limited progress toward developing truly sustainable systems of production.
- Indicators relating to the social and economic aspects of sustainability are not currently accommodated easily by the framework. There is a need to expand the framework and include these aspects as well as worker well-being and product sustainability.
- Management indicators are of particular interest to organizations and are not well accommodated by the framework in its current state.
- The term *indicator* is not always understood well and is sometimes confused with goals or issues. For example, workshop participants sometimes mention "safety" or "increase energy from renewables" as indicators. However, "safety" is an issue for which an indicator might be "number of accident-free days," and "increase energy from renewables" is a goal for which an indicator might be "percentage of energy from renewables."

CONCLUSION

There are many questions that need to be addressed in the future in order to improve the LCSP indicator framework. Testing of the framework is of key importance. In 2001 the Lowell Center for Sustainable Production worked with three companies to pilot test the framework and develop additional guidance for indicator use (Veleva & Ellenbecker, 2001b). The Center welcomes all comments and suggestions for improving its training curriculum and the indicator framework.

Regardless of the long road ahead, our work with industry shows that there is a need to clarify and simplify the numerous indicator systems in the literature today. The Lowell Center framework is one attempt to do so. Its use as a training tool, particularly for reviewing existing indicators sets, heightens awareness about sustainable production, and promotes learning and improved measurement practices.

ACKNOWLEDGMENTS

The authors would like to acknowledge the funding for this research from the Merck Family Fund and the Switzer Environmental Fellowship Program of the New Hampshire Charitable Foundation.

APPENDIX A: PRINCIPLES OF SUSTAINABLE PRODUCTION (ADAPTED FROM THE LOWELL CENTER FOR SUSTAINABLE PRODUCTION)

- Products and services are
  - safe and ecologically sound throughout their life cycle;
  - as appropriate, designed to be durable, repairable, readily recycled, compostable, or easily biodegradable;
  - produced and packaged using minimal amounts of most environmentally benign materials and energy.
- Processes are designed and operated such that
  - wastes and ecologically incompatible by-products are continually reduced, eliminated, or recycled on-site;
  - chemical substances or physical agents and conditions that present hazards to human health or the environment are continually eliminated;
  - energy and materials are conserved, and the forms of energy and materials used are most appropriate for the desired ends;
  - work spaces are designed to continually minimize or eliminate chemical, ergonomic, and physical hazards.
- Workers are valued and
  - their work is organized to conserve and enhance their efficiency and creativity;
  - their security and well-being is a priority;
  - they are encouraged and helped to continually develop their talents and capacities;
  - their input to and participation in the decision-making process is openly accepted.
- Communities related to any stage of the product life cycle (from production of raw materials through manufacture, use, and disposal of the final product) are respected and enhanced economically, socially, culturally, and physically; and
- Continued economic viability does not depend on an ever-increasing (i.e., unsustainable) consumption of materials and energy.

DISCUSSION QUESTIONS

Chapter 9: Indicators of Sustainable Production

1. What is "sustainable production"? What is the role of indicators in advancing sustainable production?
2. What are the five levels in the Lowell Center for Sustainable Production (LCSP) indicator framework? Provide specific examples of indicators for each level and analyze the challenges and opportunities companies face when implementing such indicators.
3. Select a company (preferably a multinational corporation) and research the sustainability indicators that it reports on. Describe what level most of the indicators are at?
4. What is the Global Reporting Initiative? Discuss its main weaknesses and describe how integrated reporting is aiming to address these?

REFERENCES

Adriaanse, A. (1993). *Environmental policy performance indicators—A study on the development of indicators for environmental policy in The Netherlands.* The Hague: SDU.

Farrow, P., Johnson, R., & Larson, A. (1999, November 13–16,). *Entrepreneurship, innovation and sustainability strategies: The case of Walden Paddlers, Inc.* Greening of Industry Network Conference, Chapel Hill, NC.

Global Reporting Initiative (GRI). (2000, June). *Sustainability reporting guidelines on economic, environmental, and social performance.* Retrieved from http://www.global reporting.org/

Greiner, T. (1999, November 13–16). *Indicators of sustainable production: The case of Stonyfield Farm.* Greening of Industry Network Conference, Chapel Hill, NC.

International Organization for Standardization (ISO). (1998). *Draft International Standard ISO/DIS 14031.* Geneva, Switzerland: Author.

Organization for Economic Cooperation and Development (OECD). (1998). *OECD work on sustainable development. A discussion paper on work to be undertaken over the period 1998–2001.* Retrieved from http://www.worldcat.org/title/oecd-work-on-sustainable-development-a-discussion-paper-on-work-to-be-undertaken-over-the-period-1998-2001/oeclc/40708823

Sustainable Seattle. (1998). [Home page]. Retrieved from http://www.sustainableseattle.org/

United Nations Conference on Environment and Development, Rio de Janeiro, Brazil. (1992). *Agenda 21: Programme of action for sustainable development.* New York, NY: United Nations.

U.S. Interagency Working Group on Sustainable Development Indicators. (1998). *An experimental set of indicators.* Washington DC: Author.

Lowell Center for Sustainable Production (LCSP). What is sustainable production? 2014. Retrieved from http://sustainableproduction.org/abou.what.php

World Business Council for Sustainable Development (WBCSD). (1999, April). *Eco-efficiency indicators and reporting. Report on the status of the project's work in progress and guidelines for pilot application.* Retrieved from http://www.wbcsd.ch

World Commission on Environment and Development. (1987). *Our common future.* Oxford, UK: Oxford University Press.

Veleva, V. (1999, November 13–16). *A proposal for measuring business sustainability: addressing shortcomings in existing indicator frameworks*. Greening of Industry Network Conference, Chapel Hill, NC.

Veleva, V., & Ellenbecker, M. (2001a). Indicators of sustainable production: A new tool for promoting business sustainability. *New Solutions, 11*(1), 41–62.

Veleva V., & Ellenbecker, M. (2001b) Indicators of sustainable production: framework and methodology, *Journal of Cleaner Production* (9): 519-549.

UPDATE TO CHAPTER 9: INDICATORS OF SUSTAINABLE PRODUCTION

Since the Lowell Center for Sustainable Production Indicator Framework was developed, the use of sustainability indicators by companies has increased significantly. Driven by stakeholder demands, regulatory pressures in the European Union and large companies such as Walmart and Staples, a growing number of companies have been adopting Level 3 (facility effect indicators) and Level 4 (supply chain and product life-cycle) indicators.

Some of the most notable recent developments include:

- The *Global Reporting Initiative (GRI)* became the golden standard for reporting worldwide. More than 90% of the world's 250 largest companies used the GRI guidelines and indicators in 2013 (Yelton, 2014). Since first launched in 1997, the GRI guidelines were revised four times and sector-specific guidelines were developed to further advance industry reporting (GRI, 2014). The most recent GRI guidelines issued in 2013, G4, emphasize materiality and environmental and social impacts.

- Launched over a decade ago, *the Climate Disclosure Protocol (CDP)* has further advanced the use of Level 3 and Level 4 indicators by offering a standardized framework for measuring and reporting Greenhouse Gas Emissions (GHG) and water impacts within a company's supply chain (CDP, 2014). In 2014 CDP worked with over 767 institutional investors holding over $92 trillion in assets under management. Thousands of companies and others (e.g., cities, non-profit organizations) have used the guidelines. More than 4,100 companies responded to CDP data collection inquiry in 2012, compared to 235 in 2003 (CDP, 2014).

- In response to consumer demand for greater transparency and more information about product sustainability, in 2009 Walmart launched the Sustainable Product Index initiative – an effort to develop a standardized methodology and labeling of products which reflects their life-cycle impacts and overall sustainability performance. Led by the Sustainability Consortium, this initiative has three main stages – i) initial supplier sustainability assessment; ii) creating of a life-cycle analysis database, and iii) finalizing the index and presenting to customers. As of 2014 the group was still compiling lifecycle analysis data for the various product categories by a number of working groups including industry, academics and NGOs (Sustainability Consortium, 2014).

- In April 2014 the European Parliament passed a law that requires publicly-held companies with more than 500 employees to report on their policies, risks and results in relation to "social, environmental and human rights impact, diversity and anti-corruption policies" (Environmental Leader, 2014). The law is going into effect in 2017 and is expected to further increase the use of sustainability indicators and the number of reporting companies from 2,500 presently to 7,000 by 2017.

• Despite the increasing adoption of sustainable production indicators, including Levels 3 and 4 indicators, existing measures still have limited value in predicting a company's true sustainability commitment and performance, potential financial risks and long-term value (Veleva, 2011). In response to these concerns the International Integrated Reporting Council (IIRC) was created to address this challenge and develop more effective indicators which link sustainability performance and financial performance. In December 2013 IIRC published the first Integrated Reporting Framework (IIRC, 2014). As of April 2014, over 100 companies from around the world had joined the IIRC Pilot Programme Business Network, including Danone, Deutsche Bank, Deloitte LLP, Microsoft, Natura, NovoNordisk, PepsiCo, Petrobras S.A., Rosneft and Sanofi (IIRC, 2014).

REFERENCES

Climate Disclosure Protocol. About CDP. 2014. Retrieved from https://www.cdp.net/en-US/Pages/HomePage.aspx

Environmental Leader. European Parliament Requires Sustainability Reporting. April 16, 2014. Retrieved from http://www.environmentalleader.com/2014/04/16/european-parliament-requires-sustainability-reporting/

Global Reporting Initiative (GRI). *G4 sustainability reporting guidelines.* 2014. Retrieved from https://www.globalreporting.org/reporting/g4/Pages/default.aspx

International Integrated Reporting Council (IIRC), Integrated Reporting, 2014. Retrieved from http://www.theiirc.org/

Sustainability Consortium. About Us. 2014. Retrieved from http://www.sustainability consortium.org/who-we-are/

Veleva V., "Response to Lewis's Lessons on Corporate "Sustainability" Disclosure from Deepwater Horizon," Commentary, *New Solutions*, Vol. 21 (2), 215-217, 2011.

Yelton, G. "What does sustainability reporting mean for smaller companies?" *GreenBiz*, March 27, 2014. Retrieved from http://www.greenbiz.com/blog/2014/03/27/how-do-smaller-companies-fit-sustainability-reporting

Chapter 10

MANAGING CORPORATE CITIZENSHIP: A NEW TOOL FOR COMPANIES[1]

ABSTRACT

In today's global economic downturn, identifying a company's strengths and weaknesses for better aligning resources and strategies is becoming more important than ever. Organizations that look at corporate citizenship as a critical part of business for providing new market opportunities, reducing risk, or improving reputation, are making greater efforts to assess their strengths and weaknesses to better prioritize resources and actions. Having the appropriate tools with which to do so is vital. This chapter discusses the challenges of corporate citizenship management and outlines key findings and lessons learned from piloting a new assessment tool for companies. It presents two examples of how companies have used the tool to advance their corporate citizenship efforts. Finally, it summarizes key findings about "gaps" and "strengths" in corporate citizenship management today and provides recommendations for further research.

Key words: corporate citizenship, corporate social responsibility, assessment, measurement, corporate citizenship management, tools, strategy

INTRODUCTION

The beginning of the 21st century has seen an explosion of corporate citizenship[2] activities—an increasing number of companies are making public commitments, reporting their performance, or positioning their products as environmentally friendly

[1] Reprinted from: Veleva V., "Managing Corporate Citizenship: A New Tool for Companies", *Corporate Social Responsibility and Environmental Management,* Volume 17, Issue 1, pages 40–51, January/February 2010, by permission of the publisher John Wiley and Sons. © 2010 Center for Business Ethics at Bentley University.

[2] Other terms used interchangeably include corporate social responsibility (CSR), sustainability, corporate responsibility, and triple bottom line.

or socially responsible. The drivers for such initiatives typically include growing customer demands, consumer expectations, government regulation (particularly in markets such as the European Union), improved risk management, talent management, and brand reputation. Corporate citizenship has become even more important in strategic planning as the financial crisis and economic recession of 2008–2009 hit the United States and global markets, caused in large part by unethical business practices by some companies involved in the origination, rating, and selling of mortgages.

At the same time, studies have shown that very few companies are aligning corporate citizenship efforts with their core business activities and management processes (Googins, Mirvis, & Rochlin, 2007). Most initiatives are local and scattered. Cross-functional work is limited, and various departments continue to work in silos. The past 10 years have seen a significant growth in guidelines, standards, and rankings of corporate citizenship performance, from the Dow Jones Sustainability Index, to the Global Reporting Initiative, the Electronic Industry Code of Conduct and the draft ISO 26000 standard. At the same time, there has been little guidance on what companies need to have in place to successfully manage their impacts on the environment and society. In fact, studies have shown that besides the lack of resources such as money, time, and people, the main barrier to greater adoption of corporate citizenship practices is "the lack of management processes" (BCCCC, 2007) and "the complexity of implementing integrated strategy across various business functions" (McKinsey Quarterly, 2007).

This was the underlying driver for the development of the Corporate Citizenship Management Framework (CCMF) and related Assessment Tool by the Boston College Center for Corporate Citizenship[3] (see Figure 1; for more information on the framework and the tool, see www.bccorporatecitizenship.org/ccmf).

Corporate Citizenship and the Management Challenge

The Boston College Center for Corporate Citizenship (BCCCC) defines corporate citizenship as "the commitment of companies to minimize risks, maximize benefits, be accountable and responsive to stakeholders and support strong financial results" (www.bcccc.net). This definition is in line with the "equivalent view of corporate citizenship" given by Matten and Crane (2005), which essentially equates corporate citizenship with corporate social responsibility (for comparison, the "limited view of corporate citizenship" identifies corporate citizenship with charitable donations, volunteering, and strategic philanthropy). This definition is most widely accepted by practitioners who often interchangeably use terms such as sustainability, corporate social responsibility, or corporate citizenship (e.g., Business for Social Responsibility, World Business Council for Sustainable Development). In this chapter, we will use this definition and not focus on the debate of what citizenship is and whether corporations can be citizens (Moon, Crane, & Matten, 2005).

---

[3] The Boston College Center for Corporate Citizenship (BCCCC) is a membership-based research organization associated with the Carroll School of Management.

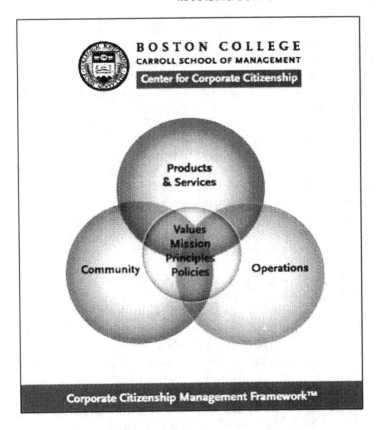

Figure 1. Corporate citizenship management framework.

Today, the debate about business responsibility has shifted from discussing whether or not to be socially responsible and what this means to *how* to become socially responsible and manage activities as an integrated part of business (Wan-Jan, 2006). Elkington (2006) also notes that corporate social responsibility or citizenship is shifting from public relations and legitimacy to issues of competitive advantage and corporate governance. Different organizations classify differently the main areas to be managed, but these typically include environmental impacts, human rights, community involvement, governance, and ethics.

Managing corporate citizenship as an integral part of business (or performance management), however, is challenging, as often companies do not have the necessary knowledge, competencies, structure, and tools. Measurement, communication, and recognition are critical elements of an effective performance management system (Stainer, 2006), but few companies have implemented good goals and metrics that are clearly communicated, tracked, and linked to financial or nonfinancial rewards (Epstein, 2008). Identifying the right performance metrics is crucial, but often companies track too many indicators, which "consumes more resources and becomes counter-productive" (Stainer, 2006).

Communication, both internal and external, is the key for effective management and engagement of all employees in support for corporate citizenship. Yet studies show that in most organizations, internal communication is still inadequate. Ziek (2009), for example, demonstrates that while far from using the perfect tools, large organizations are most advanced at communicating corporate citizenship by using frameworks such as the Global Reporting Initiative (GRI) guidelines or their annual reports. Yet internal communication is still much overlooked (Ziek, 2006). Part of the challenge is the availability of simple tools and frameworks for communicating what corporate citizenship is, assessing strengths and weaknesses and prioritizing areas to focus on. What is often measured internally may not always be appropriate to report externally (e.g., brand reputation, customer loyalty, or employee job satisfaction) and to date, there are no widely acceptable and standardized frameworks for internal measurement and communication of corporate citizenship.

Corporate Citizenship Management Framework and Assessment Tool

The CCMF was developed to help companies better understand and manage corporate citizenship as an integrated part of the business. It involves assessing and managing business practices in four closely interrelated domains (Pinney, 2009):

1. *Values, Mission, Principles, and Policies—Integration and Accountability*: Embedding corporate citizenship in the governance and management structure of the company. This dimension addresses how a company's core values, mission, vision, and governance structures support or prevent the company from understanding and managing corporate citizenship as an integrated part of business strategy.
2. *Community Support—Addressing Social Challenges*: Mobilizing the company's assets to address social issues and support social well-being beyond creating jobs and paying taxes. This can range from simple philanthropy to participation in multistakeholder social issue partnerships, engaging a range of corporate resources.
3. *Operations—Responsible Business Practices*: Utilizing responsible business practices to minimize potential negative impacts on employees, environment, and society and maximize positive impacts. This dimension addresses how a company manages a broad range of operational issues, from business ethics to health and safety, sustainable environmental practices, and human rights in the supply chain.
4. *Products and Services—Market Strategy*: Addressing societal needs with marketplace solutions that return a profit to the company. This can range from adaptation of existing products and services to be more eco-efficient or socially beneficial to a fundamental reinvention of a company's product line or services as well as their marketing and delivery.

The Corporate Citizenship Assessment Tool mirrors the CCMF and was developed as an online platform for companies to assess their management capabilities and identify areas for improvement. It focuses on the question of "What?" (what needs to be managed) rather than "How?" (how to manage the various issues). The tool is compatible with most other existing tools and frameworks (e.g., Global Reporting Initiative, Global Compact, London Benchmarking Group framework, the draft ISO 26000). It provides a real-time "snapshot" of an organization's current state of corporate citizenship management in key issue areas. It does not aim to measure performance, although one can argue that good corporate citizenship management should lead to better performance. Exploring this link, however, was not part of the present research.

The tool currently includes 79 questions covering the four CCMF dimensions. Questions can be answered as "Yes", "No", "In process", "Don't Know", or "NA" (see Figure 2). Two of the dimensions include four subcategories (e.g., operations dimension includes governance and business ethics, environment, human rights, and workplace issues).

The assessment can be completed by an individual or a team and the answers can be modified at any time as companies make progress in different areas. Each question includes detailed guidance and concrete examples. Upon completion, participants receive their scores in each of the main categories and subcategories of the tool (or a corporate citizenship "profile"). Participants are then provided with a list of available resources and tools within each of the categories, and they can schedule a debriefing to review their results and receive feedback and recommendations for improvement (for more information about the methodology, see Text Box 1).

The tool was designed to helps facilitate cross-functional discussions and follow-up actions needed to improve a company's corporate citizenship practices and elevate the role of the CSR/community involvement department. It allows tracking progress over time and identifying key gaps and opportunities in corporate citizenship management. It could also be used for external benchmarking.

While not explicitly, the tool implicitly attempts to define what is considered "excellence in corporate citizenship management." One has to remember, however, that corporate citizenship management is a journey and not a destination. No company is perfect and able to get an excellent score in all areas of the assessment. The goal is to identify strengths, weaknesses, and, respectively, opportunities for improvement. This is becoming even more important in today's global economic downturn, limited resources, and growing competition among businesses.

Tool for Advancing Corporate Citizenship Strategy

Just as there is no one-size-fits-all approach to corporate citizenship in a company; there is no single way of using the assessment tool. Companies have different culture, corporate citizenship structures, and are in different stages of their corporate citizenship journey, as a study by the Center has found (BCCCC, 2008). Yet study results demonstrate there are some critical elements for the effective

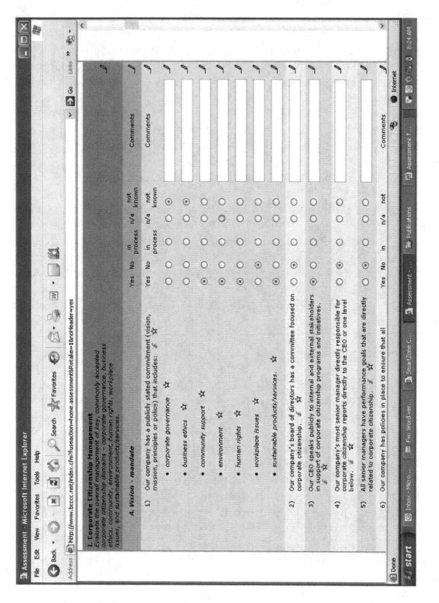

Figure 2. Screenshot of corporate citizenship assessment tool.

Text Box 1. Assessment Tool Methodology

The tool includes 79 questions that are scored equally (there is no weighting). Each subcategory is calculated as the average of all questions included. The scores for the four main dimensions are calculated as an average of the subcategories within them (e.g., Community dimension does not have subcategories; Operations dimension has four subcategories).

When calculating the scores and generating a company "profile" (see Figure 3), every question is counted. Scores for each question range between 0 and 3, depending on the answer—"Yes", "No", "In process", "NA", or "Don't Know." Finally, for easier communication, the scores are converted into percentages.

The default answer for all questions is "Don't Know", and it can be changed at any time.

Based on analysis of the alpha and beta results, and expert judgment, the following outcome categories for level of management have been defined: Excellent (91%–100%), Very Good (76%–90%), Good (61%–75%), Average (46–60%), and Need Improvement (0%–45%). The research team is currently working with an expert panel on identifying the weights for the four dimensions in order to provide an overall score in addition to the "profile."

---

use of the tool, the main one being involving key people from different business functions across the organization.

Below are provided two examples of how companies are using the CCMF and the tool to advance their corporate citizenship management efforts and strategic planning.

Underwriter Laboratories

Founded in 1894, Underwriters Laboratories (UL) is an independent, not-for-profit product safety testing and certification organization. There are probably few people in the United States who have not seen the UL mark on many household items—appliances, electronics, safety devices, water filters, to name a few. The company and its global network of offices services customers in 99 countries. UL has developed more than 1,200 standards for safety. Its product certification work involves testing, evaluation, and factory surveillance of products to ensure that they meet the UL safety standards. Annually the company evaluates more than 19,000 types of products, components, materials, and systems, and each year the UL mark appears on 21 billion products manufactured by 72,000 companies.

UL's mission since its founding has been to advance safety. Its mission statement includes eight commitments, such as promoting safe living, physically and environmentally safe products, investing in safety science and education, investing in people, and being a good example of corporate citizenship, and social responsibility (see Text Box 2).

In 2007, UL launched a formal corporate citizenship initiative, which coincided with the launching of the Corporate Citizenship Assessment tool's alpha pilot. Jane Coen, Global Manager—Corporate Citizenship, began using the assessment tool and

---

Text Box 2. Our Mission: Working for a Safer World Since 1894
(http://www.ul.com/global/eng/pages/aboutul/ourmission/)

- To promote safe living and working environments for people by the application of safety science and hazard-based safety engineering

- To support the production and use of products which are physically and environmentally safe and to apply our efforts to prevent or reduce loss of life and property

- To advance safety science through research and investigation

- To concentrate our efforts and resources on public safety in those areas where we can make valuable contributions

- To work with integrity and a focus on quality to enhance the trust conveyed by our certification marks

- To charge fair prices that allow us to meet our obligations, sustain our growth, and invest in safety science and education

- To invest in our people and encourage our people to invest in themselves

- To be a good example of corporate citizenship and social responsibility

---

quickly realized she was able to answer just about half of the questions alone. She invited others at UL to participate in the assessment: the director of Global HR Operations, the Global EHS manager, the general manager Asia Pacific Corporate Strategy, and the SVP and public safety officer, among others. The logical next step was for all of them to meet (virtually through a conference call) and discuss their answers. Going over the questions, the group very quickly came to a consensus about what the right answers were for UL.

According to Coen, using the tool helped improve internal corporate citizenship awareness and communication as it

- Revealed what they knew and what they did not know about their CC management policies, processes, and practices;
- Helped identify who in the organization would know the answer, and;
- Helped identify who at the company needs to be involved in developing integrated corporate citizenship strategy, policies, and practices.

To further build its internal corporate citizenship capabilities, UL sent members of the team to several executive education courses, including "Integrating Corporate Citizenship Across the Firm" and "Measuring, Managing and Reporting Corporate Citizenship Performance."

Using the tool enabled UL to begin the process of internal engagement and integration of corporate citizenship across the organization, building on the existing momentum and excitement. The logical next steps involved identifying appropriate frameworks and tools for integration and performance management, setting goals and targets, and measuring performance. According to Coen, UL intends to continue using the tool on an annual basis as a "reality check"—to see whether or not it is making progress in managing corporate citizenship. The company is interested in benchmarking to other similar companies and in using the tool to identify differences and discrepancies among its different regions.

Tennant Company

Tennant is a U.S. company that few consumers have heard about, as it only sells products to other businesses. Yet the company is a leader in the cleaning industry with a 12% share of the $5 billion worldwide market (Brat, 2008). Founded by George Tennant in 1870 as a private wood-flooring business, Tennant has evolved into a publicly held, global cleaning products manufacturer, selling industrial vacuums, street cleaners, floor scrubbers, and carpet extractors. Its customers include schools, state and federal government, healthcare facilities, the food and beverage industry, manufacturing, and the hospitality industry, among others.

Tennant has a long history of supporting a corporate culture of strong values, governance, and ethics. In the 1980s, it was recognized as a leader in Total Quality Management (TQM) for its Zero Defects. It has also been recognized as one of the Top 100 Ethical Companies by Business Ethics magazine (in 2000, 2001, 2002, and 2006), and the 200 Best Small Companies by Forbes (in 2007 and 2008).

With the arrival of the company's new CEO, Chris Killingstad, Tennant made the decision to take the path toward product innovation and providing environmental cleaning solutions instead of cost-cutting and outsourcing manufacturing of core products overseas. In 2007, the company spent $23 million on R&D—an increase of 38% from 2003, of which 10% went to development of new products. Today, its "green" cleaning solutions include ReadySpace carpet cleaning technology, ec-H2O™ electrically converted water, and FAST foam-activated scrubbing technology, among others. Its products provide high-quality cleaning and reduce toxic residues, improve indoor air quality and the health and safety of people who manufacture and use them. And the success was easy to measure: Between 2003 and 2006, the total number of employees increased from 2,351 to 2,800, sales were up almost 50%, and the share price in early 2008 was double what it was in 2003 (Brat, 2008). Tennant continues to expand and currently has facilities in the United States (in Minneapolis and Holland, Michigan), The Netherlands, England, Scotland, Brazil, China, and Australia.

To embed sustainability into the company DNA and support its brand promise, the Tennant CEO wanted to develop a clear sustainability vision, strategy, performance measurement, and reporting. In November 2007, Stan Mierzejewski was named the senior manager for sustainability at Tennant with the primary goal of building a cross-functional sustainability team and a road map for the company in 6 months.

The core sustainability team (CST) was formed at the end of 2007 and included the senior manager for sustainability; the communications director, corporate counsel, and co-leader of the team; the head of risk management; the director of finance; the director of organizational development; and the VP of human resources. The team regularly communicates with and reports to the senior management team (SMT), which includes the CEO, CFO, global operations manager, international VP, VP of R&D, North American VP of sales, and the general counsel.

The first task of the group was to define a sustainability vision for the company (see Text Box 3).

In April 2008, Mierzejewski and his team began using the assessment tool, which helped them "get organized, focus, and identify priorities." Key people from different departments had to be involved in order to complete the assessment. At the end, the team had a good sense of where the company was. Using the tool, they created a CSR baseline, which included information about the company's strengths and weaknesses (e.g., the company had a strong vision and mandate but showed vulnerabilities in measurement, reporting, and accountability).

Once Mierzejewski had the baseline, he created a spreadsheet using the assessment tool to assist internal strategy discussions and CSR planning. For each question, he noted the current state, desired state, priority, actions need to be taken, lead person, and time frame for accomplishing (see Figure 3).

After using the CCMF and the Assessment Tool and studying the Global Reporting Initiative, the CST quickly realized that it had to focus on a small number of issue areas for which to set goals and key performance indicators (KPI) for 2009. When prioritizing issues and gaps to focus on, the team looked at which areas were most "material" or likely to bring both social and business benefits (Mierzejewski, 2008).

For example, Tennant's energy consumption is significant, and implementing energy efficiency measures would not only help reduce the company's carbon footprint but also its energy bill by 5% to 10% annually, which translates into hundreds of thousands of dollars. In addition, greenhouse gas reporting is expected to become mandatory in the near future in many countries, including the United States. Some customers such as Walmart and GCA have already begun to ask suppliers for such information. Prioritizing energy management for 2009 would prepare Tennant to meet its own and third-party energy use and reporting requirements, both voluntary and mandated.

Text Box 3. Tennant Company Sustainability Vision

At Tennant Company, our core value is stewardship which drives our commitment to sustainability. For us, sustainability means that we balance the economic, environmental and social implications of the business decisions we make.

We produce a superior return for our shareholders because sustainability creates a customer focus, fosters innovation and drives lean operations. We work to decrease our impact on the eco-system in everything we do, while delivering on our commitments of quality and value to our stakeholders. We create a supportive workplace for our employees and provide a great place to do business for our partners.

We aspire to be stewards of all that we touch—people, products, places and profits—for today and tomorrow. (Mierzejewski, 2008)

Assessment Tool Question	Current state	Desired state	Priority	Actions	Lead	Begin	Complete
6b. Our company has policies in place to ensure that all employees understand the environmental policy/principles/ goals	Current environ- mental policy is compliance focused	Environmental policy covers our goals, stewardship of the environment, as well as compliance	A	Develop environ- mental policy	SRM, PG	4Q08	4Q08

Figure 3. Tennant Co.: Sustainability baseline and planning spreadsheet (sample).

As a result of the assessment and prioritization, Tennant's CST identified four areas on which to focus its efforts for the next 3 years. These make up the "pillars" of Tennant's sustainability strategy and will drive the KPIs on which the company plans to report progress in its 2009 CSR report, to be published in 2010:

1. Energy
2. Waste and emissions
3. Products (environmental cleaning solutions)
4. People (including employees, suppliers, customers, and communities).

After identifying these key areas, the CST commenced development of a detailed corporate citizenship work plan. The members of the CST first met with the SMT member for each pillar to confirm the baseline, gaps, and proposed priorities.

With Tennant's SMT invested in the pillars, the CST next began developing the KPIs and the specific goals and action items to achieve those goals for each KPI. Throughout this process, Tennant's CST team regularly solicited feedback from outside experts such as the Boston College Center for Corporate Citizenship (BCCCC). Once the goals and action items are finalized and agreed upon internally at the SMT level, the company plans to first measure CSR performance at its two U.S. manufacturing facilities—Holland and Minneapolis, Michigan. After finalizing the data collection and reporting methodologies in those settings, the company will begin collecting data from its overseas facilities and warehouses (Tennant owns a total of 25 buildings around the world).

Key Findings From the Assessment Tool Pilots

More than 70 companies have used the tool since the first pilot was launched in March 2007. These include large and small, private, public, and nonprofit organizations (for a full list of companies using the tool, see Figure 4). Almost all found the tool particularly valuable for raising awareness and building cross-functional collaboration on corporate citizenship management. Only when all key departments are involved can companies effectively identify strengths, weaknesses, and opportunities and thus advance their CC strategic planning.

With top management often focused on hard data and indicators, it is critical for corporate citizenship practitioners to have tools providing more quantitative information, assessment, and benchmarking. According to Barbra Anderson, director of social responsibility at Sabre Holdings, "Our field is desperate for measurements and needs hard and fast data. Every other part of the business has that, but we don't" (BCCCC, 2008).

The tool has also proved valuable for fostering internal communication and collaboration on corporate citizenship initiatives, especially for companies that are just beginning their journey toward more integrated and strategic management of corporate citizenship. General Mills, for instance, has a long history of addressing diversity, workplace issues, and environmental issues. But tracking and integrating

Adobe Systems Inc.	Farm Credit Corp.	Sabre Holdings
Aetna Foundation	Franklin Templeton Investments	SCF Arizona
Alliance Data Systems	FW Murphy	T. Rowe Price Associates
American Century Investments	Gartner, Inc.	Tacoma Public Utilities
Amway Corp.	General Mills	Telefonica S.A.
Applied Materials	Genzyme Corp.	Tennant Co.
Arizona Public Service Co.	Great River Energy	Teradata
Best Buy Co.	Green Mountain Coffee Roasters	Texas Instruments Inc.
Blue Cross Blue Shield of MI	Haley & Aldrich	The Brick Companies
Blue Cross Blue Shield of RI	Hewitt Associates	Thrivent Financial for Lutherans
Boeing Co.	Intel Corp.	Timberland Company
Brady Corp.	Investors Group	Time Warner Foundation
Burger King Corp.	Jones Lang LaSalle Inc.	Tyson Foods Inc.
Business Objects	Kaiser Permanente	U-Haul International Inc.
Cardinal Health	Levi Strauss & Co.	UBS AG
CenterPoint Energy	LifeScan Inc.	Underwriters Laboratories, Inc.
Chesapeake Energy Corp.	Lockheed Martin Corp.	United Communities Credit Union
Choice Hotels International	Merck & Co., Inc.	UNUM Provident Corp.
Coast Capital Savings	Mohawk Fine Papers, Inc.	Verizon Communications
Dow Chemical	New Balance Athletic Shoe, Inc.	Wells Fargo
Dunkin's Brands, Inc.	Nexen Inc.	West Marine Inc.
ESL Federal Credit Union	NuUnion Credit Union	Westminster Savings Credit Union
Exelon Corp.	Petro-Canada	Wisconsin Public Service Corp.
Expedia	Piper Jaffray & Co.	XL Capital Ltd.
Exxon Mobil Corp.	Ritchie Bros. Auctioneers	Great River Energy

Figure 4. List of companies that have used the assessment
tool as of May 1, 2009.

the initiatives across the organization is not an easy undertaking. When she first accessed the tool, Mary Jane Melendez, manager of programs and operations at General Mills, could answer only a fraction of the questions. She went around the company and talked to numerous colleagues to find out what the company is doing in each of the corporate citizenship areas. The result was a more comprehensive understanding of where General Mills is strong, where the "gaps" are, and how to engage people across the organization in developing a comprehensive CSR strategy.

While the tool allows the use of internal and sensitive information that cannot be found in publicly available CSR reports and thus provides more precise assessment than external rankings, it relies on self-assessment, and therefore the data is only as good as the answers provided. Additional verification is needed in order to improve validity if tools like this are to be used for external benchmarking. Yet, as imperfect as they are presently, results correlate with other studies of corporate citizenship practices (BCCCC, 2007; EIRIS, 2007):

- The weakest areas for most companies are "Measurement, Reporting and Accountability," followed by "Strategy," and then "Products & Services." Yet these are the areas providing greatest opportunities for differentiating from competitors and designing a successful corporate citizenship strategy that is aligned with the business strategy.
- The strongest areas for participating companies are "Workplace Issues," "Governance and Ethics," and "Community." Other studies have also found that globally, U.S. companies are leaders in the areas of diversity, charitable contributions and overall community support, but lag behind European and Japanese companies in the environmental area (Brussels Rules, 2007; EIRIS, 2007).

Further analysis of specific issues revealed the following common "gaps" in corporate citizenship management today:

- Very few companies are implementing performance goals for all managers and senior executives directly related to corporate citizenship—a critical step in moving from strategy to action (Epstein, 2008). Companies such as Walmart are linking senior executive compensation to sustainability goals in order to ensure senior management engagement, support, and accountability (Veleva, 2008).
- Very few companies are measuring the business value of their corporate citizenship initiatives, although this can demonstrate the business case and lead to more initiatives. For example, a recent study by BCCCC and McKinsey (2009) found that environmental, social, and governanace (ESG) programs can create significant quantifiable financial value. Another study found that volunteering leads to quantifiable business benefits such as improved reputation, employee skills, and sales (Boccalandro, 2009). However, measuring and quantifying improved reputation, faster permitting, or customer loyalty due to corporate citizenship is not easy.
- Measuring the social value of corporate citizenship initiatives can be even harder. Many of the assessment tool piloting companies measure the hours of

volunteering by employees or the dollars donated, but very few quantify the actual impacts of their foundation giving or emergency relief efforts. While some companies do not see this as a priority, a growing number of stakeholders are questioning the impacts of corporate giving and demanding greater transparency and accountability.

- Few companies report thoroughly on their social and environmental initiatives and even fewer use third-party verification for their information—a crucial element of building trust and credibility among stakeholders. While the number of U.S. companies reporting sustainability data has doubled since 2005, according to KPMG (2008), this is mostly true for large publicly held corporations. Among smaller companies, privately held and nonprofit organizations, the reporting is still very rare.

- A small number of companies are attempting to measure the greenhouse gas emissions of their facilities, and almost none has successfully measured greenhouse gas emissions across the entire supply chain. With growing customer pressures, government regulation, and consumer demands, this will become a priority area for many companies across various sectors.

- Very few companies have demonstrated leadership in product/service transparency by disclosing the social and environmental impacts on labels and packaging. Timberland and Patagonia are among the leaders in this area. Such an approach will become increasingly important for brand differentiation as consumers are increasingly punishing companies with poor social and environmental practices and rewarding companies that empower them to make positive social and environmental changes (Edelman, 2008; Trudel & Cotte, 2008).

- Most companies track consumer or customer preferences as they relate to their product performance. But very few ask questions related to protection of human rights, environment, or business ethics—issues that are increasingly affecting reputation and bottom line. Edelman's 2008 Good Purpose study found that 82% of consumers globally say they can personally make a difference by supporting good causes, and 83% of consumers are willing to change their own consumption habits to help make tomorrow's world a better place (Edelman, 2008). Even during the recession of 2008–2009, demand for green products continued to grow (BCG 2008; GreenBiz, 2009). Without proper tracking of such changing consumer preferences, companies are missing key opportunities for market positioning and growth.

Recommendations for Future Research

This chapter began the discussion about the need for better tools to support corporate citizenship/CSR executives and managers who are struggling with the complexity of managing various issues across their organizations. The study, which included interviews with over 30 companies, identified the following opportunities for further research and development of tools and resources for corporate citizenship practitioners:

- Examples of best practices for each issue area so companies can learn from and benchmark themselves to leaders in the field;
- Case studies of best-in-class companies that emphasize "the process" rather than the final result of their strategy;
- Industry-tailored assessment tools to better focus on issues specific for particular sectors and industries;
- Benchmarking tools to allow companies to compare themselves to peers or leaders in particular areas of corporate citizenship management;
- Standards of excellence in corporate citizenship management that outline best policies and practices;
- Research and analysis linking corporate citizenship management to actual corporate citizenship performance;
- Tools for identifying "material" issues for companies and helping prioritize the areas to focus on.

CONCLUSION

With growing public expectations of business, increasing regulation, customer and shareholder demands, companies today need to improve their ability to track and manage emerging social, environmental, and governance issues across their entire product/service supply chain. The CCMF/Assessment Tool presents an initial attempt to address this challenge by providing a practical framework and easy-to-use online platform for better communication, integration, and alignment of corporate citizenship and the core business strategy.

ACKNOWLEDGMENTS

The author would like to thank the following contributors: Steve Lydenberg, Sandra Waddock, Bradley Googins, Charles Levenstein, and Rich Liroff for reviewing the draft tool and providing expert feedback on the topics and questions; and the assessment tool workgroup including Josh Shortlidge, Susan Thomas, Colleen Olphert, Alyssa Dver, Chris Pinney, Cheryl Kiser, and Peggy Connolly for their excellent work on developing the online platform, assisting with the alpha and beta pilots, and the official rollout of the tool.

DISCUSSION QUESTIONS

Chapter 10: Managing Corporate Citizenship: A New Tool for Companies

1. What are the four main dimensions of the Corporate Citizenship Management (CCMF) framework? Select a specific company and use the framework to identify key corporate citizenship/sustainability issues for this company.
2. How are companies like UL and Tennant Co. using the CCMF Assessment Tool to advance their corporate citizenship/sustainability strategy?

3. What are the main gaps presently in managing corporate citizenship/ sustainability according to the study? What steps would a company take to address these gaps?

REFERENCES

Boccalandro, B. (2009). *Mapping success in employee volunteering: The drivers for effectiveness in employee volunteering and giving programs and Fortune 500 performance.* Boston, MA: Boston College Center for Corporate Citizenship.

Boston College Center for Corporate Citizenship (BCCCC). (2007). *State of corporate citizenship in the US: Time to get real: Closing the gap between rhetoric and reality.* Retrieved May 3, 2009, from http://www.globescan.com/pdf/StateofCorporate Citizenship.pdf

Boston College Center for Corporate Citizenship (BCCCC). (2008, December). Profile of the practice survey. Retrieved May 3, 2009, from www.bccorporatecitizenship.org

Boston College Center for Corporate Citizenship (BCCCC) and McKinsey. (2009). *How virtue creates value for business and society: Investigating the value of environmental, social and governance activities.* Retrieved May 3, 2009, from www.bccorporate citizenship.org

Boston Consulting Group (BCG). (2008). *Capturing the green advantage for consumer companies.* Retrieved May 28, 2009, from http://www.bcg.com/documents/file15407.pdf

Brat, I. (2008, January 28). How a firm got smart to fight grime, rivals. *The Wall Street Journal.*

Brussels Rules OK. (2007, September 22). *The Economist.*

Edelman. (2008, December 15). *Good Purpose: 2nd annual Good Purpose study.* Retrieved from http://purpose.edelman.com/

EIRIS. (2007, September). *The state of responsible business: Global corporate response to environmental, governance and social (EGS) challenges.* Retrieved November 22, 2008, from http://www.eiris.org/files/research%20publications/stateofespbusiness execsumsep07.pdf

Elkington, J. (2006). Governance for sustainability. *Corporate Governance: An International Review, 14,* 522–529.

Epstein, M. (2008). *Making sustainability work: Best practices in managing and measuring corporate social, environmental and economic impacts.* Sheffield, UK: Greenleaf.

Googins, B., Mirvis, P., & Rochlin, S. (2007). *Beyond good company: Next generation corporate citizenship.* New York, NY: Palgrave Macmillan.

GreenBiz. (2009). *Green product trends: More launches, more sales.* Retrieved May 3, 2009, from www.greenbiz.com

KPMG. (2008). *KPMG international survey of corporate responsibility reporting.* Retrieved December 31, 2008, from http://www.kpmg.com/EU/en/Documents/KPMG_International_ survey_Corporate_responsibility_Survey_Reporting_2008.pdf

Matten, D., & Crane, A. (2005). Corporate citizenship: Toward an extended theoretical conceptualization. *Academy of Management Review, 30,* 166–179.

McKinsey Quarterly. (2007, October). *CEOs on strategy and social issues.* Retrieved November 22, 2008, from http://www.socialinnovationexchange.org/sites/default/files/ event/attachments/McK_Strategy-social-issues.pdf

Mierzejewski, S. (2008, September 2). *Internal memo to senior management team.*

Moon, J., Crane, A., & Matten, D. (2005). Can corporations be citizens? Corporate citizenship as a metaphor for business participation in society. *Business Ethics Quarterly, 15,* 429–453.

Pinney, C. (2009). Framework for the future: Understanding and managing corporate citizenship from a business perspective [briefing paper]. *Boston College Center for Corporate Citizenship*. Retrieved May 3, 2009, from www.bccorporatecitizenship.com/ccmf

Stainer, L. (2006). Performance management and corporate social responsibility: The strategic connection. *Strategic Change, 15,* 253–264.

Trudel, R., & Cotte, J. (2008). Does being ethical pay. *MIT Sloan Management Review, 50,* 61–69.

Veleva, V. (2008). Product stewardship in the U.S.: The changing policy landscape and the role of business. *Sustainability: Science, Practice and Policy, 4,* 29–35. Retrieved May 28, 2009, from http://sspp.proquest.com/static_content/vol4iss2/communityessay.veleva.pdf

Wan-Jan, W. S. (2006). Defining corporate social responsibility. *Journal of Public Affairs, 6,* 176–184.

Ziek, P. (2009). Making sense of CSR communication. *Corporate Social Responsibility and Environmental Management, 16*(3), 137–145.

Chapter 11

TOWARD DEVELOPING A FRAMEWORK FOR MEASURING THE BUSINESS VALUE OF CORPORATE COMMUNITY INVOLVEMENT[1]

ABSTRACT

Business today is a key player in addressing social and environmental challenges. Every year companies contribute significant resources—cash, in-kind donations, and employee volunteers—to nonprofit organizations and community support initiatives. This support is critical for community development. Yet many companies have a limited understanding of the value their initiatives add to the community or to their business. In most cases, they measure inputs and outputs but not actual *impacts*. Measuring and communicating the business value of community-focused programs, however, is critical to maintaining funding for such programs in downturns such as the recession of 2007–2009. This chapter provides critical analysis of existing efforts to measure the business value of corporate community-involvement programs and offers guidance for developing indicators of business impact. Building on lessons learned, it identifies key criteria and makes recommendations for the development of an effective measurement framework and indicators. The chapter concludes with a discussion on how such a framework can lead to social change.

Key words: corporate-community involvement, indicators, business impact, social impact, framework, benchmarking.

[1]With kind permission from Springer Science+Business Media: *Applied Research in Quality of Life,* Toward Developing a New Framework for Measuring the Business Value of Corporate Community Involvement Initiatives, Vol. 5, No. 4, Fall 2010, pp. 309-324, by V. Veleva. © Copyright Springer.

INTRODUCTION

Business today is a key player in addressing major social and environmental challenges. It has both the resources and the responsibility to do so, and a growing number of executives recognize the value of such involvement to their company or brand reputation, license to operate, and ability to attract and retain talent. In addition, no company can succeed in isolation from the communities where it operates.

Every year companies contribute significant resources—cash, in-kind donations, and employee volunteers—to nonprofit organizations and community support initiatives. But many companies have a limited understanding of the value their community involvement initiatives add to the community or to their business. This chapter focuses only on measuring the *business value* of corporate-community involvement programs as a critical tool for increasing business involvement in solving social problems. For the purposes of this research, corporate community involvement (CCI) is defined as all initiatives and programs that a company has in place to support the communities where it operates or has an impact—from donations and employee volunteerism to strategic philanthropy and community partnerships. It is viewed as a subset of corporate citizenship, which includes four main domains: responsible operations, products and services, company governance, and community involvement (Pinney, 2009). CCI focuses primarily on how a business impacts the communities where it operates and engages in addressing social issues beyond its facilities' boundaries.

Measuring the business value of corporate community involvement initiatives helps companies demonstrate the business case for community involvement internally and allows them to better align their community involvement strategy with the core business strategy. For environmental initiatives such measures are more common. A growing number of companies measure savings from improved energy efficiency, reduced packaging, or increased revenue from new green products. But for CCI, efforts such as employee volunteering, signature programs,[2] or emergency response initiatives, there are rarely good indicators of business impact. Most research in the area of sustainability and social responsibility measurement has focused on company-level impacts and less on project or program-level impacts (Veleva & Ellenbecker, 2000; Veleva, Hart, Greiner, & Crumbley, 2001). Being able to measure and evaluate individual programs and projects, however, is critical for better decision-making and integration of community involvement in the business strategy.

Research has also shown that most companies are measuring inputs and outputs (e.g., number of volunteer hours, donation as percentage of pretax net income) versus the actual *impacts* of their CCI programs (Veleva, 2009a). Measuring impacts is still, to a large extent, underdeveloped. Most research is anecdotal, and there is no

---

[2]A signature program is typically a major investment by a company in a social program and its external communication with the goal to generate branding and recognition. One example of such a program includes the Dove Campaign for Real Beauty by Unilever.

commonly accepted framework and indicators to measure business impacts of CCI. A small but growing number of leading companies, however, have begun to develop measures to track such impacts (e.g., Starbucks, Green Mountain Coffee Roasters, IBM, and Allstate).

Research Background and Methodology

The findings in this chapter are based on a research project at the Boston College Center for Corporate Citizenship (BCCCC),[3] which began in early 2009 with the support of nine member companies—Aetna, Altria, Amway, BestBuy, Hewlett Packard, Intel, Lockheed Martin, Merck, and Underwriters Laboratories. The main goal of the project was to develop a simple and practical framework and indicators for measuring the business value of corporate community involvement programs. It was launched in response to increasing demand by corporate community involvement professionals[4] for such tools to assist business decision-making. Supporting companies did not have to be advanced in impact measurement in order to participate in the study. The research involved identifying leading companies and examples of best practices in impact measurement and using these as the basis for designing a new framework and indicators to be piloted by participants before making these publicly available.

As a first step, the research included interviews with community involvement practitioners from participating companies to better understand why they were interested in impact measurement,[5] why they were not implementing such measures, and what was the current state of measurement in their organizations. The next step involved conducting a literature review to understand what the state of impact measurement was, who the leading companies were, and how to build on existing best models to advance the field of impact measurement. This chapter outlines findings from these first two steps and proposes some criteria and recommendations for the development of the framework. Next steps will include development of the framework and indicators for measuring the business impact of CCI programs and piloting these with participating companies to test their value and applicability at a wide range of business enterprises with a global reach.

The target audience for the research includes community involvement practitioners and other company staff who are designing and evaluating CCI programs and need to demonstrate their business value internally. The audience also includes external stakeholders such as researchers, students, and others interested in indicators. A key

---

[3] The Boston College Center for Corporate Citizenship is a membership-based research organization associated with the Carroll School of Management. As of May 2010, it had 346 corporate members, the majority from Fortune 1000 companies.

[4] Common job titles for community involvement practitioners include Manager Philanthropy, Charitable Programs Manager, Community Affairs Manager, Community Investment Manager, Community Relations Manager, Director Community Grants and Investments, Volunteer Program Coordinator.

[5] In this chapter, impact measurement refers to measuring the business impacts and not the social impacts, unless explicitly noted.

assumption of the research was that a CCI program would not have any business value unless it generates social value.

Do CCI Programs Generate Business Value?

An important first question to explore is Do corporate community involvement programs indeed generate business value? What research has been done to date to examine this issue?

An initial literature review identified a small number of studies at a macrolevel that focused on evaluating the intangible assets or corporate social responsibility practices (including community involvement) and linking these to bottom-line benefits.

A 2009 study by the Boston College Center and McKinsey & Company found that two thirds of CFOs agree environmental, social, and governance activities do create measurable value for their shareholders (Bonini, Brun, & Rosenthal, 2009; BCCCC, 2009a).

At a macrolevel, researchers analyzed whether or not a company's inclusion in a social index as an indicator of CSR practices affects corporate performance controlling for size, industry, business cycle, and time (Beccehetti, Di Giacomo, & Pinnacchio, 2008). A number of other studies have linked better social performance to improved financial performance (Edmans 2009; Orlitzky, Schmidt, & Rynes, 2004; PwC, 2003).

Volunteering by employees has been linked to greater retention, job satisfaction, and team building (Boccalandro, 2009). In addition, volunteering has been demonstrated to help build various skills and competencies, such as communication skills, teamwork, adaptability, and leadership (City of London, 2010; Tuffrey, 1998).

A 2008 Gallup Consulting study on employee engagement[6] showed that "engaged organizations have 2.6 times the earnings per share growth rate compared to organizations with lower engagement in the same industry" (Gallup Consulting, 2008).

Valentine and Fleischman (2008) collected the perceived corporate responsibility information from employees and analyzed its relationship to individual work attitudes, namely, job satisfaction. Tuffrey (2003) provided a 7-step model to measure the impact of CCI and good corporate citizenship on HR management priorities, such as pride in company, awareness, advocacy, satisfaction, and retention.

Jones, Willness, and Madey (2010) conducted an experimental study on how CCI and environmental practices affect recruitment. The study found positive correlation between greater communication of CSR activities and increased interest in working for the company.

While such macrolevel studies are valuable in demonstrating that CCI programs do indeed generate business value, they are difficult for community involvement practitioners to use to justify funding for various community involvement programs. For

---

[6]Gallup defines "engaged employee" as one who is fully involved in, and enthusiastic about, his or her work and thus will act in a way that furthers their organization's interests.

such purposes, company-level and program-level studies and indicators are needed to allow for evaluation and benchmarking of individual programs and initiatives.

The field of measuring the business value of community involvement at a program level, however, is still highly underdeveloped and often based on anecdotal information. A growing number of companies, however, have begun to develop and implement more sophisticated indicators.

For example, Aetna added a question to the company's standard employee morale survey about employees' participation in a volunteer program and analyzed it against rating Aetna as "a good place to work" and other well-being measures, controlling for other variables. The Gap collected data showing that its T-shirt created for the Red cause-marketing campaign (established by Bono to support AIDS eradication in Africa) is the best-selling T-shirt ever. Verizon launched a new product to meet the needs of the elderly and people with physical disabilities and as a result, increased sales and added 100,000 new customers. Green Mountain Coffee Roasters had an academic analyze the relationship between participation and awareness of a time-off-for-volunteering policy and employee pride, loyalty, and identification with the organization (Jones, Willness, & MacNeil, 2009). ABN-AMRO measured effects of volunteering on participants' and nonparticipants' attitudes and behavior, such as attitude toward work, intention to leave company, identification with company, and organizational citizenship behavior (Gilder, Shuyt, & Breedijk, 2005). Sears developed a model to measure the employee-customer-profit chain connection and found that a 5-point improvement in employee attitudes drives a 1.3-point improvement in customer satisfaction, which in turn drives a 0.5% improvement in revenue growth (Rucci, Kirn, & Quinn, 1998).

Obtaining information about the specific indicators and methodologies for data collection, however, has proven particularly challenging, as the information is often proprietary or companies are not willing to share it publicly. No commonly accepted and publicly available framework and indicators exist presently for measuring the business impacts of CCI programs and initiatives similar to the Global Reporting Initiative framework for sustainability reporting. There is a need to build on existing efforts and develop such a framework that would lead to greater use of common indicators and, respectively, benchmarking and transparency.

Why Measure the Business Value of CCI Programs?

As with any corporate initiative, measurement is critical in strategic planning and making decisions about the future of CCI programs. In times such as the deep recession of 2007–2009, such measures became even more important as budgets were slashed and companies cut everything that was not contributing to their bottom line (MIT Sloan, 2009). While green initiatives continued to expand during the recession of 2007–2009, community involvement programs experienced cuts, such as reduced giving, staff layoffs, and reduced volunteering opportunities for employees. For example, 38% of American companies reduced their philanthropy and giving in 2009 compared to a year earlier (BCCCC, 2009b).

Initial research from project participants revealed that companies are generally at different levels of measuring the business impact of CCI initiatives. Some are still very new to measurement and focus primarily on inputs and outputs (e.g., dollars donated, hours of volunteer work), while others are more advanced and have used consultants and various indicators to measure some business impacts (e.g., reputation, ROI, employee engagement). But community involvement practitioners from all participating companies admitted they were not sure which frameworks and tools are valid and credible and therefore they did not know what to measure and, often, how to measure it (Veleva, 2009b).

According to project participants, the main reasons companies are interested in measuring the business impact of their community programs include (see also Text Box 1):

- To gain support and funding for CCI initiatives
- To enhance CCI decision-making
- To facilitate benchmarking to industry peers or other companies
- To better integrate CCI strategy with their core business strategy
- To show CCI's contribution to the achievement of strategic business objectives
- To increase the power of CCI communications, both internally and externally

Interviews with participants revealed that the key stakeholders interested in measuring the business value of CCI initiatives are internal to the company—from the board of directors to senior leadership, the HR department, executive committees, and shareholders. External stakeholders, such as community organizations, socially responsible investors (SRI), authorities, nonprofit organizations, customers, and the public, appear much more interested in the *social* impacts than the business impacts.

The initial research revealed a clear need to advance the field by creating a commonly accepted and publicly available framework, which includes a small number of indicators for measuring the business value of CCI initiatives and allows for benchmarking among companies. Such a framework should also teach companies how to think about measurement and move beyond measuring inputs and outputs to measuring impacts. Indicators of business impacts would provide companies

---

Text Box 1. Why Companies Want to Measure the Business Impact of CCI Initiatives

"We want to demonstrate to board and senior management that there is a positive correlation between well-aligned CI investment and reputation/standing within community, positive name recognition and brand recognition . . . To demonstrate correlation with employee satisfaction and ability to attract and retain top quality employees."

"It will give us a tool we just don't have. When we are asked to demonstrate ROI there is just no data—only anecdotal."

"One driver is to internally communicate and generate value to business (the big one!). Second, to benchmark" (Veleva, 2009b).

with a strategic and operational management tool to help them better align CCI initiatives with the strategic business priorities and gain greater support internally. While indicators for measuring the business impacts of CCI programs would be very different from indicators measuring the social impacts, the process of developing such measures would be similar and could help companies advance their social measurements as well.

Overview and Analysis of Existing Measurement Frameworks

One barrier to better measurement of business impacts from CCI appears to be the lack of commonly accepted and credible frameworks and indicators. Attempts to advance triple-bottom-line measurement and accounting have not proved successful, as senior executives pay attention to indicators and metrics that address the financial bottom line (Norman & MacDonald, 2003). The Global Reporting Initiative, which has become the standardized framework worldwide for measuring and reporting sustainability performance, also does not attempt to measure the business impacts of social and environmental initiatives in terms of dollars saved, increased market share, or improved employee productivity (see www.globalreporting.org). Nevertheless, it has become the most widely accepted and used framework for sustainability reporting by large companies worldwide, as it allows for benchmarking and was developed in a participatory process with a large group of stakeholders globally. There is no such equivalent in the area of measuring the business value of CCI activities. A few frameworks exist, but these are often proprietary or do not provide sufficient guidance for using in practice.

Another key barrier to impact measurement appears to be the complexity and challenges in measuring impacts. For example, one project participant pointed out that measuring brand reputation is not an area of interest to his company because the issue is influenced by so many factors that may not be possible to control even in an experimental study. Measuring employee morale and retention and the ability to attract talent and build team skills is also not an easy undertaking. Accomplishing this may require more time and resources than tracking the number of volunteer hours or the total company/foundation giving (input indicators). Companies need more guidance on *how* to measure business impacts—a more standardized approach to collecting, analyzing, and reporting data.

Despite the importance of measuring the business impact of CCI initiatives, the field is still underdeveloped. Part of the reason is that corporate community involvement began as "doing the right thing" and was not intended to generate business value. As companies' corporate social responsibility (CSR) activities matured and became more strategic, community involvement initiatives were increasingly seen as a powerful tool for improving reputation, license to operate, spurring product and service innovation, or increasing employee engagement (Porter & Kramer, 2007). CSR branding, for example, has continued to grow as more studies demonstrate the value of social and environmental initiatives on brands (Holding, 2007).

In order to analyze existing frameworks and identify the gap in impact measurement, the research team established several criteria. First, a framework must measure the business impacts and not just the social or environmental impacts. Second, in order to advance the field, a framework must be publicly available and applicable for use by any company. Only a publicly available framework can promote greater social change and business responsibility as it increases transparency and enables stakeholder involvement and wider use by companies. Third, to truly move companies toward greater adoption of corporate citizenship practices, a framework must allow for benchmarking. For example, both companies and stakeholders have used published CSR reports based on the GRI framework to benchmark and identify best and worst performers. Another criterion used in the analysis is that a framework must be applicable at a project/program level and designed for use by businesses. For example, FSG Social Impact Advisors has developed an excellent system for measuring the social impact of grants. The framework, however, is applicable mostly to nonprofit organizations and foundations interested in sharing measurement and expanding their impacts (FSG, 2010). In order to measure business impacts and be able to communicate to top management, a framework should include quantitative indicators and data that could easily be linked to common business goals such as an increase in sales, reduction in turnover, improvement in customer service, or market share.

A critical analysis of existing measurement models[7] revealed that just a few frameworks exist that provide guidance on how to measure the business value of CCI initiatives at a program or project level, but in many cases these are proprietary. Four models stand out in terms of measuring the business value of CCI programs: the London Benchmarking Group Model, the True Impact ROI methodology, the Walker CPI model, and the Corporate Citizenship Company Model (see Table 1).

The London Benchmarking Group model measures both social and business impacts and focuses specifically on the impacts of a company's community involvement programs. The model is a management tool based on input-output analysis that consists of a set of standardized accounting principles to place a value on all investments (cash, time, in-kind, management costs) into community involvement programs. The model can be used for assessing short-term benefits as well as the longer-term impacts of CCI programs. Benchmarking data is available only to participating companies (LBG, 2009).

The *True Impact model* is based on a return-on-investment approach. Similar to the London Benchmarking Group model, it measures both social and business impacts of community involvement programs. Its major guiding principle is that what ultimately matters about any corporate program is how it affects the bottom line, that is, revenues, costs, and social goals. The model is developed as an online tool, and its underlying methodology is to map and then measure. Mapping includes determining who the internal and external stakeholders are, how the community

---

[7] Much of the information about existing frameworks for measuring the business value comes from an internal paper: Lee (2009).

Table 1. Comparative Analysis of Impact Measurement Frameworks[a]

	Measures social value	Measures business value	Provides benchmark	Targeted toward companies	Focus on project/ program level	Quantitative (not just yes/no or checklist)	Publicly available
London Benchmarking Group	△	△	△	△	△	△	
True Impact ROI	△	△	△	△	△	△	
Walker CPI	△	△		△		△	
MDG Measurement Framework[b]	△		△	△		△	△
Corporate Citizenship Co. Employees Model	△	△	△	△	△	△	△
Oxfam: Footprint Analysis[c]	△			△		△	△
New Economics Foundation: SRO[d]I	△			△	△	△	△
Boston College Center Standards of Excellence[e]	△			△	△		
WBCSF Impact Indicators[f]	△		△	△		△	△

[a]Source: Lee (2009).
[b]For more information, see http://www.un.org/en/development/desa/millennium-development-goals.html
[c]For more information, see Unilever's case study at http://www.unilever.com/Images/es_Exploring_the_Links_Executive_Summary_tcm13-43083.pdf
[d]For more information, see http://www.neweconomics.org/issues/entry/social-return-on-investment
[e]For more information, see http://bccorporatecitizenship.org/index.cfm?fuseaction=page.viewPage&pageID=2096&nodeID=1
[f]For more information, see www.wbcsd.org

involvement programs affect them, and finally, how these programs affect the company's bottom line. The measurement involves placing quantitative values (in terms of U.S. dollars) on the items that are mapped (True Impact, 2009).

The *Walker Corporate Philanthropy Index* (CPI) is a framework for measuring the business value of corporate philanthropy. The index can be used to determine whether there is a link between an individual company's giving initiatives and outcomes related to its business success. The major guiding principle of the model is that corporate activities increase shareholder value. Stakeholders who perceive a company as a responsible corporate citizen will have a favorable attitude toward the company and respectively behave in ways that increase the company's success (i.e., employees stay with the company longer, customers continue to purchase from the company, community leaders view the company as a neighbor of choice). The model is standardized and based on a survey of a company's key stakeholder groups (employees, customers, community influentials) (Walker Consulting, 2009).

The *Corporate Citizenship Company* has conducted a series of research studies around linking community involvement to improved workforce capacity and meeting the strategic HR goals of their organizations. While the model is limited to just employee impacts, such as morale, motivation, commitment, and performance, the 7-step approach and related case studies provide practical guidance for HR professionals interested in leveraging their community involvement programs for achieving strategic business goals related to employees (Tuffrey, 1998, 2003).

Other measurement frameworks and models identified include the Millennium Development Goals framework, WBCSD impact indicators, and the Global Reporting Initiative. These frameworks and models, however, focus only on measuring the social/environmental impacts of CCI initiatives and not the business impacts.

Several key findings emerged from the research on existing frameworks for measuring business impacts of CCI.

Currently, there are very few models that help measure the business impact of community involvement initiatives. Most of the models focus on measuring the social impacts. Some models look at the impact of the company as a whole and do not measure the impact of a particular CCI program or initiative to allow for benchmarking different programs.

Some business impacts are easier to measure than others. For example, it is much easier to measure the monetary value of a product sold at a volunteering event than to quantify the value of improved reputation (and respectively, sales) from a company logo being displayed at a charity event.

Some approaches to impact measurement are more effective than others. For example, when the measurement system is built into the community involvement initiative from the very beginning, indicators can be used "before" and "after" the program begins in order to allow for comparisons and better measurement of generated business value.

When measuring impacts, it is better to measure both social and business impacts instead of one or the other. Business impacts often affect social impacts and vice versa. In some cases, the business impact cannot be separated from the social impact.

Since each company is part of the communities where it operates, activities that benefit the community can also benefit the company, directly or indirectly.

In order to allow for benchmarking among companies and the impacts of their programs, it is important to use a common approach and methodology. If companies are not using the same approach and methodology to measure impacts, true comparisons cannot be made.

Most of the existing frameworks to measure business impacts are based on proprietary methodologies developed by private companies and/or consultancies. When companies have their own methodology for measuring business impacts of CCI initiatives, often they are not willing to openly share it. Many companies believe they should publicize only the social impacts of their community involvement initiatives to avoid being accused of trying to benefit from community support activities.

Recommendations for Developing a Framework for Measuring Business Value of CCI

Based on the interviews with participating companies and the key findings from the literature review, the research team established a set of criteria for developing the new framework for measuring business impacts of CCI initiatives. The framework should

- Raise awareness and help community involvement managers and other staff to move from measuring inputs and outputs to measuring impacts of community involvement programs;
- Focus on unmet need: providing a publicly available framework, guidance, and indicators for measuring business impacts by building on best efforts to date;
- Provide a comprehensive, disciplined approach to measurement;
- Include sample indicators, with detailed guidance on how to implement these in practice;
- Allow for benchmarking among companies and/or among various CCI programs within a company;
- Be applicable for a specific CCI program or an entire CCI initiative globally;
- Although not explicitly focused on measuring social impacts, the framework's overall approach should be easy to adapt for measuring social value.

In order to lead to program improvement and social change, the developed framework needs to focus both on the final product (indicators) and the process for selecting programs, impact indicators, and evaluating results. Below are included some recommendations for the development of the new framework.

A critical first step in measuring the business value of CCI initiatives is to understand what are the key business impacts pursued by the company. For example, a consumer-oriented company may be focused on selling more products or services, while a business-to-business organization may be more concerned with recruitment and retention of employees or its license to operate.

Unless a community involvement practitioner has a particular program in mind to measure, she or he needs to select among often numerous programs or initiatives. Measurement is a costly exercise, and it is important to target a program that is most likely to show business benefits. A good framework would provide detailed guidance on selecting a program to measure, such as whether it is clearly defined and operationally strong, whether it is integrated into the business and feasible to measure, and whether it is known to be effective and successful in providing public benefits.

To advance the field, the new framework needs to be both flexible (to reflect differences between industries and business models) and standardized (to allow for benchmarking). A flexible framework would provide guidance on how a company can develop its value-creation model (to understand how CCI is likely to add value to business) but not offer one model for all companies. Such a value creation model could involve linking inputs, activities, key stakeholders involved, and the resulting attitudinal and behavioral business impacts. Developing a value creation model allows for better decisions about what to measure.

Identifying indicators for measuring the business impact of interest is a key part of the proposed framework. While there are some indicators that will be common for companies across industries (e.g., workforce capacity measures such as retention, loyalty, and productivity), others will differ from company to company. In order to advance the field and allow for benchmarking, it is crucial to identify a small number of widely applicable indicators and develop detailed guidance on how to use them in practice. Additional guidance on how to develop company-specific or program-specific indicators should be included. For example, it is always best to build on indicators already measured by the company (e.g., add a question on employee volunteering in a companywide job satisfaction survey or a question on a community support initiative in a consumer marketing survey).

Table 2 provides examples of potential indicators for key business impacts and goals within three main categories:

- Growth/return on capital
- External relations/reputation
- Workforce capacity building

Each of these categories includes different business impacts that are linked to corporate goals and can be measured with specific indicators. Table 2 also includes examples of companies that have developed and/or implemented such indicators.

In many cases, a major challenge in measuring impacts is the complexity of the methodology for data collection. Often, indicators that are easy to measure have low validity. Obtaining high-validity results, however, is expensive, as it takes more time and resources (e.g., to hire external experts to design and conduct an experimental study). As a general rule, it is often better to first implement a low-validity measure, such as self-reporting, which can help to quickly check for positive correlation between a CCI program and a specific business impact. Having such information at hand can be either sufficient to demonstrate value to management or help build the case for more rigorous (and expensive) measurement such as triangulation or experimental design.

Data collection will be easier in some cases than others, but in all cases it will require developing a data-collection protocol. Such a protocol can include data from sales or marketing (e.g., number of new customers, sales of a particular product) or developing a survey. New Balance, for example, tracks sales of shoes at each Susan G. Komen Walk for Breast Cancer event. If each sale of a pair of shoes brings $30 profit, each try-on is estimated to be worth $3, and each impression $0.01, the business value of this social marketing initiative can easily be calculated. In another case, Eli Lilly asked the question, "To what extent was the Day of Service a meaningful team-building event for you?" in its post-project survey. This allowed it to track and evaluate the value of this volunteering program for improving employee job satisfaction.

Evaluation is a critical component of any effective program management. Involvement of a greater number of stakeholders—both internal and external—in discussion of the measurement findings would help identify weaknesses in the program or the measurement as well as the most effective ways to address them. It remains to be seen, however, how willing companies will be to share measurement findings externally.

DISCUSSION AND CONCLUSION

While the proposed framework will focus only on measuring the business impacts of CCI initiatives, it is critical to link it to other frameworks that measure social impacts or develop an integrated framework in the future that helps measure both. To truly foster social change, social impact indicators need to be measured together with business impact indicators and communicated to stakeholders. While this research did not include a comprehensive literature review on social impact measurement, studies have demonstrated that companies "generally remain uninterested in measuring the impact of their social initiatives" (Arli & Zappala, 2009). Measurements are focused primarily on inputs and outputs, not on the social impacts of CCI initiatives. The main barriers to social impact measurement seem to be the lack of time and resources to measure such impacts, the lack of interest in such measures, and the lack of standardized frameworks and measures.

To foster business or social change, one needs to look at the entire system and engage a wide array of stakeholders in the process (Foster-Fishman & Behrens, 2007). While business implementation of the proposed framework remains to be seen, legitimate questions from community stakeholders include: How do businesses select the programs to support? Are they going to disclose the indicators, and are they considering some unintended consequences of measuring business impact? For example, a program may demonstrate the lack of significant business impact, but it could be helping to address a critical social issue. Would that mean that a company needs to discontinue its support for it? Is strategic philanthropy always a good idea? Some NGOs and community-based stakeholders have questioned

Table 2. Examples of Indicators for Measuring Business Impacts of CCI Programs

Category of business value	Impact	Potential indicators	Company
1. Growth/Return on capital	New markets	• Number and value of new markets entered • $ revenues generated	Novo Nordisk
	Innovation/New products/services	• Number and value of new products developed and sold • Number and market value of new patents developed	The Gap
	New consumers/Customer retention	• Number and value ($ sales) of new customers • Number or percentage of customers retained as result of CCI	Verizon, New Balance
2. External relations/Reputation	Corporate reputation	• Change in reputation ranking/stakeholder opinion	Intel, British Gas
		• Dollar sales to top customers with philanthropic tie • Amount of positive media coverage	Aetna
	Differentiation/Customer loyalty	• Customer loyalty (percentage of consumers citing CI program as key to loyalty) • Visibility index	JCPenney, Allstate, UGI Utilities
	License to operate	• Reduction in time/$ for obtaining permits	Intel
	Investor interest/Confidence/stock performance	• Percentage of investors with increased interest in company • Inclusion in social indices	

3. Workforce capacity	Managerial/leadership skills/employee development	• Percentage improvement in employee key competencies as result of volunteering • Percentage improvement in performance	IBM, Bank of America
	Productivity	• Number of percentage of "highly engaged" employees	
	Loyalty/morale/job satisfaction	• Employee loyalty • Change in ranking of CCI involvement in job satisfaction survey	Green Mountain Coffee Roasters, Aetna
	Recruitment	• Number of new talent added as result of program • Importance of CCI program to young workers	Deloitte
	Retention	• Percentage of employees citing CCI program among top factors for staying in company • Cost of training new employees	BAE Systems

strategic philanthropy.[8] While the proposed framework is based on the assumption that there could be no business value without creating social value first, more research is needed to explore this assumption.

Developing standardized indicators is one of the key drivers for companies interested in impact measurement. Such indicators allow for benchmarking, which can be a powerful driving force for business change and social change. Developing such standardized indicators, however, is challenging as it involves some trade-offs (Kreger, Brindis, & Mannuel, 2007; Veleva & Ellenbecker, 2000). One common trade-off is between simplicity and comprehensiveness—if the framework is to be easy to use, it needs to be simple and based on a small number of steps and indicators. If it is to be comprehensive and follow a disciplined approach to identifying all possible business impacts from CCI, it would be more complex and based on a larger number of indicators. Finding the right balance is always a challenge, but it is critical for successful implementation.

Finally, business impact indicators are only tools, and they alone cannot lead to social change. Top management support, stakeholder involvement, and greater transparency are among the key factors that can foster wider use of such indicators and ultimately lead to business change and social change. What such indicators can do, however, is raise awareness, inform decision-making, and promote accountability and continuous improvement.

ACKNOWLEDGMENTS

The author would like to thank the following organizations for funding the research: Aetna Foundation, Altria Client Services, Amway, Best Buy, Hewlett Packard, Intel, Lockheed Martin, Merck, and Underwriters Laboratories. In addition, the author would like to thank Bea Boccalandro, Allison Lee, Chris Pinney, Phil Mirvis, Jane Coen, and Maureen Hart for their work on the project.

DISCUSSION QUESTIONS

Chapter 11: Toward Developing a Framework for Measuring the Business Value of Corporate Community Involvement

1. What is "corporate community involvement" and how does it help create business value?
2. What are some existing frameworks for measuring the business value of community involvement initiatives? What are their key weaknesses?
3. Provide examples of indicators for measuring the business value of community involvement in each of the three categories: a) growth/return on capital, b) external relations/reputation, and c) workforce capacity. Which indicators are the most difficult to measure and why?

---

[8]Based on discussion in the conference breakout session: Veleva, Coen, & Hart (2009).

4. Select a company and research the use of indicators for measuring the business value of community involvement. Report on your findings and discuss gaps found, if any.

References

Arli, D., & Zappala, G. (2009, August). Why do companies ignore measuring the social impact of their corporate community involvement programs? *The Centre for Social Impact*. CSI Briefing Paper No. 4.

Boccalandro, B. (2009, April). Mapping success in employee volunteering: The drivers of effectiveness for employee volunteering and giving programs and Fortune 500 performance. *Boston College Center for Corporate Citizenship*. Retrieved April 30, 2010, from http://www.bccc.net/index.cfm?fuseaction=document.showDocumentByID &DocumentID=1308

Becchetti, L., Di Giacomo, S., & Pinnacchio, D. (2008, March). Corporate social responsibility and corporate performance: Evidence from a panel of U.S. listed companies. *Applied Economics*.

Bonini, S., Brun, N., & Rosenthal, M. (2009, February). Valuing corporate social responsibility. *The McKinsey Quarterly*.

Boston College Center for Corporate Citizenship (BCCCC). (2009a). *How virtue creates value for business and society: Investigating the value of environmental, social and governance activities*. Retrieved April 30, 2010, from http://www.bcccc.net/index.cfm?fuseaction= document.showDocumentByID&DocumentID=1269

Boston College Center for Corporate Citizenship (BCCCC). (2009b). *Weathering the storm: The state of corporate citizenship in the United States 2009*. Retrieved April 30, 2010, from http://www.bcccc.net/index.cfm?fuseaction=document.showDocumentByID &DocumentID=1333

City of London. (2010, May). *Volunteering—The business case*. Retrieved April 27, 2010, from http://www.cityoflondon.gov.uk/business/economic-research-and-information/research-publications/Document/research-2010/Volunteering_The%20Business%20Case.pdf

Edmans, A. (2009) Does the stock market fully value intangibles? Employee satisfaction and equity prices. *University of Pennsylvania, The Wharton School*. Retrieved May 3, 2010, from http://papers.ssrn.com/sol3/papers.cfm?aabstract_id=985735

Foster-Fishman, P., & Behrens, T. (2007). Systems change reborn: Rethinking our theories, methods and efforts in human services reform and community-based change. *American Journal of Community Psychology, 39,* 191–196.

FSG Social Impact Advisors. (2010, March 24). *Breakthroughs in shared measurement systems: Systemic approaches to evaluation* [webinar presentation]. Retrieved from http:// www.fsg.org/Portals/0/Uploads/Documents/PDF/breakthroughs_webinar_presentation. pdf?cpgn=Webinar%20DL%20-%20Coll%20Imp%20Shared%20Measurement%20ppt

Gallup Consulting. (2008). *Employee engagement: What's your engagement ratio?* Retrieved April 30, 2010, http://www.memphisbusinessgroup.org/assets/1441/employee_engagement_ overview_brochure.pdf

Gilder, D., Shuyt, T., & Breedijk, M. (2005). Effects of an employee volunteering program on the work force: The ABN-AMRO case. *Journal of Business Ethics, 61,* 143–152.

Holding, C. (2007, August 23). CSR's impact on brands grows. *Policy Innovations*. Retrieved May 4, 2010, from http://www.policyinnovations.org/ideas/commentary/data/csr_ brand_impact

Jones, D. A., Willness, C. R., & MacNeil, S. (2009). Corporate social responsibility and recruitment: Person-organization fit and signaling mechanisms. In G. T. Solomon (Ed.), *Proceedings of the 69th annual meeting of the Academy of Management.* ISSN 1543-8643.

Jones, D. A., Willness, C. R., & Madey, S. (2010). Why are some job seekers attracted to socially responsible companies? Testing underlying mechanisms. In L. A. Toombs (Ed.), *Proceedings of the 70th annual meeting of the Academy of Management.* ISSN 1543-8643.

Kreger, M., Brindis, C., & Mannuel, D. (2007). Lessons learned in systems change initiatives: Benchmarks and indicators. *American Journal of Community Psychology, 39,* 301–320.

Lee, A. (2009, June). *Discussion paper on landscape analysis and next steps in impact measurement project.* Boston College Center for Corporate Citizenship.

London Benchmarking Group (LBG). (2009). What is The LBG Model? Retrieved April 30, 2010, from http://www.lbg-online.net/about-lbg/the-lbg-model.aspx

MIT Sloan Management Review. (2009, September). *The business of sustainability.* Retrieved April 30, 2010, from http://www.mitsmr-ezine.com/busofsustainability/2009#pg1

Norman, W., & MacDonald, C. (2003). Getting to the bottom of the "triple bottom line." *Business Ethics Quarterly, 14*(2), 243–262. Retrieved May 4, 2010, from http://www.jstor.org/pss/3857909

Orlitzky, M., Schmidt, F., & Rynes, S. (2004, December). Corporate social and financial performance: A meta-analysis. *Social Investment Forum Foundation.* Retrieved May 4, 2010, from http://www.freewebs.com/marcorlitzky/Papers/orlitzkyschmidtrynes2003os.pdf

Pinney, C. (2009). Framework for the future. *Boston College Center for Corporate Citizenship.* Retrieved April 27, 2010, from http://www.bccc.net/index.cfm?pageId=2008

Porter, M., & Kramer, M. (2007). Strategy and society: The link between competitive advantage and corporate social responsibility. *Harvard Business Review, 85,* 136–137.

PriceWaterHouseCoopers (PwC). (2003). *Integral business: Integrating sustainability and business strategy.* Retrieved May 4, 2010, from http://www.pwc.com/en_GX/gx/sustainability/integralbusinessreport.pdf

Rucci, A., Kirn, S., & Quinn, R. (1998, January/February). The employee-customer profit chain at Sears. *Harvard Business Review, 1998,* 82–97.

True Impact. (2009). *About Us.* Retrieved April 30, 2010, from http://www.trueimpact.com/about.html

Tuffrey, M. (1998). Valuing employee community involvement: Practical guidance on measuring the business benefits from employee involvement in community activity. *The Corporate Citizenship Company.* Retrieved April 27, 2010, from http://corporate-citizenship.com/wp-content/uploads/Valuing-Employee-Community-Involvement.pdf

Tuffrey, M. (2003). Good companies, better employees: How community involvement and good corporate citizenship can enhance employee morale, motivation, commitment and performance. *The Corporate Citizenship Company.* Retrieved May 4, 2010, from http://www.centrica.com/files/reports/2005cr/files/csr_Good_companies_better_employees.pdf

Valentine, S., & Fleischman, G. (2008). Ethics programs, perceived corporate social responsibility and job Satisfaction. *Journal of Business Ethics, 77,* 159–172.

Veleva, V. (2009a). Managing corporate citizenship: A new tool for companies. *Corporate Social Responsibility and Environmental Management.* Retrieved April 30, 2010, from http://www3.interscience.wiley.com/cgi-bin/fulltext/122456956/PDFSTART

Veleva, V. (2009b, June). *Summary of key intake interview findings: Impact measurement project* [internal paper]. Boston College Center for Corporate Citizenship.

Veleva, V., Coen, J., & Hart, M. (2009, October 1–2). *Measuring the business value of corporate community initiatives.* Community Indicator Consortium 2009 International Conference: Community Indicators as Tools for Social Change, Bellevue, WA.

Veleva, V., & Ellenbecker, M. (2000, Autumn). A proposal for measuring business sustainability: Addressing the shortcomings in existing frameworks. *Greener Management International, 31,* 101–120.

Veleva, V., Hart, M., Greiner, T., & Crumbley, C. (2001). Indicators of sustainable production. *Journal of Cleaner Production, 9,* 447–454.

Walker Consulting. (2009). Knowledge Center. Retrieved April 30, 2010, from http://www.walkerinfo.com/knowledge-center/

Section III.
Case Studies in CSR and Environmental Management

Chapter 12

STONYFIELD FARM—THE BUSINESS MODEL FOR SOCIAL AND ENVIRONMENTAL RESPONSIBILITY: A CASE STUDY[1]

ABSTRACT

Founded in 1983 as a small family-owned yogurt firm, Stonyfield Farm became a $96.8 million company in 2002, with over 4% of the yogurt market in the United States and the largest producer of organic yogurt nationwide. Despite its impressive growth, the company has held to its founding mission to support small family-run dairies in New England, provide a healthful, productive and enjoyable workplace for all employees, and serve as a model to show that environmentally and socially responsible businesses can also be profitable. This case study analyzes the drivers and incentives for environmental and social decision-making that have driven the company on the way to sustainability. It demonstrates that even small companies with limited resources can achieve business success while following sustainability principles.

Key words: sustainability drivers, organic agriculture, environmental and social responsibility, sustainability indicators.

[1] Reprinted from: Veleva V., "Stonyfield Farm – The Business Model for Social and Environmental Responsibility", *REAd – Revista Eletrônica de Administração*, Special Issue 36, Vol. 9, No. 6, December 2003, pp. 223-246, by permission of the publisher.

1 INTRODUCTION

This chapter presents the case of Stonyfield Farm—a small, family-owned yogurt firm, which grew to become a $100 million company in 2003, while holding to its founding mission to support small family-run dairies in New England; provide a healthful, productive, and enjoyable workplace for all employees; and protect the environment.

One of the objectives of the case study is to demonstrate that companies that are environmentally and socially responsible in their business practices can also be profitable. At the same time, the chapter raises the question why some companies choose to go green or even pursue sustainability. Is this a response to outside pressures, an attempt to build a competitive advantage, or expression of their values "to do the right thing?" Another key objective of the chapter is to explore the key sustainability drivers and capabilities behind Stonyfield Farm's success and thus provide valuable lessons to other companies that have chosen to pursue sustainability.

The data for this case were collected during the period 1998–2000, when the author participated in developing the company's first mission report as part of a joint project with the Lowell Center for Sustainable Production. Additional information was collected in 2002 in an interview with the company's Vice President of Natural Resources, Nancy Hirshberg.

The chapter begins with an overview of the yogurt industry followed by Stonyfield Farm's story and its social mission. Next comes a discussion of the key drivers and capabilities behind socially and environmentally responsible business practices. The chapter then presents some of Stonyfield Farm's key achievements within the five mission areas. It concludes with a discussion of the corporate capabilities and factors for success, the company's future plans, and how these relate to sustainability.

2 COMPANY BACKGROUND AND MARKET PROFILE

2.1 Industry Profile

The yogurt-making business is highly competitive. It began in the United States in 1929. The Colombosian family, Armenians who lived in Andover, Massachusetts, started Colombo and Sons creamery. Later the company was purchased by General Mills and incorporated as Colombo. In 1919, near Barcelona, Isaac Carasso came out with Danone. He brought it to the United States in 1941. In 1998, the company, called Danone Group, had over 15% of the world fresh dairy market. In 2002, its U.S. subsidiary, Dannon, had 29% of the national grocery yogurt market (see Table 1).

The annual sales of yogurt in grocery stores[2] in the United States for fiscal year 2002 were $2.5 billion and grew at a rate of 10% (see Table 1). The main companies in the sector included Yoplait, Dannon, Breyers, Stonyfield Farm, and Colombo.

---

[2]Grocery store sales are the sales at the retail level, and these differ from the wholesale level, usually tracked by a company.

Table 1. U.S. Yogurt Grocery Sales
(52 weeks ending December 29, 2002)

No.	Company	Dollar share, %	Dollar sales	Dollar sales % change from a year ago
1	Yoplait	34.0	$868,333,888	11.5%
2	Dannon	29.0	$741,708,544	8.3%
3	Breyers	13.4	$341,536,576	10.4%
4	Private Label	5.4	$138,505,840	(12.3%)
5	Stonyfield Farm	4.1	$103,649,064	7.6%
6	Colombo Inc.	2.7	$68,931,880	(8.0%)
7	Yofarm Corp.	2.0	$50,082,984	31.2%
8	La Yogurt	1.3	$32,111,098	3.1%
9	Mountain High	1.2	$29,693,450	5.6%
10	Axelrod	0.7	$17,557,054	84.1%
	TOTAL	100.0	$2,555,894,784	10%

Source: IRI (Information Resources, Inc.).

Over the past 3 years, Stonyfield Farm managed to move its position from the fifth to the fourth branded[3] yogurt in the sector, passing the well-known brand Colombo.

The 2002 sales of yogurt in the natural foods market[4] were $105.5 million, of which Stonyfield Farm had 38.3% (or $40.4 million), followed by Brown Cow, Horizon, Wholesoy, and White Wave. In 2003, Stonyfield Farm acquired Brown Cow and thus further increased its share in this market.

Stonyfield Farm's business success is impressive considering how the company started two decades ago.

2.2 Stonyfield Farm's History, Products, and Market

The founder of Stonyfield Farm, Samuel Kaymen, had only modest aspirations and never intended his company to capture a market share when he first began making yogurt. In fact, he entered the yogurt-making business unintentionally. In 1978, he was running the Rural Education Center in Wilton, New Hampshire, to "teach organic agriculture and care of earth." Kaymen started making yogurt because "the

---

[3] "Private label" is not a company but an aggregation of store brands and is therefore not considered a competitor.

[4] Natural foods market is tracked separately from the grocery store sales.

funding for the school dried up." At that time, he was making small amounts of yogurt for the family needs. A few years later, in 1983, Kaymen decided to found a yogurt company—Stonyfield Farm—with Gary Hirshberg as CEO.

Before becoming Stonyfield Farm's CEO, Hirshberg was director of the ecological research group New Alchemy Institute in Falmouth, Cape Cod. Disappointed by the limited power of NGOs (nongovernmental organizations) to affect changes, he seized a different approach, that of a businessman. Business interfaces with millions of consumers daily, which is an enormous opportunity to reach a large audience. In addition, business has the resources, the global reach, and the responsibility to move the world toward greater sustainability. Therefore, Hirshberg was determined to find a way to harness the power of corporate America to advance his cause (Gray, 1998).

In 1989, after 6 years of struggling to survive, Stonyfield Farm began to grow and moved to a new plant in Londonderry, New Hampshire, to provide more capacity for its expansion. Since then, the company has achieved an annual growth of 25% to 30%. Its sales in 1996 were $31.5 million, in 1999 they were $53 million, and in 2002 they were $96.8 million, compared to $2.5 million in 1990. The percentage growth would likely slow down over time, but Stonyfield Farm would still remain one of the fastest growing companies in the sector (see Table 1), achieving its goal of $100 million a year in 2003. In 2002, the company employed 180 people and had one production facility in Londonderry, New Hampshire, which was expanded to meet the increasing production needs.

With over 4% share of the yogurt market in the United States, Stonyfield Farm distributes its production to all 50 states. Some 67% of its 2002 sales were certified organic, up from 30% only 3 years ago (Greiner, 2000). This made Stonyfield Farm the largest producer of organic yogurt in the country. In 2002, its product line included over 80 different products, such as

- YoBaby Organic Whole Milk Yogurt for babies and toddlers
- YoSqueeze Organic Portable Lowfat Yogurt
- Organic Whole Milk Yogurt
- O'Soy Organic Cultured Soy
- Organic Drinkable Lowfat Yogurt
- Organic Super Premium Ice Cream
- Organic Frozen Yogurt (nonfat and low fat). (Stonyfield Farm, 2002)

The company uses only natural ingredients in its products. No artificial colors, sweeteners, preservatives, or thickeners are used. Its entire yogurt contains six live, active cultures, and in 2002, it was the only brand in the United States with L. reuteri, which was scientifically proven to boost immune system defenses and enhance the body's resistance to gastrointestinal disease. Recently, Stonyfield Farm began to add inulin to its products—a natural dietary fiber and prebiotic that has been clinically shown to increase calcium absorption up to 20%.

Following its founding mission to support small family farms, Stonyfield Farm receives milk from local co-ops. St. Albans Cooperative Creamery in St. Albans, Vermont, supplies the company with conventional milk. The organic milk is provided by CROPP, a co-op based in Wisconsin, which includes dairy farms in Vermont and

Maine. No milk comes from New Hampshire, since it is not a dairy state and had only 160 dairy farms in 2002, none of which organic (for comparison, Vermont had 1,433 dairy farms in 2002) (N. Hirshberg, interview, July 1, 2002). According to Stonyfield Farm's requirements, participating farmers do not treat the cows with the synthetic bovine growth hormone (rBGH).

3 STONYFIELD FARM'S MISSION AND SUSTAINABILITY

Stonyfield Farm rarely uses the word "sustainability." However, its mission and accomplishments are examples of social, economic, and environmental responsibility.

According to CEO Gary Hirshberg, the model business should have environmentally sound business practices. It must be a place where employees enjoy working and feel personally fulfilled. In the case of yogurt making, it would produce high quality all natural products made with ingredients grown with sustainable agricultural practices that are environmentally sound and return a fair price to the farmers. Perhaps most importantly, the business would be profitable and provide an exceptional return on investment. Otherwise, it would not be a viable model (Stonyfield Farm, 2000).

In developing the original business plan for the company in 1984, Gary Hirshberg crafted Stonyfield Farm's mission and its five key components: quality, environmental responsibility, profitability/return on investment, employee well-being, and support of family farms (see Figure 1). For most of its first decade, the company was focused on staying in business and making a quality product. In the second decade much more work was devoted to trying to fulfill the founding mission and, in doing so, be a model for others (Stonyfield Farm 2000).

In 1998, the Lowell Center for Sustainable Production[5] approached Stonyfield Farm with an offer to work with the company to develop a set of sustainability indicators. Stonyfield Farm responded willingly and a 2-year partnership ensued. This project allowed Stonyfield Farm to revisit its mission, further define the five key areas, and develop a set of indicators to measure progress toward its mission and goals (see Figure 2).

Stonyfield Farm's interest in developing a suite of sustainability indicators came with one significant constraint: The effort could not require a large time investment of the company's senior and middle managers. This time constraint recognized the Herculean efforts that managers were devoting to the rapidly expanding production. Setting aside considerable time to focus on sustainability training and education would force managers to divert time needed to manage the company's rapid growth. This constraint was especially problematic because the understanding of sustainability concepts among line workers and most managers was quite poor, according to

[5]The Lowell Center for Sustainable Production (LCSP) was established in 1996 at the University of Massachusetts Lowell to promote sustainable production practices. It includes faculty members from several departments and has been involved in numerous projects with businesses, NGOs, and communities in the United States and abroad.

Stonyfield Farm Mission Statement

1. To provide the very highest quality, best-tasting, all natural and certified organic products.
2. To educate consumers and producers about the value of protecting the environment and of supporting family farmers and sustainable farming methods.
3. To serve as a model that environmentally and socially responsible businesses can also be profitable.
4. To provide a healthful, productive and enjoyable work place for all employees, with opportunities to gain new skills and advance personal career goals.
5. To recognize our obligations to stockholders and lenders by providing an excellent return on their investment.

Figure 1. Stonyfield Farm's mission statement.

Family Farm Indicators
- Percentage of organic sales
- Organic acres supported
- Number of small family dairy farms supported

Profitability/Return on Investment Indicators
- Net sales
- Stock price
- Market share

Environmental Indicators
- Solid waste
- Pesticides
- Supply-chain greenhouse gas emissions

Enjoyable Workplace Indicators
- Compensation
- Vacation time
- Holidays
- Turnover rate
- Length of service
- Stock ownership

Figure 2. Sample mission indicators at Stonyfield Farm.

Nancy Hirshberg, Vice President of Natural Resources. At the onset of the project, half of the company's 18-member senior- and middle-management team had been with the company for 2 years or less.

Led by Gary and Nancy Hirshberg, the program involved top and middle management throughout the company's Leadership Team. The latter was a cross-functional/cross-departmental group, which included representatives from all main departments: production, sales, marketing, human resources, and environmental department, among others. The Team met regularly to address some problems or initiate new projects. The key obstacle in the beginning was to get "buy-in" from the staff for this project. Overwhelmed with responsibilities related to company growth and expansion, people did not have the time for any additional work, according to Ms. Hirshberg. Line workers and the Board of Directors were not involved in the program, but this might change in the future. Stonyfield Farm recognized that it was communicating its mission better externally (to its customers and general public) than internally (to its employees). Wider employee education and involvement in sustainability projects became one of the key goals, according to Ms. Hirshberg.

4 SUSTAINABILITY DRIVERS

Why do some companies choose to go green or even pursue sustainability? Is this a response to outside pressures, an attempt to build a competitive advantage, or an expression of their values to "do the right thing?" Past research on organizations and environment typically referred to four drivers of corporate ecological response: legislation, stakeholder pressures, economic opportunities, and ethical motives (Bansal & Roth, 2000, p. 717). For example, projects to reduce energy use and waste can lead to significant savings (Veleva, Bailey, & Jurczyk, 2001, p. 327). Legislative bans on chemicals can lead to innovation and use of environmentally benign substitutes.

New research on corporate drivers, however, has demonstrated that there are more complex dynamics between what is happening within an organization and in the field it operates. According to Hoffman (2001, p. 135), how a company acts is determined by an entire web of interactions between two types of factors: institutional and cultural. The institutional factors (also called "occupational communities") include suppliers and buyers, consumers, financial institutions, shareholders, investors, insurance underwriters, trade associations, academic institutions, and religious organizations. The cultural factors represent the different approaches (or cultural frames) an organization may take. Hoffman classifies these into eight basic frames: operational efficiency, risk management, capital acquisition, social responsibility, market demand, strategic direction, human resource management, and regulatory compliance (p. 140). Often organizations may have multiple institutional pressures and cultural frames, which lead to a greater variety of responses.

Based on extensive qualitative study, Bansal and Roth (2000, p. 717) identified three key motivations for companies to go green: competitiveness, legitimation, and ecological responsibility. Competitiveness relates to developing and sustaining a competitive advantage. Legitimation is defined as "the desire of a firm to improve the appropriateness of its actions within an established set of regulations, norms, values, or beliefs." Ecological responsibility represents the activities targeted at improving a firm's impact on the environment (Bansal & Roth, 2000, p. 726).

What does the case of Stonyfield Farm demonstrate to the theory and practice of sustainability? The following sections explore the motivations and the key external and internal factors behind the company's pursuit of sustainability.

4.1 External Drivers

According to Ms. Hirshberg, the key external driver for Stonyfield Farm was the current state of the environment—constantly increasing pollution, resource depletion, and biodiversity loss, among others (N. Hirshberg, interview, July 1, 2002). This was the key motivating factor behind the company's founding mission. Stonyfield Farm simply wanted to be a good corporate steward, which corresponds to what Bansal and Roth (2000) call "ecological responsibility." This motivating factor represents the ethical aspect of environmental action, which emerges from the "concern for the social good" (Bansal & Roth, 2000, p. 728). Instead of acting only for pragmatic reasons, companies act because it is "the right thing to do."

Competitiveness has also been a motivating factor for Stonyfield Farm, although somewhat less significant. Bansal and Roth (2000, p. 724) argue that firms motivated by competitiveness "actively innovate ecologically benign processes and products to enhance their market position." Striving for sustainable practices has allowed Stonyfield Farm to differentiate itself from competitors and has provided clear public relation benefits. For example, in 1999 alone the company estimated that the received media attention was worth over $66,000. Although there were some attempts to mimic Stonyfield Farm's approach,[6] most of the companies in the sector were still in the pollution control/compliance stage (Ehrenfeld, 1996).

Stonyfield Farm has constantly sought to "improve the appropriateness of its actions within the established set of regulations, norms, values or beliefs," which Bansal and Roth (2000, p. 726) call "the legitimation factor." Developing strong connections with local communities, environmental advocates, customers, and suppliers—the stakeholders who are establishing the new norms of corporate behavior—are examples of how an organization can be an active participant in defining the norms rather than been trapped in a constant struggle for compliance.

Regulations and government relations were not a driving force behind Stonyfield Farm's sustainability efforts, according to Ms. Hirshberg. However, these were important for highlighting key environmental problems and areas of concern (N. Hirshberg, interview, July 1, 2002).

4.2 Internal Drivers

The key internal driver for Stonyfield Farm's sustainability efforts had always been top management commitment, led by the Hirshbergs. As discussed earlier, Mr. Hirshberg was a former NGO activist who turned to business in order to make a greater impact on people and the environment. Ms. Hirshberg has been with the company since 1991. She is a passionate proponent of sustainability at Stonyfield Farm, and some of her major efforts included starting the company's organic program, managing the solid waste minimization program, developing

---

[6]In 1994, Dannon started the "Danimals" campaign, which put messages about wild animals on its yogurt containers and promised to donate a percentage of its profits to the National Wildlife Federation. In 1999, Colombo began the production of organic yogurt. Both efforts were short-lived and not very successful.

partnerships with NGOs for educational campaigns, and spearheading the mission program to get employees to improve the company mission performance. She had been active with the Business for Social Responsibility, Organic Trade Association, and EcoPartners. Both Mr. Hirshberg and Ms. Hirshberg were guest speakers at many national and international conferences and meetings, such as the International Dairy Federation, the National Town Meeting on Sustainability, and Business for Social Responsibility.

Another driver behind Stonyfield Farm's unique approach was its shareholders' support. The company's initial investors included individuals and foundations with clearly expressed environmental and social values.

5 STONYFIELD FARM'S SUSTAINABILITY ACHIEVEMENTS

Developing mission indicators allowed Stonyfield Farm to evaluate in a more consistent way its progress within each of the five key mission areas. The indicators were published in a Mission Report, used only internally (Stonyfield Farm, 2000). A growing number of companies today are using some form of environmental or sustainability indicators to better manage their operations as well as to communicate results to interested stakeholders (Veleva & Ellenbecker, 2000). Figure 2 presents some of Stonyfield Farm's mission indicators. Evaluating the indicators revealed that the company was doing well in the areas of quality, profitability, and environment. The key challenge identified by the Leadership Team in year 2000 was employee turnover rate (particularly among hourly workers), which was partially due to the strong economy and related labor movement. Additional areas for improvement included operations/office policies, employee involvement and education about family farming, product packaging, and climate change. This section provides highlights of Stonyfield Farm's numerous achievements in the main mission areas.

5.1 Quality Organic Products and Family Farms

Stonyfield Farm was established in order to support and revive interest in New England's declining family farmers. Some 20 years later, it was still following this mission. Stonyfield Farm was buying milk mainly from family-run diaries that produce organic or conventional milk without genetically engineered bovine growth hormone (rBGH). Such hormones are added to a cow's feed to increase milk production. According to Mr. Hirshberg, "The wide use of genetically engineered bovine growth hormones (rBGH) could raise milk supply and lower prices to a point at which family-owned dairies could not compete with large producers" (Stonyfield's Hirshberg, 1998). Stonyfield Farm, along with Ben & Jerry's, and Organic Valley, successfully fought an Illinois ban on labeling rBGH-free products.

Organically grown food promotes biological diversity, recycling of nutrients, and preservation of soil fertility. It prevents the introduction of toxic and persistent chemical pesticides and fertilizers into the environment and food chain. In addition, to achieve "certified organic status," farmers must not use growth hormones and antibiotics. Many studies have related the use of pesticides and hormones to some cancers (Levy & Wegman, 1995, p. 668). Thus, Stonyfield Farm provided more jobs while at the same time protecting the environment and human health. The dairy industry nationwide has been drastically changing its structure. Between 1954 and 1992, the number of farms in the United States decreased 95% (Outlaw, Jacobson, Knutson, & Schwart, 1996, p. 2). This shift from small, family-run farms to large, typically confined animal feeding operations (CAFOs) has led to loss of local jobs, increasing environmental pollution (animal waste and water contamination), and the use of genetically engineered hormones and antibiotics.

5.2 Consumer and Producer Education

Stonyfield Farm has always been an education-oriented firm. According to Mr. Hirshberg, the company has done "a very good job of closing the gap between consumers and the environment." To promote consumer awareness of small farms, Stonyfield Farm initiated the "Have-a-Cow" program, whereby consumers were encouraged to "adopt" a cow. Stonyfield Farm also targeted global warming in its "Put a Lid on Global Warming" campaign. The firm partnered with the Union of Concerned Scientists (UCSs) in an effort to combat the $13 million advertising campaign by industries opposing global warming. During the campaign, Stonyfield Farm printed a global warming message on more than five million yogurt container lids.

Stonyfield Farm has a special Visitor's Center and offers tours of its facility. The visitor center's purpose is mainly educational. It offers souvenirs, yogurt, and information about the company. Approximately 20,000 people visit the plant annually, which has been another opportunity to educate consumers about family farming, organic agriculture, and environmental protection. The Center offers various cookbooks and other publications to educate consumers on organic food and healthy living, such as "A Practical Guide to Understanding Organic."

5.3 Environmental Responsibility

One of Stonyfield Farm's main goals was to reduce carbon dioxide emissions associated with its manufacturing and production. Figure 3 demonstrates that the CO_2 emissions per unit of product decreased significantly since 1994. In addition, Stonyfield Farm initiated several projects that completely offset its facility CO_2 emissions[7] (N. Hirshberg, interview, July 1, 2002). The projects included reforestation in the Northwest, building energy efficient straw-bale homes in China, replacing inefficient oil boilers with natural gas boilers in schools, and methane recovery from coal mines in Ohio and other states. Each of these projects led to specific reductions in the atmospheric CO_2 emissions and when subtracted from Stonyfield Farm's facility emissions, the total was net zero.

For its unique approach and significant achievements with regard to global warming, in May 1999, the President's Council for Sustainable Development awarded Stonyfield Farm the National Award for Sustainability (NTM, 1999).

---

[7]Facility CO_2 emissions include the emissions from the production processes within a facility. They do not count emissions from transportation, raw materials extraction, or product use.

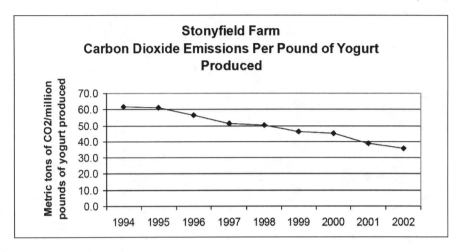

Figure 3. Stonyfield Farm CO_2 emissions.

At the same time, Stonyfield Farm recognizes that most of its impacts on climate change are in the supply chain, such as product packaging and methane from cows. This became particularly clear after implementing the sustainability indicators and measuring the company's global warming potential over the supply chain. To address this issue, Stonyfield Farm has constantly been searching for more environmentally friendly packaging materials.

Energy use is directly linked to global warming, but it also generates air pollutants, such as sulfur dioxide and nitrogen oxides, and promotes the formation of ground-level ozone. Through lighting retrofits, a hot water recovery system (to capture "waste" heat), and redesigning the yogurt-making process, Stonyfield Farm significantly reduced its energy intensity (kWh per pound of yogurt) and saved $147,216 in year 2000 alone. Figure 4 demonstrates that the energy use per unit of products was significantly reduced over the past 8 years. At the same time, due to expansion in production volumes, the total energy use and CO_2 emissions increased.

Packaging has been a major challenge for Stonyfield Farm, since the company ships millions of yogurt containers annually. Packaging contributes to climate change, waste, and air pollution. Over the past several years, Stonyfield Farm has continuously worked to address this issue. In 1996, in order to select the packaging with the lowest environmental impact, Stonyfield Farm used the results of a life-cycle assessment undertaken by the Boston-based Tellus Institute consulting group. By switching to polypropylene, in 1998 alone the firm prevented the manufacturing and disposal of over 85 tons of plastic[8] as well as the use of chlorine and the release of dioxin (a by-product in the production of bleached paper).

---

[8]Using polypropylene instead of high-density polyethylene allowed Stonyfield Farm to use less plastic by making yogurt containers thinner.

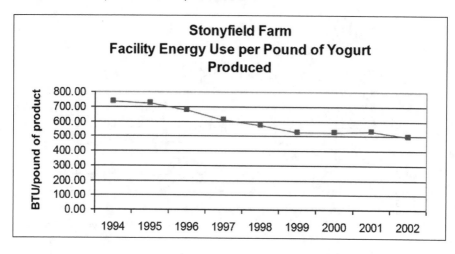

Figure 4. Stonyfield Farm energy use 1994–2002.

In 1999, Stonyfield Farm partnered with Polytainers, its principal packaging supplier, to sponsor two life-cycle studies that examined the impacts of its yogurt-delivering system. Conducted by the University of Michigan's Center for Sustainable Systems, the studies assessed the total environmental burden of Stonyfield Farm yogurt product-delivery system and made a series of recommendations. Some of the recommendations, such as eliminating the lids on small cups, were implemented by 2003; others, such as educating consumers about the environmental benefits of buying in larger containers, would be implemented in the future (N. Hirshberg, interview, July 1, 2002).

Stonyfield Farm was recognized by the Environmental Protection Agency's Waste Wise Program for its achievements in waste minimization. The company had always put a strong emphasis on waste prevention and elimination whenever possible, then on reduce, reuse, and recycle. Over 60% of the generated solid waste was either reused or recycled. Recovered materials included cardboard, metals, paper, yogurt containers, and wooden pallets. In partnership with Recycline, Stonyfield Farm recycled its waste yogurt containers to make toothbrushes. The company was accepting back its empty containers, which consumers could drop off or mail on their expenses to Stonyfield Farm's facility in Londonderry, New Hampshire. Waste yogurt was used to feed local pigs. The direct savings from the solid waste program in year 2000 were estimated at $83,791. In 2003, Stonyfield Farm replaced the rigid lids of its small containers with foil, which further reduced waste.

Stonyfield Farm donates 10% of its annual profits to environmental groups through its "Profits for the Planet" program. For example, in 1997 alone the company gave out $164,008 (Gray, 1998). The company had given away millions of cups of free yogurt at nonprofit events, such as Earth Day, the Walk for Hunger, and Share Our Strengths. Each year, Stonyfield Farm donates a couple hundred pounds of yogurt to local food banks.

Yogurt making is a water-intensive manufacturing process, and Stonyfield Farm initiated several projects to reduce its water consumption. Rinsing water was recirculated and reused, leading to $40,299 estimated financial savings in year 2000 alone (N. Hirshberg, interview, July 1, 2002).

5.4 Employee Well-Being

In addition to its environmental and community responsibility, Stonyfield Farm cares about its employees and aims to provide healthy and safe workplaces and rewarding jobs. In 2002, the firm employed about 180 people (up from 150 in 1999). All full-time employees have good benefits and are offered alternative healthcare and tuition reimbursement. Stonyfield Farm relied heavily on teams. Examples included organic team, events team, and line efficiency teams. Teams meet periodically, and the entire company meets biannually to review progress. Various surveys are conducted to track employee job satisfaction (new employee survey, exit surveys, climate survey[9]). In addition, every employee has the right to schedule a lunch meeting with the CEO to discuss issues of concern.

6 CORPORATE CAPABILITIES AND FACTORS OF SUCCESS

Mr. Hirshberg takes a very strong position on the role of business. He believes that "any problem on earth will be solved if business makes it a priority; any problem that has not been solved yet is because business has not made it a priority" (Sillanpää, 1998). Stonyfield Farm's story demonstrates that a company can be at once profitable as well as socially and environmentally responsible. The question, then, is why aren't more companies like that? What are the factors and corporate capabilities behind Stonyfield Farm's success? Has it influenced the business community? And can such a model be replicated in another business environment or industry?

The transformation toward business sustainability is long and complex. As Ehrenfeld (1996) points out, there are three main stages: compliance, prevention, and sustainability. In countries with a long tradition of environmental protection, like the United States, almost all companies have moved to the compliance stage. Many progressive firms have moved into the second stage, best characterized with preventive approaches such as pollution prevention, life-cycle assessment, eco-efficiency, and industrial ecology. Very few companies, however, have moved toward the third stage, sustainability.

Sustainability requires an expansion of the firm's strategic horizons in both time and organizational dimension (Ehrenfeld, 1996). A second industrial revolution is needed, according to McDonough and Braungart (1998, p. 6), to move companies from eco-efficiency to eco-effectiveness. Eco-efficiency means to produce more with less, but it still promotes the same production paradigm that has brought us to the present environmental crisis. The concept of eco-effectiveness introduces a completely new paradigm whereby industry is regenerative rather than depletive.

---

[9]This is a job satisfaction survey, which asks a series of questions related to compensation, benefits, work hours, career opportunities, and social environment, among others.

It involves design of products that work within the cradle-to-cradle life cycles rather than cradle-to-grave. It separates the biological nutrients from the technical nutrients (which are reused or recycled). It sells services rather than products (McDonough & Braungart, 1998, p. 6). Such a move toward eco-effectiveness or sustainability, however, involves risk, innovation, and long-term planning—key aspects that deter many companies from undertaking it. Furthermore, companies have traditionally been driven by governmental regulations in the environmental and social areas. The inertia of such patterns is difficult to overcome.

This research indicates that Stonyfield Farm is one of a handful of companies that has chosen to make the step toward sustainability, and the result is clearly a success. Yet this is not just good luck. It is the company's *visionary approach.* In their book "Built to Last," Collins and Porras (1994) present one of the most comprehensive studies of successful companies. This study is based on comparisons between visionary and non-visionary companies. They define visionary companies not just as successful or enduring. They are "the best of the best in their industries and have been that way for decades." Many of them "have served as role models for the practice of management around the world" (Collins & Porras, 1994). Contrary to business school doctrine, "maximizing shareholder wealth" and "profit maximization" are not the primary objectives or the dominant driving forces for most visionary companies. Making money is only one, and not necessarily their primary, objective. In fact, the study revealed that visionary companies have had core ideologies to a greater degree than comparison companies. The authors call this paradox "the Genius of the AND": a visionary company does not "simply balance between idealism and profitability, it seeks to be highly idealistic *and* highly profitable" (Collins & Porras, 1994).

Another key factor for Stonyfield's success is *top management support.* Its founder, Samuel Kaymen; CEO Gary Hirshberg; and Vice President of Natural Resources Nancy Hirshberg, were people with high ideals, goals, and personal missions. Their stories reveals that Stonyfield Farm had become merely a tool to achieve their goals to make a larger impact on society and environment than any individual or even nonprofit organization can do.

No company can succeed in business if it does not provide high-quality products or services. Making the very highest quality, best-tasting yogurt is the first priority for Stonyfield Farm. The company relies on continuous innovation in product formulations and packaging. The use of six live cultures, natural fiber, and organic ingredients as well as original messages on its yogurt containers and lids has clearly differentiated the company from its competitors. In this way, Stonyfield Farm has successfully integrated a wide array of stakeholders, including consumers, NGOs, suppliers, distributors, and shareholders.

Customer loyalty is another factor in Stonyfield Farm's success. The company is growth-oriented and consumer driven. Demand for Stonyfield Farm's products continues to grow rapidly, even when other companies' products are on sale. And surprisingly, this has happened while Stonyfield increased the average price of their products. The company's unique approach to put concerns about health and environment first has increased the number of customers. There is a growing market for environmentally preferable products. Surveys show that a growing number of people in the developed countries are willing to pay a premium for such products. The business world realizes this too. Surveys of top corporate executives have found that they believe "greater opportunities in the management of environmental affairs come from producing environmentally friendly products and services to differentiate their companies from competitors" (Dillon & Baram, 1993).

Cross-disciplinary coordination is another key corporate capability at Stonyfield Farm. The company relies heavily on teams to address problems and come up with original ideas for further product innovation, packaging improvement, and reducing employee turnover. According to Bolino, Turnley, and Bloodgood (2002), social participation behaviors on the part of employees are likely to facilitate the creation of network ties, which are the basis of creating a social capital. The latter is a critical source of sustainable organizational advantage (Nahapiet & Ghoshal, 1998). Evidence of the good management-employee ties at Stonyfield Farm is also the culture of open communication. For example, an employee survey in 1999 revealed that insufficient vacation time was the most prevalent complaint among the workers. Comparisons with other companies in the sector revealed that Stonyfield Farm's vacation time was below the average for the industry. As a result, top management decided to give each employee additional vacation days.

Product stewardship calls for reduction of the life-cycle environmental effects of products (EPA, 2003). Very few companies, however, have embraced this idea and are taking concrete steps toward its practical application. Among the best-known examples are Interface, which is taking back its old carpet for recycling; and Xerox, which has eliminated many toxic chemicals from its products and is leasing its products instead of selling them. Stonyfield Farm has developed product stewardship capabilities that make it unique in the entire sector. The life-cycle assessment of its packaging and taking-back as well as recycling its waste containers are only two examples of extended producer responsibility. With no legislation currently to demand product stewardship, proactive companies like Stonyfield Farm are both improving their image and getting ready for any future regulatory changes.

Part of Stonyfield Farm's success is result of having a market niche. There is a growing demand for organic products, and Stonyfield Farm has grasped this market opportunity. For example, sales of organic milk nearly doubled from about $16 million in 1996 to almost $31 million in 1997, according to dairy industry figures. Overall, the demand for organic food is expected to grow even more in the future (Gilbert, 1999). In fact, one may argue that the company actually helped drive the organic food market by its numerous educational initiatives.

7 FUTURE PLANS AND SUSTAINABILITY

Despite its success, Stonyfield Farm has its challenges. According to Ms. Hirshberg, the three priority areas in the near future are (a) goal setting with employee involvement; (b) climate change, packaging, and distribution; and (c) environmental management system. Addressing those will bring the company further ahead on the way to sustainability.

Stonyfield Farm is committed to strong growth and expansion. In October 2001, the Danone Group purchased 40% of Stonyfield Farm's shares and raised concerns among many of its friends and customers. Would the company manage to follow its mission in the future and keep its high profile or would it lose its identity eventually? What did this partnership mean for both sides?

According to the top management, the agreement allowed Danone initially to purchase 40% of Stonyfield Farm's shares, providing liquidity exit for the nearly 300 Stonyfield Farm shareholders, many of whom were friends and employees who helped the company with crucial financial assistance during its start-up phase. In 2003, subject to a successful mutual partnership, Danone had the right to purchase all remaining nonemployee stock, resulting in Danone's majority ownership and financial consolidation. Stonyfield Farm would remain a completely independent private firm, with Mr. Hirshberg having a long-term arrangement to continue as Chairman, President, and CEO. Stonyfield Farm welcomed two Danone appointees to its five-member board. Provisions were made to keep all current employees, suppliers, brand names, and the ability to make donations to environmental causes.

According to Ms. Hirshberg, this was a strategic partnership that would not change Stonyfield Farm's mission and approach. The agreement was signed after a long and careful consideration of different candidates. Danone Group was chosen, since both companies had compatible missions when it comes to environmental responsibility, health, and nutrition.

It remains to be seen how this partnership will affect Stonyfield Farm. According to the company management, it was an excellent model for enabling emerging value-driven firms to gain in strength and stature while remaining loyal to the growing base of consumers who seek organic and natural products.

8 CONCLUSION

The case of Stonyfield Farm of New Hampshire demonstrates that it is possible to be a responsible corporate citizen and at the same time be highly profitable; one is not necessarily at the exclusion of the other. The process of business transformation toward greater social and environmental responsibility requires overcoming the inertia of the existing business paradigm, taking risks, and developing innovative approaches. There is no prescribed path to follow but rather an array of options. Yet visionary companies like Stonyfield Farm have seen the new opportunities and chosen to lead the way and serve as a model company in the 21st century.

DISCUSSION QUESTIONS

Chapter 12: Stonyfield Farm – The Business Model for Social and Environmental Responsibility: A Case Study

1. What are the main drivers – internal and external – for Stonyfield Farm to pursue sustainability?
2. What are the key sustainability impacts and challenges for a yogurt company like Stonyfield Farm?

3. List the company's key achievements in each of its mission areas: a) providing quality products and supporting family farms, b) consumer and producer education; c) environmental responsibility; and d) employee well-being?
4. Today Stonyfield Farm is part of Danone Group. What are some of the pros and cons of a company focused on sustainability becoming a part of a large multinational corporation?

REFERENCES

Bansal, P., & Roth, K. (2000). Why companies go green: A model of ecological responsiveness. *Academy of Management Journal, 13*(4), 717–736.

Bolino, M., Turnley, W., & Bloodgood, J. (2002). Citizenship behavior and the creation of social capital in organizations. *Academy of Management Review, 27*(4), 505–522.

Collins, J., & Porras, J. (1994). *Built to last. Successful habits of visionary companies.* London, UK: HarperBusiness.

Dillon, P., & Baram, M. (1993). Forces shaping the development and use of product stewardship in the private sector. In K. Fisher & J. Shot (Eds.), *Environmental strategies for industry.* Washington, DC: Island.

Ehrenfeld, J. R. (1996). *Integrated environmental management: Strategies for the sustainable firm.* Symposium on adaptive strategies for future-oriented techno-industries, Kon-Kuk University, Seoul, Korea.

Environmental Protection Agency (EPA). (2003). *Product stewardship.* Retrieved May 3, 2003, from http://www.epa.gov/epawaste/conserve/tools/stewardship/index.htm

Gilbert, S. (1999, January 19). Fears over milk, long dismissed, still simmer. *The New York Times.*

Gray, S. (1998, April 9). Entering another world. *The Chronicle of Philanthropy. The Newspaper of Non-Profit World, 10*(12).

Greiner, T. (2000). *Indicators of sustainable production: A case study on measuring sustainability at Stonyfield Farm, Inc.* Unpublished paper, Lowell Center for Sustainable Production.

Hoffman, A. (2001). Linking organizational and field-level analysis: The diffusion of corporate environmental practice. *Organization and Environment, 14*(2), 133–156.

Levy, B., & Wegman, D. (1995). *Occupational health: Recognizing and preventing work-related disease* (3rd ed.). Boston, MA: Little, Brown.

McDonough, W., & Braungart, M. (1998, October). The next industrial revolution. *The Atlantic Monthly.*

Nahapiet, J., & Ghoshal, S. (1998). Social capital, intellectual capital, and the organizational advantage. *Academy of Management Review, 23,* 242–266.

National Town Meeting (NTM) for Sustainable America. Indicators of Sustainable Production. Poster Presentation. Detroit. (1999, May 1–4). Detroit, MI.

Outlaw, J., Jacobson, R., Knutson, R., & Schwart, R., Jr. (1996, March). Structure of the U.S. dairy farm sector. *Dairy Markets and Policy: Issues and Options.*

Sillanpää, M. (1998, Autumn). A new deal for sustainable development in business: Taking the social dimension seriously. *Greener Management International, 23,* 93–115.

Stonyfield Farm. (2002). *Products.* Retrieved December 1, 2002, from http://www.stonyfield.com/products

Stonyfield Farm. (2000, August 3). *Stonyfield Farm mission report* (available only for internal company use).

Stonyfield's Hirshberg: Profitable and progressive. (1998, March 22). *The Telegraph* (Hudson, NH).

Veleva, V., Bailey, J., & Jurczyk, N. (2001). Using sustainable production indicators to measure progress in ISO 14001, EHS system, and EPA achievement track. *Corporate Environmental Strategy, 8*(4), 326–338.

Veleva, V., & Ellenbecker, M. (2000, Autumn). A proposal for measuring business sustainability: Addressing shortcomings in existing frameworks. *Greener Management International, 31,* 101–120.

UPDATE TO CHAPTER 12: STONYFIELD FARM – THE BUSINESS MODEL FOR SOCIAL AND ENVIRONMENTAL RESPONSIBILITY: A CASE STUDY

Over the past decade Stonyfield Farm has continued to boldly pursue its mission and sustainability goals. Its partnership with Danone Group has proven beneficial both in terms of its bottom line and sustainability mission – Stonyfield was able to expand further both domestically as well as in Canada, France and other European countries while continuing to buy milk only from local dairy farms and achieving its goal of selling 100% organic yogurt. As of 2012 the company had over $370 million in revenue and about 300 employees in its Londonderry facility.

Some of its most notable sustainability achievements over the past decade include (Fisher, 2013):

- Reducing solid waste by 50% between 2007 and 2012;
- Increasing recycling rate by 49% between 2006 and 2012;
- Reducing trash per ton of production by 80% between 2007 and 2012;
- Achieving 36% absolute reduction in transportation greenhouse gases (GHG) between 2006 and 2012;
- Introducing plant-based packaging for yogurt containers based on polylactic acid (PLA);
- Installing anaerobic bio-digester at Londonderry, New Hampshire, which has enabled it to utilize liquid waste for generating biogas (with payback period of just 2 years).

As result of all eco-efficiency and sustainability initiatives, Stonyfield Farm saved over $30 million between 2006 and 2012 (Fisher, 2013).

Stonyfield Farm has continued its commitment to employees as well. In 2011 it was named one of the Top Five Largest Companies to Work For in New Hampshire by Business New Hampshire Magazine and NH Businesses for Social Responsibility (Londonderry News, 2011). The company has also continued to launch new, sustainable products, all 100% organic, including Greek yogurt, YoBaby and YoToddler Pouches (Stonyfield, 2014).

In January 2012, after leading the company for 29 years, Gary Hirshberg stepped down as Stonyfield CEO in order to become more active in "pushing for change in national food and agriculture policies" (Ireland, 2013). He however, continued to serve as the company Chairman. Ms. Hirshberg also left Stonyfield in 2013 and currently leads her own consulting company Hirshberg Strategic. It remains to be seen whether the sustainability mission and vision have been engraved deep into the firm culture so its sustainability journey continues strong even without the former leaders.

REFERENCES

Fisher, M. (2013). "Stonyfield and Eco-Efficiency." Guest lecture. MGT481 Introduction to Environmental Management and Clean Energy. UMass Boston. March 3.

Ireland, D. (2013). Stonyfield CEO to Step Down. *Eagle Tribune*. January 13. Retrieved from http://www.eagletribune.com/newhampshire/x1561257565/Stonyfield-CEO-steps-down

Londonderry News. (2011, January). Londonderry Company Named One of Top Five Best in NH. Retrieved from http://www.londonderrynh.net/tag/best-companies-to-work-for-in-nh

Stonyfield. (2014). Products. http://www.stonyfield.com/products

IVEY | Publishing

Chapter 13

NEW BALANCE: DEVELOPING AN INTEGRATED CSR STRATEGY

Copyright © 2010, Ivey Management Services   *Version: (A) 2010-01-28*

Katherine Shepard, social responsibility manager at New Balance, understood that New Balance faced new challenges in terms of corporate social responsibility (CSR):[1] how to maintain its social responsibility culture when acquiring new brands, how to become more transparent and thus increase stakeholder trust and support and how to position itself as a responsible leader in the industry to obtain business benefits without having to "chase" peers, as Nike and Timberland. She was struggling with some issues due to her intimate familiarity with the company, and she recognized its high potential and the changing operating environment for business. Shepard also knew that New Balance needed someone outside the company to

---

[1] *In this case, the term corporate social responsibility is used interchangeably with corporate citizenship, responsible leadership and sustainability.*

look at the current level of CSR management and performance and provide an independent and credible evaluation and list of recommendations. The Boston College Center for Corporate Citizenship (BCCCC)[2] came to mind as it was an organization with which New Balance was familiar and comfortable.

Both chief executive officer (CEO), Rob DeMartini, and vice-chairman and co-owner, Anne Davis, liked the idea and, in December 2008, the company engaged the BCCCC research team to conduct an assessment and provide recommendations for developing an aligned CSR strategy to the Responsible Leadership Steering Committee and senior leadership. That strategy could also serve as the basis for developing New Balance's first publicly available CSR report. In 2009, New Balance began a process to assess, redefine and integrate its CSR strategy with the core business strategy.

NEW BALANCE MISSION

"Demonstrating responsible leadership, we build global brands that athletes are proud to wear, associates are proud to create and communities are proud to host."

INTRODUCTION

In October 2008, Shepard was driving to the Burlington, Vermont area to spend the weekend with her family. As she was enjoying the beautiful foliage, she recalled her first experience with New Balance 18 years earlier. It was an uncomfortably hot August day in Boston, but Shepard was determined to get her father a birthday present. Since he wanted some running shoes, she took him to a nearby retail outlet. Being surrounded by hundreds of sneakers that all looked very much the same was an overwhelming experience for her father, and for her as well. After a moment of silence, Shepard's father said to the salesman, "Tell me which ones are made in the U.S." The salesman immediately suggested New Balance shoes. They had never heard of the brand before but Shepard's father liked the fit and style and they walked out with a birthday gift — a pair of New Balance sneakers. That "made in USA" label made it an easy decision and became something that Shepard remembered.

A year later, in the spring of 1991, Shepard was looking for a new job. She saw a newspaper advertisement from New Balance looking for a corporate communica-tions manager. The job description seemed a perfect fit, and she already knew one thing about the company that was very important to her and her family: New Balance was committed to domestic manufacturing. She applied for the job and, after an extensive interview process, joined New Balance later that year. A few years later she was promoted to senior corporate communications

---

[2]*The Boston College Center for Corporate Citizenship (BCCCC) is a membership-based research organization associated with the Carroll School of Management. New Balance had been a member of the Center since 1999.*

manager and in 2007, she became the social responsibility manager for New Balance (see Exhibit 1).

Since its founding more than 100 years ago, New Balance had followed its mission and demonstrated social responsibility to its employees and communities where it had operations. A strong culture of "doing the right thing" was developed and maintained over the years, as New Balance remained the only large footwear manufacturer with production in the United States. With rapid growth in the late 1990s, however, the company turned into a global brand, which required moving CSR to the next level — from "doing what's right" to fully integrating CSR into the business strategy.

NEW BALANCE: HISTORY AND BUSINESS OVERVIEW

New Balance was founded in Boston in 1906, when a 33-year-old waiter named William J. Riley began building arch supports to alleviate pain for people who spent all day on their feet. In 1925, Riley designed his first running shoe for a Boston running club, known as the Boston Brown Bag Harriers. The shoe was so successful that in the 1940s, New Balance began making custom shoes for running, baseball, basketball, tennis and boxing. In 1960, it began manufacturing running shoes in multiple widths and significantly expanded production.

In 1972, New Balance was purchased by James Davis, who remained the owner together with his wife Anne (in 2009, James was New Balance chairman and Anne was vice-chairman and executive vice-president, administration: see Exhibit 2). After graduating from Middlebury College in 1964, James Davis worked as a sales representative for an electronics firm, but his long-term objective was to own and manage his own business. A friend told him about New Balance, whose owner at the time, Paul Kidd, was looking to sell the business. After doing some research on the company, talking with athletic coaches in New England and trying the New Balance sneakers himself, he was convinced of the high potential for the company: "I felt leisure-time products would be a high-growth market, and I found that New Balance had a good product," he recalled. "After running in them myself I was very impressed with the shoe."[3] Using his own savings and taking a long-term bank loan, Davis purchased New Balance for $100,000.[4]

Sports shoes remained the focus of New Balance business operations, and the company experienced tremendous growth over the next 37 years. This growth was especially significant in the late 1990s, when the company began a series of acquisitions involving various brands, such as Dunham, Warrior and Brine,[5] among others. In 2009, New Balance was a global company with 4,100 employees

---

[3] Kim B. Clark, "New Balance Athletic Shoes," Harvard Business School Publishing, 1980, p. 680-710.

[4] All funds are in US$ unless otherwise stated.

[5] The acquired brands included men's traditional and everyday shoes, apparel, footwear and equipment for lacrosse, hockey and volleyball, among other sports.

worldwide (2,634 of them in the United States) and sales of $1.61 billion in 2008 (see Exhibit 3). It was the second-largest manufacturer of athletic footwear in the United States after Nike, and the fourth largest in the world (see Exhibit 4). The company was the only global footwear manufacturer with production in the United States (about 25 per cent of production). It had five company-owned factories in the United States — Boston and Lawrence, Massachusetts, and Norridgewock, Norway and Skowhegan, Maine — and one in the United Kingdom. It had approximately 200 footwear suppliers in the United States, the United Kingdom, China, Vietnam, Indonesia, Mexico, Japan, Taiwan and Cambodia.

In addition to footwear, New Balance had a small but growing apparel and accessories business (less than five per cent of sales in 2008). The apparel and accessories were manufactured through suppliers and licensees from 27 countries around the world, including the United States, China and Taiwan.

New Balance was probably best known among consumers for its "Endorsed by No One" campaign. While it saw athletes as its critical market segment, in contrast with much of the industry, the company chose not to spend money on endorsements from individual professional or "celebrity" athletes or use them in advertisements.

In 2006, New Balance implemented a lean production system[6] (modeled after Toyota's lean manufacturing) in all domestic operations, which led to significant productivity improvements and reduced waste, worker exposures and costs; for example, the time it took to make a pair of shoes in the Lawrence facility was reduced from eight days to three hours. Between the years 2005 and 2009, productivity improved 49 per cent as a result of waste reductions. Associates were trained and encouraged to make suggestions for continuous improvements. In 2007, a new CEO from the consumer product industry, Rob DeMartini, was brought on board to lead the company on the journey to becoming a truly global brand.

FOOTWEAR INDUSTRY OVERVIEW AND CSR DRIVERS

In 2009, the U.S. footwear industry consisted of approximately 100 manufacturers, 1,500 wholesalers and 30,000 retail outlets with a combined annual revenue of $25 billion.[7] Major brands, such as Nike, Reebok, Brown Shoe and Timberland, were mainly owners of brand names that sourced their shoes from independent

---

[6]*Lean production was pioneered by Toyota and represents flexible manufacturing technologies to deliver goods on demand, minimize inventory, maximize the use of multi-skilled employees, flatten management structure, and focus resources when and where they were needed.*

[7]*Source: Hoovers, "Industry Overview: Footwear Manufacture, Wholesale and Retail," www. hoovers.com/footwear-manufacture,-wholesale,-and-retail-/—ID__130—/free-ind-fr-profile-basic. xhtml.2009, accessed December 4, 2009.*

manufacturers. The retail chain market was highly concentrated: the largest 50 chains represented approximately 80 per cent of the market.

One extremely important factor in the footwear business was the logistics of delivering product to retailers. Manufacturers had to be able to respond to requests within days or even hours; therefore, most footwear companies had several distribution centers, typically 500,000 to one million square feet, and sophisticated computer systems to track inventory, orders and deliveries.

Footwear demand was driven by fashion and demographics. The industry had three main segments: athletic shoes, women's shoes and men's shoes, which represented 30 per cent, 25 per cent and 15 per cent, respectively (the remaining 30 per cent was miscellaneous). Domestic manufacturing of shoes had been rapidly declining and in 2009, it was estimated at less than $3 billion annually. The typical U.S. manufacturer was small, with an annual revenue of $10 million and fewer than 100 employees, and able to compete with larger companies through superior design or marketing. U.S.-made products were mostly private-label men's shoes. Average revenue per employee was $100,000. Materials, mainly leather, amounted to 50 per cent of costs. Over the past two decades, footwear manufacturing had been rapidly moving overseas to countries, such as China, because of the large labour cost savings. Despite technological advances, footwear was still largely assembled by hand.

As a result of moving operations to developing countries with known human and labor rights violations, the footwear and apparel sectors faced significant social and environmental challenges, underlining the urgency of implementing an integrated CSR strategy. Companies such as Nike, Adidas, Timberland and Gap had long recognized the costs and reputational risks of poor CSR management and had devoted staff and resources to developing clear strategies to not only mitigate risks, but also take advantage of emerging opportunities related to regulatory changes and consumer preferences (see Exhibit 5). Four areas of existing or emerging issues with high potential to affect New Balance or any other company in the footwear/apparel industry included:

- **Human and labour rights issues in the supply chain**: While this was the first major CSR issue that the industry had to face (e.g. boycott of Nike products in the 1990s), it still remained an area of top focus in 2009. Over the years, there had been a shift in the specific issues. The initial non-governmental organization (NGO) campaigns focused on development of codes of conduct and implementation of supplier monitoring. In 2009, issues such as maximum work hours, health and safety in overseas factories, use of temporary workers, transparency, responsible purchasing practices and "exit strategies" when closing factories overseas dominated the agenda.
- **Increasing demands for transparency**: While privately held companies such as New Balance did not face the same disclosure pressures as publicly held peers, "size invites scrutiny" and demands were growing from NGOs and other stakeholders for greater transparency (e.g. the 2008 Play Fair campaign

at the Beijing Olympics[8]). While not every company would be ready to disclose all suppliers as Nike and Timberland had done,[9] a greater transparency could build trust and mitigate unexpected reputation risks from recalls or incidents in the supply chain. It also could help build an emotional bond with ethical consumers and lead to greater customer loyalty.

- **Greenhouse gas (GHG) emissions regulation**: With fast changes in the United States in this area, regulation was just around the corner. Massachusetts, where New Balance was headquartered, introduced mandatory GHG reporting by companies effective January 2009.[10] The U.S. Senate and House of Representatives were drafting a federal climate change regulation. Some of New Balance's peers, such as Timberland and Patagonia, had already begun to prepare for the forthcoming regulation (and also attract ethical consumers) by measuring and reporting their GHG emissions and product carbon footprint.

- **Health, safety and product stewardship**: Adoption of REACH[11] (Registration, Evaluation, Authorization and Restriction of Chemical substances) by the European Union in 2006 changed the way chemicals were regulated. REACH imposed greater responsibility on companies to assess environmental, health and safety impacts of their product ingredients and to identify safer alternatives. The potential for liability from using dangerous chemicals or materials significantly increased. Nanotechnology in particular could bring a new level of health and safety concerns for workers and consumers as traditionally safe materials like carbon and silver, for example, can become toxic to human health and aquatic life when their molecular structure is changed (e.g. carbon nanotubes and nano silver). With growing pressures to reduce waste, regulatory changes were also expected at the end of products' useful lives (e.g. requiring manufacturer product take-back or imposing a fee for product disposal).

All of these social and environmental issues for the footwear and apparel industry necessitated a process aligned with the core business in which product

---

[8]*The Play Fair campaign was an alliance of Oxfam, Global Unions, the Clean Clothes Campaign and their constituent organizations worldwide, which aimed to push sportswear and athletic footwear companies, the International Olympics Committee (IOC) and national governments toward eliminating the exploitation and abuse of workers in the global sporting goods industry. For more information, see www.playfair2008.org. While Oxfam did not participate in the 2008 campaign, it remained a member of the Play Fair Alliance.*

[9]*The list of Timberland supplier factories in 2008 is available at www.justmeans.com/user content/companydocs/docs/company_docs_1213368647.pdf; Nike's list of suppliers in 2009 is available at www.nikebiz.com/responsibility/documents/Dec09_Collegiate_Disclosure.pd, both accessed January 13, 2010.*

[10]*See Massachusetts Department of Environmental Protection, Global Warming Solutions Act Implementation, www.mass.gov/dep/air/climate/index.htm, accessed on December 7, 2009.*

[11]*See EUROPA Environment, "What is REACH?" http://ec.europa.eu/environment/chemicals/ reach/reach_intro.htm, accessed on December 7, 2009.*

design, operations, communications, marketing, sourcing and procurement and other functions in companies work together to address challenges and identify new opportunities for business growth and meeting social and environmental responsibilities.

CSR AT NEW BALANCE:
THE RIGHT THING TO DO

In 2006, as New Balance celebrated its 100th year, owners James and Anne Davis made a commitment to corporate responsibility as a central part of the organization's values and mission. Corporate responsibility was seen as a way of differentiating a company that "thrives" from a company that just "survives." While the explicit commitment brought new focus to corporate responsibility, the notion of responsibility was not new at New Balance: ever since the Davises became the owners, the company had strongly supported corporate philanthropy, encouraged employee volunteering and ensured compliance in factories overseas that made New Balance products.

The company did not have a CSR department, but instead had one social responsibility manager, Shepard, who reported to the vice-president of Intellectual Property. Its most formalized CSR structure was the CSR Steering Committee, which was established in 1997, the aim of which was to focus on overseas footwear suppliers and elevate overall working conditions in those factories. In 2007, it was renamed the Responsible Leadership Steering Committee (RLSC) and included four areas of responsible leadership (RL):

- Philanthropy and community investing,
- Environmental sustainability,
- Socially responsible compliance,
- Product life cycle.[12]

The committee was chaired by Shepard and included senior executives from key functional areas. In April 2009, as part of the process for greater alignment and integration with the core business, a fifth area of responsible leadership was added — New Balance domestic manufacturing — and a few additional executives were included from key divisions, such as marketing and branding (see RLSC chart in Exhibit 1). For each RL area there was a sub-team, which met on average every six weeks and focused on specific issues and tangible outcomes; for example, the team working on environmental sustainability made significant progress toward identifying restricted materials, ensuring compliance with the European Union REACH

[12] *2007 Corporate Social Responsibility Report (published in 2008 and available only internally).*

initiative and exploring how recycled, recyclable and renewable natural resources-based materials could be incorporated into product design and packaging.[13]

Throughout the years, the company's private ownership status had allowed it to take risks and make choices that publicly held companies might not have been able to do; at the same time, private ownership also meant lower pressures to disclose social and environmental performance. Strong believers in "doing what's right for employees and communities," the owners were always very "humble" and hesitant to talk aloud about social responsibility; thus, despite its numerous initiatives, very little information had been made available publicly about New Balance's work in this area.

CSR AS A BUSINESS IMPERATIVE FOR A GLOBAL COMPANY

As a global player in the footwear and sport apparel industry in 2009, the challenge for New Balance became to move CSR to the next level and fully integrate it into the core business. For global companies, CSR was a critical tool for safeguarding and maintaining brand reputation in a world where up to 50 per cent of a company's value could be dependent upon reputation and intangibles. A 2008 survey by the BCCCC and the Reputation Institute showed that CSR was the second most important driver of reputation at 16.3 per cent, following the quality of products and services at 17.6 per cent.[14]

Global companies faced much greater scrutiny and demands for transparency than domestic brands, particularly in regards to CSR issues, such as supply chain practices (e.g. the Play Fair campaign); at the same time, CSR could be a powerful tool for improving brand awareness, increasing customer loyalty and differentiating from competitors, as companies such as Starbucks, Gap and Nike had demonstrated. Studies had continued to demonstrate the increasing numbers of ethical consumers.[15] In this context, it was a strategic concern that both internal and external surveys of consumers showed New Balance at the bottom of its peer group on CSR performance. Internally, the New Balance marketing department was conducting such surveys of 2,000 consumers annually; externally, Rice University's Brand Management Study in 2004 came up with similar findings and concluded that "as a person is more aware of New Balance, has good feelings about the brand, and

---

[13] Michael Blowfield, "New Balance Case Study," unpublished paper prepared for the Business Network on Integration at the Boston College Center for Corporate Citizenship, November 2006.

[14] Reputation Institute and Boston College Center for Corporate Citizenship, "Building Reputation Here, There and Everywhere: Worldwide Views on Local Impact of Corporate Responsibility," March 2009, www.bcccc.net/index.cfm?fuseaction=document.showDocumentByI D&nodeID=1&DocumentID=1270, accessed January 13, 2010.

[15] For more information see: Boston Consulting Group (BCG) 2008 Survey, "Capturing the Green Advantage for Consumer Companies," www.bcg.com/publications/files/Capturing_ Green_Advantage_Consumer_Companies_Jan_2009.pdf, accessed January 13, 2010, Remi Trudel and June Cotte, "Does Being Ethical Pay?," MIT Sloan Management Review, Winter 2009, 50.2.

likes the brand's personality, the more willing he or she is to purchase a New Balance running shoe."[16]

In 2009, the challenge for New Balance was to build on the strong implicit values and culture of corporate responsibility and develop a comprehensive and publicly visible global CSR strategy. This strategy had to be able to support the development of New Balance as a highly successful global business capable of making a significant and meaningful contribution to global social development through its core business as well as its community investment and philanthropic programs.

To address this challenge and move toward a more integrated CSR strategy, New Balance began two initiatives in early 2009:

1. **Assessment of CSR management and performance:**[17] The purpose of this initiative was to evaluate the company's strengths, weaknesses and opportunities in CSR management in order to identify a few areas to focus on and align with core business strategy;
2. **Development of a CSR report:** This involved the compiling of information, goals and indicators on social and environmental performance in order to develop New Balance's first publicly available CSR report (in 2007 the company published a CSR report that was available only internally).

The company engaged a research team from BCCCC to conduct an in-depth CSR assessment and provide recommendations, as well as the Center for Reflection, Education and Action (CREA) to help develop the CSR report.[18]

CORPORATE CITIZENSHIP MANAGEMENT FRAMEWORK

In order to assess its current understanding, organizational readiness and performance in CSR, New Balance used the Corporate Citizenship Management Framework[19] (see Exhibit 6). The CCMF was developed to help companies better understand and manage corporate citizenship as an integrated part of the business.

---

[16] Harada, C., Hawthorn, A., Kilbride, J., and Redding, C., "New Balance Athletic Shoe, Inc.: Brand Audit," Jones Graduate School of Management, Rice University, December 2004. Unpublished report.

[17] A separate but related initiative included an assessment of the New Balance Foundation's charitable contributions and provided recommendations for improving the focus and alignment with the company's business strategy.

[18] This case focuses only on the first initiative. There was, however, communication between the research team and CREA to ensure that key findings and recommendations from the assessment were taken into consideration when developing the CSR report.

[19] For more information on the framework see Christopher Pinney, "Framework for the Future: Understanding and Managing Corporate Citizenship from a Business Perspective," Boston College Center for Corporate Citizenship, briefing paper, February 2009, www.bcccc.net/index. cfm?fuseaction=document.showDocumentByID&DocumentID=1259, accessed January 13, 2010.

It involves assessing and managing business practices in four closely inter-related domains[20]:

- **Overall governance — Values, mission, principles and policies**: Embedding corporate citizenship in the governance and management structure of the company. This dimension addresses how a company's core values, mission, vision and governance structures support or prevent the company from understanding and managing corporate citizenship as an integrated part of business strategy.
- **Community support — Addressing social challenges**: Mobilizing the company's assets to address social issues and support social well-being beyond creating jobs and paying taxes. This can range from simple philanthropy to participation in multi-stakeholder social issue partnerships, engaging a range of corporate resources.
- **Operations — Responsible business practices**: Utilizing responsible business practices to minimize potential negative impacts on employees, environment and society, and maximize positive impacts. This dimension addresses how a company manages a broad range of operational issues, from business ethics to health and safety, sustainable environmental practices and human rights in the supply chain.
- **Products and services — Market strategy**: Addressing societal needs with marketplace solutions that return a profit to the company. This can range from adaptation of existing products and services to be more eco-efficient or socially beneficial, to a fundamental reinvention of a company's product line or services, as well as their marketing and delivery.

ASSESSMENT OF CSR MANAGEMENT AND PERFORMANCE

Using the CCMF framework, the research team conducted industry research, visited the Lawrence, Massachusetts, factory and interviewed 29 internal and external stakeholders between January and April 2009. Internal stakeholders included senior executives across all key functions, factory workers and supervisors; external stakeholders included an NGO and a retailer. What follows are the key findings from the assessment.

1. Overall Governance: Values, Mission, Principles, and Policies

New Balance's top strengths, according to almost all interviewees, included its history, values and integrity. Before CSR became a "buzz word" almost 30 years

---

[20] *For more information on the framework see: Vesela Veleva, "Managing Corporate Citizenship: A New Tool for Companies," Corporate Social Responsibility and Environmental Management, 17, 2010, pp. 40-51, published online in Wiley InterScience, www.interscience. wiley.com, June 15, 2009, DOI: 10.1002/csr.206, accessed January 26, 2010.*

ago, the company was committed to being responsible to its employees and the communities in which it had operations. People were proud to work at New Balance, stating that "management is responsive" and "takes things very seriously." Employees felt personal accomplishment and pride in what the company was doing. As one supervisor at the Lawrence factory summed it up, "This is an exceptional company; there is no other company like New Balance, with focus on people and domestic manufacturing."

The interviews with senior management at New Balance revealed a strong basic support for CSR. The company commitment to corporate responsibility as a central part of the organization's values and mission was well understood; at the same time, there appeared to be no clear consensus or understanding of what this should encompass. Few understood what New Balance's current RL priorities or goals were. Some believed that RL was about philanthropy and volunteering, for others it was about compliance in overseas factories. Most executives still saw CSR as a cost rather than a strategic business driver with measurable social and business benefits.

While the RL platform covered many key aspects of CSR, it left out critical areas, such as transparency and accountability, employee support and domestic manufacturing; therefore, it did not provide sufficient guidance for managers on how to identify potential business risks and opportunities. New Balance's commitment to retain a portion of its manufacturing base in the United States and avoid layoffs in the economic recession of 2007-2009, for example, were clear demonstrations of social responsibility that were not captured in the RL framework. In response to this finding, New Balance focused on strategy and initiatives in the domestic manufacturing aspect of its RL platform, an area that clearly differentiated the company from competitors.

The CSR assessment found that New Balance lacked a clear process for setting CSR goals that were linked to the core business strategy. Four of the company's six strategic business priorities could easily be linked to responsible leadership:

- Inspire an engaged and committed workforce,
- Transform New Balance into a top-tier global brand,
- Build an emotional bond with athletic consumers,
- Practise continuous improvement.

Overall communication appeared to be a challenge for New Balance and a key barrier to positioning itself as a responsible leader. "Capturing all the good things" that associates were doing in the United States and abroad and communicating on an ongoing basis was critical if the company wanted to embed CSR into the core business, further empower associates and create an emotional bond with consumers. Pressures for external reporting were growing both from inside and outside the company. Organizations such as the Maquila Solidarity

Network[21] wanted to see more disclosure on supplier factories, whereas New Balance associates wanted to see more about the "wonderful work" they did. While James and Anne Davis were very "humble," they also admitted they "need to be transparent and report — we owe it to our associates and our consumers."[22]

While the assessment revealed numerous impressive CSR initiatives (e.g. worker conditions in supplier factories, greening of U.S. facilities and significant reductions in volatile organic compounds emissions domestically), these were not well connected and aligned, nor were they always measured and communicated to top management; for example, domestic manufacturing, use of renewable energy and greening New Balance stores and factories all contributed to a lower company carbon footprint, but this had not been measured or communicated internally or externally. RL was not seen as an "umbrella" initiative and "thus got a little silo'd," according to one interviewee. Initiatives were often driven by personal passion and interests rather than top-level policy or mandate. The lack of clear policies on how to address the tension of cost versus sustainability presented a challenge in some segments as employees had to balance costs, profitability and aesthetics.

The company assessment found a significant difference between the footwear and apparel divisions' experience and capability to manage CSR, particularly on the operational side; New Balance had good monitoring and control of its footwear manufacturers to ensure compliance to labour practices and restricted materials. This was not the case for apparel, where factory orders were small, suppliers were changed frequently and resources were limited.[23] There was also a gap between the level of CSR management in the U.S. facilities and overseas supplier factories (for more information about this see the Operations section).

Many executives indicated in interviews that the lack of clear leadership was a major obstacle to developing an integrated CSR strategy, and that unless there was a senior-level champion for CSR on the leadership team, there was little possibility for CSR to advance significantly. In contrast to most peers, New Balance did not have a CSR department or a vice-president-level executive in charge of CSR. Some commented on the "lack of focus" of the RL Steering Committee, and the need to change its mission and purpose if it was to play a leadership role in developing an integrated CSR strategy.

---

[21] *Established in 1994, the Maquila Solidarity Network (MSN) is a group of labor and women's rights organization committed to supporting the efforts of workers in global supply chains to win improved wages, working conditions and a better quality of life. For more information see http://en.maquilasolidarity.org, accessed January 13, 2010.*

[22] *Source: Interview with Anne Davis, February 12, 2009.*

[23] *For example, in the footwear division, New Balance was the only company that its overseas factories manufactured for. In the apparel and accessories division, however, New Balance was one of many customers and therefore it had limited leverage in enacting changes.*

2. Products and services

Through its products, New Balance had the greatest opportunity to bring positive social and environmental changes as well as bottom-line benefits. With the 46.2 million pairs of sneakers sold around the world in 2008, as well as a growing array of apparel and accessories, the company had a truly global reach. This area included issues concerning how New Balance designed its products, sourced materials and worked with suppliers, marketed and delivered products, and how it took responsibility at the end of products' useful life. This category also included measuring and reducing the carbon and toxicity footprint of products.

From product design to marketing and delivery, this domain should include strategic innovation and "out of the box" thinking on what the next generation of footwear and apparel would look like, and how to minimize negative environmental and social impacts and maximize social benefits along the supply chain. This area was of critical importance for achieving a win-win case, with environmental, social and business benefits; however, the research team's analysis revealed that there was still a lack of complete understanding of how this domain linked to CSR and how the company could better leverage its existing environmental and social initiatives to generate business benefits.

While most footwear and apparel companies aimed to have one or two product lines that were considered "green" or "sustainable," New Balance had taken a different approach — to include recycled content and environmentally preferable materials in all footwear. This started with 20 per cent in 2008, and aimed to increase to 25 per cent of product weight by the end of 2009. The Outdoor Group division of New Balance had been particularly active in incorporating sustainable design criteria in the development of new footwear: it developed and implemented an "eco score card" to evaluate all new products (considering cost-effectiveness, functionality and other design criteria in addition to environmental impacts). Clearly, the impact from such an approach was much greater from an environmental point of view; the business benefits were less clear but could include cost savings and attracting ethical consumers.

New Balance appeared to be the first among peers to completely eliminate polyvinyl chloride (PVC) from all footwear[24] (both Timberland and Nike were still using PVC in 2009, albeit in very small amounts). While there was no regulation in 2009, pressures had been growing worldwide (from NGOs, regulators, socially responsible investors, etc.) to eliminate PVC from all consumer products. Retailers such as Target and Wal-Mart had agreed to stop selling products that contained PVC. New Balance's proactive effort to eliminate this potentially harmful substance was not just a good environmental decision but a smart business move as well.

---

[24] *With the lack of corporate-wide policy on PVC it was not clear whether all acquired brands were also PVC-free.*

New Balance's retail group had worked to implement a "green" store design, even though there was no top management mandate. The project, which was strongly supported by James Davis, had slightly higher upfront costs but a short payback period. With the growth of environmentally conscious consumers, such steps could positively impact how consumers viewed New Balance, since retail locations were often seen as the "face of the company."

While the footwear division, and particularly the Outdoor Group, had been very active in the area of developing and introducing more sustainable products (e.g. the 070 shoe, which came to market in the third quarter of 2009 and was New Balance's first "green" shoe[25]), the apparel and accessories division had limited resources, faced a high degree of business growth pressures and was "trying to keep . . . afloat." Apparel faced much greater and more complex environmental and social challenges as production lines and factories changed quickly. It also relied on many licensees and a greater variety of materials. Although apparel represented a small fraction of the business at the time of the assessment, it could expose the company to significant risks or liabilities, even from promotional items; for example, in response to increasing media attention and consumer concerns over polycarbonate bottles containing Bisphenol A, in 2009 the company had to remove them from store shelves.

New Balance did not have a system in place to assess the life-cycle impacts of products (both footwear and apparel/accessories), a system which could help position it as an industry leader; for example, its practices of domestic manufacturing and use of rail instead of trucks for shipping products or parts significantly reduced products' carbon footprint, but this was not measured or communicated. Much more education was needed to "push design teams toward using environmentally preferred products and manufacturing."

More research was also needed on new materials and their performance. Sometimes environmentally preferred materials used in footwear and apparel did not provide good performance and durability: in the past coconut shells were found to be cost effective, but consumers did not like the material because it was too hard.

With the increasing amount of waste and shrinking landfill capacity, there was a growing trend toward product stewardship or implementing policies that would require manufacturers to take back their products at the end of their useful life;[26] for example, Germany instituted a landfill fee on footwear in 2008. While competitors such as Nike had been taking back and recycling old products for some time, this was an expensive undertaking. Developing industry collaboration was one possible

---

[25] *The 070 shoe was made with recycled materials, reduced waste and water-based adhesives. For more information see www.nbwebexpress.com/newbalanceME070SN.htm, accessed on January 13, 2010.*

[26] *For more information on product stewardship see www.productstewardship.us and Vesela Veleva, "Product Stewardship in the U.S.: The Changing Policy Landscape and the Role of Business," Sustainability: Science, Practice and Policy, Fall/Winter 2008, 4.2, http://ejournal.nbii.org/archives/vol4iss2/communityessay.veleva.html, accessed on January 13, 2010.*

approach, although historically New Balance had been unsuccessful in developing such a partnership with other footwear manufacturers. Other possible approaches included partnering with NGOs or regulators to find a cost-effective solution.

3. Operations

Integration of CSR into operations was one area where New Balance was particularly strong and could provide leadership for the entire industry. Most of the initiatives had demonstrated clear business value in terms of dollar savings, reduced costs or increased productivity. Intangible benefits included improved worker safety and morale. New Balance had a robust environmental program and good restricted materials program in its footwear division. It had achieved compliance with the European Union REACH regulation — a safeguard against potential fines, market exclusion or damaged reputation. The ability to reduce the number of suppliers from almost 400 to 200 had allowed New Balance to increase its control, reduce costs and improve efficiency. Partnering with organizations, such as the British Leather Group, provided the benefit of a third-party certification standard for selecting materials suppliers with good environmental compliance and safety.

One of the best examples of a win-win approach was the "spectacular reduction in volatile organic compounds" in domestic factories. According to John Wilson, executive vice-president of manufacturing, the program was "really a poster child for sustainability." It began in the late 1990s as a partnership with Henkel, New Balance's German supplier and one of the sustainability leaders in the chemicals/materials sector. The result was a process called "moisture cured reactive hot melt," which as of May 2009 was 98 per cent implemented in domestic footwear production. This process eliminated the use of solvent cements, which resulted in 2.7 to 5.0 per cent cost savings, translating to more than $6 million in savings from increased productivity and reduced emissions and waste. Productivity went up from 9.5 pairs per team person/hour to 19.3 pairs per team person/hour. Compared to its peers, who used water-based adhesives, New Balance had achieved much lower volatile organic compounds (VOCs) emissions per pair in its U.S. facilities — 0.33 grams per pair, compared to a former 14 grams per pair.

Another example of responsible leadership was the adoption and enforcement of a maximum 60-hour workweek for Chinese suppliers, down from more than 70 hours. According to Jim Sciabarrasi, vice-president of Sourcing and Procurement, the initiative led to increased productivity in the range of 35 per cent in the first year. In 2009, New Balance agreed to work with the Maquila Solidarity Network to help publicize these productivity improvements as a way to get more companies to adopt responsible supply chain practices.

Waste reduction was another strong area for the company and a good example of cost savings. In 2008, New Balance recycled 99 per cent of its waste, which together with the reduced emissions of VOCs from manufacturing and cleaners led to a change in its status to a "small quantity hazardous waste generator," and thus reduced the costs for disposal, worker training and insurance.

In 2007, New Balance implemented a new job coaching program in the United States to reduce work-related injuries. The program used early symptom intervention and included ergonomic evaluation (840 evaluations were completed in 2008). Setting a goal of less than eight work-related injuries per 200,000 hours of work (or 100 full-time workers), New Balance achieved an actual rate of 6.2 to 6.3, which translated into improved productivity, reduced absenteeism and lower insurance costs; in addition, the program had improved morale among associates as they felt that management truly cared about them.

Switching to green cleaners in all U.S. facilities in 2008 had proved to be another win-win initiative that put New Balance ahead of its peers. Working with a green janitorial product company, it identified four green chemicals that replaced the previously used 20 conventional cleaners. At the end, the program saved New Balance $240,000 compared to the previous year, according to John Campbell, corporate manager of Corporate Services. This number did not include the additional benefits of improved worker health, safety and morale.

Improving energy efficiency was identified as another strong area for New Balance. Replacing lighting, servers and improving processes were among the actions that allowed the company to reduce energy use and therefore lower costs by $340,000 in 2008 alone; as a result, New Balance was able to increase its portion of renewable energy to 30 per cent in all domestic facilities at no additional cost. This was a smart business move considering the forthcoming GHG emissions regulation in the United States.

One unique operational area for New Balance was its commitment to employees. Despite the difficult economic times in 2008 and 2009, the company avoided layoffs. This focus on domestic manufacturing and protecting jobs in the United States could have won it a particularly strong reputation among U.S. consumers and helped further differentiate the brand. Studies had shown that 86 per cent of American consumers wanted to see companies manufacture their products in the United States.[27] Treating employees well also improves associates' morale, engagement and productivity.

While the footwear division had made some remarkable strives in the operations domain, apparel, accessories (done mostly through licensees) and promotional items were found to pose significant risks. According to one interviewee, New Balance did not have the same leverage with suppliers as it did for footwear. Since these items carried the New Balance logo, the company could potentially be blamed should a problem arise. The cost of compliance was a challenge, as the batches were very small: for example, the company spent $2,000 to test 400 promotional lip balms before the 2008 Olympic Games).

Another challenge in the operational domain was the gap between CSR management in domestic operations compared to supplier facilities overseas. While there were business reasons for this discrepancy (e.g. low-skilled work force, high

---

[27] See *Boston Consulting Group 2008 Survey "Capturing the Green Advantage for Consumer Companies," http://209.83.147.85/impact_expertise/publications/files/Capturing_Green_ Advantage_Consumer_Companies_Jan_2009.pdf accessed January 13, 2010.*

employee turnover and technical issues), they had to be addressed or the gap could expose the company to some potential reputational risks.

To keep domestic jobs, New Balance was considering closing some of its overseas factories. The question then became, was the company going to take measures to minimize the negative social impacts on the workers overseas (e.g. through compensation and retraining)? Organizations such as the Maquila Solidarity Network provided guidelines for responsible transitions for multinational companies forced to close down production in countries such as China. Use of contract labour in overseas factories was an area that "raise[d] a red flag," according to Sciabarrasi. While New Balance monitored for any violations and took corrective action, it did not have a standard on short-term contracts used to hire temporary workers overseas, a concern voiced by stakeholders, such as the Maquila Solidarity Network. The situation was also complicated by different cultural perceptions; for instance, some migrant workers in Asian countries may prefer to work longer hours in order to earn more in a short period of time before returning to their homes.

4. Community support

A key part of New Balance's mission included supporting the communities where it had operations. Philanthropy and volunteering were an important factor in employee retention and job satisfaction. As one interviewee pointed out, "New Balance employees feel highly empowered to help others and engage in the community to do our part, inside and outside our work hours." New Balance had a "sincere and deep belief in philanthropy which came from the top — its owners Anne and Jim Davis." Between 1997 and 2007, the New Balance Foundation's giving increased from $142,750 to $6,494,388 annually.

Volunteering was very active and people were proud of the company's involvement. Studies have demonstrated that volunteering also helps improve public relations, branding and reputation, employee team and skill building, recruitment and sales.[28] In 2007, 614 associates in the United States contributed more than 3,847 hours of service to local communities, which was a 25 per cent increase compared to the previous year. The 2008 job satisfaction survey demonstrated that 96 per cent of employees "[felt] good about the way they contribute[d] to the community."

The community support strategy "received strong support across all levels in the company and in all geographies." There was good awareness about the programs, such as the Susan Komen breast cancer initiative, which had become a 20-year tradition. New Balance had developed a good system to measure the return on investment (ROI) for this social marketing initiative: it assigned dollar value and calculated ROI based on the cost of the event, shoe sales, expected value from shoe "try-ons," giveaways and advertising impressions. Shoe sales at events were easy

---

[28] For more information see: Bea Boccalandro, "Mapping Success in Employee Volunteering: The Drivers for Effectiveness in Employee Volunteering and Giving Programs and Fortune 500," Boston College Center for Corporate Citizenship, April 2009, www.bcccc.net/index.cfm?fuseaction=document.showDocumentByID&DocumentID=1308, accessed January 13, 2010.

to track and drove ROI. For a $100 pair of shoes, with a profit of $30, 100 per cent of the profit would contribute to the ROI for the event. Another level of the hierarchy was a "try-on." New Balance estimated the value of "try-ons" based on internal marketing benchmarks; for example, it knew that approximately 10 per cent of customers who try on shoes actually buy them. If the profit on a $100 pair of shoes is $30, then the value of a "try-on" would be $3.

Despite its strong community involvement culture, New Balance community involvement strategy (including New Balance Foundation giving) was not aligned with the business strategy: it was mostly U.S.-centered and insufficiently communicated both internally and externally (to customers and other stakeholders). Employees felt that the brand did not get enough recognition for all the great work that had been done. The community support strategy was also poorly focused. Areas of involvement included childhood obesity, breast cancer, Boys and Girls Clubs and the YMCA, among others; however, these were not issues that were relevant to all people worldwide, and employees did not always feel passionate about them.

OPPORTUNITIES AND CHALLENGES IN BUILDING AN INTEGRATED CSR STRATEGY

The assessment revealed that New Balance had many of the key elements required for the development of an effective CSR strategy to address the challenges that the company faced as a global business. It identified several key **strengths**:

- Strong commitment to corporate responsibility as a central part of the organization's values and mission;
- Readiness to support the development of an integrated CSR strategy by key leaders from across the company, as well as the CEO and the owners;
- Good range of practical knowledge and experience in CSR initiatives distributed across the organization from supply chain management to community involvement and employee volunteering.

Identified **weaknesses** that had to be addressed in order to move forward included the following:

- Lack of clear and effective leadership either in the form of executive leadership or the RL Steering Committee;
- Lack of a comprehensive definition and organizational understanding of what RL meant for New Balance;
- Lack of a framework for systematically identifying CSR risks and opportunities that were material to the business;
- Lack of a strategy for aligning and integrating CSR into the core business and measuring the business and social value from various initiatives under way;
- Lack of communication and reporting systems to create awareness and measure progress in CSR and communicate progress with internal and external stakeholders.

As the fourth-largest footwear brand in the world, New Balance had the opportunity and responsibility to take CSR to the next level and give new meaning and value to responsible leadership. As a growing global brand in an environment of high consumer expectations, public awareness and concerns about social and environmental issues in the footwear and apparel industry, the time was right for New Balance to create a "breakthrough" strategy on CSR; however, developing and implementing such a strategy required addressing some key questions and challenges:

- What was the right structure for adopting a unified, company-wide approach to CSR? To what extent should such a structure be formalized? Should New Balance create a CSR department or continue to rely on the RL Steering Committee for driving CSR?
- What should New Balance focus on to have the greatest impact in terms of both social and business results? Should it concentrate on two to three areas where it is particularly strong or address two to three areas identified as posing the highest risks?
- How should New Balance maintain its culture and values of social responsibility given its fast growth through acquisitions of different brands? Is it possible to promote growth and social responsibility at the same time?
- What does an industry leader look like? Is leadership about continual internal improvement or about being a strong public champion? Should the company partner with industry peers, NGOs and governments to address issues beyond its reach today?
- What are the roles of the CEO and the owners— James and Anne Davis — in moving forward with an integrated CSR strategy? Who should be leading the process?
- What is the role of senior management? Is it sufficient for senior management to fire the starting pistol and expect that people will feel empowered to move forward? Or should it take a more active role in mapping the direction, providing goals, guidance, recognition and continuous communication?[29]

From its strong values of ethical responsibility and community support to the way it addressed key social and environmental issues, such as preserving U.S. jobs and "greening" its manufacturing processes and products, New Balance had a strong foundation on which to build this strategy. With the CSR assessment, engagement of key executives and the work on the first CSR report, New Balance had begun the transformation. The challenge for the company going forward was to discern how to make CSR and responsible leadership a powerful force for driving global business success while increasing the contribution of New Balance to developing a just and sustainable world. Building the business case for an integrated CSR strategy was the next critical step for moving forward.

---

[29] *Some of the questions came from an earlier assessment of New Balance conducted by the Boston College Center for Corporate Citizenship: Blowfield, Michael, "New Balance Case Study," October 2006.*

Exhibit 1

RESPONSIBLE LEADERSHIP ORGANIZATIONAL CHART, APRIL 2009

```
┌─────────────────────────┐
│   Chairman and          │
│   Vice-chair            │
└─────────────────────────┘

┌─────────────────────────┐
│   Chief Executive Officer│
│                         │
└─────────────────────────┘
```

Responsible Leadership Steering Committee
- Social Responsibility Manager, Committee Chair
- Vice-chair, NB and EVP Administration
- EVP Commercial Operations
- VP Sourcing and Procurement
- EVP Apparel
- VP Intellectual Property
- VP Global Design and Development
- Director Global Marketing and Brand Management

RL Category Sponsors and Structure (Includes international operations)

Philanthropy and community investing	Environmental sustainability	Domestic manufacturing	Product and life cycle	SR compliance

All company associates
Part of every associate's responsibility

Exhibit 2

SENIOR EXECUTIVE STAFF

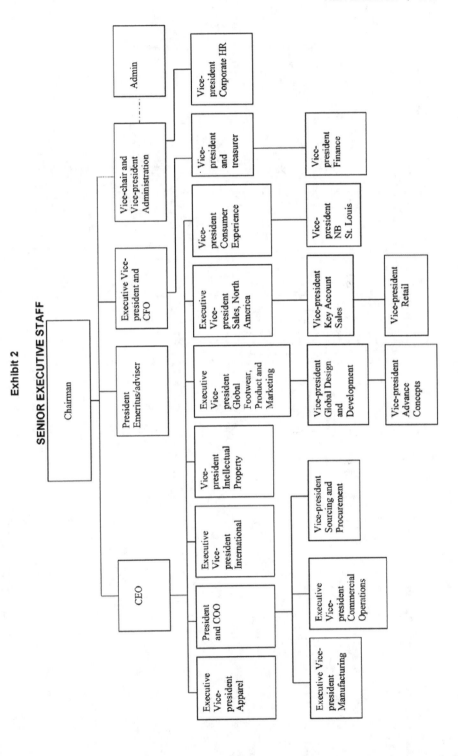

Exhibit 3

NEW BALANCE WORLDWIDE SALES GROWTH (US$), 1991 – 2008

1991	1999	2005	2008
$210 million	$890 million	$1.54 billion	$1.61 billion

Exhibit 4

ATHLETIC FOOTWEAR MARKET, 2008

#	Company	Sales (in millions of US$)	Market share (%)
1	Nike (incl. Nike Golf, Converse)	$5,192	41.70
2	Adidas (incl. TMaG, Reebok)	$1,531	12.30
3	Skechers	$1,084	8.71
4	**New Balance**	**$920**	**7.39**
5	VF Corp. (1)	$570	4.58
6	ASICS	$449	3.61
7	Collective Brands (2)	$415	3.33
8	Puma	$404	3.24
9	Quiksilver (3)	$275	2.21
10	Crocs	$261	2.10

Notes: (1) VF Corp. includes Vans, Reef Brazil and The North Face.
         (2) Collective Brands includes Keds, Hilfiger, Sperry and Saucony.
         (3) Quiksilver includes DC, Roxy and Quiksilver brands.
Source: Sporting Goods Intelligence, www.sginews.com, April 20, 2009, Vol. 26, No. 16.

Exhibit 5

FOOTWEAR AND APPAREL INDUSTRY: SELECTED CSR BENCHMARKS, 2008

Company	Business structure				Annual CSR report	Independent human rights monitoring	Disclosing supplier list	Operations			Structure		
	Status	# of employees (2008)	Revenue 2008 (in US$ mil.)	Priority issues				Steps to reduce energy/footprint	Restricted substance policy	% of products with recycled content	CSR dept. home	Title of CSR head	CSR reports to:
New Balance	Private	4,100 (2,634 in the U.S.)	$1,540	Breast cancer, obesity	No	Yes- footwear only	No	Improved energy efficiency; renewable energy in the U.S. facilities - 30%	No policy but in compliance with REACH. Continuous improvement & "eco score card" for footwear	All	Intellectual property Corporate	Social responsibility manager	VP of Intellectual Property
Adidas Group	Public	39,000	10,799 Euro	Health (reproductive & HIV/AIDS), education, youth, disaster relief	Yes	Yes (Fair Labour Association)	Yes	Reducing use of air freight; environmental guidelines and training for suppliers; energy audits of own sites & retail stores	Yes – goal of average VOC emission of 20 g/pair of shoes	Unknown, "experimenting" with use	Legal	Global director Social & Environmental Affairs	General Council
Nike	Public	30,000	$16,325	Sport for youth inclusion – Let me Play; refugees; disaster response	Yes	Not consistently – in FY05-06 researchers from MIT investigated factories	Yes	Sustainable design guidelines; Climate neutral by 2011; participation in WWF Climate Savers program	Aim for 100% of Nike footwear to meet baseline; Considered standards by 2011, all apparel by 2015, and all equipment by 2020. Plan to maintain current VOC g/pair (95% reduction from a 1998 baseline)	Not reported	Stand alone	VP Corporate Responsibility	CEO
Timberland	Public	6,300	$1,436	Environment, community greening	Bi-ennial, quarterly KPIs	No	Yes (posted on Just Means website)	Increasing renewable energy; Green Index™ rating; Env. Code of Conduct; Green Building principles for new stores; $3,000 employee bonus for hybrid car	Working on completely phasing out PVC across entire footwear line	79.5%	Corporate Culture	VP of CSR	Corporate Culture officer

Exhibit 5 (continued)

Business structure				Priority issues	Operations						Structure		
Company	Status	# of employ-ees (2008)	Revenue 2008 (in US$ mil.)		Annual CSR report	Independ-ent human rights monitoring	Disclos-ing supplier list	Steps to reduce energy/ footprint	Restricted substance policy	% of products with recycled content	CSR dept. home	Title of CSR head	CSR reports to:
Levi Strauss	Private	11,550	$4,200	Disaster relief found., bldg. assets (poverty), preventing spread of HIV/AIDS, workers' rights, environ. sustainability	No	No	Yes	Environmental provisions in sourcing guidelines, use of organic cotton, "Cradle-to-cradle" life cycle assessment of select products, completed GHG inventory and Facilities Environmental Impact Assessment	Unknown	Unknown	Unknown	Unknown	Unknown
Gap	Public	25,000	$15,763	Youth (developed world) & women - work and life skills (developing world)	Yes	Yes (SAI & Verite)	No	Three focus areas: 1) energy conservation, 2) output/ waste reduction, 3) cotton/ sustainable design. Pledged to reduce U.S. GHG emissions by 11%/sq. ft. from 2003-2008. Monitoring energy consumption in about 40% of U.S. stores. Env. procurement guidelines into RFP process for all non-merchandise suppliers. EMS training for factories.	Yes - have developed "Restricted Substance List" that dictates which chemicals cannot be used when producing their clothing. Restricts several chemicals, including formaldehyde, lead and carcinogenic dyes.	Working to include recycled material in packaging & labels - not discussed for products	Legal and Admini-stration	Senior VP of Social Responsi-bility	Chief Legal and Admini-strative officer

Exhibit 6

CORPORATE CITIZENSHIP MANAGEMENT FRAMEWORK

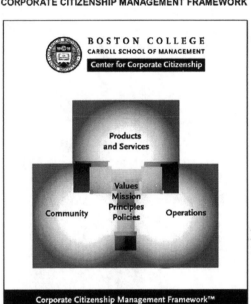

Source: Vesela Veleva, "Managing Corporate Citizenship: A New Tool for Companies," *Corporate Social Responsibility and Environmental Management*, 2009, DOI: 10.1002/csr.206, www3.interscience.wiley.com/cgi-bin/fulltext/122456956/PDFSTART, accessed January 13, 2010.

DISCUSSION QUESTIONS

Chapter 13: New Balance: Developing an Integrated CSR Strategy

1. For each of the four Corporate Citizenship Management Framework (CCMF) dimensions, identify key strengths and weaknesses for New Balance.
2. Based on the analysis of strengths and weaknesses, identify one to three areas for New Balance to focus on and develop a CSR strategy that is integrated with the business strategy.
3. List the key steps for implementing an integrated CSR strategy (e.g., who should be involved? What would the communication plan consist of? What resources are needed? What is the timeline? What are the measures of success?)

IVEY | Publishing

Chapter 14

SOLUTIONS CARE ASSOCIATION: DEVELOPING AN INTEGRATED CSR STRATEGY[1]

Marcus Delerton, senior vice-president of Community Benefit, Research and Health Policy at Solutions Care Association, understood the challenges facing the organization in terms of corporate social responsibility (for organizational chart see Exhibit 1). It was a mid-size nonprofit health care organization which was quickly growing in the United States and was widely considered an emerging leader in the environmental area with its initiatives around phasing out toxic chemicals, investing in clean energy and promoting disease prevention. The company was deeply involved in numerous community benefit initiatives and programs and its employees were highly engaged in volunteering and proud to support its mission. But there was limited awareness internally and externally about all social and environmental initiatives, which were often neither aligned nor well communicated. Delerton realized that developing an integrated strategy and becoming more transparent about

---

[1] *This case has been written on the basis of published sources only.*

One time permission to reproduce granted by Richard Ivey School of Business Foundation on June 24, 2013.

Solutions Care Association's social and environmental performances were critical for maintaining the organization's reputation as an imminent leader in corporate social responsibility (CSR) and protecting its nonprofit status. At the same time, he knew that without developing an integrated CSR strategy and setting specific goals and targets, a CSR report would have limited value to the company's internal and external stakeholders.

With the increasing focus on health care from the Obama administration and growing pressures on nonprofit organizations to demonstrate public benefit, the time was right for Solutions Care Association to assess its existing capabilities for launching an integrated CSR strategy.

To obtain a comprehensive assessment of its current CSR capabilities and independent and credible recommendations on developing an integrated strategy, Solutions Care Association engaged The Center for Corporate Social Responsibility Strategies, an organization with which the company was familiar and comfortable. Olivia Stanning, national director of Community Engagement and Philanthropy at Solutions Care Association, began coordinating the work, starting in 2008 (for CSR organizational chart see Exhibit 2). The assessment laid out the basis for developing and implementing an integrated CSR strategy for Solutions Care Association that could also serve as the basis for preparing the company's first CSR report.[2]

SOLUTIONS CARE ASSOCIATION MISSION

To provide our members and all communities with easy, quick, affordable access to health care services, without sacrificing quality of care.

HEALTH CARE INDUSTRY OVERVIEW AND CSR DRIVERS

In 2009, health care in the United States was provided by many separate legal entities, and included three main groups: health care facilities (hospitals and other facilities), health insurers and pharmaceutical companies. The health care facilities included more than 820,000 hospitals, doctor offices, emergency care units, nursing homes and social service providers. Major companies in this category included Kaiser Permanente, HCA, Solutions Care Association and Ascension Health. The sector was highly fragmented and the top 50 organizations generated just 15 per cent of the revenue.[3] The industry was labor-intensive and the annual revenue per employee was $80,000. Solutions Care Association had become an increasingly important company in this category.

In contrast with most of the world, health care in the United States was led by for-profit entities. For example, about 75 per cent of the 6,000 U.S. hospitals

---

[2] *Solutions Care Association had begun publishing a Community Benefit Annual Report in 2006.*

[3] *"Industry Overview: Healthcare Sector," Hoovers, www.hoovers.com/free/ind/fr/profile/basic.xhtml?ID=120, accessed April 5, 2010.*

were for-profit. At the same time, federal and state governments were involved in the U.S. health care sector either as a direct-care provider (e.g. the Department of Veterans Affairs), an operator of health insurance (e.g. Medicare for the elderly and Medicaid for the low-income and disabled), or a provider of various social services. Overall, about 60 per cent of Americans were covered by employer-sponsored health insurance, five per cent were on individual insurance, and 15 per cent were enrolled in public insurance programs such as Medicaid and Medicare.[4] In 2009, before the U.S. Congress passed the Health Care and Education Reconciliation Act of 2010,[5] about 15 per cent of the U.S. population was uninsured (around 45 million). On average, a family of four paid $11,000 for health insurance per year, of which 75 per cent was typically covered by the employer (in cases of employer-sponsored health insurance).

Health care had emerged as one of the top concerns for Americans and American companies and, not surprisingly, became one of the first issues to be addressed by the Obama administration. According to a report by the Committee for Economic Development,[6] "despite the fact that the U.S. had some of the best care for seriously ill patients, the U.S. employer-based health insurance system was failing." The cost of insurance had been rising more quickly than wages or total income in the economy. According to McKinsey estimates,[7] in 2010 consumers paid more than employers in health care costs and the total consumer bad debt reached $65 billion. Despite U.S. leadership in health care technology, scientific advances and medical research, the quality of health care and population health outcomes were worse than they should have been, due to inefficiencies, lack of competition, medical errors, and a focus on treating diseases rather than prevention. In 2009, the United States spent $2.5 trillion on health care (about $8,047 per resident), which accounted for 17.3 per cent of the country's Gross Domestic Product (GDP) and was the largest one-year increase in history, when comparing to the 2008 spending of $2.3 trillion or 16.2 per cent of GDP (see Exhibit 3). By 2019, national health spending was expected to reach $4.5 trillion and comprise 19.3 per cent of GDP.[8]

[4] *Medicaid and Medicare were governmental programs that provided medical and health-related services for the poor and elderly, respectively. For more information, see www.medical newstoday.com/info/medicare-medicaid/whatismedicare.php, accessed November 24, 2010.*

[5] *For more information on the Health Care and Education Reconciliation Act of 2010, see www.govtrack.us/congress/bill.xpd?bill=h111-4872&tab=summary, accessed April 5, 2010.*

[6] *"Quality, Affordable Health Care for All," Committee for Economic Development, 2007, www.ced.org/library/reports/45/134-quality-affordable-health-care-for-all-moving-beyond-the-employer-based-health-insurance-system, accessed November 24, 2010.*

[7] *"The next wave of change for US health care payments," McKinsey Quarterly, May 2010, www.mckinseyquarterly.com/Health_Care/Strategy_Analysis/The_next_wave_of_change_for_US_health_care_payments_2585, accessed November 24, 2010.*

[8] *Center for Medicare and Medicaid Services, www.cms.gov/NationalHealthExpendData/downloads/proj2009.pdf, accessed November 24, 2010.*

Several factors contributed to the high health care costs. First, due to the fragmented, multi-payer system, U.S. health care had significant administrative costs — estimated between 21 per cent and 31 per cent of health care spending.[9] Second, there was "zero-sum competition in the health care." In any industry, competition helps reduce costs, improve quality and drive up value for consumers. In the health care industry, however, "system participants divided value instead of increasing it.... Costs were shifted from the payer to the patient, from the hospital to the physician, from the insured to the uninsured, and so on."[10] Third, the U.S. system had focused on treating diseases rather than on health management (educating and empowering people to live healthier lifestyles).[11] Finally, the high prices of drugs, outpatient procedures, and medical staff salaries also contributed to the high costs (for a breakdown of U.S. health care expenses see Exhibit 4). Pressures were growing to reduce health care costs without sacrificing the quality of service, and a growing number of studies had demonstrated that CSR practices such as improving energy efficiency, reducing waste, eliminating toxic chemicals and focusing on disease prevention could lead to significant cost savings.

As many developed countries experienced growth in the population of people 65 and older, health care expenses were projected to continue to rise.[12] Chronic and preventable diseases such as cancer, heart disease and diabetes were a key factor behind increasing health care costs. Measures to reduce obesity and smoking and to promote a healthy lifestyle required implementing an integrated strategy to engage various stakeholders such as employees, patients and local community organizations.

In addition to the economic impacts, health care organizations had significant environmental and social impacts. A 2009 study found that the industry spent $8.5 billion on energy costs and made up eight per cent of U.S. greenhouse gas emissions (in contrast, health care in the United Kingdom contributed to three per cent of the country's emissions).[13] Hospitals alone generated about two million

---

[9] Steffie Woolhandler, M.D., M.P.H., Terry Campbell, M.H.A., and David U. Himmelstein, "Cost of Health Care Administration in the U.S. and Canada," New England Journal of Medicine, 349, 2003, pp. 768-75, www.pnhp.org/publications/nejmadmin.pdf, accessed April 6, 2010; "Accounting for the cost of US health care: A new look at why Americans spend more," McKinsey Global Institute, November 2008, www.mckinsey.com/mgi/publications/US _healthcare/pdf/ US_healthcare_Chapter1.pdf, accessed April 6, 2010.

[10] Michael Porter and Elizabeth Olmsted Teisberg, "Redefining Competition in Health Care," Harvard Business Review, June 2004, www.hbr.org, accessed April 5, 2010.

[11] Studies had shown that 97 per cent of OECD spending on health went to health care, and only three per cent was spent on keeping people healthy; see "A Healthy Tomorrow? Health Systems: Facts and trends," World Business Council of Sustainable Development, 2006, www. wbcsd.org/DocRoot/UTun4bgJpUSac3AbDFOR/health-facts-trends.pdf, accessed April 6, 2010.

[12] According to Center for Medicare and Medicaid Services, per person personal health care spending for the 65 and older population was $14,797 in 2004, or 5.6 times higher than spending per child ($2,650) and 3.3 times spending per working-age person ($4,511); see www.cms.gov/ NationalHealthExpendData/downloads/2004-highlights.pdf, accessed April 5, 2010.

[13] Jeanette Chung and David Meltzer, "Estimate of the Carbon Footprint of the US Health Care Sector," Journal of American Medical Association, 302:18, 2009, pp. 1970-1972.

tons of solid waste per year (an average of 15 pounds per patient) and while most (about 85 per cent) of the waste was non-hazardous, toxic waste was still a major problem as hospitals were the fourth-largest discharger of mercury into the environment.[14] Besides the well-known impacts of energy use and air pollution from facilities, there were also growing concerns about water contamination with drugs and other pharmaceutical products. A 2008 Associated Press investigation found that U.S. hospitals and long-term care facilities flushed an estimated 250 million pounds of drugs each year that contaminated U.S. drinking water. Government regulations[15] and consumer/NGO demands had emerged as a powerful driver for change.

Many health care organizations had come to realize that healthy people need healthy communities and a clean environment. Social responsibility for the health care industry did not only include helping the poor, uninsured and underinsured, and supporting universal health coverage, but also helping build healthy communities by supporting community development. The latter could be achieved in many ways: through employee volunteering, local sourcing, green building, promoting healthy living and socially responsible investing (e.g. through employee retirement plans or other investments).

Despite its significant environmental, social and economic impacts, the health care industry had one of the worst disclosure records among all industries in 2009.[16] Outside the pharmaceutical and biotechnology companies, only a few health care organizations provided comprehensive CSR information on their website or had published a CSR report (e.g. Catholic Healthcare West, WellPoint). Most health care organizations published community benefit reports focused primarily on philanthropy and giving to local communities. Pressures for increased transparency and reporting were growing, including on nonprofit organizations, as a way to protect their tax-exempt status and demonstrate community benefit beyond philanthropy and volunteering.

While nonprofit health systems such as Solutions Care Association had been established to address many of the issues of charity care and community service, there had been growing evidence of "convergence in nonprofit and for-profit behavior" and "convergence of pricing between nonprofit and for-profit hospitals."[17] The media had increasingly portrayed nonprofit hospitals as building luxury facilities, charging large premiums and reducing their services for the poor, while paying significant amounts to their executives and employees. Such trends increased

[14] Thera Kalmijn, "Healthcare Heal Thy Footprint," GreenBiz, March 30, 2010, www.greenbiz.com/blog/2010/03/30/healthcare-heal-thy-footprint, accessed April 16, 2010.

[15] Examples of changing regulatory policies in the United States included the pending greenhouse gas emissions regulation, the 2009 EPA decision to include pharmaceutical contaminants under the Clean Water Act, and increasing local initiatives to restrict the use of mercury, phthalates, PVC, Bisphenol A, and other toxic chemicals.

[16] For more information, see www.CorporateRegister.com, accessed April 16, 2010.

[17] Jack Needleman, "The Role of Nonprofits in Health Care," Harvard School of Public Health, Journal of Health Politics, Policy and Law, 26:5, 2001, pp. 1113-1130.

the pressures to re-examine the status of tax-exempt health care providers in a market-driven health care system.

Through its products and services the health care industry had the greatest impact and, accordingly, the greatest opportunity to make a positive contribution to society. Defining what was a "sustainable" health care product or service required thinking "out of the box" about the next generation of the health care delivery system. Was it sustainable to build and operate so many concrete buildings, using vast amounts of energy, materials and toxic chemicals, and have people, physicians and other medical staff go there in order to deliver health care? What were the social and environmental determinants of diseases? This information could help health care organizations begin to deliver health instead of treating diseases. Some leading organizations had begun to partner with technology companies such as Google, Intel and Microsoft to invent the next generation of health care where the focus was on prevention and where people could get most of their routine care in their homes. Such an approach would mean significant savings for people, health care organizations, the environment and society as a whole. With the introduction of electronic records (about 30 per cent of U.S. doctors used electronic medical records, or EMRs, in 2009), the basis was laid out for transformation of the health care industry through improved information and communication.

SOLUTIONS CARE ASSOCIATION: BUSINESS OVERVIEW

In 2009, Solutions Care Association was regarded as a mid-size nonprofit health care provider, and an emerging leader, in the United States. With headquarters in Glenbrook, Nevada, it served 4.3 million members in five states and had approximately 80,000 technical, administrative and clerical employees and caregivers, and 7,000 physicians (see Exhibit 5). Many people knew Solutions Care Association was different from other health care providers but few understood how and why. The company consisted of four distinct groups:

- **Solutions Care Health Plans**: Established as a non-profit corporation, the Health Plans contracted exclusively with the Solutions Care Medical Groups and Solutions Care Hospitals for medical and hospital services offered to members.
- **Solutions Care Hospitals**: This nonprofit, public-benefit corporation operated community hospitals in Texas, Nevada and Florida, owned outpatient facilities in several states, and provided hospital and educational services in other states.
- **Solutions Care Medical Groups:** The medical group included about 7000 physicians, who served exclusively Solutions Care Health Plans members.
- **Coalition of Solutions Care Unions**: The unions were a key player in the organization and represented about 80 per cent of the company's employees. In 1998, the Unions signed an agreement with management to promote greater dialogue around labor issues, safety and performance.

With its integrated structure, Solutions Care Association represented a unique model for health care delivery, which could serve as an example of what the U.S. health care system ought to look like. The fact that Solutions Care Association was a payer as well as a provider allowed the improvement of quality of care, cost structures and communication among all the people providing care.

CSR AT SOLUTIONS CARE ASSOCIATION: THE IMPLICIT MISSION-DRIVEN ACTIVITIES

As a values-based social purpose organization, corporate social responsibility was engraved into Solutions Care Association's business model and its orientation to society. While growing and changing over the years, Solutions Care Association had actively pursued an agenda to meet its commitment of improving people's health via quality care. For example, in 2009 its Community Benefit expenditures were about 12 per cent higher than the expenditures in 2008. Its largest spending in 2009 was for Medicaid (see Exhibit 6).

The company had a CSR Sponsor Group and an Environmental Stewardship Sponsor Group providing overall guidance and direction for Solutions Care Association. In addition, the company had a CSR Workgroup and an Environmental Stewardship Workgroup, which consisted of mid-level managers from across the company and the specific regions who were in charge of implementing the overall strategy in Community Benefit (CB) and Environmental Stewardship (ES) (for more information on the structure and how these groups were linked, refer to Exhibit 2).

Established in 2000, Community Benefit at Solutions Care Association had evolved over the years through several phases; what had begun as an initiative to provide care and coverage for low-income people had evolved into a group focused on developing and disseminating knowledge through research, education and empowering consumers.

In 2009, Solutions Care Association was considered a leader in environmental stewardship — the company's strategy was to minimize its environmental impacts and promote sustainability as the basis for improving individual and community health. In 2008, the company formally adopted environmental stewardship principles, strategies and guidelines. With its commitment to clean energy, waste reduction, phasing out of toxic chemicals, and green procurement, it demonstrated industry leadership and won numerous awards. Collaborating with other organizations focused on environmental stewardship, the company even helped launch a nationwide initiative in 2007 (*Healthy People-Healthy Planet-Healthy Workers*) as an attempt to move the entire industry toward greater sustainability.

From a CSR perspective, there were three questions that had to be continually asked as Solutions Care Association pursued its social mission:

- How well were Solutions Care Association's values and mission reflected in the way the company was managed internally?

- Did Solutions Care Association's contribution to, and impact on, the communities it served add up to a meaningful "social benefit" that clearly distinguished Solutions Care Association from its for-profit competitors who were rapidly innovating to meet increased demands for corporate social responsibility?
- Was Solutions Care Association's "social benefit" clearly understood and valued by the organization's key internal and external stakeholders?

CSR AS A PLATFORM FOR SOLUTIONS CARE ASSOCIATION'S LEADERSHIP IN THE 21ST CENTURY

As an emerging leader of the integrated health care plan in the United States, Solutions Care Association had both the responsibility and the opportunity to be a model of what American health care should look like. With growing concerns and scrutiny of the health care industry, there was no better time for Solutions Care Association to continue to strengthen its leadership position in addressing key social and environmental problems such as delivering affordable health care, reducing climate change impacts, phasing out toxic chemicals and creating a safe, culturally sensitive and supportive environment for employees, patients and suppliers. Corporate social responsibility was not a new concept for Solutions Care Association, but it could become a powerful tool in assessing risks and opportunities from a new angle and implementing a more integrated and aligned strategy for becoming a "leader in social justice."

The following sections present key findings from an initial assessment of Solutions Care Association's management capabilities and structure intended to help the company implement an integrated CSR strategy, based on 15 interviews with 20 Solutions Care Association senior executives with national responsibilities from all four parts of the organization. The interviews were conducted between August 2009 and January 2010. Participants were introduced to a comprehensive framework for managing CSR and asked to provide their perspectives on key strengths, challenges and opportunities for Solutions Care Association.

CORPORATE CITIZENSHIP MANAGEMENT FRAMEWORK (CCMF)

In order to assess its current understanding, organizational readiness and performance in CSR, Solutions Care Association used the Corporate Citizenship Management Framework[18] (see Exhibit 7). The CCMF was developed to help

---

[18] *For more information on the framework, see Christopher Pinney, "Framework for the Future: Understanding and Managing Corporate Citizenship from a Business Perspective," Boston College Center for Corporate Citizenship, briefing paper, February 2009, www.bcccc. net/index.cfm?fuseaction=document.showDocumentByID&DocumentID=1259, accessed April 16, 2010.*

companies better understand and manage corporate citizenship as an integrated part of the business. It involved assessing and managing business practices in four closely interrelated domains[19]:

- **Overall governance — Values, mission, principles and policies:** Embedding corporate citizenship in the governance and management structure of the company. This dimension addresses how a company's core values, mission, vision and governance structures support or prevent the company from understanding and managing corporate citizenship as an integrated part of business strategy.
- **Community support — Addressing social challenges:** Mobilizing the company's assets to address social issues and support social well-being beyond creating jobs and paying taxes. This can range from simple philanthropy to participation in multi-stakeholder social issue partnerships, engaging a range of corporate resources.
- **Operations — Responsible business practices:** Utilizing responsible business practices to minimize potential negative impacts on employees, the environment and society, and maximize positive impacts. This dimension addresses how a company manages a broad range of operational issues, from business ethics to health and safety, sustainable environmental practices and human rights in the supply chain.
- **Products and services — Market strategy:** Addressing societal needs with marketplace solutions that return a profit to the company. This can range from adaptation of existing products and services to be more eco-efficient or socially beneficial, to a fundamental reinvention of a company's product line or services, as well as their marketing and delivery.

ASSESSMENT OF CSR MANAGEMENT AND PERFORMANCE

Using the CCMF framework, the research team conducted industry research and interviewed senior executives from across the organization. The goal was to evaluate executives' understanding and approach to CSR both within their domains of responsibility, as well as within Solutions Care Association in general. What follow are the key findings from the assessment.

---

[19] *For more information on how companies had used the framework, see Vesela Veleva, "Managing Corporate Citizenship: A New Tool for Companies," Corporate Social Responsibility and Environmental Management, 17:1, 2009, pp. 40-51, www3.interscience.wiley.com/journal/ 122456956/abstract?CRETRY=1&SRETRY=0, accessed April 16, 2010.*

1. Overall governance:
Values, mission, principles, and policies

Solutions Care Association's mission was what had attracted the majority of its employees, including many senior executives, to join the organization. As one interviewee clearly stated it, "Our purpose is to help humanity." Solutions Care Association had a history of delivering on its mission and supporting health care reforms and the communities where it operated. Solutions Care Association's remarkable structural characteristics (being a federation of four distinct organizations — health plans, hospital facilities, medical groups and labor unions), however, "also carried with them some downsides." The four groups were not always aligned in their goals and priorities. Finding the "sweet spot" for the four groups and the mechanism to effectively engage them all was one of the most critical conditions for implementing an integrated CSR strategy. Despite this, one interviewee believed that the structure was in place, and that it allowed management to spread issues quickly across the entire organization. This included the Environmental Stewardship Executive Committee and the CSR Executive Committee, which were linked to the groups working at the regional levels (refer to Exhibit 2).

Solutions Care Association had a history of supporting public health reforms, including the proposal for expanded health care coverage in California. Its public policy work had become even more important with the U.S. health care law passed by Congress in March 2010 and the implementation of health care reform.

Solutions Care Association had been successful in working with various stakeholders — suppliers, NGOs, community organizations, government, customers and other health care organizations, among others. This was a crucial element of successful CSR strategy in the 21st-century business environment. In fact, Solutions Care Association actively engaged with many NGOs and community organizations to address social and environmental problems. Health Care Without Harm,[20] for example, had been instrumental in many decisions around procurement and supply, greening facilities and other initiatives focused on worker safety, patient safety and environmental safety.

Public polling had demonstrated increased positive news coverage of Solutions Care Association according to its Communications Department, which was an indicator of the organization's brand strength and good reputation. In an environment of declining trust in business, such a brand reputation was a critical asset in delivering on Solutions Care Association's mission and commitments.

Communication, both internal and external, was identified by many participants as the key weakness of the organization. There was very limited knowledge across the organization and outside of all the great work that Solutions Care Association's employees, physicians, National Facilities Services, procurement and supply, and

---

[20] *Health Care Without Harm was an international coalition of hospitals and health care systems, medical professionals, community groups, labor unions, environmental and environmental health organizations and religious groups, which worked to promote the health of people and the environment (for more information, see www.noharm.org).*

other departments were doing. There was also a lack of communication from the leadership/national level on what CSR was, how it related to the work Solutions Care Association was already doing, such as Community Benefit initiatives, and why it was important for the company to be pursuing an integrated CSR strategy. One participant in the interviews pointed out that she was not sure about the role of the CSR Sponsor Group. Several other participants appeared to have little knowledge about the CSR Sponsor Group and its role. More conversations and communications were needed on this and the link to strategy.

Developing and implementing an integrated CSR strategy require getting a strong focus. Solutions Care Association employees "had a huge portfolio of diverse responsibilities" and in order to make CSR a priority, there was a need for clear communication and constant focus on goals, objectives, measures and accomplishments.

Some Solutions Care Association employees had the perception that "the execution of CSR initiatives was quite costly." Being able to measure and identify initiatives where CSR helped save money would be critical to overcoming this barrier. Studies had found that the main barrier to more successful execution of CSR strategies by business was the difficulty in defining the business case or how CSR helped avoid liabilities, save money, differentiate the brand and retain customers, consumers and employees.[21]

While most of the executives interviewed were familiar with the notion of corporate social responsibility, they believed "employees could not differentiate between CB and CSR; articulating how they are different was challenging."

One internal contradiction and barrier to more aligned and integrated CSR strategy was the brand strategy dilemma — "helping individuals who contributed financially but who were not particularly in need of medical help versus helping those who did not contribute but required medical assistance," as stated by one interviewee.

2. Products and services

Through its products and services, Solutions Care Association had the potential to bring positive social and environmental changes as well as benefits for business. With its 80,000 employees, 7,000 physicians, 4.3 million members, dozens of suppliers and many others served by the company, it had a relatively good reach. The area of products and services included issues such as how Solutions Care Association sourced its products and worked with suppliers, how it delivered services to market, how it helped the uninsured and underinsured, how it provided affordable health care services, and how it minimized the carbon and toxicity footprint of its products and services.

---

[21] *For more information, see "The Business of Sustainability," Special Report, MIT Sloan Management Review, www.mitsmr-ezine.com./busofsustainability/2009#pg1, accessed April 16, 2010.*

This domain included strategic innovation and "out of the box" thinking on what the next generation of health care delivery would look like and how to minimize negative environmental and social impacts and maximize community benefits. This area was of critical importance for achieving the company's mission of providing affordable, easily accessible care of the highest quality. But analysis revealed that there was still no complete understanding of how this domain reflected CSR and how it could be used to leverage Solutions Care Association's initiatives for social change and community health.

According to several interviewees, no other health care organization in the United States had Solutions Care Association's model of integration — between the medical group, hospital facilities, health care plans and labor. Such integration allowed the achievement of greater efficiency in delivering more affordable health products as a result of savings from improved material and energy efficiency, and greater collaboration and innovation among the four parts of the business. This integration also allowed for better communication and collaboration on key new initiatives and product/service changes.

Solutions Care Association was well known for its focus on the prevention of diseases, particularly chronic ones, which were the main factor behind increasing health care costs in the United States and worldwide. One interviewee said Solutions Care Association was in a unique position to do so because its health care delivery model was not defined by health care forces, but rather was based on an integrated system.

In 2009, Solutions Care Association had a small but extremely valuable medical data bank and 250 researchers in its medical research institute who published and provided research to the public. For instance, Solutions Care Association's researchers were behind an important medical-drug case, finding an increased incidence of seizures among users of a particular drug. The company had a unique ability to use patients' data to generate studies.

As one interviewee pointed out, in his long experience in the health care field he had not come across another organization that had environmental goals as part of its product and service development and delivery. Solutions Care Association, for instance, was the first among its peers to phase out the use of the plasticizer DEHP in intravenous bags in hospitals and other facilities. It took five years to identify and work with a vendor willing to develop a safer alternative of the product, which did not exist in the marketplace previously.

With the push toward better and faster access to customer health records, Solutions Care Association had managed to stay on the frontline of developing and implementing an electronic system for data collection and maintenance. This system was a key factor for improving the efficiency and, consequently, the cost of providing medical services, as well as providing patients with greater access and control over their medical history. The ability of patients to take their medical records with them when they traveled to other jurisdictions was an enormous innovation in medical records management. It also reduced paper use and related environmental impacts such as waste, water pollution and air emissions.

The affordability of Solutions Care Association's health insurance products was identified by several interviewees as the biggest challenge in the area of products and services. According to one senior executive, five to 10 years prior, Solutions Care Association had a significant lead in providing affordable insurance products but "times have changed and in 2009 Solutions Care Association could not provide competitive pricing." As simply put by the executive, "Solutions Care Association needed to stay fresh and unique in order to guarantee its position as price leader; unfortunately, it lost its identity." With Wal-Mart's $4 price for many common prescription drugs, it was critical for Solutions Care Association "to be innovative and somehow manage to come up with a solution for price competition," as one senior executive stated. One participant mentioned that a big barrier to providing affordable products was the "perception" that affordable services were not high quality.

At a time when the market demanded greater access to facilities and services outside the delivery system, Solutions Care Association did not provide such access. For example, in 2008 a large customer put out a request for proposal for one provider for all of its employees nationwide. Solutions Care Association, which operated in just five states, could not compete with larger, for-profit companies in cases like this. Such market demands were expected to increase as institutional customers looked for ways to cut constantly increasing health insurance costs.

With the growing awareness of water contamination and the related negative health impacts of drugs (both from sewer flow and improper disposal), the pharmaceutical and health care industries would be under increasing pressure to act responsibly and help address the problem. Moreover, in December 2009 the Environmental Protection Agency added pharmaceutical contaminants to the list of pollutants to be monitored under the Clean Water Act. While Solutions Care Association had been tracking these developments, it did not have a publicly stated policy for or commitment to the collection and disposal of unused or old medications.

3. Operations

Integration of CSR into the operations dimension was one area where Solutions Care Association was particularly strong and had provided leadership for the entire industry. Examples included the work on greening hospital facilities, implementing strong diversity and workforce development programs, and supporting minority suppliers through training and capacity building, among others. Overall, this domain of corporate citizenship management was the strongest of all four and the key questions were how to learn from these successful initiatives, how to better communicate the results both internally and externally, and how to leverage this area to better support and align with the work in Community Benefit and products and services.

Solutions Care Association had provided strong leadership on greening its operations both among its peers and among other companies, from improving energy efficiency, to eliminating DEHP-containing products, to using renewable energy and building Leadership in Energy & Environmental Design certified facilities. At the same time, no clear approach to environmental issues had been articulated organization-wide (e.g. where to go for information, who to partner with), according to interviewed executives.

As part of its increasingly dominant position in the industry, Solutions Care Association was able to influence suppliers and promote the development of environmentally friendly products (e.g. eliminating mercury, DEHP, and other toxic chemicals from products and operations). However, participants in the interviews pointed out that "while the promotion of environmentally friendly products is obviously desirable, they are not cheap," which posed a challenge. An external barrier to greater adoption of environmental stewardship, according to the Solutions Care Association procurement group, was that manufacturers were very slow in responding to environmental procurement requests due to intellectual property concerns.

Diversity was another very strong area for Solutions Care Association. The value proposition was well defined and strongly supported by all four Solutions Care Association groups. There was good communication on diversity goals, initiatives and achievements. The work included not only employees, but also suppliers and customers. With changing demographics, diversity was clearly one of the material areas addressed by the organization.

Solutions Care Association had a highly unionized work force and the unions were a key player in the organization. There was good labor-management collaboration and a strong commitment to work force development. For instance, interviewees said Solutions Care Association provided "plenty of education to its employees outside of their regular jobs, including workshops, seminars, and team-building exercises" and it was "extremely dedicated to its employees and stood by its pledge to provide its employees with job security."

According to interviewees, there were good measures in place in the area of operations. Examples included measuring the environmental and business impacts of green initiatives, carbon footprint, eco-toxicity footprint, and diversity data, among others.

According to a senior executive in charge of ethics and compliance, Solutions Care Association had "an unprecedented management of compliance." It voluntarily implemented the Sarbanes-Oxley Act and had no instances of fraud or non-compliance with its internal policies.

Although its 2007 sustainability initiative (*Healthy People-Healthy Planet-Healthy Workers*) was one of the most significant initiatives in moving the entire industry toward greater environmental stewardship, there was little awareness and insufficient support for it among all four Solutions Care Association groups. Many of the interviewed senior executives were unfamiliar with the initiative and did not know why Solutions Care Association had taken a leadership role with it. Some even expressed concerns about "losing its unique position by partnering with its competition."

As part of its commitment to employees, Solutions Care Association placed a strong emphasis on worker health and safety. Each Solutions Care Association region had developed a safety plan as part of its quality plan that reflected Solutions Care Association's strategic goals of safe culture, safe care, safe staff, safe support systems, safe place and safe patients. At the same time, despite its efforts to promote health and wellness among patients (e.g. by emphasizing prevention and providing healthy, organic food in many hospitals), the health profile of its employees was poor and, according to one interviewee, "our customers are in better shape than we are!" While it was not uncommon for health care workers to have a higher cost of health insurance, Solutions Care Association could focus more on addressing this issue and, consequently, cutting costs.

4. Community support

Supporting the communities in which it operated was a key area for Solutions Care Association that was managed by the Community Benefit group. It involved three types of activities: a) programs to support access to health care for the uninsured and underinsured, b) programs designed to support community health through employee volunteering, grants and contributions, and c) public policy initiatives designed to advance health care policy to better serve all Americans. The Community Benefit program area was of vital importance for protecting the organization's tax-exempt status and delivering on its mission. Many of the participants in the interviews agreed that while CB was getting stronger, much of the work was not recorded and communicated to the rest of the organization or externally.

All interviewees emphasized the great work of many Solutions Care Association employees and physicians volunteering in the community. Volunteering, in particular, was "a significant aspect of the medical group." According to one senior executive, however, the company "was not at all successful at advertising all of our great work in volunteering." There was no system in place to record and communicate internally or externally all the great initiatives by the Community Benefit Department and Solutions Care Association employees.

One interviewee pointed out that Solutions Care Association did more than others in helping uninsured and low-income people. A significant portion of Solutions Care Association "losses" included services to Medicaid patients and the uninsured. There was a need to better understand and communicate the link between Solutions Care Association's mission and Medicaid. This work was probably one of the most significant contributions to the community, but it was not explicitly elaborated upon or communicated internally or externally.

Solutions Care Association was particularly strong in "granting access to various community clinics and its eagerness to share its best practices," according to another employee. But most interviewees agreed that CB was often "taken for granted" and "it's a shame we don't address it more consistently, as we do diversity." This was happening at a time of greater demand for transparency and reporting and a growing need to protect the nonprofit status of organizations such as Solutions Care Association, another senior executive emphasized.

OPPORTUNITIES AND CHALLENGES IN BUILDING
AN INTEGRATED CSR STRATEGY

The assessment revealed that Solutions Care Association had many of the key elements required for the development of an effective CSR strategy to address the challenges that the company faced as a global business. Its **key strengths** included:

- A powerful social mission that was highly attractive to employees and stakeholders, and set the basis for corporate social responsibility (all senior executives recognized this as a competitive advantage for Solutions Care Association)
- An integrated delivery system from insurance to patient care, allowing for more efficient and potentially cost-effective health care for members and giving members more control over their health care management
- A comprehensive approach to member health with strong emphasis on keeping members well through "healthy" lifestyle programs (e.g. Empower Myself Campaign[22])
- Strong commitment and leadership in supporting environmental stewardship through supply chain procurement and tendering practices and through a commitment to "green" facilities development and management
- A strong medical research program to promote innovation in health care and health care delivery and a willingness to share this research and Solutions Care Association's flourishing medical history database with others to advance health care in America and worldwide
- A social responsibility commitment to serve the underinsured and the uninsured through dues subsidy programs, charity care and participation in relevant government programs
- Strong stakeholder involvement and good brand reputation

Key weaknesses that had to be addressed in order to develop an integrated CSR strategy included:

- Poor communication and coordination — both internally and externally — about the many CSR-related programs in the organization
- Lack of alignment or knowledge between the four groups at Solutions Care Association — the Health Plans, Medical Groups, Hospitals and Labor — on all social and environmental initiatives being undertaken
- Shrinking lead for Solutions Care Association in providing affordable insurance products
- Greater focus on measuring *inputs* (e.g. community grants, uninsured people served) rather than *impacts* of CSR initiatives on both Solutions Care Association and the community

---

[22] *Empower Myself was an advertising campaign emphasizing the power of individuals over their health.*

- Poor understanding of the link between Medicaid, helping the uninsured and underinsured, and how sustainable operations could be linked to health care affordability

As an emerging leader of integrated health care plans in the United States, Solutions Care Association had both the responsibility and the opportunity to be a model of what American health care should look like. With health care overhaul and increasing scrutiny of the health care industry, there was no better time for Solutions Care Association to strengthen its leadership position in addressing key social and environmental problems, such as reducing the cost of health care, mitigating climate change impacts, eliminating toxic chemicals in products and operations, and creating a safe, culturally sensitive and supportive environment for employees, patients, and suppliers. With the CSR assessment, engagement of key executives and the work on greater transparency and reporting, Solutions Care Association had begun the transformation. The challenge for the company going forward was to use CSR as a powerful tool in assessing risks and opportunities from a new angle and implementing a more integrated and aligned strategy for becoming a "leader in social justice." Building the business case for an integrated CSR strategy and engaging the leadership at a regional level were the next critical steps for moving forward.

Exhibit 1

SOLUTIONS CARE ASSOCIATION ORGANIZATIONAL CHART — EXECUTIVE TEAM, 2010

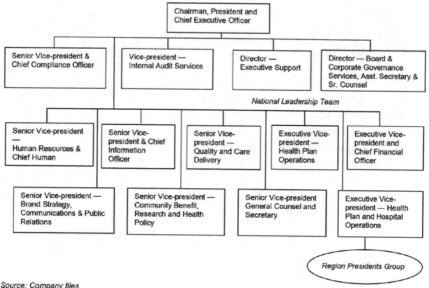

Source: Company files.

Exhibit 2

**CORPORATE SOCIAL RESPONSIBILITY MANAGEMENT
AT SOLUTIONS CARE ASSOCIATION, 2010**

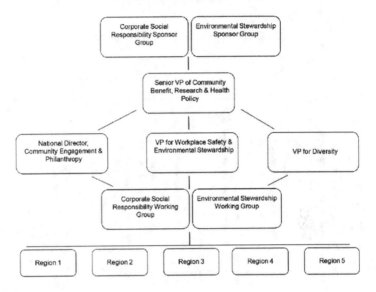

Source: Company files.

Exhibit 3

HEALTH EXPENDITURES AS A SHARE OF GDP, 2007

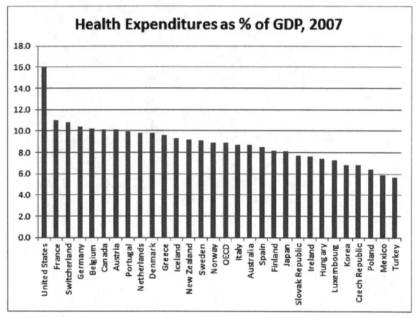

Source: OECD Health Data, 2009,
www.oecd.org/document/21/0,3343,en_2649_33929_44219221_1_1_1_1,00.html, accessed March 3, 2011.

Exhibit 4

U.S. HEALTH CARE EXPENDITURE, 2008

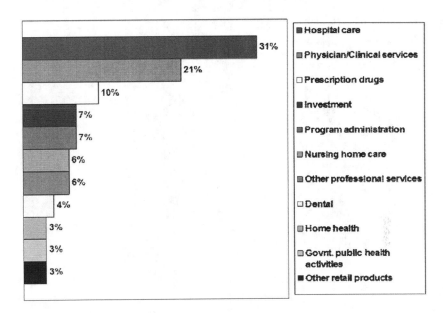

Source: Centers for Medicare and Medicaid Services, Office of the Actuary, National Health Statistics Group.

Exhibit 5

SOLUTIONS CARE ASSOCIATION — KEY STATISTICS AS OF DEC. 31, 2009

Health Plan Membership: 4.3 million

Medical facilities and physicians
- Medical centers: 17
- Medical offices: 200
- Physicians: 7,000
- Employees: 80,000

Operating revenue:
- 2008: $20.1 billion
- 2007: $18.9 billion
- 2006: $17.2 billion
- 2005: $15.1 billion

Local markets:
- Nevada
- California
- Florida
- Texas
- Missouri

Source: Company files.

Exhibit 6

**2009 SOLUTIONS CARE ASSOCIATION TOTAL COMMUNITY SPENDING
BY INVESTMENT CATEGORY
(in millions)**

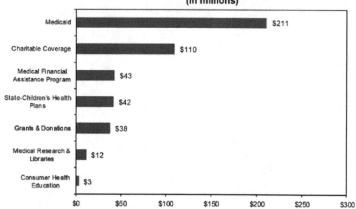

Source: Created by authors.

Exhibit 7

CORPORATE CITIZENSHIP MANAGEMENT FRAMEWORK

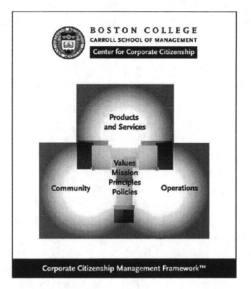

Source: Vesela Veleva, "Managing Corporate Citizenship: A New Tool for Companies," *Corporate Social Responsibility and Environmental Management* (2009), DOI: 10.1002/csr.206, www3.interscience.wiley.com/journal/110497535/issue, accessed March 3, 2011.

UPDATE TO CHAPTER 14: SOLUTIONS CARE ASSOCIATION: DEVELOPING AN INTEGRATED CSR STRATEGY

On March 23, 2010 President Obama signed into a law the Patient Protection and Affordable Care Act (ACA, also known as Obamacare) and thus made United States the last developed country to move towards providing universal health coverage (US GPO, 2010). In contrast to many other countries, the law built on the U.S. system of employer-provided insurance (Gawante, 2009). It introduced the *personal mandate*—a requirement that everyone purchase health insurance (or pay a penalty) either through existing employer provided plans or through the new state and federal insurance exchanges. For people below 400% of the federal poverty level the law provided a subsidy. Companies with over 50 employees were required to offer basic insurance plans or pay penalty. By expanding coverage and the number of people insured the ACA aimed to insure an additional 32 million people in the United States, and reduce health care costs by focusing on prevention, less emergency care and greater transparency (Kaiser, 2013).

Some of the ACA's *most popular features* included:

• People can no longer be denied coverage because of pre-existing conditions;
• Children are eligible under parents' insurance until age 26;

- All insurance plans have to include coverage for outpatient and emergency services, hospitalization, maternity and newborn care, mental health disorders, prescription drugs, rehabilitation services and devices, laboratory services, preventive and wellness services and chronic disease management, and pediatric services;
- Preventive care services such as annual exam, mammograms, and immunizations, must be covered without co-payment;
- The law eliminated cost discrimination based on gender (Kaiser, 2013).

The ACA had numerous flaws and problems, including technical issues with the online state and federal health exchanges which prevented millions of people from registering initially, move by some employers to restrict the hours of part-time employees (below 30 hours/week) to avoid offering health insurance, increasing costs for some employees and employers to add better coverage, and the delay of the large-employer mandate to 2015, among others. Nevertheless, when the March 31st 2014 deadline for open enrollment for the first year passed, the government had exceeded its goal of registering 7 million Americans through the health exchanges (Shear & Pear, 2014).

Early data also show that during the period 2009–2013 spending on health care slowed and in 2013 represented 17.9% of GDP (World Bank, 2014). A 2014 study found that when the Affordable Care Act fully goes into effect in 2014 and 2015, the cost of health services will grow at 6.5% per year, significantly less than the double digit increases in the early 2000s and the 7.5% increase estimated for 2013 (Hicken, 2014).

A recent survey of 249 health care executives about the main outcomes of the law found that "68% believed the act will lead to greater *industry consolidation*, 66% anticipated greater *transparency*, and 75% expected a greater *focus on value-pricing and cost-cutting*" (PRWeb, 2014). As of 2014 these outcome were already taking place:

- According to a 2013 report by the American Hospital Association (AHA), 10% of community hospitals have been acquired or merged between 2006 and 2012, with particular increases registered in 2011 and 2012 (Wood, 2013).
- Studies have estimated that the health care industry can save over $100 billion over 10 years as result of better disclosure of health care prices. In May 2014 three of the largest health care systems—UnitedHealth, Aetna, and Humana—announced that they would "develop and provide consumers free access to an online tool that will offer the most comprehensive information about the price and quality of health care services" (Mayer, 2014).
- Driven by the ACA and the technologic advances, the health care industry was moving fast into launching new, innovative products and services, such as telemedicine. The University of Virginia Health System was among the first to use Skype for connecting patients and physicians, "saving Virginians over 7.9 million miles in travel for health care" and improving health outcomes such as 25% reduction in preterm deliveries in high-risk pregnancies. Partners

HealthCare system reduced by 50% the readmission of 1,200 heart-failure patients in Boston by implementing a home telemonitoring program (Rhodan, 2013).

Over the past several years the health care sector has continued to embrace sustainability as key strategy for reducing costs and demonstrating its commitments to healthy people, healthy planet and healthy employees. In 2012 Health Care Without Harm, the Center for Health Design and Practice Greenhealth launched the *Healthier Hospital Initiatives*, a new national campaign focused on advancing environmental health and sustainability in the health care sector. The initiative provides guidance and seeks commitments by hospitals around the United States in six priority challenge areas: a) engaged leadership, b) healthier food, c) leaner energy, d) less waste, e) safer chemicals, and f) smarter purchasing (HHI, 2014). As of May 2014 the initiative included 12 of the largest U.S. health systems with about 500 hospitals and more than $20 billion in purchasing power, including Partners HealthCare, Dignity Health (formerly Healthcare West), Kaiser Permanente, and Tenet Healthcare (HHI, 2014). The initiative aims to "enroll at least 2,000 hospitals in 50 states and the District of Columbia over the next three years to implement sustainable operations, and will measure the impact on improved patient, worker and community health and reduced costs" (HHI, 2014).

Some believe the United States is headed towards a single payer system, much like the rest of the world (Goodman, 2013). Only the future will show if and whether this can happen. In the meantime, health care organizations such as Solutions Care Association remain critical for providing leadership and best practices in how social responsibility and sustainability can lead to better outcomes for patients, environment, and employees, while saving costs and improving the bottom line.

DISCUSSION QUESTIONS

Chapter 14: Solutions Care Association: Developing an Integrated CSR Strategy

1. For each of the four Corporate Citizenship Management Framework (CCMF) dimensions, identify key strengths and weaknesses for Solutions Care Association.
2. Based on the analysis of strengths and weaknesses, identify one to three areas for Solutions Care Association to focus on and develop a CSR strategy that is integrated with the business strategy.
3. List the key steps for implementing an integrated CSR strategy (e.g., who should be involved, what would be the communication plan, what resources are needed, what is the timeline, measures of success, etc.).
4. What are the main factors for the high healthcare costs in the United States? How has the Affordable Care Act of 2010 affected the health care industry? What are some of its key provisions? What are some emerging industry initiatives around healthy people—healthy planet—healthy employees?

REFERENCES

Gawante, A. 2009. Getting there from here: How should Obama reform health care? January 29. *The New Yorker*. Retrieved from http://www.newyorker.com/reporting/2009/01/26/090126fa_fact_gawande

Goodman, A. 2013. There's a single payer prescription for what ails Obamacare. The Athens News. October 13. Retrieved from http://www.athensnews.com/ohio/article-40830-thererss-a-single-payer-prescription-for-what-ails -obamacare.html

Healthier Hospitals Initiative (HHI). 2014. About HHI. Retrieved from http://www.healthierhospitals.org/about-hhi

Hicken, M. 2014. Health care costs to slow in 2014. *CNN Money*. Retrieved from http://money.cnn.com/2013/06/18/pf/healthcare-costs/index.html

Kaiser, R. 2013. Patient Care and Affordable Care Act. Guest lecturer, UMass Boston, MGT330, Nov. 26.

Mayer, K. 2014. More transparency can save health industry billions. BenefitsPro.com. May 20. Retrieved from http://www.benefitspro.com/2014/05/20/more-transparency-could-save-health-industry-billi

PRWeb. 2014. Healthcare Executives Split on Impact of the Affordable Care Act – Largely By Sector. May 24. Retrieved from http://www.prweb.com/releases/ABLOrganization/SurveyResults0812/prweb9787965.htm

Rhodan, M. 2013. Saving U.S. health care with Skype. Time. September 16. Retrieved from http://swampland.time.com/2013/09/16/saving-u-s-health-care-with-skype/

Shear M. and Pear, R. 2014. Obama claims victory in push for insurance. *New York Times*. April 1. Retrieved from http://www.nytimes.com/2014/04/02/us/politics/obama-to-report-on-progress-of-health-care-law.html

The World Bank. 2014. Health expenditure, total (% of GDP). Retrieved from http://data.worldbank.org/indicator/SH.XPD.TOTL.ZS/

U.S. Government Printing Office. 2010. *Public Law 111-148 – Patient Protection and Affordable Care Act*. Retrieved from http://www.gpo.gov/fdsys/pkg/PLAW-111publ148/content-detail.html

Wood, D. 2013. Hospital mergers and acquisitions increase benefiting communities. *Healthcare News*. June 4. Retrieved from http://www.amnhealthcare.com/latest-healthcare-news/hospital-mergers-acquisitions-increase-benefiting-communities/

Chapter 15

MEASURING THE BUSINESS IMPACTS OF COMMUNITY INVOLVEMENT: THE CASE OF EMPLOYEE VOLUNTEERING AT UNDERWRITERS LABORATORIES[1]

With Shoshana Parker, Allison Lee, and Chris Pinney

ABSTRACT

This study presents findings from piloting a new framework for measuring the business impacts of corporate community involvement at Underwriters Laboratories. It focuses on evaluating the human recourse (HR) outcomes of employee volunteering in three signature programs. Five business impacts were measured—job satisfaction, morale, organizational pride, belief in the UL mission, and engagement. Using an employee survey, the research team compared signature program volunteers with others and found a positive correlation between volunteering and impacts on morale, organizational pride, belief in the UL mission, and engagement. Employee awareness (without participation) of UL signature programs was also associated with increased morale and organizational pride. While the study did not prove causation, it confirmed previous research on the link between employee volunteering and positive HR outcomes. The authors provide recommendations for further research and how companies can use the impact measurement framework to evaluate the bottom-line benefits of their community involvement programs.

[1] Reprinted from: Veleva V., Parker S., Lee A. and C. Pinney, "Measuring the business impact of community involvement: The case of volunteering at UL", *Business & Society Review*, Vol. 117, Issue 1, pp. 123-142, Spring 2012, by permission of the publisher John Wiley and Sons. © 2012 Center for Business Ethics at Bentley University.

INTRODUCTION

Business today is a key player in addressing major social and environmental challenges. It has both the resources and the responsibility to do so, and a growing number of executives recognize the value of such involvement to their company/brand reputation, license to operate, and ability to attract and retain talent. Employees, in particular Generation Y, want to work for companies that have strong values and demonstrate a commitment to society beyond providing jobs and taxes. In addition, no company can succeed in isolation from the communities in which it operates.

Every year, companies contribute significant resources—cash, in-kind donations, and employee volunteers—to nonprofit organizations and community support initiatives. Yet most companies have a limited understanding of the value their initiatives add to the community or to their business. Measuring the business value of corporate community involvement[2] (referred to as either CCI or CI) initiatives helps companies demonstrate the business case for community involvement internally and allows them to better align their community involvement strategy with the core business strategy. For environmental initiatives, such measures are more common, but for CCI efforts such as employee volunteering, signature programs, and emergency response initiatives, there are rarely reliable business indicators. Most research in the area of social responsibility has focused on company-level impacts and less on project- or program-level impacts (Veleva, 2010).

Research has also shown that most companies are measuring inputs and outputs (e.g., number of volunteer hours, donation as percentage of pretax net income) versus the actual *impacts* of their CCI programs (Veleva, 2009). Measuring impacts is still underdeveloped. Most research is anecdotal, and just a few leading companies have begun to develop measures to track such impacts (e.g., Starbucks, Green Mountain Coffee Roasters, IBM, and Allstate, among others).

This chapter presents the case of UL—how the company piloted a new framework for measuring the business impacts of community involvement—to evaluate the business benefits of employee volunteering. The initial hypothesis was that employee volunteering is associated with positive human resource (HR) impacts such as greater employee engagement, retention, and job satisfaction.

Does Employee Volunteering Have Business Benefits?

Initial literature review of macro-level studies revealed mixed findings on the business benefits of employee volunteering. On the one hand, volunteering by employees has been linked to greater retention, job satisfaction, and team building (Boccalandro, 2009). Volunteering has also been demonstrated to help build various

---

[2]For the purposes of this research, CCI is defined as all initiatives and programs that a company has in place to support the communities in which it operates or has an impact—from donations and employee volunteerism to community partnerships. It is viewed as a subset of corporate citizenship, which includes four main domains: responsible operations, products and services, company governance, and community involvement (Pinney, 2009).

skills and competencies such as communication skills, teamwork, adaptability, and leadership (City of London, 2010; Tuffrey, 1998). Tuffrey (2003) provided a 7-step model to measure the impact of CCI and good corporate citizenship on HR management priorities, such as pride in company, awareness, advocacy, satisfaction, and retention. Yet other studies did not find a significant relationship between volunteer program participation and employee commitment (Nanderam, 2010).

There is, however, extensive research linking higher employee engagement and morale to bottom-line benefits. A 2008 Gallup Consulting study on employee engagement[3] showed that "engaged organizations have 2.6 times the earnings per share growth rate compared to organizations with lower engagement in the same industry" (Gallup, 2008). A study by Marketing Innovators International (2005) demonstrated that companies in the "high morale" category outperformed their industry peers by about 20%. Thus, an employee volunteering program that can help improve HR outcomes can have measurable bottom-line benefits.

While macro-level studies are valuable in demonstrating that CCI programs and volunteering in particular could indeed generate business value, they are difficult for community involvement practitioners to use to justify funding for various community involvement programs. For such purposes, company-level and program-level studies and indicators are needed to allow for evaluation and benchmarking of individual programs and initiatives.

The field of measuring the business value of CCI at a program level, however, is still highly underdeveloped and often based on anecdotal information. Yet a growing number of companies have begun to develop and implement more sophisticated indicators.

For example, Aetna added a question to its standard employee morale survey about employees' participation in a volunteer program and analyzed it against rating Aetna as "a good place to work" and other well-being measures, controlling for other variables. Green Mountain Coffee Roasters enlisted an academic to analyze the relationship between participation in and awareness of a time-off-for-volunteering policy and employee pride, loyalty, and identification with the organization (Jones, Willness, & MacNeil, 2009). ABN-AMRO measured the effects of volunteering on participants' and nonparticipants' attitudes and behavior, such as attitude toward work, intention to leave company, identification with company, and organizational citizenship behavior (Gilder, Shuyt, & Breedijk, 2005). A Barclays Bank study found positive correlation between volunteering and job satisfaction, pride, communication, and leadership skills (Institute for Volunteering Research, 2004). A study of the IBM Corporate Service Corps volunteer program found positive correlation between participation in the program and improved cultural intelligence, leadership, and skills development (Marquis & Kanter, 2009).

Obtaining information about the specific indicators and methodologies for data collection, however, has proven particularly challenging, as the information is often

---

[3] Gallup defines "engaged employee" as one who is fully involved in, and enthusiastic about, his or her work and thus will act in a way that furthers his or her organization's interests.

proprietary or companies are not willing to share it publicly. No commonly accepted and publicly available framework and indicators exist presently for measuring the business impacts of CCI, including volunteering, similar to the Global Reporting Initiative framework for sustainability reporting.

To address this gap, a research project was launched in early 2009 to build on existing efforts and develop a framework that would lead to greater use of common indicators, and respectively, benchmarking and transparency (Veleva, 2010). The resulting Impact Measurement framework was piloted by several companies, including UL, to measure the business value of employee volunteering and other community involvement programs.

UL: COMPANY OVERVIEW AND VOLUNTEERING PROGRAMS MEASURED

Founded in 1894, UL is an independent, not-for-profit product safety testing and certification organization. There are probably few people in the United States who have not seen the UL mark on many household items—appliances, electronics, safety devices, water filters, to name a few. The company and its global network of offices services customers in 99 countries. UL has developed more than 1,200 standards for safety. Its product certification work involves testing, evaluation, and factory surveillance of the products to ensure that they meet the UL safety standards or other nationally recognized standards. Annually, the company evaluates more than 19,000 types of products, components, materials, and systems, and each year the UL mark appears on 21 billion products manufactured by 72,000 companies. UL's mission since its founding has been to advance public safety. Its mission statement includes eight commitments, including promoting safe living and working environments, working to prevent or reduce loss of property with physically and environmentally safe products, investing in safety science and education, investing in people, working with integrity and quality, concentrating efforts on public safety, being a good example of corporate citizenship, and social responsibility (UL, 2010).

For the purpose of the research, UL chose to measure the business impacts of three signature employee volunteering programs—programs designed to address social issues through volunteering while also building the company's brand reputation. The three programs were For Inspiration and Recognition of Science and Technology (*FIRST*) Robotics, UL Safety Ambassadors, and Habitat for Humanity (HFH). The first two were conducted mostly on company time, while HFH volunteers did so on their own time. Each program is briefly described below.

FIRST Robotics Competition

FIRST was founded in 1989 by inventor Dean Kamen to inspire an appreciation of science and technology in young people. Based in Manchester, New Hampsire, *FIRST* designs accessible, innovative programs to build self-confidence, knowledge, and life skills while motivating young people to pursue careers in science, technology, and engineering. With the support of many of the world's most well-known companies, the not-for-profit organization hosts the *FIRST* Robotics Competition and the *FIRST* Tech Challenge for high-school students, the *FIRST* LEGO League for children 9–14 years old, and the Junior *FIRST* LEGO League for 6–9 year olds (for more information about *FIRST*, see www.usfirst.org).

UL serves as the safety partner of the *FIRST* Robotics Competition for high schoolers. UL's contributions in 2009 included 2,336 employee volunteerism hours as safety advisors at 47 events across North America, site sponsorships and mentoring of local *FIRST* teams, providing seven judges at the regional and championship events, judging safety animation awards, producing videos, and providing support to the *FIRST* marketing team.

UL Safety Ambassadors

Established in 2003, Safety Ambassadors is a key signature program for UL. The Ambassadors are current or retired UL employees committed to spreading UL's public safety messages. They promote safety education, awareness, and outreach, cultivating a safety-conscious public to make safety-smart decisions within their homes, their communities, and their schools. Safety Ambassadors are the face of UL to the communities where they serve. They deliver safety messages to children and adults within the communities in which they live using safety curricula developed by UL or in conjunction with Disney Educational Productions.

HFH

HFH is one of the eight charitable organizations that participated in UL's 2009 *Changing Lives* annual Giving Campaign in the United States and Canada. In 2009, UL piloted project workdays from UL's corporate headquarters (Northbrook, Illinois) with the local HFH location. UL funded five local build days, both financially and with the necessary volunteer staff. Interest from staff was so great that a waiting list was created for future project workdays for staff to participate in. The company expanded the program and project workdays to other U.S. offices and its office in Toronto in 2010, involving more of its staff in this community activity.

Framework for Measuring the Business Impacts of CCI

Figure 1 presents the framework for measuring the business impacts of CCI initiatives used by UL (BCCCC, 2010). It was developed as a result of a year-long research project and represents a continuous improvement model involving seven steps. The main goal of the framework was to raise awareness and help community involvement practitioners to move from measuring inputs and outputs to measuring impacts of their programs. It also aimed to provide a publicly available, comprehensive framework that would be applicable for a specific program or an entire CCI initiative.

Step I in the framework includes generating a short list of potential business impacts and then deciding which ones are important to measure. Step II aims to define

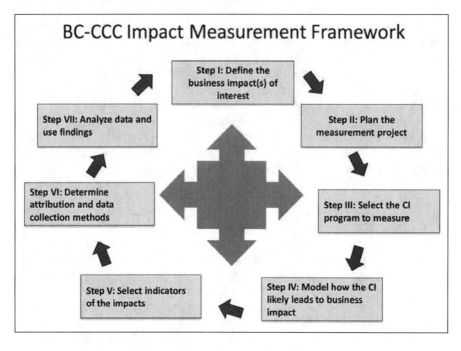

Figure 1. Boston College Center for Corporate Citizenship framework for measuring the business impacts of corporate community initiatives.

the purpose of the measurement and ensure that people, time, and other necessary resources are in place. Unless a CCI practitioner has a particular program in mind to measure, s/he needs to select among often numerous programs or initiatives. Measurement is a costly exercise, so it is important to target a program that is most likely to show business benefits. Step III provides guidance on selecting a program to measure, such as whether it is clearly defined and operationally strong, whether it is integrated into the business and feasible to measure, and whether it is known to be effective and successful in providing public benefits. The framework is flexible and allows for measuring a range of programs—from a multifaceted global community involvement initiative to an extremely focused local program.

Step IV allows a company to develop its own value-creation model of how CCI is likely to add value to business. It involves linking inputs, activities, key stakeholders involved, and the resulting attitudinal and behavioral business impacts. For example, after volunteering, employees might develop a more positive view of the company, which can translate into higher retention, morale, and productivity. Customers, clients, or consumers might develop greater awareness of the company, which could translate to greater loyalty and increased sales. Having developed a value-creation model allows a company to make better decisions about what to measure. Using internal or external resources, a company may want to further customize its value-creation model.

A key step in the process for measuring the business impacts of interest involves selecting appropriate indicators (Step V). In some cases, the impacts may not be possible to measure directly and will require using survey questions. For example, employee engagement cannot be measured directly and therefore is typically measured using one or more survey questions. While some indicators are common for companies across industries (e.g., measures of workforce development such as job satisfaction, retention, and engagement), others differ from company to company.

Once indicators are selected, the next step is to decide on the *method* for conducting such measurement and attributing the results to the CI program. Available methods vary in their ease of implementation and validity of results. As a general rule, the higher the ease, the lower the validity of the results, and vice versa, the higher the validity, the lower the ease. Obtaining high validity results is often expensive as it takes more time and resources (e.g., to hire external experts in designing and conducting an experimental study). Examples of different methods for attributing business impact include opinion, self-reported connection, correlation, triangulation, pre/post, and experimental design.

Once the method for attributing impact is selected, the next step includes developing and following a data-collection protocol, which may include designing and conducting a survey, comparing results to previous data, or calculating the business benefit based on collected data (e.g., in a cause marketing campaign, sales of new product, or comparing retention and performance of employees involved in a volunteering program to those who were not involved).

The final framework step has three main goals: to establish whether or not the CCI program appears to be associated with greater business impact(s), to communicate results internally and in some cases externally, and to identify options for improving the CI program and the measurement process (e.g., by moving toward higher validity indicators). It also provides guidance on calculating the return on investment (ROI).

The ROI is often used to calculate the return on a specific investment or to compare among different potential investments/projects. To calculate ROI, the benefit (return) of an investment is divided by the cost of the investment, and the result is expressed as a percentage or a ratio: ROI = gain from investment/investment x 100.

Calculating the ROI is a straightforward process as long as conversion factors are available. Conversion factors allow a company to "monetize" the value of a particular program. For example, if a volunteering program is associated with greater employee engagement, in order to calculate the ROI, one needs to know what additional revenue the company generates from engaged employees compared to non-engaged employees and how many employees "move" from being not engaged to "highly engaged" as result of the CI program. Companies often have such conversion factors internally. If internal conversion factors are not available, standard external factors could be used in some cases.

Finally, once the project is completed, it is important to evaluate the process and the results. Indeed, evaluation is a critical component of any effective program management. Involvement of a greater number of stakeholders (mostly internal but in some cases external) in this process helps identify weaknesses in the program or the measurement and effective ways to address them.

Measuring the Business Impacts of Signature Volunteer Programs at UL

In January 2010, UL formed a cross-functional team to participate in piloting the impact measurement framework. The team was led by Jane Coen, Global Manager, Corporate Citizenship, and comprised company representatives from the Corporate Social Responsibility, Consumer Affairs, Customer Advocacy, Engineering, HR, and Marketing departments.

As a first step, the team discussed the business impacts of interest to the company as they related to volunteering. Potential impacts of interest included morale, a more positive view of the company, productivity, retention, engagement, and teamwork.

The next step was to apply parameters to selected volunteering programs. The team agreed to focus only on the programs in the United States and to use one year as the timeframe. Compiling program information included identifying the total number of participants in each program and all program inputs such as staff time, monetary costs, in-kind donations, and such. This information was used to construct a value-creation model for each program (see Figure 2 for the value-creation model for Safety Ambassadors). The model involved entering inputs, activities, and attitudinal and behavioral impacts on key stakeholders.

After evaluating each program and its potential impacts, the team decided to focus on measuring five business impacts: connection to mission, engagement, job satisfaction, morale, and organizational pride.

The team then discussed potential indicators to measure the five selected impacts and a mechanism to collect data. Every 2 years, UL conducts its *Global Voices* employee survey, which involves relevant indicators for measuring business impacts of interest to the company. While it is usually recommended to use existing indicators, there were internal reasons that led the team to use the post-*Changing Lives* annual giving campaign survey to collect data and to include slightly modified versions of the *Global Voices* survey questions to measure business impacts. With the help of the BCCCC research team, and using a list of sample indicators, the team added the following questions to the post-*Changing Lives* annual giving campaign survey:

- *Job satisfaction*: "If you participated in any UL-sponsored volunteer opportunities during 2009, including volunteer opportunities that were part of the *Changing Lives* campaign, how did your participation impact your job satisfaction?" (5-point scale from "Significantly decreased my job satisfaction" to "Significantly increased my job satisfaction")
- *Morale*: "I would recommend UL to others as a good place to work." (5-point scale from "Strongly disagree" to "Strongly agree")
- *Organizational pride*: "I am proud to say I work at UL." (5-point scale from "Strongly disagree" to "Strongly agree")
- *Belief in mission*: "UL's mission is one that I believe in." (5-point scale from "Strongly disagree" to "Strongly agree")
- *Engagement:* "I'm willing to contribute beyond what is required in my job to help UL succeed." (5-point from "Strongly disagree" to "Strongly agree")

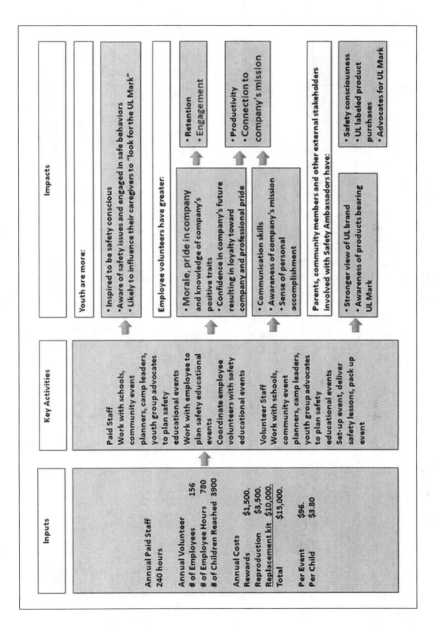

Figure 2. Safety Ambassadors' value-creation model, UL (2010).

For assistance on survey design, programming, and data analysis, the UL team brought in two members of its market research group. The questionnaire was finalized in early April 2010 and was piloted among half a dozen employees. The online survey was launched on April 13, 2010; survey invitations were emailed to 3,850 U.S.-based employees. The average completion time was approximately 5 minutes. As an incentive, UL offered a sweepstakes for two domestic roundtrip airline tickets. By the end of the 2-week field period, 1,427 employees completed the survey (resulting in a 40% response rate).

The sample was representative of the population of U.S.-based UL employees by place of work, internal organization, and type of work. The scores from the new questions were consistent with the scores from the questions on which they were based in the 2008 *Global Voices* survey, providing additional assurance that the sample represented the population.

Results from the three signature programs were similar and were aggregated in order to have a sufficient number of volunteers for data analysis (335 U.S. employees participated in at least one of the three signature programs in 2009).

After conducting statistical analyses using the z-test and Pearson chi-square test, a positive correlation was found between volunteering and impacts on morale, organizational pride, belief in UL mission, and engagement. In addition, employee *awareness* of UL signature programs was associated with positive workforce outcomes:

- *Belief in UL mission was higher among signature volunteers vs. non-volunteers*: 100% of signature program volunteers versus 95% of employees who did not participate in any UL-sponsored activity said they believed in the UL mission (answered "Agree" or "Strongly agree") (see Figure 3);

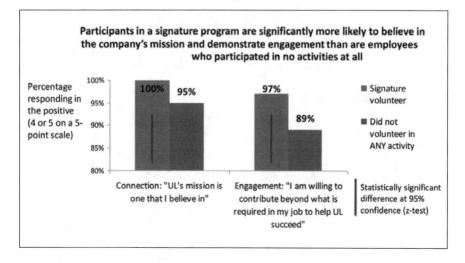

Figure 3. Signature volunteering impacts on connection to
mission and engagement.

- *Engagement was higher among signature program volunteers vs. non-volunteers*: 97% of the volunteers in the signature programs versus 89% of employees who did not participate in any activity said they were willing to contribute beyond what is required to help UL succeed (answered "Agree" or "Strongly agree") (see Figure 3);
- *Signature program volunteers reported higher job satisfaction as a result of participating in a program compared to volunteers in non-signature programs*: 70% of participants in the signature programs reported that their participation "significantly increased" or "somewhat increased" their job satisfaction compared to 53% for volunteers in non-signature programs (see Figure 4).
- *Awareness of signature programs was associated with higher morale and pride*: Employees aware of at least one signature program (and who did not participate in a signature program) reported higher morale (87% vs. 81%) and organizational pride (94% vs. 88%) than those who were not aware (see Figure 5).

Discussion and Research Limitations

The study findings presented in the previous section demonstrate statistically significant differences in outcomes for signature program volunteers versus others. It also confirmed previous research findings that awareness (without participation) of employer-sponsored volunteering opportunities can have measurable

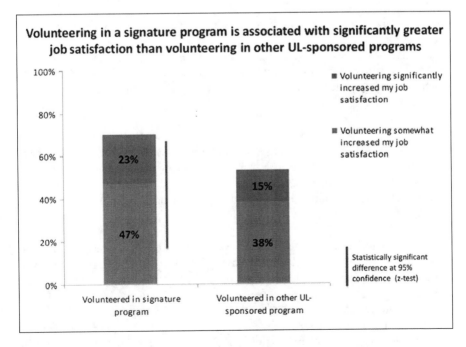

Figure 4. Self-reported change in job satisfaction from volunteering.

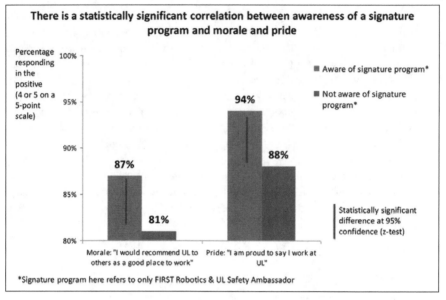

Figure 5. Awareness of signature programs and impacts
on morale and pride.

effects on employee pride, loyalty, and identification with the organization (Jones et al., 2009).

Although study results were compelling, there are several limitations worth mentioning. While signature program volunteering appears to be associated with much greater job satisfaction (17% higher) than participation in other community support events (e.g., Bring Your Child To Work Day; Life Source Blood Drive; Adopt a Beach Clean-up Event; Salvation Army Food, Clothing and/or Toy Drive), the research did not analyze each individual nonsignature initiative but rather evaluated them in aggregate. It could be possible, for example, that a local school-mentoring program would also be associated with higher morale, engagement, and job satisfaction.

While retention was initially identified as one of the business impacts to measure, discussions with the HR team revealed that it was not an issue of concern at UL and was therefore not worth measuring. The high retention (and, conversely, low turnover) is another indicator that overall workforce morale, engagement, and job satisfaction at UL are expected to be higher than at organizations with lower retention. This could potentially explain the small differences in morale, engagement, and belief in company mission between signature program volunteers and non-volunteers (in the range of 5%–8%).

It is not surprising that people who work at UL (and most people in general) strongly believe in its safety mission. While the research team found a statistically significant difference between signature volunteers and non-volunteers, the difference is very small (100% vs. 95% using the top two boxes of a 5-point scale). Even analyzing results for the top box only ("Strongly agree") revealed the same 5% difference (77% vs. 72%) between volunteers in signature programs and volunteers in low-engagement activities such as Life Source Blood Drive, Bring Your Child To Work Day, and Salvation Army Drive. Results could be very different for a company in a different sector and with a different mission.

Another limitation of the UL study was the inability to prove causation. Using an employee survey allows for the identification of statistically significant correlations but only an experimental design can begin to establish causation. For example, the study did not look at the demographic characteristics of UL volunteers (e.g., age, gender, family status, having young children), which may influence the decision to volunteer (Gilder et al., 2005). In addition, engaged employees could be more likely to participate in company-sponsored events.

Because of the very specific nature of and variability in volunteering programs, one cannot generalize on their business value across companies or even among different programs that a company may have. Additional research needs to be undertaken to identify the factors determining the effectiveness (in terms of bottom-line benefits) of an employee volunteer program. Such research could also explore the finding from the UL study that skill-based volunteering programs are associated with greater business benefits than non–skill-based volunteering programs.

Despite the study limitations, results were compelling and formed the basis for a series of internal presentations that focused on estimating the signature programs' ROI and the benefits to UL of further expanding these programs. For instance, the team began to evaluate and recommend a policy for paid time-off for volunteers in company-sponsored community involvement activities.

CONCLUSION

While the described study focused solely on measuring the business impacts of volunteering, to truly foster social change, social impact indicators need to be measured together with business impact indicators and then communicated to stakeholders. Critics of community involvement and corporate social responsibility have questioned "the sincerity of these activities and argued that firms are simply attempting to stave off stakeholder pressures without providing a corresponding benefit to society" (Hess & Warren 2008). While this research did not include a comprehensive literature review on social impact measurement, studies have demonstrated that companies "generally remain uninterested in measuring the impact of their social initiatives" (Arli & Zappala, 2009). Measurements are focused primarily on inputs and outputs, not on the social impacts of CCI initiatives. The main barriers to social impact measurement seem to be the lack of time and resources to measure such impacts, the lack of interest in such measures, and the lack of standardized frameworks and measures (Veleva, 2010).

To foster business or social change, one needs to look at the entire system and engage a wide array of stakeholders in the process (Foster-Fishman & Behrens, 2007). While business implementation of the presented framework remains to be seen, one potential outcome could be that companies begin to support programs and initiatives that have demonstrated the greatest bottom-line benefits. Not surprisingly, such an approach could attract strong criticism from community stakeholders, who often question how businesses select which programs to support and whether they would disclose the indicators for measuring business impacts. If a program does not show a significant business impact but does help address a critical social issue, should a company discontinue its support for it? While the study and the BCCCC impact measurement framework were based on the assumption that there could be no business value without creating social value first, more research is needed to explore this assumption.

Finally, it is important to remember that business impact indicators are only tools and that they alone cannot lead to social change. Top management support, stakeholder involvement, and greater transparency are among the key factors that can cultivate wider use of such indicators and ultimately lead to business change and social change. What such indicators can do, however, is raise awareness, inform decision-making, and promote accountability and continuous improvement.

ACKNOWLEDGMENTS

The authors would like to thank Jane Coen and the entire UL team for their work on the project, and to the following organizations for funding the research: Aetna Foundation, Altria Client Services, Amway, Best Buy, Hewlett Packard, Intel, Lockheed Martin, Merck, and UL. The authors also would like to acknowledge the important contribution of Bea Boccalandro and Vera Works in the development of the Impact Measurement Framework.

DISCUSSION QUESTIONS

Chapter 15: Measuring the Business Impacts of Community Involvement: The Case of Volunteering at Underwriters Laboratories

1. What are the main steps for measuring the business value of community involvement programs according to the Impact Measurement Framework? What did the study identify as key business benefits of employee signature volunteering at UL?
2. Discuss and analyze how employee volunteering helps create business value.
3. What are the pros and cons of measuring and reporting the business benefits of community involvement internally and externally?

REFERENCES

Arli, D., & Zappala, G. (2009, August). Why do companies ignore measuring the social impact of their corporate community involvement programs? [CSI briefing paper No. 4]. *The Centre for Social Impact.*

Boccalandro, B. (2009, April). Mapping success in employee volunteering: The drivers of effectiveness for employee volunteering and giving programs and Fortune 500 performance.

Boston College Center for Corporate Citizenship. Retrieved December 23, 2010, from http://www.bcccc.net/index.cfm?fuseaction-document.showDocumentByID &DocumentID=1308

Boston College Center for Corporate Citizenship (BCCCC). (2010). *Impact measurement framework.*

City of London. (2010, May). *Volunteering—The business case.* Retrieved December 24, 2010, from http://www.cityoflondon.gov.uk/business/economic-research-and-information/research-publications/Documents/research-2010/Volunteering_The%20 Business%20Case.pdf

Foster-Fishman, P., & Behrens, T. (2007). Systems change reborn: Rethinking our theories, methods and efforts in human services reform and community-based change. *American Journal of Community Psychology, 39,* 191–196.

Gallup Consulting. (2008). *Employee engagement: What's your engagement ratio?* Retrieved December 24, 2010, from http://download.employee5.com/employee-engagement-whats-your-engagement-ratio-gallup-consulting-1898.html

Gilder, D., Shuyt, T., & Breedijk, M. (2005). Effects of an employee volunteering program on the work force: The ABN-AMRO case. *Journal of Business Ethics, 61,* 143–152.

Hess, D., & Warren, D. (2008). The meaning and meaningfulness of corporate social initiatives. *Business and Society Review, 113*(2), 163–197.

Institute for Volunteering Research. (2004). *Community investment: The impacts of employee volunteering at Barclays Bank.* Retrieved December 30, 2010, from http://www.value network.org.uk/Documents%20for%20Website/Subgroup%20B/Background%20papers/ IVR%20-%20Barclays%20R%20Bull.pdf

Jones, D. A., Willness, C. R., & MacNeil, S. (2009). Corporate social responsibility and recruitment: Person-organization fit and signaling mechanisms. In G. T. Solomon (Ed.), *Proceedings of the 69th annual meeting of the Academy of Management,* ISSN 1543-8643.

Marketing Innovators International. (2005). *The effects of employee satisfaction on company financial performance.* Retrieved December 30, 2010, from http://www.marketing innovators.com/wp-content/uploads/2011/09/TheEffects.pdf

Marquis, C., & Kanter, R. M. (2009, March 27). IBM: The corporate service corps. *Harvard Business School.* Case study 9-409-106.

Nanderam, D. (2010, April). *Corporate social responsibility and employee engagement: An exploratory case.* PhD dissertation. Capella University. UMI Number: 3398748.

Pinney, C. (2009, February). Framework for the future: Understanding and managing corporate citizenship from a business perspective [briefing paper]. *Boston College Center for Corporate Citizenship.* Retrieved April 16, 2010, from http://www.bcccc.net/index.cfm? fuseaction-document.showDocumentByID&DocumentID=1259

Tuffrey, M. (1998). Valuing employee community involvement: Practical guidance on measuring the business benefits from employee involvement in community activity. Corporate Citizenship Company. Retrieved December 24, 2010, from http:// corporate-citizenship.com/wp-content/uploads/Valuing-Employee-Community-Involvement.pdf

Tuffrey, M. (2003). Good companies, better employees: How community involvement and good corporate citizenship can enhance employee morale, motivation, commitment and performance. *The Corporate Citizenship Company.* Retrieved May 4, 2010, from http://www.centrica.com/files/reports/2005cr/files/csr_Good_companies_better_ employees.pdf

Underwriters Laboratories. (2010). *About UL.* Retrieved December 24, 2010, from http:// www.ul.com/global/eng/pages/corporate/aboutul/

Veleva, V. (2009). Managing corporate citizenship: A new tool for companies. *Corporate Social Responsibility and Environmental Management, 17*(1), 40–51. Retrieved April 30, 2010, from http://onlinelibrary.wily.com/doi/10.1002/csr.206/abstract

Veleva, V. (2010, Fall). Toward developing a new framework for measuring the business value of corporate community involvement initiatives. *Applied Journal of Quality of Life, 5*(4), 309–324.

IVEY | Publishing

Chapter 16

PERKINELMER: OLD INSTRUMENT REUSE AND RECYCLING

Jonathan Lese, corporate social responsibility manager at PerkinElmer, a global technology company developing diagnostics and biomedical products for the environmental and human health sectors, was facing new challenges in the area of product end-of-life (EoL) management. As of 2012, PerkinElmer provided maintenance services but was not responsible for instrument recovery and EoL management in the United States. The situation was different in the European Union, which in 2002 had enacted legislation mandating product take-back by manufacturers. While no federal action was expected in the United States in the near future, a growing number of individual states had enacted laws for product take-back.

Considering the company mission and its strong commitment to product stewardship, Lese believed this was not only an important area to address but also that it would lead to new business opportunities. He wanted to further investigate whether there were already some take-back initiatives in some North American regions, what PerkinElmer's competitors were doing in this area, what options for EoL management there were and whether or not there was a business model for taking back old products company-wide, given the absence of U.S. federal mandates.

PERKINELMER MISSION

"At PerkinElmer, a global technology leader, we're taking action to improve the health and safety of people and their environment. Engaged in a proactive fight against illness, contamination and threats to our well-being, we're committed to transforming risk into safety, mystery into knowledge and ideas into action for a healthier today and a better tomorrow."[1]

INTRODUCTION

In January 2012, Lese participated for a second time in the Green Innovation and Eco-efficiency Strategy for Business course at the Carroll School of Management, Boston College. He was very pleased with the students' work the year before and believed that it was a great opportunity to explore the issue of responsible EoL instrument management. As part of the course curriculum, students were assigned in teams to work with a specific company on a real life problem. The PerkinElmer student team was formed in February 2012 with the main goal of better under- standing the existing practices at the company, exploring the challenges and oppor- tunities of a company-wide product take-back program and providing recommen- dations to implement a strategy with both business and environmental benefits. Over the following three months, the student team spoke with representatives from the company's departments of environmental health and safety, strategic partnerships and materials optimization, North America Repair Depot, sales, product manage- ment and OneSource® Laboratory Services. A survey of sales representatives was conducted to gain insights into customer actions, preferences and opportunities for responsible instrument EoL management.

PERKINELMER: HISTORY AND BUSINESS OVERVIEW

PerkinElmer was founded in New York City in 1937 by Charles W. Elmer, a court clerk nearing retirement, and Richard Perkin, a young investment banker. The two met at an astronomy lecture delivered by Elmer at the Brooklyn Institute of Arts & Sciences and soon became friends bound by their common interest in astronomy. Following their passion, the two men successfully turned their hobby into a business partnership in precision optics.[2] Elmer contributed $5,000 from

---

[1] PerkinElmer, "Mission," www.perkinelmer.com/aboutus/ourcompany/mission/default.xhtml, accessed July 25, 2012.

[2] "The PerkinElmer Corporation History," International Directory of Company Histories, Vol. 7, James Press, 1993, www.fundinguniverse.com/company-histories/the-perkin-elmer-corporation-history/, accessed December 12, 2012.

his savings and Perkin raised $15,000 from his relatives for startup capital, which they used to order equipment from Europe.

The company began its operation as a consulting business in a small Manhattan office, but by the end of its first year, it was making optical components in Jersey City, New Jersey. After incorporating in 1939, the company moved to Connecticut's Fairfield County in 1941. Business flourished during World War II as a result of the increased demand for precision instruments. In addition to wartime instruments and components, PerkinElmer continued to conduct research and in 1944 introduced the world's first commercially available spectrophotometer.[3] Additional products developed by PerkinElmer included infrared and mass spectrophotometers, gas chromatographs and atomic absorption spectrometers. Most of the company's laser work in the 1960s related to defence and space applications.

In 1999, the analytical instrument division of PerkinElmer was acquired by EG&G, a photonics company founded in 1931 by MIT professor Harold Edgerton. The newly merged company assumed the name PerkinElmer with a focus on developing advanced precision instruments for the health and environmental sciences.[4]

In 2012, PerkinElmer was a global technology company with operations in more than 150 countries, about 7,200 employees worldwide, over 3,300 patents and sales of $1.9 billion (see Exhibit 1). About half of its sales (49 per cent) were in the Americas, with the rest in Europe (31 per cent) and Asia-Pacific (20 per cent). PerkinElmer traded on the New York Stock Exchange under the symbol "PKI" and was a component of the S&P 500 Index. Its growth over the past decade had been fuelled primarily by acquisitions. Among the companies acquired in 2011 were Caliper Life Sciences, Inc. (provider of imaging and detection solutions for life sciences research, diagnostics and environmental markets), Geospiza, Inc. (developer of software systems for the management of genetic analysis and laboratory work-flows) and ID Biological Systems, Inc. (manufacturer of filter paper-based sample collection devices for neonatal screening and prenatal diagnostics).

Approximately half of PerkinElmer products were focused on human health such as diagnostics and biomedical (e.g., clinical lab testing, blood cord banking, medical imaging, in-vitro to in-vivo imaging) and the other half on environmental health (e.g., air, water, soil, and hazardous waste analysis; bio-monitoring; food safety testing; toy safety testing; wind, solar cells and biofuels testing).[5] In 2011, the company reported that "we touched over one million lives through cancer screening with our advances in digital imaging technology, we improved the pro-ductivity of over two million research scientists with our informatics software, we

---

[3] A spectrophotometer is a device that measures light intensity as a function of wavelength. It is used by scientists to determine the chemical composition in a particular sample (e.g., soil, water, air).

[4] Vicki Sato, Christopher Jaeker and Kareen Reda, "PerkinElmer — Developing Products in China for China," Harvard Business School Case # 9-612-032, December 2011.

[5] Jonathan Lese, Presentation about PerkinElmer, MD841 Green Innovation Class, Boston College Carroll School of Management, February 6, 2012.

helped ensure the health of over 31 million babies in more than 90 countries with our screening technologies and we analyzed over two billion environmental samples with our detection capabilities."[6]

One of the signature services offered by PerkinElmer was OneSource® Laboratory Services, a comprehensive yet flexible and customized program for professional lab services ranging from asset management to continuous improvement, managed maintenance, instrument qualification, training, relocation, parts supply and other related capabilities.

As did most multinational companies, PerkinElmer had a strong commitment to corporate social responsibility (CSR). Its CSR work was organized around three main pillars: community engagement, sustainable and ethical business practices, and eco-innovative products.[7] In 2010, the company launched its first CSR report, "Making a World of Difference."[8]

RESPONSIBLE EOL MANAGEMENT: OPTIONS, DRIVERS AND BEST PRACTICES

Responsible product EoL management is a component of product stewardship, which the U.S. Environmental Protection Agency (EPA) defines as "a product-centered approach to environmental protection which calls on those involved in the product lifecycle — manufacturers, retailers, users and disposers — to share responsibility for reducing the environmental impacts of products."[9] Product stewardship includes changing the design of products to eliminate toxic and hazardous materials and/or the responsible management of products at the end of their useful lives through reuse, remanufacturing, recycling or disposal. While a company can pursue either of the two approaches, they are often related since green product design facilitates recycling and remanufacturing and product take-back can lead to innovations in redesign. The Boston College student project only focused on product EoL management.

Product reuse is the most desirable option for responsible EoL product management. Often customers will replace their instruments for new ones with better capabilities although their old products are still working. In such cases, reselling or donating the old instruments extends their useful life and thus reduces related environmental and health impacts from the manufacture of new products and the disposal of existing ones. Such an approach can also yield financial benefits for the owner of the product. Cars, furniture, baby clothes and toys are all

---

[6]*PerkinElmer 2011 Annual Report, http://files.shareholder.com/downloads/PKI/1987249438 x0x553226/7e5397ea-7e45-4a61-8026-48d6b3a834c9/2011_Annual_Report_PKI.pdf, accessed July 26, 2012.*

[7]*PerkinElmer, "Corporate Social Responsibility," www.perkinelmer.com/ourcompany/corporate reponsibility/corporatesocialresponsibility/default.xhtml, accessed July 26, 2012.*

[8]*PerkinElmer, "Making a World of Difference," Corporate Social Responsibility Report 2010, www.perkinelmer.com/PDFs/Downloads/BRO_CSR_2010.pdf, accessed July 26, 2012.*

[9]*U.S. EPA, "Product Stewardship," 2012, www.epa.gov/epawaste/conserve/tools/stewardship/ index.htm, accessed August 4, 2012.*

examples of products with well-established and profitable business models for product reuse.

Remanufacturing is the next most desirable EoL product management option as it not only minimizes environmental impacts but can also create new market opportunities and higher profits than the manufacture of new equipment. According to one PerkinElmer representative, India and China provide excellent market opportunities for the selling of remanufactured instruments. Research has also demonstrated that the average profit margin for product reconstruction activities is 20 per cent compared to typical profit margins of 3 to 8 per cent in the manufacturing industry.[10] However, for many global supply chains, this option is not viable as the processing costs of remanufacturing are often higher than the selling price of new products.[11]

When reuse or remanufacturing is not feasible, **recycling** can be the next option for responsible EoL management. Recycling allows for the extraction of valuable materials such as metals, plastics and glass, which are then used in the manufacture of new products. A reduction in waste generation would not only lessen the environmental burden but can also have bottom line benefits as the cost of waste disposal declines or additional revenue is obtained (when recyclers pay for the materials). As of 2012, the recycling of complex medical instruments was challenging, however, due to the assortment of varied materials that were not always properly labeled. Paying for collection and shipping was another challenge, since, compared to reuse or remanufacturing, the extracted value could be insufficient to cover this cost. As the growing number of mandates require elimination of toxic chemicals from products and as shortages of raw materials increase, recycling is expected to become more financially viable in the future.

Disposal — where a device is thrown away — is the least preferred EoL management strategy. Such an action not only has negative environmental impacts but can also expose a company to two types of risks: regulatory risks in case a take-back mandate is enacted and financial/competitor risks in case another company collects, remanufactures and sells the refurbished devices.

Drivers for Sustainable EoL Management

EoL product management has become an increasingly important business concern as result of a growing number of product take-back regulations and changing customer expectations. Since 2001, the Product Stewardship Institute in the United States had led numerous successful dialogues between businesses and federal, state and local governments around take-back policies in many product categories such as electronics, leftover paint, phone books and compact fluorescent bulbs, among

---

[10] John A. Pearce II, "The Profit-making Allure of Product Reconstruction," *MITSloan Management Review* 50.3, Spring 2009, pp. 59–65.

[11] M. Pagell, Zhaohui Wu and N. Murthy, "The Supply-chain Implications of Recycling," *Business Horizons* 50, 2007, pp. 133–143.

others. Several of these dialogues led to the adoption of product take-back mandates at the local and state levels.[12]

The main drivers for product stewardship and responsible EoL management in 2012 included:

- **European Union RoHS and WEEE directives**: These two European Union directives adopted in 2003 were the main drivers for greater product stewardship by electrical and electronic equipment manufacturers globally. The Restrictions of Hazardous Substances (RoHS) Directive (2002/95/EC) restricted the use of lead, mercury, cadmium, hexavalent chromium, polybrominated biphenyls (PBBs) and polybrominated diphenyl ethers (PBDE) in electrical and electronic equipment. The Waste Electrical and Electronic Equipment (WEEE) Directive (2002/96/EC) imposed the responsibility for the collection and disposal of such equipment at the end of a product's life. It covered 10 categories of products, two of which related to PerkinElmer products: Category 8 (medical devices), and Category 9 (monitoring and control instruments). Both directives applied to all companies involved in manufacturing or selling electrical or electronic equipment in the European Union.[13]
- **State and local take-back mandates**: As of 2012, 25 U.S. states had passed legislation mandating statewide electronic waste (e-waste) recycling. Several more states were working on passing new laws or improving existing ones. All laws except those in California and Utah used a producer responsibility approach, by which manufacturers were liable for the costs of recycling.[14] Though medical devices and monitoring and control instruments were not covered in the mandates, this could change in the future.
- **Increasing customer expectations**: In the absence of federal regulations, customer demands for "green" products were the main driver for product stewardship in the United States. In a 2010 survey, 58 per cent of CEOs cited customer demand as the most significant driver for sustainability and "green" product development in their companies.[15] Another study found that as the demand for sustainable products was growing significantly, "it was becoming

---

[12] V. Veleva, "Product Stewardship in the United States: The Changing Policy Landscape and the Role of Business," Sustainability: Science, Practice and Policy 4, Fall/Winter 2008, pp. 29–35.

[13] European Commission, "Frequently Asked Questions on Directive 2002/95/EC (RoHS) and Directive 2002/96/EC (WEEEE)," http://ec.europa.eu/environment/waste/pdf/faq_weee.pdf, accessed October 1, 2012.

[14] Electronics Take Back Coalition, "State Legislation," www.electronicstakeback.com/promote-good-laws/state-legislation/, accessed July 31, 2012.

[15] UN Global Compact-Accenture CEO Study, "A New Era of Sustainability," 2010, www.unglobalcompact.org/docs/news_events/8.1/UNGC_Accenture_CEO_Study_2010.pdf, accessed July 31, 2012.

increasingly clear that being sustainable can drive new growth that capitalizes on a rising demand for environmentally friendly and energy-efficient products."[16]

- **Disposal bans of products containing hazardous materials**: As of 2012, many medical instruments and supplies contained hazardous materials such as lead, cadmium, hexavalent chromium, radioactive material and mercury. Despite an absence of federal legislation banning their disposal in landfills, a growing number of product categories considered hazardous waste were restricted from waste disposal at state levels. Such bans typically followed enactment of e-waste regulations; this was the case of the State of Oregon, which banned the landfill disposal of computers, monitors and televisions in January 2010, just three years after it passed its e-waste bill.[17]

- **Company commitments to social responsibility and good reputation**: Increasingly, companies' reputations have been linked to operational issues such as offering safe and "green" products versus options such as giving money to charities.[18] In the era of social media and more widely informed consumers and customers, companies often began adopting sustainable practices to improve their reputation and attract talent.

- **Opportunity to innovate, increase market share or enter new markets**: Leading companies had recognized that remanufacturing requires an in-depth knowledge about products and the application of new technologies, thus promoting innovation and competitive advantage. For example, Xerox Corporation not only saved $200 million annually by remanufacturing copiers but also "inhibited competition by placing state-of-the-art remanufactured copiers back into service against competitors' higher cost new models."[19]

Best Practices in Product EoL Management

Leading companies had long recognized the business opportunities in product EoL management. Xerox was among the first companies that began taking back and remanufacturing its copiers in addition to offering customers competitive leasing contracts, achieving significant savings and inhibiting competition. Back in 2000, Sony began a five-year partnership with Waste Management[20] to promote electronics recycling in Minnesota. Under the partnership, Sony electronics products were accepted for free for recycling at a number of Waste Management facilities located throughout the southern part of the state. Electronic products made by other

---

[16] PriceWaterhouseCoopers, "Green Products: Using Sustainable Attributes to Drive Growth and Value," December 2010, www.pwc.com/en_US/us/corporate-sustainability-climate-change/assets/green-products-paper.pdf, accessed July 31, 2012.

[17] Oregon Department of Environmental Quality, "Disposal Bans," www.deq.state.or.us/lq/pubs/docs/sw/prodstew/AppendixEDisposalBansAndProductStewardship.pdf, accessed July 31, 2012.

[18] V. Veleva et. al. "The State of Corporate Citizenship 2009: The Recession Test," www.hitachifoundation.org/storage/documents/socc_report_2009.pdf, accessed July 31, 2012.

[19] Pearce, "The Profit-making Allure of Product Reconstruction," p. 64.

[20] www.wmtwincities.com/electronic, accessed January 10, 2013.

manufacturers were also accepted but required a recycling fee. In another instance, Dell Computer implemented product take-back initially to ensure compliance with the European Union WEEE Directive but soon realized that there could be business benefits. It adopted a worldwide program for product take-back, which in addition to recycling offered consumers a trade-up program and an on-line auction for used PCs and a donation program. Dell partnered with Staples and other retailers to collect used computers and worked with the National Cristina Foundation to promote product donations.[21]

In the area of medical instruments, Siemens had adopted a robust company-wide program for take-back, refurbishing and remarketing of pre-owned equipment and systems. The company had found that "recycling and remarketing can be a successful business model in some product segments." Its refurbished ecoline systems included a wide range of medical systems such as angiography, computer tomography, magnetic resonance, molecular imaging, fluoroscopy, mammography, radiography, urology and surgical C-arms. It offered de-installation by an authorized service provider, transportation in special packaging, refurbishing, re-installation, training and a regular warranty of 12 months along with spare parts for five years. Its old X-ray generators, for example, were shipped to a plant in Germany where the "the low-wear parts were disassembled, refurbished and, after a detailed quality check, were reused in the manufacture of new generators." The company reported that some components were reused two or more times.[22]

Competitor Approaches to Instrument EoL Management

The global market for analytical and life science instruments had been growing steadily: between 2002 and 2007, it increased from $26 billion to over $36 billion and was projected to reach $49 billion by the end of 2012. As of 2012, there were over 100 companies working in different geographic regions, but the market was highly consolidated as the top 25 industry players accounted for over 60 per cent of the total market sales. Companies in the sector were pursuing aggressive growth primarily through acquisitions as competition increased. The sector was experiencing rapid growth, fueled primarily by the pharmaceuticals and biotechnology research industry.[23]

Among the main PerkinElmer competitors (see Exhibit 2), Agilent Technologies had the most advanced system for trade-in of products and a wide selection of used

---

[21] K. Palmer and M. Walls, "Economic Analysis of Extended Producer Responsibility Movement: Understanding Costs, Effectiveness, and the Role for Policy," International Forum on the Environment, February 2002, eweber.ucsd.edu/~carsonvs/papers/4002.doc, accessed October 1, 2012.

[22] Siemens, "Product Take-back and Conservation of Resources," www.siemens.com/sustainability/en/core-topics/product-responsibility/facts-figures/product-return-and-conservation-of-resources.htm, accessed August 3, 2012.

[23] Laboratory Equipment World, "Laboratory Analytical Instruments Industry is Growing Despite Odds," 2008, www.laboratoryequipmentworld.com/laboratory-analytical-instrument-industry.html, accessed August 3, 2012.

equipment with the same warranty, return policy and product support as new ones. Refurbished products from competitors Beckman Coulter and Bio-Rad Laboratories were offered through a third party, but it was not clear whether or not there was an established partnership. The largest among the five selected competitors, Roche Holdings, had published a position statement on product stewardship but did not provide any details about product-take back in the United States. Millipore offered take-back and recycling options for a very limited number of products (mostly consumables) and was exploring additional opportunities for product recycling. All five competitors were compliant with the WEEE Directive and had established systems for product take-back in the European Union.

ASSESSMENT OF PERKINELMER EXISTING PRACTICES IN EOL MANAGEMENT

In 2012, developing eco-innovative products was one of the three pillars of PerkinElmer's CSR strategy. The company had publicly stated its commitment to product stewardship: "We design, develop and manufacture our products in a manner that minimizes the health and environmental impacts throughout the product lifecycle, all of which are completed in compliance with customer and product regulations."[24]

In order to assess PerkinElmer's existing practices in instrument EoL management and the feasibility of implementing a company-wide take-back program in the United States, the Boston College research team spoke with several PerkinElmer representatives and visited a OneSource® Laboratory Services lab at Merck that was managed by PerkinElmer engineers. It also conducted a survey of the company's North American sales force.

Since about a third of PerkinElmer sales were in Europe, much of its business fell under the influence of the WEEE and RoHS directives. While products in the medical devices category (Category 8) and the monitoring and control instrument category (Category 9) were originally exempted from the RoHS Directive, the 2011 recast of the directive eliminated this exemption. Medical devices and monitoring/control instruments will become subject to RoHS restrictions starting in 2014, with compliance dates extending into 2017 for certain product types. The compliance date for PerkinElmer products classified as in-vitro medical devices is July 22, 2016. For industrial monitoring and control instruments, the compliance date is July 22, 2017.[25]

To conform to instrument take-back rules, PerkinElmer had partnered in most European countries with the European Advanced Recycling Network (EARN).

[24] PerkinElmer, "Product Stewardship," www.perkinelmer.com/ourcompany/corporate responsibility/corporatesocialresponsibility/productstewardship/default.xhtml, accessed August 1, 2012.
[25] PerkinElmer Letter to Customers regarding Directive 2011/65/EU (RoHS recast); see also official European Union announcement at http://ec.europa.eu/environment/waste/rohs_eee/index_en.htm, accessed December 12, 2012.

EARN helped companies meet WEEE requirements by managing the logistics for the handling and treating of all equipment. PerkinElmer covered the costs of treatment, recycling and recovery of the equipment on arrival at the EARN facility by collecting a small fee as part of the standard terms and conditions for equipment sale. PerkinElmer did not work with EARN in every European country as it had other partnerships with organizations such as Recupel in Belgium or L&T in Finland. In some cases, PerkinElmer was taking part in a program rather than making a partnership. For example, the firm took part in the B2B Compliance scheme in the United Kingdom. In Denmark, businesses could participate in local authority collection schemes (as of 2012, Denmark was the only country that had implemented such measures).

The research revealed that as of 2012, PerkinElmer customers in the United States had several available options for instrument EoL management. One was to throw away the old equipment. Another was to take advantage of the market for used machines online and in developing countries. A third was to take the initiative to recycle the machines themselves. A fourth was a trade-in program in which customers who returned their instruments to PerkinElmer were given a 10 per cent discount on their next purchase. In California, PerkinElmer had a program where customers were provided with a recycling option for $1/pound as well as an Elan/NeXION trade-in promotion. Robert Hazen, global product manager at PerkinElmer, stated, "customers were generally interested in safe disposal and recycling options that contribute to their firm's brand equity."[26]

Sales Team Survey

In order to understand customers' preferences for EoL management, the research team conducted a survey of PerkinElmer's North American sales force. Of the 746 salespeople to whom the survey was sent in April 2012, 117 (or 16 per cent) responded. Most of the respondents worked in the United States; a few were based in Canada. The survey was anonymous, but participants were invited to provide their contact information if they wanted to answer additional questions. Below key findings from the survey are outlined.

When asked what customers usually did with their PerkinElmer instruments once decommissioned, the majority of salespeople (61 per cent) said they trashed some or all of their old machines.[27] About one-third of customers (32 per cent) used the available equipment trade-in and recycle program for discounted future purchases. The other EoL options ("sell to auction house," "send to recycler" and "don't know") trailed behind at 22 per cent, 19 per cent and 19 per cent, respectively (see Exhibit 3).

The survey asked the salespeople which EoL options would be of greatest interest to their customers. Results revealed that customers were most interested

---

[26] *Phone interview with Robert Hazen, March 29, 2012.*
[27] *Survey participants were able to select more than one option for instrument disposal; therefore, the total percentage was greater than 100.*

in a trade-in package that would include responsible disposal in exchange for discounted future purchases of PerkinElmer products (this program was already employed in California for some products and to some extent for consumables). The second most favourable option was to allow PerkinElmer to salvage parts for use through a service agreement of their instrument. The least desired option was to send the machines directly to a recycler at the customers' expense (see Exhibit 4). In the comments section, one respondent pointed out that most customers sought a low cost option and were not willing to pay extra for instrument disposal. In some cases, customers were able to sell old equipment through auctions.

In addition to asking about customer preferences, the survey also sought to identify the degree of importance of a responsible EoL management program (it used the scale of 1 to 5, where 1 was "not important at all" and 5 was "very important"). Findings demonstrated that most respondents believed a responsible disposal program was worthwhile for customers, since "important" was the most frequent result, chosen by 34 per cent of survey participants, followed by "somewhat important" (25 per cent) and "very important" (14 per cent) (see Exhibit 5).

When asked if aware of any forthcoming regulations that would impact their clients' ability to dispose of their equipment in the manner that they were currently employing, one salesperson cited the California Electronic Waste Recycling Act of 2003 and another one pointed out that state environmental authorities regulate EoL management.

The survey sought to identify any potential differences based on client location.[28] Results revealed that some regions of the United States were more concerned about EoL management than others. For instance, while 28 per cent of respondents working in the south and southeast believed it was "important" or "very important" to offer responsible EoL management options for customers, the percentage was 57 per cent for the northeast and 55 per cent for the midwest (see Exhibit 6).

The size of customers' labs did not seem to play a major role in shaping customer preferences for EoL instrument management. The majority of PerkinElmer's clients were identified as having small (using one to 10 instruments) to mid-size (using 11 to 50 instruments) labs. About one-third (32 per cent) of survey respondents stated that they served customers that used a mix of small and mid-sized laboratories.

To gain further insight into the issue, the research team reached out to the salespeople who had provided contact information with the following question: "Considering your customers' alternatives and preferences for equipment disposal, what would you say is the most practical way (if any) for PerkinElmer to recoup value from these used instruments?" Six responses were received suggesting that incoming old instruments could be refurbished and resold, harvested for parts, recycled or scrapped; that engineers should be able to determine the uses and hidden

---

[28] Due to the small number, salespeople working in Canada were excluded from the analysis.

values of each machine; and that there were intangible benefits of EoL management, primarily around customer relations.

From the salespeople's perspective, there seemed to be value that could be recovered from the refurbishing and harvesting parts of used machines. Taking back old instruments would also protect the company from potential competitors who could refurbish and resell the equipment and thus threaten PerkinElmer's market position. However, the company had to identify the most cost-effective take-back approach.

OPPORTUNITIES AND CHALLENGES FOR ADOPTING RESPONSIBLE INSTRUMENT EOL MANAGEMENT AT PERKINELMER

The main challenge for sustainable EoL management was devising a model that was not only practical for customers but also profitable or at least profit neutral for the company. The research team findings suggested there was a business case for taking back used equipment as there was a strong customer demand for responsible EoL management and many competitors were already doing it. Moreover, PerkinElmer was facing business risks from competitors who could collect its old instruments and sell them for a lower price to its current customers. There was a large second-hand market — particularly in countries such as India and China — that could bring bottom line benefits for the company. The intangible benefits related to brand equity, customer relations and public relations were also significant.

Lese believed that with the growing number of take-back mandates and increasing costs of raw materials, it was just a question of time before all companies in the industry begin to take back old instruments. What was the right approach for PerkinElmer at this time so it could be ahead of competitors without sacrificing profits?

The main questions for the research team to answer included:

- What are the business benefits of adopting a corporate-wide product take-back strategy? What are the reasons for not adopting such a strategy at this time?
- What is the best option for adopting a corporate-wide EoL management strategy? Should PerkinElmer simply take back and recycle the old equipment or refurbish and resell it?
- Should the company train its own employees to examine, disassemble and refurbish the old instruments or partner with another company with core expertise in this area?
- What does an industry leader in instrument take-back look like? Is leadership about continual internal improvement or about being a strong public champion? Should the company partner with industry peers, non-governmental organizations and government to address issues beyond its reach today?

Exhibit 1

PERKINELMER SELECTED FINANCIAL DATA

	Jan 1, 2012	Jan 2, 2011	Jan 3, 2010	Dec 28, 2008	Dec 30, 2007
		Fiscal years ended (in thousands, except per share data)			
Statement of Operations Data:					
Revenue	$ 1,921,287	$ 1,704,346	$ 1,550,766	$ 1,659,668	$ 1,436,470
Operating income from continuing operations	91,128	157,568	115,946	75,882	133,509
Interest and other expense (income), net	26,774	(8,383)	15,787	44,039	15,890
Income from continuing operations before income taxes	64,354	165,951	100,159	31,843	117,619
Income from continuing operations, net of income taxes	1,172	138,908	73,461	45,333	102,055
Income from discontinued operations and dispositions, net of income taxes	6,483	252,075	8,620	23,973	42,317
Net income	$ 7,655	$ 390,983	$ 82,081	$ 69,306	$ 144,372
Basic earnings per share:					
Continuing operations	$ 0.01	$ 1.19	$ 0.63	$ 0.39	$ 0.86
Discontinued operations	0.06	2.15	0.07	0.20	0.36
Net income	$ 0.07	$ 3.34	$ 0.71	$ 0.59	$ 1.21
Diluted earnings per share:					
Continuing operations	$ 0.01	$ 1.18	$ 0.63	$ 0.38	$ 0.85
Discontinued operations	0.06	2.14	0.07	0.20	0.35
Net income	$ 0.07	$ 3.31	$ 0.70	$ 0.58	$ 1.20
Weighted-average common shares outstanding:					
Basic:	112,976	117,109	116,250	117,659	118,916
Diluted:	113,864	117,982	116,590	118,687	120,605
Cash dividends declared per common share	$ 0.28	$ 0.28	$ 0.28	$ 0.28	$ 0.28
Balance Sheet Data:					
Total assets	$ 3,834,198	$ 3,208,946	$ 3,058,754	$ 2,932,923	$ 2,948,996
Short-term debt	---	2,255	146	40	562
Long-term debt	944,908	424,000	558,197	509,040	516,078
Stockholders' equity	1,842,216	1,925,391	1,628,671	1,569,099	1,574,936
Common shares outstanding	113,157	115,715	117,023	117,112	117,585

Source: SEC Filing 10-K, 2012, www.sec.gov/Archives/edgar/data/31791/000144530512000499/pki-2011_10k.html#s95214F8CF7833664FF5EB84AA59548AD, accessed December 12, 2012.

Exhibit 2

SUMMARY OF EOL INSTRUMENT MANAGEMENT AT SELECTED COMPETITORS

Company	# of employees	Revenues (2011, in US$)	Instrument EoL Management Practices
Agilent Technologies	20,000	$6.6 billion	In compliance with the European Union WEEE Directive in Europe. Well-established instrument trade-in program offered cash or up to 50 per cent less for new products. Wide selection of used equipment with the same warranty, return policy and support for 20 to 50 per cent less.
Beckman Coulter Inc.	12,000	$3.7 billion	Compliant with the European Union WEEE directive. Refurbished company instruments were offered online by companies such as GMI and BioSurplus, but it was not clear if this was a result of established partnership.
Bio-Rad Laboratories, inc.	7,000	Over $2 billion	In compliance with the European Union WEEE Directive in Europe. Partnered with GMI to offer trade-in discount toward new equipment.
Millipore	10,000	$869 million Part of The Merck Group	In compliance with the European Union WEEE Directive in Europe. Offered take-back and recycling options for a very limited number of products (mostly consumables) but was exploring additional opportunities for product recycling.
PerkinElmer	7,200	$1.9 billion	In compliance with the European Union WEEE directive. Some trade-in programs available to customers in some regions. Recycling option for $1/pound available to customers in California.
Roche Holdings	80,129	$47.4 billion	The company had published a position statement on product stewardship which stated that "Roche takes responsibility for their products over their whole life-cycle and is in compliance with all relevant regulations." No specific details on product take-back, however, were found.

Sources:
Agilent Technologies, "Premium Used Equipment,"
http://savings.tm.agilent.com/index.cgi?PageImage:CONTENT_ID=107&User:LANGUAGE=en#, accessed August 1, 2012;
Beckman Coulter, "Automated Labware Positioners," April 2012,
https://www.beckmancoulter.com/wsrportal/techdocs?docname=987836, accessed October 1, 2012; GMI: Trade-In and
Trade-Up, www.gmi-inc.com/Trade-In-Trade-Up-Program.html; accessed October 1, 2012; BioSurplus, "About Us,"
www.biosurplus.com/about-us/our-partners/ , accessed October 1, 2012; GMI, www.gmi-inc.com/trade-in-trade-up.html,
accessed December 12, 2012; Millipore, "WEEE and RoHS Compliance," www.millipore.com/company/sup3/weee-home,
accessed October 1, 2012; Millipore, "Products," www.millipore.com/sustainability/flx/srproducts&tab1=3&tab2=5, accessed
October 1, 2012; GMI: Trade-In and Trade-Up, www.gmi-inc.com/Trade-In-Trade-Up-Program.html; accessed October 1,
2012; BioSurplus, "About Us," www.biosurplus.com/about-us/our-partners/ , accessed October 1, 2012; Roche Holdings,
"Roche Position on Product Stewardship — We minimize the negative health and environmental impacts of our products,"
November 29, 2011.

Exhibit 3

SALES TEAM SURVEY — CUSTOMER EOL PRACTICES

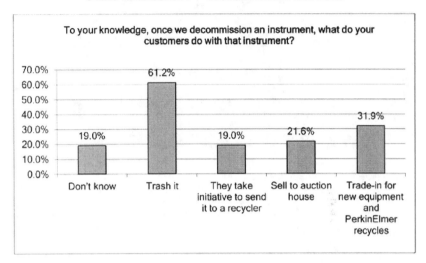

To your knowledge, once we decommission an instrument, what do your customers do with that instrument?

Source: PerkinElmer Sales Team Survey, April 2012.

Exhibit 4

SALES TEAM SURVEY — CUSTOMER PREFERENCES FOR EOL MANAGEMENT (0=NOT INTERESTED, 1=SOMEWHAT INTERESTED, 2=INTERESTED, AND 3=VERY INTERESTED)

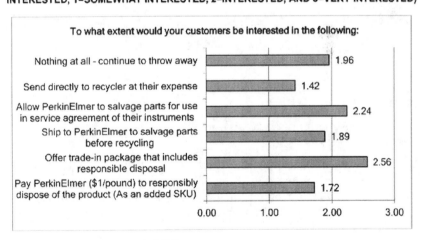

To what extent would your customers be interested in the following:

Source: PerkinElmer Sales Team Survey, April 2012.

Exhibit 5

IMPORTANCE OF RESPONSIBLE EOL MANAGEMENT TO PERKINELMER CUSTOMERS

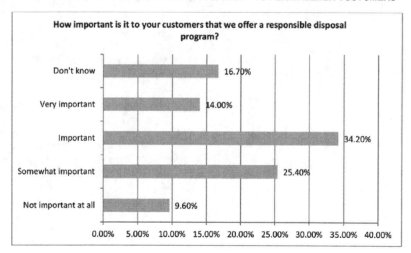

Source: PerkinElmer Sales Team Survey, April 2012.

Exhibit 6

CUSTOMER DEMAND FOR RESPONSIBLE EOL MANAGEMENT IN DIFFERENT U.S. REGIONS (%)

Region\Importance	Very important	Important	Somewhat important	Not at all important	Don't know
West and Southwest	22	22	22	17	17
South and Southeast	4	24	28	20	24
Northeast	19	38	14	5	24
Midwest	11	44	33	6	6

Source: PerkinElmer Sales Team Survey, April 2012.

DISCUSSION QUESTIONS

Chapter 16: PerkinElmer: Old Instrument Reuse and Recycling

1. What are the main drivers for adopting a corporate-wide product take back strategy for PerkinElmer? What are the key barriers presently?
2. What is the best option for adopting a company-wide take-back strategy? Should PerkinElmer simply take-back and recycle the old equipment or re-furbish and re-sell?
3. Should the company leverage its own employees to examine, disassemble and refurbish the old instruments, or collaborate with another company with core expertise in this area?
4. What policies are needed to advance greater product take-back in the United States?

INDEX

ABOUT THE AUTHOR

Dr. Vesela R. Veleva is a Lecturer in the Department of Management and Marketing, and Co-Director of the Center for Sustainable Enterprise and Regional Competitiveness at the College of Management, UMASS Boston. In her capacity she manages the interdisciplinary programs in *Clean Energy and Sustainability* and promotes applied research, workforce training, and collaborations that advance the green, sustainable economy. Her areas of expertise include sustainability indicators, corporate social responsibility, occupational and environmental health and sustainable production and consumption. Dr. Veleva has 19 years' experience in the environmental and sustainability fields and previously worked at Boston College Center for Corporate Citizenship, Citizens Advisors, Greiner Environmental Inc., and Sustainable Measures Inc. She has a doctorate in Pollution Prevention and Clean Production from the University of Massachusetts Lowell, Master's degree in Pollution and Environmental Control from the University of Manchester, UK, and B.S. in Electrical Engineering from the Technical University of Varna, Bulgaria. Dr. Veleva teaches *Business Environments and Public Policy* (MGT330) and *Introduction to Environmental Management and Clean Energy* (MGT481). She has published articles in numerous journals, including *Business and Society Review, Journal of Cleaner Production, Corporate Environmental Strategy, Sustainability: Science, Policy and Practice,* and *CSR and Environmental Management,* among others. She has been invited to present at many conferences and other events including the SCORAI International Conference, NCSE Annual Conference, Community Indicator ConsortiumInternational Conference, Massachusetts Sustainable Communities Conference, and Business Value Creation Through Green Chemistry Conference, among others.